Jim Bishop: Reporter

JIM BISHOP
REPORTER

by Jim Bishop

RANDOM HOUSE   NEW YORK

Dedicated
To the Reporters
On "Overnight"—
Mark Hellinger, Damon Runyon, Bill Corum,
Gene Fowler, Floyd Gibbons, Fulton Oursler,
Irvin S. Cobb, Frank Ward O'Malley,
Richard Harding Davis, Ben Hecht, Meyer Berger,
Ernie Pyle, Charles MacArthur and Heywood Broun

Contents

For the Record:

The current era is always the most exciting. Vanity goads man to feel that, in his time, the world has reached peaks of culture, progress and conflict, and that, from now on, the urge to do noble and horrible things will subside. He looks backward with pity and forward with apathy.

Great events—unless they are natural phenomena, or cataclysmic—are devised by great people, and I am possessed of the certainty that the middle part of the twentieth century will go down in history as the time of the big minds and the small souls. More technological progress was made in this era than in all the ones which preceded it, but man knew not what to do with it, or with himself. For the first time, he became completely materialistic and he discovered universes which were terrifyingly small and powerful, and it was cowardice to be one's brother's keeper.

It was and is a poor time to be alive. This is not a judgment; it's a fact. And yet, in this period of man's march toward the stars, it was my duty to be as good a journalist as my talents would permit, and these talents were bent toward people rather than historical events. In people I found a sense of balance. They came in many sizes and shapes and with varying degrees of goodness and evil; they were fruitful and barren.

This book is a close-up of people in my time. There are presidents and popes and paupers and politicians inside. There are also the unknowns who have a story to tell; people who aren't much more than a loose thread in the tapestry of current history. Each one moved me to the point of writing, which is a lot of motion because, after thirty-five years of facing blank paper and a typewriter, the once-sensitive fingers are calloused.

I cannot speak for you, but I love people, whole hosts of them, and the more fallible we become, the deeper is the attachment. But love is not blind. Sometimes love has twenty-twenty vision.

When one hefts our civilization, our culture, our progress, in both hands, love of fellow man begins to die a little. We are in a time of rebellion, a sick discontent pervades the world. In America, over a hundred years have passed since Abraham Lincoln freed the slaves. Now, twenty million Negroes fight for acceptance.

The mosaic of Victoria's empire is in fragments. Africa has burst one big chain into many small links. China refuses to acknowledge Soviet Union leadership in the struggle for despotic socialism. The two great powers of the earth live in sleepless tension: scorpions sealed in a bottle. Our stomachs jump when an announcer says, "We interrupt this program for a news bulletin . . ."

The threat of annihilation is a boarder in every home and sleeps in every bed. Few are patriotic. Fewer volunteer to serve their country. The youth of the land listen to their parents' opinion so that they may select the opposite course. The day of loyalty to an employer and a full measure of work for full pay is gone.

This is time-payment time. The people want more missiles, bigger pensions, more security and less taxes; bigger freezers and more steaks; shorter hours, of course. Chiseling is respectable. The only crime left on the books is being caught. We take pills to sleep, and other pills to wake up. We need liquor to make us jolly, and laughter to make us forget.

Love is sex. When it isn't sex it isn't love. If you don't love me, I despise you. Am I my brother's keeper? I can't remember his name. Church? That's where they take you when you die. God is an ideological misfit. Life? That's a long heartache stretching between the cradle and the grave. Liberty? That's my right to do it to him before he does it to me. The pursuit of happiness? It can be achieved on the back seat of a parked car.

I'm a gray-haired fiftyish man who has seen much. I was paid well to see it. Often, I found that there were more than two sides to a story, and I had to train myself to look at all the sides. It was necessary, in many cases, to slam the door on my personal feelings. In my time, I have written twelve thousand stories and fourteen books, and I don't recall any which completely pleased the people who were in them.

Nor have all of them pleased me. The stories in this book come close to saying what I wanted to say.

JIM BISHOP

Hallandale, Florida

Jim Bishop: Reporter

Races

After hundreds of years, the Negro emerged from the shadows, but, even in sunlight, many white men saw him as a shadow. The fight was for higher stakes than equality; it was for acceptance. It was also a battle of hypocrites on both sides. Many of the Negro's political proponents among the Caucasians would not have a Negro in their homes; a big segment of the Negro leadership had moved out of Negro communities long before the fight started, and they used the Civil Rights struggle as a political echo chamber.

For a decade, the United States was in convulsion. The weapons ranged all the way from the antiseptic opinions of the Supreme Court to bottles of flaming gasoline thrown into moving automobiles; from the legalistic goading of Attorney General Robert F. Kennedy to the rape of a Negro girl at Tallahassee by four white males. The twenty million dark-skinned people had the law and the moral right at their side; the whites had guilt and fear working for them.

The minorities themselves began to break into fragments. The Jews of New York fought for the Negro. The Jews of Atlanta sat in silence. Jewish shops in New York were looted. A synagogue in Atlanta was bombed. Negro leaders in Harlem said that their people were not ready for desegregation; white politicians said they were. The moderate South was overwhelmed by the White Supremacy councils. The reasonable men on both sides whispered; the extremists shouted.

This section of the book deals with the people and events which were alive and hot throughout the struggle. It was the only fight within my memory which had no winners.

Thunder Over Dixie

The air is warm. The streets are lacquered with last night's rain. A pencil of a spire lifts a cross toward God. Two white women walk down East Capitol, in Jackson, Mississippi. They stare absentmindedly into a shopwindow as dark waves of Negroes curve around them on the sidewalk.

A bullhorn snorts as an electric-diesel loafs into Jackson from New Orleans. A fat Negro woman rocks on her porch and squints through the screen at the morning pedestrians. In the Edwards Hotel, four men in a descending elevator stare at the back of the Negro girl who is running it. At the third floor, a white girl gets on. The men remove their hats.

There is tension here and there is tension all over the South, but the knuckles and lips of the State of Mississippi are white with it. This is a land of impatient men. Some of them are sick unto death of the United States Supreme Court. Their voices become shrill with anger when they talk about the decision of May 17, 1954, which said that separate schools for white and Negro are unconsitutional and which gives the South "a reasonable time" to bring all children before the same blackboard.

Six segregation bills are pending on Capitol Hill in Jackson. This is like writing an epitaph in smoke. The Negroes say nothing. They can read. They know better than the white man that desegregation will come. It will take years; maybe a whole generation. It will come. And the Negro, in his atavistic wisdom, sees no happiness in it for him.

The white men who fight the hot glacier have a certain uniformity. They wear snap-brim hats and they have red, wrinkled necks and their paunches are held by broad, brown belts. They appear to be close to sixty and they barely move their lips when they talk. They seldom laugh; what comes out is a desiccated cough. They own the blue minks on their women's backs. They own the black Cadillacs and the houses on the hills and the whining beagles, and they can stare through tiny blue eyes at a Negro and tell a "good boy" from a "bad one" in a few seconds.

These men are trying to protect the white man from his brother. So, starting in Sunflower County in July, 1954, they organized themselves into white "Citizens' Councils." There is one in almost every city and hamlet. The members do not wear sheets and they burn no crosses. They are like plane watchers, except they watch people. They watch white people as well as black. And they report to local headquarters about Negroes who like white schools and about white people who like Negroes. The "Citizens' Councils" are persuasive. In two years, almost forty thousand Negroes left Mississippi.

The Red Necks are Christians. They go to church and they bow knee and head to Christ. They believe they have done more for the Negro of the South than anybody, including Lincoln. They point out that they even built separate schools for the Negro. They lend him money, hold his mortgage, seldom coerce his women, permit their children to play with his, and bid him a civil time of the day. When you get to know the Red Neck pretty well, he talks. And, when he talks man-to-man, your stomach knots a little because, deep down, he admits that he is afraid of the Negro on two counts: (1) "If he gets into our schools he will soon take over our state"; (2) "The male Negro will force intermarriage on our women."

The "Citizens' Councils" represent a pinch of the population. Some have ten members in a town. Some have fifteen. Around them are a fistful of emotional adolescents of all ages. They wring fear from the other whites in a town because they have the power to hurt by tongue and by boycott. The average family can win the grudging approval of the "Citizens' Council" by being merciless to Negroes at all times.

Up in Holmes County, Mississippi, two men are still fighting desperately to save their farm by denying again and again that they permitted Negroes to use their swimming pool. Down here, the "Citizens' Council" has an opposite number. This is the National Association for the Advancement of Colored People. It is called the NAACP.

Here in Jackson, it is small and secretive and as hard to hold under a thumb as a soft grape. When you ask Negro educators or doctors about it many say, "Don't know anything about it and don't want to."

The local group used to have an office on North Farish, but they moved to a new building over on Lynch (of all streets) and

Mr. Medgar Evers* is the president but he isn't in the office and nobody knows where he is. I phoned, and I drove over to the office; I phoned again and I left my name and my number, but Medgar Evers was not found.

A few doors away from the NAACP office, an old white wooden building stands behind a pool of brackish water. Inside, in a small office, a big, good-looking man with mahogany skin sits behind a flat desk. He is James Gooden, director of the Board of Education (Negro) of the City of Jackson. Behind him lie thirty years of work in the school system. He is no fool. Before talking to me, he phoned the superintendent of schools and asked for permission.

The reply was concise: "Go ahead and talk to him. Give him the answer to anything you feel qualified to answer." Gooden lowered his head and smiled sadly at the green blotter.

"It took a couple of hundred years for this problem to come up," he said softly, "and now everybody wants answers overnight. What do you want to know? How many schools? We have eight thousand children in ten buildings in Jackson. Negro children, of course. There are maybe four hundred children who should be in school and who aren't."

He talked on. A ball-point pen danced over the pages of a notebook. Gooden knows his subject. Only twice did he refer to the files for figures. Negro school enrollment in this city is about 40 per cent of the total.

The white Board of Education spends forty cents out of every dollar on Negro schools. Negro schools are bigger than white schools because Negro families live in congested areas and need bigger schools. Negro schools are newer and brighter than white schools because the white people didn't begin to take Negro education seriously until twenty years ago.

Negro teachers are paid 10 per cent less than white teachers in Jackson. Living expenses for the white teacher are higher. The average white teacher pays fifty dollars a month for an apartment. The Negro teacher pays thirty. The Negro teacher, on less pay, has more purchasing power.

All schoolbooks come from a common printer and are the same in the white and Negro schools. Even the city requisition blanks for rulers and inkwells and erasers are the same. The desks are the same.

Gooden does not alter the soft tone when he is about to shock you. He continues softly, almost prayerfully, "No Negro parent

---

* Evers was later murdered.

has asked me to transfer a student to a white school. Most of my people are opposed to desegregation of schools."

He cups his hands behind his head. "Very few people have stopped to think that we too have pride. Most children would rather be Negro students in a Negro school than to be unwelcome in a white child's school. Go over and talk to the children at recess. Ask them. Speak to the mothers," he said. "They know real good. You tell a mother that her little boy or girl is going to go to the nice white school and watch how sad her face gets. You know why? I'll tell you why. Her little girl dresses as good as the Negro children, but not as good as the white children. Her little boy is as good as any boy in his own school, but how is she going to tell him that, in the new school, if a white boy gets fresh with him, he must not hit back or answer back? What Supreme Court is going to make the white students take the Negro children into their games at recess?"

Millions of words, hot and cold, have been spoken and written about this matter and nobody asked the little girl with the cute black pigtails how she feels about it. James Gooden smiled and slammed both hands on his desk. "You know what?" he said. "There are nine million Negroes within three hundred miles of where we're sitting. Know what they want? What they really want? They want to feel as good as you—in public. That's all. Let us bring up our children in our own schools. But don't make us get off the sidewalk to let you pass; don't make us take a back seat in a bus; don't make us sit in a separate waiting room. You want the whole truth? There you have it.

"The races have character. Each has his own. Every time my church tries to put on nice quiet services like the white people, the people don't come to the church any more. They go down to another church where they can shout and weep. What makes the colored boy laugh may not be funny to the white boy at all. Vice versa, too. But the only real trouble we have is the result of two hundred years of bad treatment. Now we're neurotic. We need adjusting. Deep down we don't feel as good as the whites. That's why our men buy flashy clothes and flashy cars. The Negro is trying to convince himself that he's as good as anybody. If integration comes, who is going to teach the colored children how to get used to the snobs sitting around them? Do you know how cruel children can be to each other? Mister, there are more sides to this question than I can count."

I talked to some Negro women. They agreed with Gooden. One said that, in the city of Jackson, there may be as many as fifty families who would want to put their youngsters in white schools.

They talked about status, and used the word several times. What, I asked, is status?

They grinned, wiped their hands on aprons, and all started to talk at once. The best example of status, it seems, is the Negro maid in the white household. She has status. She excites envy among the Negroes. She runs the white kitchen. She is trusted. They give her money to go shopping. They make a fuss over her cooking. When she goes to a movie with the white children, she sits in the white section.

Status. That's what the Negro wants.

At Sallie Reynolds Elementary School, the children have it. They also have it at the Jim Hill High School. These are modern structures, schools which look like sunlit bakeries. There are 852 students in grades one to six. There are twenty-six rooms; about thirty-three students to a room. All of the teachers graduated from Negro colleges. Their salaries range from $2,200 a year to $3,200.

The Sallie Reynolds school cost $360,000 to build in 1952. In a city of 135,000, it is one of seven elementary Negro schools. There are two junior high schools and two junior-senior high schools. Here, they study chemistry and astronomy in the sixth grade. The children are gifted with good manners and rich laughter.

The old Nash staggered through the road holes in Tuxedo Junction and the yellow headlights bucked the walls of the Negro shanties. "You want to see a Negro district?" the cop said. "This is one." In the cold starry night, the unpainted houses leaned against each other like frightened ghosts. This is Birmingham, Alabama.

A thin man slouched beside the cop on the front seat—Edward Strickland. He covers his baldness with good gray hats. A few years ago he exposed the viciousness of Alabama politics in a book called *Phenix City*, but he is first of all a reporter. A good reporter. He has been covering the Negro district of Birmingham for fourteen years.

The policeman was another Eddie—Edward L. Quinn, a big crew-cut who works the Negro district out of the detective bureau. In conversation, he sounds as solicitous as a bridegroom. But the words are hard and the sympathies have been blunted by years of cop callousness.

Who knows a city better than a policeman and a reporter? Who? The Mayor? A preacher? A bellhop or a sociologist? A reporter and a policeman have to know the city down to its sox, and neither one is paid for finding anything good about it.

The car bounced through Tittusville and on up the steep little hill where the rich Negroes live in their modern ranch homes with the matching Cadillacs in the driveway and are waited on by Negro servants from down in Tuxedo Junction. It's a realistic world, this one.

Children play in front of the houses of prostitution in daylight hours. After dark, they are indoors, eating or studying or sleeping —three and four to a bed in drafty rooms separated from other rooms by faded cotton curtains. By sight and sound, they learn much more at home than they do at school.

We stopped in at Big Mike's place. This is a coffeehouse for whites only. All public places are marked "White Only" or "Colored Only" and, in some towns, a white man can be fined twenty-five dollars for ordering something in a restaurant for Negroes. The Negro never makes the opposite mistake unless he is badly drunk and belligerent.

Birmingham is the newest of the Southern cities—nearly ninety years old. It was born out of a mountain of iron ore and it spreads out in neat squares across two valleys. Now three hundred sixty thousand people call it home, and two hundred ten thousand of them are dark of skin. There are rich whites and rich Negroes and poor whites and poor Negroes. As befits a big Southern city, Birmingham has its white "Citizens' Council."

But, in Birmingham, of all the Southern cities, the "Citizens' Council" has not been sufficient to give the white man peace of mind. He needs something stronger. So, for the first time in years, Ku Klux Klan pamphlets were dropped on all whites' front porches. The literature was the same as in 1865—anti-Catholicism, anti-Semitism, anti-Negroism. Birmingham is in a mood to read.

Detective Quinn stirred his onyx coffee slowly and said that the trouble was that the North does not understand Negroes, and the South does. "In Birmingham," he said, "the Negro commits eight out of each ten crimes. He requires the services of more than half the police department. He lives different. He thinks different.

"Take the Smithfield project," says Quinn. "That's exactly the same as the white housing projects, brick for brick, room for room. Take a look at any of the white ones, and then look at the Negro one. They throw garbage on the front lawn."

Quinn is a tough cop. He is also a Southerner. Strickland is a tough reporter. He is also a Southerner. The white man's code of supremacy comes easily to them.

Quinn, for example, has a contempt so deeply ingrained that he does not know it exists. Once, when we talked of Negro disorderly houses, he drawled, "Ah don't have to point them out to you folks.

They are all disorderly houses and you can take a picture if you please and what can anybody say?" There are millions of men like Quinn in the South.

Strick hung his hat and sat. "Wait a minute," he said. "Admit that the schools haven't given the Negro the educational, the cultural advantages he should have. The fact is that the law now says we have to give him these advantages quickly. O.K. We'll admit we were wrong. But we still can't obey the law at once.

"The truth of the matter is that the Southern Negro is a sensual child. He wants only what pleases his several senses. There is a black belt in Alabama—it runs from Meridian, Mississippi, all the way to a spot twenty miles south of West Point, Georgia—and there the Negroes run from five to one to seven to one over the white man. You're white. How would you like to have a house down there? Try it awhile and then tell us about the law."

"It's just this," said Quinn. "We're not going to have integration in this generation. Sometime maybe. But not now. And, if you think I'm anti-Negro, go out to Scratch Ankle and ask the people about me. They know me as good as I know them. Ask them."

Strick chuckled. "Some of these Negroes want to run him for public safety commissioner."

Officer Quinn is a Bible student. His best girl is his five-year-old daughter Kathy, a pale, pretty blonde. "You know what the Negro wants?" the cop said.

"I'll tell you," said Strick. "I'll tell you what the Negro really wants. He wants good wages and fair treatment, that's what he wants. That's the extent of it. He doesn't want to go to your house and nothing embarrasses him more than to see you in his."

Quinn marveled at such succinct wisdom. "I think I know the Negro as well as anybody and I don't know one yet who wants to be bothered with a white school. You ever see our Parker High School? It's Negro. I don't know about now, but it used to be called the biggest in the country."

We paid for the coffee and left a little tip and walked out into the night. To the south, we could see Red Mountain in the moonlight. It is full of dolomite and iron ore and coal and the three get along well in the same mountain and each maintains its integrity until all three get into the smelting furnaces across town. Then they come out shiny bars of steel.

Something is wrong. Terribly wrong. All the white evidence shows that the Negro is content, but all the daily news shows that he feels miserable. Rosa Parks sat in front of a Montgomery bus. Trouble started. Negroes began to walk to work. The ensuing boycott almost wrecked the bus company. A girl named Autherine Lucy drove to the University of Alabama in a limousine, stepped out in the height of fashion, and was shown to the head of the line of registering white students. There was a riot.

Integration? For years, the rich white families of Birmingham have offered good upstairs rooms to their maids and butlers, good furniture and a radio, the saving of thirty-four cents a day bus fare and many dollars in rent—and yet not one maid or butler in fifty will live with the white families, each one announcing in a whisper, with eyes downcast, that if madam doesn't mind we would prefer to go on living in the shacks of Tuxedo Junction.

Why? The Southern Negro living in a white house feels that he is in a plush strait jacket. He is a second-class boarder in a first-class home. If there is any conversation, his part of it is "Yes, sir" and "Yes, ma'am." He must also remember to smile when he says it. In Tuxedo Junction, he can yell "No" without fear. He can get drunk, stay sober, shoot pool, crack dirty jokes, sleep all day, read, prowl for a woman, play the numbers, eat as he pleases when he pleases, stop smiling, stare at pedestrians, do nothing.

A hundred years ago on Palm Sunday—a quick wink in the eye of time—Richmond, Virginia, lay gasping and defeated in its own dust. Lee left it. Grant took it. For a time it almost died of rage and shame; and, intellectually, Richmond is in almost the same emotional storm today. No one likes to be compelled to do anything, but Richmond likes it less than anyone else. The city, and with it the state, has been fighting the Supreme Court for years. And Virginia will lose the final engagement in this war too.

Here, the level of argument is loftier than in Birmingham or in Charleston or Jackson. Here there are no generalizations against the Negro without documentation. You can talk to a bank president or a preacher or shopkeeper and each will tick off the statistics on his fingers. The epitome of the fighters is a blue-eyed, balding man who sits in the office of the *Richmond News-Leader*.

His name is James Kilpatrick, but everyone calls him Jack. He is the editor. He writes the editorials and some of them sting. Kilpatrick is a Roman Catholic, and is the father of three sons— twelve, eight and five. He was born in Oklahoma City and is as Southern as the bottom of a mint julep. The Catholic Church in the South has led the fight to admit Negroes in the churches and the schools, but Jack Kilpatrick could hardly be in deeper disagreement with the hierarchy of his own church.

This man is so grim as to be humorless. "I've worked on this matter for almost two years to the exclusion of nearly everything else," he says. "No matter how you say it, the Supreme Court has, in effect, tried to amend the Constitution. That's what it comes to." He taps a cigarette and lights it. In the smoke, he sees a side to segregation which could not occur to a Northerner. "You grow up from the cradle with a black mammy, and you know that there is a bond of affection between you." He slams his hand on the modern desk before him. "But you always know that you're different and she knows that she's different.

"It would take hours to tell you how different. I've known colored people all my life, and it is hard to generalize about a whole race of people, but it is still almost impossible to know when a colored man is telling the truth and when he isn't. That's one difference.

"Another one is that—well, let's take school children. They may be playing happily, you've seen them do it, and suddenly they are in passionate argument. These things happen over nothing. Nothing at all. Negroes are emotional children. They are worse than others in this respect. And, in school or anywhere else, they can be violent." He placed one arm over the back of his swivel chair. "And will you please bear one thing in mind: the good never rubs off as easily as the bad!"

This is a young man who is as sincere, and as certain of his convictions, as you are. He is as sure that the Negroes are not ready for integration as he is of one more breath. At the slightest challenge, he yanks open steel filing drawers and whips out charts and tables and hands them to you to read.

For example, if you maintain that Negro immorality may lie solely in the white man's mind, Kilpatrick's fingers execute a swift mambo over the yellow file folders and he comes up with a chart of 1954 showing that the Negroes of Virginia had 24,192 babies that year and 5,207 of them were illegitimate. Roughly, one out of five.

"In themselves," he says, "these statistics prove little. The thing that impresses me is that the South did not begin to help the Negro culturally and economically until perhaps twenty years ago —fifteen maybe. Since then, more has been done for colored people than in all the time before. And you know what? In 1954, these people had a higher percentage of illegitimate babies than ever before."

The State of Virginia has three and a half million people, of which 22 per cent, about seven hundred seventy thousand, are Negroes. "If the Negroes," the young editor says, looking at the ceiling, "were more responsible, more mature, the bulk of my objections to their admittance in our schools would be removed. I can't imagine this happening, but even if it did, many would still object on the ground that our cultures are different." Including him.

The word different comes up all the time. And, the Negroes use the word as a vague crutch for limping thoughts, too. Different. One of the reasons why the Catholic Church has progressed slowly among Negroes in the South, the young man says, is that the Negro insists on participating in worship and wants to holler and sing and cry. "The Negro gets to play no part in the Mass except to say three Hail Marys out loud at the end," he adds.

The Virginia State Department of Education used nationally standardized tests to grade students. It still does. The most recent tests are cited by Southerners to support their view that, when integration comes, the white student will be yanked downward as the Negro student is pulled upward. They claim they tested thirty-five thousand eighth graders of both races in the Iowa Silent Reading Test and, if all things had been equal, everyone would have scored 8.8—which means eighth grade, eighth month. The white city children averaged 9.2 (ninth grade, second month) and the Negro city children averaged 6.5 The white rural children scored 8.5; the Negro rural child 6.1. In Mental Maturity Tests the white city eighth graders were shown to have a reading age of thirteen years, six months. The Negroes, ten years, seven months.

Some of this is undoubtedly due to neglect of the Negro students on the part of white Boards of Education. How much? There are no figures available on that subject. It will require two generations for the scholastic aptitudes of the two races to approximate each other. One generation will not be enough because the Negro student is going to need at least one older generation at home sufficiently educated to encourage him to study and to understand his ambitions.

It is a sleepy, sunny Sunday morning with a crayon of blue wood smoke in the sky. From a window in the Carolina Hotel in Raleigh, North Carolina, I can see a prim young lady on her way, I suppose, to church with her young man, and I can see a diesel locomotive moving a solitary boxcar down a siding. The tops of the trees show a conceited spring green and the traffic lights wink from red to green, but there are no automobiles waiting and there is something of impotence about the majesty of the law telling someone to stop and someone else to go and no one there to obey.

There are times like that in the South.

From what I have seen on this trip, the South is economically sprightlier than it used to be, and a shade less stubborn. It is a land of long-legged women and short tempers; two-lane highways and one-track minds; good industry and bad cooking; a place where the decay is deeper in the mansions than in the shacks; a matriarchal shadow of courtly manners and vague fears; magnolias and bootleggers and pickaninnies and rebel banners and fine universities and poor whites and women who live in a mental Tara Hall.

To me, Raleigh is churches; Richmond is department stores; Charleston is a gorgeous hussy; Augusta is a man with his sleeves rolled up; Atlanta is a finger of suspicion; Birmingham is a lazy boy under a tree; New Orleans is a woman promising more than she can give; Jackson is an old man trying to stop a fight before it starts; Lexington, Mississippi, is a hot pistol free to point in any direction.

There is interposition, a word that changes direction in mid-syllable. There is a lot of talk in all the states about interposition, but it is a legal nothing. The word was first heard in Virginia in 1798 and it means that, theoretically, a state can interpose itself between the Supreme Court and the Constitution in an effort to protect the Constitution. It was used to protest a court decision against the Alien and Sedition Act. The act died before the case of interposition could be heard.

In 1814, the States of Massachusetts and Connecticut tried interposition in protest against the conduct of the War of 1812. The war ended before the case could be heard.

Just before the Civil War, the State of Wisconsin interposed to protest the return to the South of a fugitive slave. The war started before the case could be heard, so there is no precedent for interposition.

Another Southern device is to propose a new Constitutional amendment which would ask for integration under Federal control in all schools. This sounds as though the South is giving itself a judicial hot-foot, but the reasoning is subtle. Constitutional amendments usually require years for ratification. Besides, any thirteen states can block an amendment and the South is confident that it can stop its own proposition. Meanwhile, Louisiana has a law which says that the State Board of Education must close any school in which the students are mixed. South Carolina is prepared to make segregation more rigid. In Texas, integration was started in most southwest and western public schools in 1955. Alabama, Georgia and Mississippi will be the most difficult states to desegregate. In Arkansas, there is integration in three towns, and more will follow. Florida has a primary coming up in May and does not want to discuss the question until afterward.

It isn't a bad record. Anyone who has a nodding acquaintance with Southern customs is bound to consider it a good record. The fear of the white man for the Negro is real. It does no good to tell the Southerner that the sins of his fathers are on his shoulders. He knows it better than you do.

He hurts the most when he thinks about the things he has done in the past twenty years to help the Negro advance—the near elimination of lynchings and violence; the modern schools which have been built for Negroes; the accreditation of Negro colleges with graduates in law and medicine and the arts; the tentative extension of the vote to Negroes in some counties; the building of many Negro clinics and hospitals out of public funds; free school buses; Negro policemen; libraries, taverns, taxicabs, and public welfare departments solely for Negroes.

Now the white South is being led by the ear to do something that it is not ready to do.

Then too, it must be said that the Northern Negro and the Southern Negro have little in common at present except complexion. Most Northern Negroes—like their white neighbors—are sophisticated citizens. Many Southern Negroes aren't.

The argument that once the Negroes get into white schools they will move into white beds is dishonest and shameful. Most Negroes are too poor to afford white wives, even assuming they want them or that any sizable number of white women are willing to marry Negroes. And if the economic condition of the Negro improves to a point where it is comparable with that of a white man, there will still be no reason to expect an epidemic of intermarriages.

The Negro will not "mongrelize" the races. Is a baby from a white father and a black mother a shade different in hue from a baby coming from a white mother and a black father? Negro children seem to be uniformly bright and mannerly and healthy. I saw no resentment among them; just silent envy of white children.

I was told repeatedly that the morals of the average Negro woman in the South were far below those of her white sisters. I do not know. But I do know that economic pressures are great and that it is doubly difficult to defeat evil and hunger at the same time.

I look out the window at the blue wood smoke, and the traffic lights winking yes and no to no one, and I wonder why men expend so much energy on fights they cannot win. Integration is more than a law; it is a moral obligation. The specious arguments of a Southern editor; the eagerness of a Negro to thrust his simpering son into the fight; the deep-down ineradicable fear of ignorant white men that their women, in time, will prefer to sleep with colored men, all seem to soil the law. Something simple has been made complex.

The Supreme Court decision of May, 1954, does not require the Negro to socialize with me, or me with him. It wasn't easy to get an invitation to visit Negroes in their homes. I could smell suspicion at each front door. The white Southerner says: "Nobody knows the Negro like we do," but I never heard a Negro say it. Only the Negro truly knows the Negro. Often, he is ashamed of his knowledge.

The Larks and the Sparrows

It was a warm bright night and the moon shone on all without favor in Tallahassee, Florida. It caught the late Friday shoppers on Monroe Street and it flecked the big oaks with little rhinestones. It hushed the evening talk of the locusts and it tossed long blue shadows across the campus of Florida State University.

It caressed the dome of the old capitol and, with equal fervor, brightened the campus of Florida A. & M. University for Negroes. If the man in the moon learned anything about Tallahassee on May 1, 1959, he learned that this is a sedate and proper town; a capital and a college town; a place of old houses and older tradition; a community of forty-seven thousand persons who have dignity and who think of themselves as being above the petty spite of racism.

They point out that the larks and the sparrows often share the same oak tree, but they do not mingle. It is that way among people who are of separate colors. There are thirty-two thousand whites, and fourteen thousand Negroes.

There is no rancor here. No smoldering hate. The Negro is restricted, but no more so than elsewhere in the South. He cannot dine in a white restaurant, but he can work in the kitchen and cut up the food for whites and finger the dishes. The ironies of color have been with these people so long that they do not see them.

The Seaboard Airline tracks—two silvery rails—separate the sparrows and the larks. North of the tracks is a good part of white Tallahassee. South is the colored section and, if you can stand an irony within an irony, they too have their caste system; their slum poor and their professional rich. There are some fine homes with spacious lawns around Owens and Osceola streets, and there are some pretty poor-looking huts on Dade Street.

It was in the poor section, on this night, that Betty stood quietly as her sister flicked the last dark curl in place, hooked the final eye on the gold and white evening dress, and pulled the short net down for the last time. Betty swung back and forth in front of the bedroom mirror. She was pleased with what she saw.

She was a Negro girl, nineteen years old, and pretty. She was slender, and could have been a little bit fuller here and there, but she had dark satiny skin and the eyes of a young doe. Life had been pretty good to Betty.

She was a freshman at Florida A. & M. and she was president of the board of ushers at the Philadelphia Primitive Baptist Church. She was studying to be a secretary, and, even if she met a boy she liked, she wanted a career. Also, Betty wanted to do something for her mother.

Momma deserved a break. The father had left this family a long time ago. Momma, a short, dark articulate woman who knows nothing but hard work and morality, had strained to keep the brood together. There were three daughters and a son and Grandma to care for and feed and clothe. Momma got a job as janitor of the Motor Vehicle Bureau in Tallahassee and she kept the place spotless.

The woman watched the final fitting of the gown. She must have felt a little pride. Her work was almost over. Freddie was twenty; Betty was nineteen; Melinda, eighteen, and Doris, seventeen. She had good children.

At ten thirty Thomas Butterfield knocked on the screen door. Betty had told him that she didn't want to get to the Orange and Green Ball too early. It would be the last big social affair at the college before summer vacation, and Roy Hamilton was going to be there in person. He would, of course, sing "I Need Your Lovin'." That was his big hit.

Momma told Tom Butterfield to come in. He brought a friend, Richard Brown. Both were nineteen; both were Negro freshmen; both came from Miami. This was Betty's first date with Butterfield. He was tall and thin and mannerly. A little diffident. It had taken him some time to ask for this date and he worked up his nerve exactly one week before the ball.

Betty had said yes, and she had to find a girl friend for Tom's friend, Richard Brown. She had asked her girl friend Edna, who was also a freshman, and now it was to be a foursome. Edna was tiny, and had a good sense of humor and was a good dancer.

Momma watched them go. "Have a nice time and get home on time," she said. Betty said yes. She kept looking at Tom. He looked so good. So manly, all dressed up. She picked her way carefully down the front steps of the old unpainted house. At the curb, Tom slid into the driver's seat. Betty sat next to him. Richard dropped into the back seat.

The car moved off, and, in the dim light of the dashboard, the three talked of how a big part of the college cafeteria had been cleared away for dancing, of the thrill of hearing Roy Hamilton in person, of how Betty's brother Freddie had gone off earlier with his own date. Betty really didn't have to be home until after one.

They stopped on Abraham Street for Edna. She was ready, and she came out wearing a full-length white gown. Now the conversation began to bubble. The boys came to life, and the girls felt like queens. It is a short ride to Florida A. & M. and, when they arrived outside the proper building, cars were parked everywhere. Tom drove on a little, and found a space, and he locked the 1952 Chevrolet as though it were a new Cadillac.

All the classes were present. The place jumped with the big sound. Some sat at tables and sipped punch, and some danced. There were dreamy numbers and lively bounces and, when Roy Hamilton sang, the students stopped dancing and just stood in front of the bandstand swaying.

It was twelve thirty. The band stopped playing, and the hundreds of couples began to break up. There were shouts and kidding and laughter, and the two boys escorted Betty and Edna back into the car. The boys didn't want to take the girls directly home, and the girls didn't exactly want to go right home.

The whole game is to find a place to park. The moon was still high. There was a softness in the night breeze. Tom Butterfield drove south on the Boulevard, turned right on Osceola, left on Pasco Street, and right on Bragg Drive. He moved up a hundred yards to a big lonesome oak, and swung right around it and pulled up to a barbed wire fence and turned off the ignition.

They were facing the big blank screen of the Lincoln outdoor theater. No cars were inside. The show was over. Behind the car, on the other side of the street, was Jake Gaither Park, a Negro recreational center with a nine-hole golf course.

The windows were rolled down. Next to the fence, they could

hear the night trill of the locusts in the wild blackberry bushes. This is the time when a boy, for the first time, must find the nerve to place his arm across the seat behind the girl; it is also the time when a girl offers no encouragement and a little resistance.

Richard, in the back seat, found that he had a talking girl on his hands. Tom, in front, was inching his hand around to the top of the seat, still speaking softly and gravely. Some cars had parked nearby. Now, at 12:45 A.M. the others left. There were no street lights; no car lights.

It was easy to spot the other car coming up the road. It came up fast, with the brights on, and it turned off the road at the last second and pulled to a stop on the left side of the Chevy.

Tom thought it might be other revelers from the ball. He looked, and saw four white men. All were young. They got out. Two hurried to Tom Butterfield's side of the car; two trotted around to the other side. The door on Betty's side was flung open and a shotgun was aimed in.

A man's voice said, "Get out." It wasn't loud or mean. It was an authoritative order. Betty looked at the gun, and looked at Tom, and she started to cry. In the back seat, Edna, seventeen, began to wail. One of the men in the dark said, "Shut up. You girls got nothing to worry about."

Tom said nothing. Richard said nothing. They got out. The girls followed them. One of the white men turned the Chevy lights on. Another one ordered the two boys to crouch in front of the bumper. The boys squatted, elbows on knees, eyes on the grass. The girls were ordered to crouch behind the boys. They did as they were told.

One of the four said, "Where are you boys from?" They said they were from school, but that they came from Miami. In the headlights, the shotgun could be seen. One white youth stepped forward with a knife. It was a peculiar instrument. It came down long, with an ever-narrowing blade, and the end had been split so that it had two points.

Someone prodded the colored boys. "You two get back in the car," a voice said. There was no excitement in the voice. Just an odor of stale whisky in the night air. Tom Butterfield and Richard Brown got into the car. "Now," a voice said, "back up until I tell you to stop."

Tom was so shaken that he could hardly find the key. He started the car. The man made motions for him to back, so he backed. He kept going back until he reached the road. Then he swung the car, so that he faced away from the white men.

"Now stop," a voice said. Butterfield hit the gas pedal, sunk low in his seat, and started down Bragg Drive, waiting to hear a shotgun blast. There was no such sound. He hurried toward town to look for a policeman.

Betty and Edna watched them go, and the girls stood. One man grabbed Betty by the wrist, the other clutched at Edna. Both girls were dragged to the barbed wire fence and pushed, crying, to the ground.

"Not here," one of the men said. "Not right here." The girls were yanked to their feet. They stood whimpering. The moon was on the wane. Now, for the first time, Betty and Edna knew. They started little polite pleas, but nobody listened. Now they knew.

One of the white men opened the back door of the car. "Get in," he said. Betty began to cry harder. Edna screamed. One man slapped Betty on the face. "Shut up," he said. Edna, quaking in the long white formal, turned quickly and ran. Betty watched her go. She expected the man with the gun to aim and fire. He didn't. These men couldn't afford noise, even the noise of weeping.

They let Edna go. She ran down past the entrance to Jake Gaither Park and across the first lawn she saw and up to a door. She rang and moaned and pulled at the door. Nobody was home. The nerves of the body short-circuited the mind and Edna became hysterical. She began to run around, a few steps in this direction; a few steps that way.

The four men put Betty in the back seat. She had stopped crying. Her shoulders shook. Her knees shook. Two men got in front. Two flanked her on the back seat. She thought perhaps if she appealed to them, explained. The mouth opened, but only whispers came out. She tried to speak up. The man driving said, "Shut up." She shut.

Then the crying started, and she couldn't stop it. A man on one side of her grabbed her head and jammed it into his lap. She felt the car start, bumpy over the grass, then smoothly down the road.

The men talked a little. The driver knew a place. A good place. Betty could hardly breathe. They drove a long time. There was smoothness and high speed in the sound. Then came a slowing down, and brakes being applied sporadically, then more acceleration, and bumps. A moment later, the car stopped.

Tom Butterfield drove up Pasco Street and down Railroad Avenue with his friend Richard Brown. The boys felt they had been cowardly to run off and leave the girls with the four men. Still, they kept reminding themselves, they were really looking for a policeman.

They couldn't find a prowl car in the Negro district, so they drove back to the scene, on Bragg Drive, and they saw nothing but darkness and heard nothing but the night sounds. They stopped the car. They called in the darkness. Into the headlights came Edna. Her dark cheeks were stained with old tears. The boys put her in the car and decided to look again for a policeman.

At the police station, they told their story. The cops asked a few questions. They entered the complaint at one thirty. They moved, and moved fast. They called by radio the description of the missing car, and the meager description of the four white men. They asked the state police for aid. They called in the sheriff's police; they ordered the city prowl cars to join the hunt. There was no lagging; no hesitation.

One policeman took Edna and the Brown boy in his car. A young deputy sheriff named Joe Cooke, Jr., took Tom in his car. This was Cooke's first night out alone in a squad car. He prowled the city.

The four white men stopped the car in a narrow rutted lane in the middle of a woods. The trees were thick and young. They took Betty out of the car, holding her by the arm so that she wouldn't fall among the brambles. They got her to a clearing.

"What," she said nervously, "what are you going to do with me?"

In the headlights, she could see the four now. One was a dark, mature young man. A second was slightly younger, maybe twenty-two. He was tough and he issued orders to her. A third was a good-looking youth, perhaps twenty. The fourth was a fuzzless boy.

"As long as you do as we tell you," the bossy one said, "you won't be hurt."

The older one approached her. He saw her staring at the one with the shotgun. "Lay down," he said, pushing at her shoulder. She did. She started to cry again. "What's your name?" he said. It was strange, but she couldn't remember. She just couldn't remember.

The one with the gun said, "You stop crying or you won't see home again." Another one said, "Tell us about school."

One of them knelt alongside of her and he was smiling. She didn't want to beg, but she started to and couldn't stop. "Please don't go with me," she murmured over and over again. "Please don't go with me."

The squad cars raced in and out of Tallahassee with the red

lights blinking. They hit every main road, every side road; they combed the alleys and their rubber squealed on macadam and spun red clay into the night sky. They stopped cars, asked questions. There was nothing to report.

From 1:15 until 4 A.M. Betty was lying in the leaves of the forest. The men did not permit her to sit or stand at any time. Sometimes, while one demanded her attention, the others gathered a little bit off and talked. She had stopped pleading long ago. Her new hope was that she might be permitted to live.

She was raped seven times. Around four o'clock, one man pulled her to her feet. She was taken to the car and placed in the middle of the back seat.

One of the men took a diaper from a laundry package and wound it around her eyes. Then he jammed her face into his lap and the car started to back out of the glade. The men didn't talk much. After a while, the driving became smooth and the tires began to sing with speed. Once, a man said, "Let's turn off at Orange." There was no answer, but she knew that Orange Avenue branched off the state highway into the Negro section. They were still moving fast, when one of the men said, "There's a cop behind us." The car picked up more speed, and more. One of the men grabbed the back of Betty's neck and shoved her on the floor.

She heard the high cry of a siren. Then there was some lurching, and brakes began to squeal. The car was a long time stopping. It died in front of a Cities Service station at Railroad Avenue and Osceola. The station was closed. A night light was on.

Deputy Sheriff Joe Cooke, Jr., got out of his car. A man aimed a shotgun out the window at the policeman. Butterfield watched from the prowl car. "If anybody moves," the young officer said, "I'll shoot him." The shotgun was lowered.

The men got out. Cooke lined them against the filling station wall. Their hands were above their heads. One of the men tried to crawl into some bushes at the side of the station. Butterfield told the deputy sheriff. The man was brought back.

Cooke kept his gun aimed at their backs and ordered the girl out of the car. The gold and white dress didn't look like much. "We'll just have to wait until a car comes," Cooke said. "I have no radio." They waited. The car came. The four men were booked on charge of rape. The time was 4:20 A.M. The night was over. The moon had set.

The prisoners are in the detention pen. They wait for Judge W. May Walker to order their shackles struck. They are young. They look immature and scared. They speak in whispers. They swallow when they are told they may have to die in the electric chair at Raiford for this crime. Their eyes tell you this was no crime. It was a prank. She was a colored girl. They didn't hurt her.

They told that to Deputy Cooke the night he arrested them. They made statements. They admitted their guilt. Guilt? She was only a colored girl.

Ollie Stoutamire, sixteen, is a second cousin to the police chief. His mother died at his birth. He had been attending vocational school until recently. Then Ollie got a job with a pipe company. He was once picked up by juvenile authorities on a minor charge. His attorney is City Judge John Rudd.

David I. Beagles is eighteen. He is the best citizen of the four. He was raised in Westville, Florida. He is a senior in high school and helps his parents by working part-time at a filling station. His father is a truck driver. His mother is a waitress. He has never been arrested. He is being defended by Howard Williams.

Patrick Scarborough is twenty. He is married. He was born in Tampa. His mother was shot in a tavern in 1946. His father committed suicide the same year. He was raised by his grandparents. Life with them was so irksome to Pat that, as quickly as possible, he joined the Air Force.

He has just finished a tour of duty in Alaska. He is home on leave with his wife. He once served thirty days for a motor vehicle violation. Attorney: Harry Michaels.

Ted Collinsworth is twenty-three. He is an illiterate telephone lineman. He is married, has two children, a son, two, and a daughter, eleven months. His lawyer is G. Gunter Toney and Ted will plead temporary insanity. His sisters and his wife have made written statements about Ted Collinsworth. Some of it reads like this:

A sister: "He was always stupid, he could not learn to read or write. When he was six, he was found behind a wood stove drunk and passed out. He used to complain of pains in his stomach. A doctor said not to let him use tobacco in any form.

"Neighborhood boys used to tease my father. When Ted was eight, his father gave him a gun and told him to shoot the boys. There were seven children in our family. We were poor. We got no love. My father worked in a sawmill sometimes, but most of the time he said he had erysipelas of the legs and couldn't work. My mother took in washing.

"Ted's clothes came from welfare. He never had no shoes. He couldn't learn in school and he has been drinking since he was seventeen. He married early, but arguments broke it up.

"Dad kept a special four-foot board at the end of the porch for

beating his wife. He had a double razor strop for the children
with a dipper sewed on the end for a handle. We all slept in the
same room and, at night, all the little ones watched our parents.

"My father didn't like any of us. At Christmas he gave us each
an orange. My mother died last October. She had been a drug
addict for seven years. After the funeral, my father spoke to the
children and told them that he did not love them and he never
had."

Collinsworth's lawyer, G. Gunter Toney, is a serious young
man. Since his plea will be temporary insanity, he will call a
psychiatrist to support it. The Court appointed a couple of doctors to examine Collinsworth. It is believed they will testify that
the young man may be stupid, but he knew the nature and the
quality of his acts when he was in the woods with Betty.

The prosecutor is William D. Hopkins, who is respected
among both races here as a just State Attorney. He is a citizen of
substance in this community, a man with a fleck of gray at the
temples and a soft reasonable manner. He has a good home, a fine
farm, a dairy herd, and hunting dogs. He has been known to
assist without fee Negro wives whose husbands have disappeared.

The judge, W. May Walker, is stout and gray and hearty. He is
a "self-made man" and worked his way through school. He is one
of three judges in the Second Circuit Court in Leon County and is
reputed to be stern in his judgments. He will permit no running in
and out of his court by reporters, no cameras, no delays in the
progress of the trial.

He owns a fine brick home with a curved gravel driveway, and
his colored housekeeper has remained in his service for twenty-
five years.

No one wants to serve on the jury. The men here despise the
defendants, but don't want to doom them. Most of the better
citizens have asked to be excused. The remainder of the panel,
about 230, have been augmented by sixty new names—all white
men. Each of the four defense lawyers has ten challenges. State
Attorney Hopkins has forty. It could be a slow trial. If four Negroes had raped a white girl, it would be a fast trial.

Everybody has been busy investigating the moral life of Betty.
So far, no one has found a blemish. One attorney said the investigation at Florida A. & M. College showed Betty was the only one
in her class who, when the other girls were changing to gymnasium clothes, asked permission to change in private.

A man would almost have to be a liar to make this jury. The
questions are so adroit that, to qualify, a juryman has to endorse

capital punishment, assume the innocence of four young men
charged with raping a Negro girl, have read accounts of the story
but have no opinion, be ready to acquit if doubt shadows his
mind, have children, be prepared to ask for mercy for the four,
and have no prejudice against alcoholism.

For a whole day, the contending sides asked those questions. All
day long the lawyers lounged against the jury box, looking each
man in the eye, and all day long jurymen were challenged and
excused and sent away.

In the evening, twelve men were agreed upon, and two alter-
nates were picked. Four women were waiting to be questioned,
but the lawyers didn't get to them. Four Negro men were in the
panel, too, but the sheriff didn't get to their names.

The court is on the second floor of the Leon County Courthouse. It is old, and the walls are pastel green, hung with tinted
photographs of old judges. The bench has a pencil sharpener
screwed into one side, and a big pitcher of shaved ice on top.
Behind Judge Walker, a gray-maned lion of a man, is an old
grandfather clock. The brass pendulum swings its unhurried way,
and it calls time to the four young men who face it.

These are charged with taking a colored girl named Betty, at
shotgun and knife point, and raping her in a woods outside of
town on the morning of May 2, 1959. In the silence of counsel,
they hear the clock. So do their kin who sit watching from the
downstairs white section of the court.

The leader is Ted Collinsworth, who sits quietly in a blue silk
sports shirt, watching and listening. His face is tough and handsome; his lashes are almost girlishly long. Papers are passed back
and forth along the counsel table. Collinsworth does not try to
read them because he is illiterate.

David I. Beagles fidgets. He is a blond crew-cut, a short,
vacuous boy who chews gum and who stops when he wants to
think. He has acne and picks at his skin.

Although Ollie Stoutamire is sixteen, he looks twelve. He has
big dark eyes in a pale face; he keeps cracking his knuckles and
trying to work up a smile to show he isn't afraid. He is so thin that
his plastic belt has special holes punched in it to hold his trousers
up.

Pat Scarborough could play J. Wilkes Booth if he had a mustache. His brown hair is mussed; he frowns perpetually; his
mouth droops at the edges; he looks like a troublemaker and
dissenter. He is the kind of young man who is acutely aware of
his rights, but no others.

There is a room in the front of the building. Betty sits there, all dressed up and nervous. Her mother and her brother and sisters sit with her. Betty keeps renerving herself to the ordeal. Soon they will call her and she will then sit on the stand, surrounded by white men, and she will see the four boys for the first time since the predawn hours of May 2.

She is dark and modest and has a size-ten figure, skinny and flat and lost inside the white blouse. Her response to questions is direct and unequiovocal. When she doesn't know, she says, "I'm sorry. I don't know." There is a chance that, before sundown, Betty will feel that she is on trial. Essentially, she is. Very few of her race complain of rape. If they do, sometimes the guilty men cannot be found.

The white men here hate rape cases. If a Negro is charged with raping a white woman, the entire community winces when the woman must take the stand to answer intimate questions.

None of the men will mind asking Betty these questions, and the defense counsel can spend as long as they please trying to crack her story.

That's their job. Judge Walker has been almost overly fair. He sees this as a hanging case and, many times while almost three score of men were walking in and out of the jury box he asked: "If the evidence of guilt is beyond reasonable doubt, are you ready to vote guilty?" A guilty verdict means the electric chair. A guilty verdict with a recommendation for mercy means any sentence the judge cares to render, from a suspended sentence up to life in prison.

The judge isn't stressing the mercy angle. Neither is State Attorney William Hopkins, who asked every prospective juror: "You are not opposed to capital punishment? You would not be afraid to vote for it if the evidence from the witness chair warrants it?"

Hopkins has explained to reporters again and again: "Integration is a separate problem. It has nothing to do with this case. We are trying a crime and it is going to be tried without regard to color."

John Rudd asked no questions. He passed his thoughts behind his hand to other defense counsel. Howard Williams, young Beagles' lawyer, asked the Rudd questions and used the Rudd challenges. These men are working as a team for the two younger defendants.

Harry Michaels, Scarborough's stocky and polite lawyer, wanted to be sure no one had a preconceived notion about guilt before sitting on the jury. He also leaned toward men who had children.

The loner among the lawyers is G. Gunter Toney, a short intense bright man, who pleads that his client, Collinsworth, was temporarily insane at the time of the commission of the crime. He is the only one willing to admit that a crime occurred.

There is going to be a big legal wrangle over this. Some doctors will testify against. The only item on which all seem agreed is that Ted, who owned the car used that night, also the shotgun, has the mentality of a boy of nine. And, they might add, the instincts of a grown sadist.

Ted's wife, Pearlie, paused at the counsel table to say hello to her man. I sat behind them. This is the dialogue:

Pearlie: "Are you scared?"

Ted: (no kiss for his wife) "Are you?"

Pearlie: "No."

Ted: "How are the kids?"

Pearlie: "They're all right."

Ted has two young children. The colored girl claims she was blindfolded, in the car, by a diaper.

The balcony was jammed with Negroes. So were the stairwell, the corridors, and the street in front of the court. It was a damp, misty day, but they came to lend silent support to one of their people, and they did it without giving the many uniformed deputies a chance to get excited. Many stood in the mist, watching.

One boy, son of a Negro minister, refused to move when ordered and was taken to the sheriff's office. His father came to get him and he was sent home, denying he talked insolently to the law, while the two lawmen said he did.

The only thing that brought a quick smile to all faces was when a prospective juror was being questioned about his feelings on Collinsworth's temporary insanity. He looked puzzled, stroked his chin, and said, "We tryin' to get him for insanity? Or drinkin'?"

Before the morning session opened, Judge May called the sheriff to the bench and pointed to the Negroes in the balcony. "You got a lot of people up there," the judge said. "This is an old courthouse." The sheriff nodded. "Well," the judge said, "what's going to happen if that balcony gives way?" The sheriff moved his gum over to the opposite cheek. "Instant integration," he said.

She looked like a child. She wore a big white blouse hiding the nothing underneath, and a black and salmon plaid skirt and white sandals. There was lipstick, a new wave in her shiny hair, and imitation gold circlets in her ears. This was Betty, the colored coed, testifying to her rape by four white boys.

Judge Walker didn't have to rap for order. Five hundred pairs of eyes—half of them friendly—studied every inch of Betty. No one missed a word of her whispering story. Juror Number Five—Rufus Graddy—didn't appear to be breathing. He cleaned his glasses on his jacket.

One reporter said: "She looks like a kid. Why pick her?"

She was available. That's why. All the white hoodlums had in mind was to break up a necking party and use a shotgun and a switchblade knife as big as a platter to make the Negroes crawl.

When the colored boys drove away, and Edna ran screaming into the darkness, Betty was left. And the white boys began to get better ideas. One took her by the wrist and dropped her into the grass with a knife at her neck.

But another one said, "No, no. Not here."

She told it all. State Attorney William Hopkins leaned on the edge of the jury box and led the girl, moment by moment, through the events of the whole night. Betty told it straight.

The prosecutor apologized when he asked intimate questions. When he asked who took her panties, she didn't know.

"The first one," she said. She was raped seven times in three hours, and she left the piney glen with "bruises on my chest. They came from the stiff net in the front of the dress. Somebody leaning on it."

She held her head up with a little pride when the four defense attorneys began cross-examination. Sometimes she just shook her head no to a question, and the dark waves behind her head swung back and forth. The thin-lipped man with the scorn in his voice, John Rudd, had no taste for his job and he looked away from Betty as he questioned her.

"Did he [Ollie Stoutamire] mistreat you or bite you or kick you or threaten you?"

The answer came quickly: "No."

The questions became incisive. "How many times did he get with you?"

The answer died on the lips: "Twice."

"Was he first or fourth or what?"

She hung her head. "First." This was the first proof that, in the darkness, she knew one from another.

"Betty, I'm going to ask you a question and I want you to think carefully before you answer. You're nineteen and you got a lot of years ahead of you. My boy is sixteen and he has more years in front of him—isn't it true that Ollie was so drunk that he couldn't do anything?"

"No."

"You sure?"

"I'm sure."

The defense began to stagger after that. They had to crack her story, and they hadn't. The tall lawyer, Howard Williams, scraped the bottom of the moral barrel. "Were you a virgin when this happened?"

The State Attorney got to his feet. "Objection, your honor," he said. "Even a prostitute can be raped." The objection was sustained. Betty didn't have to answer.

Lawyer Gunter Toney, who appeared to be flailing in the dark hoping to strike a solid object, sometimes walked into one.

"Betty, you testified that somebody was first. Who was fourth?"

"Collinsworth." She survived cross-examination without giving up any self-respect, without altering her story or straining to defend it. They let her go at noon recess. In the afternoon, the prosecution began to drop the little tiles in place which, when completed, make an ugly picture.

Richard A. Brown, who sat in the back of the car with Betty's friend, Edna, the night all of this happened, has tight black hair, dark skin, big brooding eyes and a tiny mustache.

The defense picked him to try to prove two points: One, that Brown and Butterfield were having relations with Betty and Edna as the white boys came along; two, that Betty was not reluctant to go with the white boys. The defense failed on both counts and, inadvertently, permitted young Brown to toss in a gratuitous remark that, when he and Tom were kneeling in front of the car headlights, one of the white boys suggested that the Negroes be killed, and that someone else said, "No, they're good boys." This, in addition to his testimony identifying the Winchester shotgun and the big knife, tends to show that Betty accompanied the white boys under threat of death.

At 4:17 P.M. Joe Cooke, Jr., came to the stand. He's twenty-one, blond, with a skin haircut. Cooke studies criminology at Florida State University. When he isn't in class, he's a part-time deputy sheriff.

He testified crisply in a honey drawl. At one o'clock on the night in question he was talking to Deputy W. W. Slappey near the courthouse when a car pulled up. In it were three Negroes: Brown, Butterfield and Edna. They told a story that four white boys had threatened them and had driven off with a girl named Betty.

Slappey spread the alarm and young Cooke took Butterfield with him. Slappey ordered Cooke to apprehend, not to arrest. In a short time, police cars were roaming the quiet streets and predawn highways, looking for a 1959 Chevy with four white boys and a colored girl.

At 4:30 A.M. Cooke said they were coming back into town

when they saw a Chevy ahead of them. It was 1959 and had no license plate. He chased it and he thinks they hit better than sixty around some of the corners. He then saw the face of a colored girl at the rear window with what appeared to be a gag in her mouth. Also, he saw the silhouette of a shotgun. He hit his siren, blinked his brights, and pulled the car to a curb.

Four men got out. One tried to crawl away. He ordered all to stand against a filling station wall and to remove their shoes and everything from their pockets. He found Betty on the floor of the Chevy, hysterical. Her eyes were swollen from weeping. She didn't make much sense.

At the hospital, while the doctors were examining the girl, Cooke examined her clothing. One panel of net was torn from her evening dress. Wire grass and pine straw were stuck to the back of the gown. He removed it and put it in an envelope and marked it for identification.

Slappey followed Cooke to the stand. When he arrived at the filling station, he saw Betty, saw the four white boys, and asked the girl one question.

"Did those boys hurt you?" he asked. She replied, "All four of them raped me."

All day long, the four defense attorneys objected and asked for a mistrial. Judge W. May Walker, a Southerner's Southerner, leaned over backward to be courteous to all. But when he heard one attorney make the same objection three times, he drawled, "Overruled that matter several times. The question has been foreclosed—and put at rest."

Thomas Butterfield got on the stand, a handsome Negro with hands composed and mind honed. He told the story of that night in detail. He told how, when he and the police reached the scene of the arrest, Betty was still in the evening dress; the side zipper was down; her brassiere was undone; her cheeks were tear-stained, and she shook in spasms.

"I couldn't talk to her," he said sadly. "She was in no condition to talk to nobody." The defense lawyers, one at a time, took careful aim at Tom Butterfield and tried to drill his story. They had tried hard to crack Betty's story earlier. They had equal luck with both: None. Q. What were you doing when those white boys came up in their car? A. Talking. Q. How long had you been parked? A. Fifteen minutes—I don't know, maybe twenty. Q. Come now, it was longer than that. A. No it wasn't, sir. Q. Were your clothes disturbed when they ordered you out of the car? A. No, sir. Q. You sure? A. Yes, Sir.

Edna Richardson took the stand after Butterfield. She is the girl who ran from rape. She's dark, nervous, rolls her eyes before she answers, wears heavy make-up and silvered nails. She, like the others, tells a story which matches in almost every detail, what the five hundred spectators have been hearing for three days.

In the afternoon, with the sun leaning on the roof of the old Leon County Courthouse and the colored people lining the edges of the stairwell waiting for balcony seats, Dr. R. L. Anderson, a Negro of Florida A. & M., was called to tell of his examination of Betty at dawn the morning of the crime. He's a distinguished-looking man with a splash of gray and he wears rimless glasses.

He examined her and found Betty to be hysterical. He helped her to remove the evening dress and the crinolines. She kept sobbing and shaking. He found no bruises or contusions. He found no signs of irritation, no sign of virginity. He made a vaginal smear and found many signs of sperm.

Officer Raymond Hamlin, who appears to have total recall, sat in the witness chair, modestly kept his small eyes aimed forward, and told everything he heard and saw the morning of the rape. In effect, his quotes of the four boys were such that he was causing one to testify against the other. He quoted Scarborough:

"Scarborough told me the couples were necking when they pulled up alongside. Collinsworth and Scarborough sat in front; Ollie and Beagles were in back. Beagles got Betty into the car and held her head in his lap. When they got to the woods, Betty was ordered to lie down. She did.

"Little Ollie was first. Scarborough was second. He told me she offered no assistance the first time, but she did the second. 'When I was with her, she whispered, "Are they going to hurt me?" I said no.' "

He quoted Beagles:

"The Negroes in the car were having intercourse, we ordered them out. When one girl ran away, I pushed the other one into the car. She pushed her head down into my lap. When we got to the woods, she whispered to me, 'If you don't tell anybody, I won't tell anybody.' "

He quoted Collinsworth:

"I'm not admitting to any rape. I admit I had intercourse with that girl, but it ain't rape." Officer Hamlin said sadly: "He didn't have a particular nimble mind."

The more Hamlin was questioned, the better he remembered. "Ollie told me that Scarborough had the gun, Beagles had the knife. Scarborough did the talking and ordered the Negroes to

kneel in front of the bumper. I asked Ollie about the second time
he was with Betty and he said, 'There wa'ant no second time.' "

Toward the end of the day, Collinsworth's attorney, Toney, got
permission to put a psychiatrist on the stand in the absence of the
jury. Dr. William Wilhoit took the stand and outlined his findings,
He is young and dark, wears glasses and has a nervous sports
shoe. His examination he said, disclosed that Collinsworth has a
defective mentality; the doctor stressed that Collinsworth is a
man of more than half Indian blood. Wilhoit said, "When alcohol
was added to his Indian blood and defective mentality, he was
easily led. I don't think he can be held fully accountable for his
behavior."

The doctor said Collinsworth has a mental age of nine, an
Intelligence Quotient of sixty, and can be called a moron. State
Attorney Hopkins asked the doctor if he found any evidence of a
psychosis. The doctor said no.

At dinnertime, Hopkins closed his case for the State of Florida.
After dinner, the defense opened its case in night session. The
court day lasted sixteen hours.

The defense opened by putting David Irven Beagles on the
witness stand. There is a feeling among the defense lawyers that
the four boys have been betrayed, in a sense, by the prosecutor.
He is actually prosecuting, hard and unremittingly. There is a fear
that he will—really will—ask the death penalty. There is a feeling
of apprehension that it is the South which is on trial this time, and
if Negroes can die for rape, or serve life sentences, white boys can
too.

Beagles testified as his mother and father sat in the second row
of spectators. His father kept studying his shoes; his mother, small
and dark, gazed out in perpetual horror over a handkerchief
clutched to her mouth. Irven, as he is called, talked in bursts,
moving only his lower lip. He kept sliding a graduation ring on
and off his finger as his attorney led him gently through his story
of what happened on the night of May 1.

He speaks deep in his throat, and he tells of how he and Ollie
Stoutamire drank whisky that night. They had a blind date, but
they didn't keep it. They went over to Ted Collinsworth's house
and met Gene [Patrick] Scarborough there. Ted was cussing
about the Negroes who park near his house and throw empty
bottles.

Ted had some gin. They drank that, too. They got in Ted's car
and, when they saw the Negro coed's automobile, Ted yelled,
"There's one of them."

"I looked in the car and saw a boy laying on top of a girl. Gene had Ted's shotgun and he told the Negroes to get out. One started running. I found a knife in the back of Ted's car. I opened the back door and Gene told the girl to get in. I pushed her head down.

"Somebody told her that if she did what we wanted her to, she wouldn't be hurt. She said she would. There wasn't much talk. She talked to us like an ordinary person would. When we got to the woods, she said, 'If you don't tell anybody, I won't.' I told her I wouldn't. On the way back, she said she wanted to be let out at the college. We were on our way back when the police stopped us."

Harry Morrison, assistant state attorney, cross-examined. He got Beagles to admit ownership of the knife, got him to swear that his friend Scarborough got out of the car with a shotgun (loaded).

"And when that other girl ran off," Morrison said, "and the colored boys got away, that Betty just got in your car freely and voluntarily like she was glad to see y'all?" Beagles swallowed and said, "Yes, sir." "Did you put the blindfold on her on the way home?" "Yes, sir." "Then she did not come back with you as voluntarily as she left?" "One of the fellows said to push her down to the floor boards, but I thought the blindfold was better."

The last day of the trial began, as had all the others, calmly. The conversation in the corridors was about Pat Scarborough, the defendant who looks like a fanatic. He had been on the stand late Friday night—a surprise witness in his own behalf—and his truculent attitude shocked some.

His brown hair is perpetually mussed; his brooding eyes hide under the dome of his forehead and he gives the impression of a youth who might, if goaded, go berserk. State Attorney Hopkins, on cross-examination, seemed to approach that point when he asked Scarborough who held the gun at the four Negro freshmen when the group was ordered from their car in lovers' lane on May 2.

Q. Who told the colored boys to go away?
A. (quickly, proudly) I did.
Q. For what purpose?
A. (starting to glare at the D.A.) I don't know.
Q. You don't know? Then why did you keep the girl?
A. (Curling of lips) I don't know why I did that either.
Q. How many times did you go with Betty?
A. Twice.

Q. (Asked innocently) Did you kiss her?

A. (After silence and staring up at giggling Negroes in balcony) No.

Q. Do you remember Officer Hamlin asking you that question? What did you say then?

A. (in a whisper) I said I kissed her . . . on the neck.

The big judge rapped for order at 8:38 A.M. He had kept the trial going the night before until ten minutes before midnight. He was pushing to keep the defense from dragging its feet.

Collinsworth, the silent, is pleading insanity. He has spent the trial looking down at his thumbs as they roll against each other. He seldom talks to the other defendants; sometimes he listens. Ted's first witness was his brother Tom, a hard-working family man.

Tom testified that young Ted is an alcoholic; that he was first found drunk and unconscious behind a wood stove at the age of six. The family blames everything on the father, Tom, Sr., who beat the children to the floor of the one-room house, then stomped on them. The mother, who died last October, took in washing to feed the children, and she was beaten with a special four-foot board.

Ted listened to his brother testify, but he didn't lift his eyes. Assistant State Attorney Harry Morrison, on cross-examination, asked another innocent question:

"Tom, weren't you brought up in the same family with Ted, at the same time, under the same circumstances, by the same father, and aren't you a responsible citizen and a good family man?"

Tom had no answer.

He was also asked if it wasn't true that, for an insane man, Ted managed to keep a job for three years as a telephone linesman, managed to get married and have two children and turn his paycheck of eighty-five dollars a week over to his wife, and do his work satisfactorily?

No answer.

Tom was followed by his father. He is tall and thin, a man of brittle step and turkey neck. Ted did not look up. The father cocked his left ear toward counsel, and said that, as he rightly remembers, Ted was a boy who "couldn't learn nothing," and threw spitballs in school. Daddy said that he personally had had eight months of schooling and it hadn't hurt him none. He got off the stand.

There is a *Tobacco Road* quality about the Collinsworth group. They live cheaply and meanly, laughing and scratching and sizing each other up, and the men drink and fish and look down upon the Negroes as though it was the last sacred right left to a bewildered white man.

Pearlie took the stand, and Ted looked up at his thin wife with the neat print dress, the whiny tone, and the freshly waved hair, and, in a trice, he rejoined the human race. He broke down and cried.

She says he beat her with a tennis racket, and he slugged her when she was eight months pregnant, but she put some fervency in her tone when she told the jury that Ted Collinsworth is the best husband that ever lived.

She broke down on the stand twice. Ted, at the counsel table, wiped his eyes with a blue handkerchief. None of the Negroes in the balcony wept. They watched, and they were quiet.

There was a group of psychiatrists who followed Pearlie, and, as always at a trial, they became enmeshed in the lengthy hypothetical questions covering insanity and its relationship to the defendants. Dr. William Wilhoit, for the defense, said these things at various times:

"He is a mental defective with an added factor—alcoholism. He is a moron with an I.Q. of sixty. He is not fully responsible. He is not psychotic. He knows the difference between right and wrong. He is sane. He did not understand the quality of his act. He was medically insane at the time of the crime."

Dr. Wilhoit was followed by court-appointed doctors. Dr. James O'Connor, a psychiatrist who looks like a prescription clerk in a drugstore, called Ted illiterate, but says the boy knew what he was doing on the night of May 1. Dr. C. H. Cronich and others agreed. Dr. Cronich said:

"He told us he knew he was doing wrong. He even told us the penalty for rape."

The streets of this old Southern town were quiet tonight as the case neared the jury after dinner. Drivers, passing the courthouse, yelled: "Jury out yet?" Negro women sat on benches under swamp oaks, fanning themselves. A few policemen sat in patrol cars, watching the Saturday night traffic. This was waiting time.

Family shoppers walked the cool sidewalks, staring into well-lighted stores. Not much was said about the trial. And yet, everyone was aware of it and everyone knew that something important could happen tonight. The retired generation of Southerners felt that the trial would end in a hung jury. The rest sensed a new uneasiness that there should be a moral difference between the raping of a white woman and the raping of a Negro. Was there a difference?

In a dramatic final summation, State Attorney William D.

Hopkins urged the jury to reject racial bias and find the four white youths guilty. Hopkins left it to the jury to decide whether to condemn the defendants to death. But he asked the panel what would happen if four Negroes had taken a single white girl at gun point and raped her seven times.

"If you're going to convict on facts in one case, you've to convict on facts in another," he said. "I'm sorry defense counsel saw fit to bring anything in, even by innuendo, about the difference in the races," he concluded. "I'm sorry they brought the race question into it. I don't think it's right."

Hopkins' pointed remarks were prompted by defense summations that implied that "these four boys" were about to be sent to the electric chair by Northern newspapers. Howard Williams intoned: "There are certain things that have been ingrained in me that I don't have to think about again. The pendulum, gentlemen, sometimes swings too far. Sometimes I wonder how we got so far off the rails."

He clasped the edge of the jury box and stared at the twelve men as though they knew what rails he meant.

"I want to tell you another thing. It's about an electric chair, a little invention we have down in Raiford. One thing I know: the evidence I've seen here removes Irven Beagles as far away as it is possible to get from the electric chair." He canvassed the eyes with his own and saw no challenge. "If the State Attorney sells you the electric chair, he's some salesman because he is selling something that is worthless.

"This case involves life and liberty." He took a deep satisfied breath. "The motives of these boys on that night were wholesome and honest and absolutely innocent."

The attorneys followed each other like knights on a jousting field. City Judge John Rudd, who conceals no contempt when he stares at the Negroes in the balcony, came up to speak for Ollie Stoutamire.

"We the defense," he said loudly, "worked under handicaps. We had no investigators. We had no money. We got no respect from the balcony. We had no respect from the four Negroes— lovers, philosophers, conversationalists—whatever you want to call them." His razor lips slice his words sidewards. "Are we going to kill that small undernourished boy for being in the wrong place at the wrong time?"

He shook his head sadly as though the jury had already committed this heinous offense. "Are you going to vote to send thirty-three thousand volts through that boy's body, or send him away for a long time? I'd like to say: 'Send him home,' but he doesn't

have one. Send him back to his father—and let them find a place
to live."

The smooth, soft, swift little voice of S. Gunter Toney got
directly to the point.

"The fact that we have a race situation here is a factor in this
case. The pressure, the clamor, the furor has been out of all
proportion to the worth of the case. I think we all expect fair
play. We are a Christian people." This sounded as though the
defendants and the jury belonged to an exclusive lodge. "My God,
when you read those newspapers, this case sounds awful. Who's
trying to agitate this case? Who's interested in a verdict? What
kind of a verdict? You won't forget this case, gentlemen of the
jury. I won't forget it."

All of it was enough to make a man think, when he wants to
know how to apply the law to a case of mass rape. Especially if
he aspires to return to Tallahassee and live after reaching a verdict.

The jury left the courtroom at 9:53 P.M. The old flat-footed
bailiff with the thick glasses led the way, feeling his way along the
rail. The twelve men followed. There were no smiles. No nods of
recognition. They accepted the final job grimly.

They entered a big square room on the second floor of Leon
County Courthouse. It was air-conditioned. They could look
down on Monroe Street, and see the little knots of white and
colored people standing around. The window was closed and they
could not hear the driver, waiting for the green light, yell out:
"Jury out yet?"

Yes, the jury was out. It had a ten-minute job. All it had to do
was to mark four sheets of paper "not guilty" or, at worst, "guilty
of assault with intent to rape." After all, the four boys wilting in
that detention cell were white. The girl was a colored coed. If the
case was turned the other way around, it would be a different
verdict but it would still require only ten minutes.

They sent out for two big pots of coffee. It felt funny to be able
to talk about the case. Since Wednesday they had been admonished by Judge Walker not even to mention the case they have
been hearing. The newspapers they were permitted to read in the
Cherokee Hotel had been butchered with shears.

The twelve men walked around the room, stretching their legs,
glad to think of home again. They elected A. H. King as foreman.
He's known as Gus, and he is a short grandfather with a grin like
a boy. He chews gum and, out on Route One, he owns a "postage
stamp" farm of 450 acres.

By now, these men knew each other pretty well. Gus King decided, after they sat to deliberate, that they would never reach a verdict if everyone was going to talk about different defendants at the same time. He asked them to be quiet for a moment and he said they would consider each boy alone, one at a time.

Someone said Betty's dress didn't look very mussed to him. If she was really raped in that thing, he couldn't understand it. Gus said the State exhibits were in the room, maybe everyone ought to have a look at them. They were in a big carton, jumbled one on top of the other.

The white and gold evening dress, with its three bouffant crinolines, was yanked out. Gus King wrinkled it between his big hands. Then he fluffed it out. "See?" he said. "I know about these things. They never wrinkle much."

The jurymen nodded. One reached for the big Winchester shotgun which Pat "Gene" Scarborough had aimed at the two Negro couples parked in a shady lane on the night of May 1. Another picked up the big knife with a bone handle and pressed the button. A seven-inch blade snapped out gleaming. Irven Beagles had held it against Betty's neck forty-four days ago.

"That knife," one of them said, shaking his head at the size of it. "Damn."

The foreman saw one of the jurymen holding the evening dress in front of him. "Why don't you try it on?" That brought the only smile of the night.

Down at the Florida Theater, people were coming out asking "any verdict yet?" Down in Frenchtown, where the Negroes live, it was achingly quiet. At the State, where the horror movies glow, some teen-agers came out and said, "Let's go over to the courthouse and see what happens."

It was a hot night. An insufferable night. The jury sat in some comfort. Across the street, a *Life* photographer trained a telescopic lens on the room. He made a few pictures. The sheriff's deputies took him under the arms and went off with him.

One juror fidgeted and said well, it was going to be useless to ask him to vote for the electric chair because he was opposed to capital punishment. Another chimed in, and said that went for him too. These two had lied when State Attorney William D. Hopkins asked them, as a condition of acceptance, whether they were opposed to capital punishment. They had said no.

Another juror spoke up and said he wasn't opposed to capital punishment, but he wouldn't vote for it unless someone could show him the girl had been beaten up. A tall thin one spoke: "I would vote all four into the chair if they beat her." There was something which outraged them more than rape: a beating.

King chewed his gum. His twinkling eyes darted from face to face. After so much silence over so many days, it was good to hear them speak their minds, whether you agreed with them or not.

A middle-aged man said, "I couldn't vote to send that little boy to the electric chair. I just couldn't."

That brought up another point: culpability. The jurors agreed all four were equally culpable. No one could say one was more guilty than any other. So, if the chair was ruled out, then so too was freedom. These boys were not going to be sent home.

John Rudd, attorney for young Ollie Stoutamire, had told this jury he had no doubt that the kid, ashamed to retreat in the presence of the older boys, had gone over to where Betty was lying in the woods, heart pounding like a rabbit's, and "he wiggled around a little and strutted off without doing anything."

Rudd is an important man here. Would the jury take his word, or Betty's? Betty said the young boy had been the first to rape her, had pulled her panties off. The jury thought it over. They took Betty's word.

In court, the air conditioner died. Reporters sat in the jury box, feet on the railing. Sheriff's deputies—big men with hard eyes—leaned against the walls. Pretty girls dressed in their best made a social session of it, chattering and swigging Cokes.

The jury narrowed it down to two verdicts. It could be "guilty, with a recommendation of mercy" or it could be "assault with intent to rape." The first often means twenty years to life. The second would be a short term in State Prison. Some of the men said assault wasn't worth considering. Rape was rape.

King turned on his grin. He now had a verdict, but he wanted these men to talk it out a little more. They did. He was pleased no one had mentioned the girl's race since the deliberations began.

They talked about Beagles. He was the good boy who had flashed the knife. His lawyer, big Howard Williams, had told the jury: "The motives of these boys on that Friday night were wholesome and honest and absolutely innocent."

The jury did not believe Williams. They voted guilty for his client. Gus marked it down—with the recommendation for mercy. One thing was sure: Irven would be in prison at least ten years or more before he would be eligible for parole.

Scarborough, the meanest-looking of the group, the twenty-year-old on furlough from the Air Force, was barely discussed. Most of the jury believed Gene Scarborough was the leader on that night in the woods off Springhill Road. He was the one who held the shotgun and drew a bead on the Negroes in the parked car. He had said, "Get out."

His attorney had told this jury: "The State has failed to prove the charge of rape against Scarborough." The jury didn't believe him.

The case of Ted Collinsworth was different. His lawyer had pleaded him insane. The jury had listened to the learned psychiatrists for and against Collinsworth. The doctors had immersed themselves in a game of semantics, juggling their opinions in such a multisyllabled pontification that the jury paid no attention to any of it.

"Collinsworth manages to keep a job, doesn't he?" Gus King said. Onc sentence. It smashed everything the psychiatrists had said. He manages to keep a job. How can he be insane if he can be a telephone linesman and not do crazy things? The jury decided Ted Collinsworth, illiterate and retarded, was not insane. He knew what he was doing when he raped Betty.

"Guilty, with a recommendation . . ."

Ollis Stoutamire's case caused a little chin rubbing. He was the first to commit rape, but he was only sixteen. Some of the jurors knew his history. His mother had died when he was born. His father placed him with other people and remarried. He didn't like school, and he didn't care much for work. Ollie couldn't wait until he became a man, and issued his own orders. The jury decided Ollie achieved his goal on the night of May 1.

They voted a man's verdict. "Guilty, with a recommendation . . ."

At 12:19 A.M. Sunday morning, Gus King peeped out inside the courtroom hall. He called the bailiff.

"Go tell the judge we're ready," he said. "We have reached a verdict."

They had. They had.

Harlem: Portrait of a Time Bomb

Harlem . . . the night is alive. Harlem . . . it's a flat cornet hitting the high thin notes. It's dark skin in darker shadows. It's neon lights on Lenox and a cube of ice fighting for its life in a highball. Night is laughter. It's a city breeze plucking the strings of the fire escapes. Night is spareribs and street fights and a white man in a prowl car. Night is love on a cinder roof, steel bars on windows, garbage cans with their lids at a rakish angle, hot stones cracking cool.

Night is the wail of an infant, a fly walking upside down on a kitchen ceiling; a drunk walking rightside up. Night is Negro women smiling on ten thousand stoops; it's a dandy in yellow shoes; a cat under a parked car; a rat poised on a crib. Night is a police call box, a little boy watching men pass a needle; a yellow light in a butcher shop.

Most of all, night is four hundred fifty thousand pairs of eyes looking, laughing, sleeping, crying, winking, scanning, flirting, scorning, cursing, dozing, despairing, desiring and dying.

Harlem is six square miles of hate. It is a Black Ghetto sitting on the northern edge of an island called Manhattan. It is twelve thousand old tenements owned almost solely by white men. They will rent a room and a half complete with cracked ceilings, leaky pipes, and filthy toilets for thirty dollars a week. Exclusively to Negroes.

There are more good people and more bad people here than anywhere else in the world. Ironically, there are no in-between people. An adolescent Negro finds himself magnetized to one extreme or the other. The 32nd precinct, on West 135th Street, tells the story in numbers of people:

"We cover two thirds of one square mile of Harlem. In our area there are seventy-four thousand five hundred people. These consist of seventy-four thousand four hundred Negroes; forty whites, and sixty Chinese." What do they produce? Crime. You want to buy a hot car, a shot, a fix, a gun, a knife, a woman, stolen goods, hubcaps, radio antennae, a side of beef, a rare cigarette, heroin? You want to be beaten up, maimed, sodomized, killed?

This is the place. You want to go to church, get a handout, beg a meal, find mercy, earn a loyal friend, see true generosity, live in Christian love? They are here. You want to see broken homes, rickety kids, fathers in the gutter, mothers in despair, sons in jail, daughters in three-dollar fleabags, old ladies with turkey skin sorting through garbage?

Harlem.

Testimony:

Patrolman Justice A. Lester, a Negro with a hairline mustache and piano teeth: "We have no juvenile gangs here. Last one was the Assassins. They disbanded three years ago." A fat waitress, no name: "You gonna write about Harlem? For God's sake, tell the truth. We ain't as bad as we painted and we ain't as good as we wanna be."

A blind drug addict, with a tapping cane: "Don't give me no

grief, mister. I'm too sick to talk. Go away. Leave Harlem alone."
Deputy Chief Inspector Daniel Daly: "I was born in Harlem.
The good family groups and the church groups far outnumber the
bad ones. But you only read about the bad ones."

Testimony:

Patrolman Archibald Sheppard, Negro: "Hundred and seventeenth street between Madison and Fifth. I'd call it the worst
street in town. Ninety per cent of the people are addicts."

Mrs. Jacqueline Lowe, educational counselor: "The Negro
child is two years behind the white child in spelling, three years
in mathematics. I don't care what the governor or the State Board
of Education says about integration; it's going to be an additional
hardship on the Negro child."

Testimony:

Madison S. Jones III, Director of Educational Research: "The
Communist Party has completely failed in its solicitation of the
American Negro. I can't understand why we're so loyal to this
country."

Glester Hinds, chairman of the People's Civic and Welfare Association: "There are too many negative-thinking people here.
They want miracles to fall out of a cloud." Reverand Oberia
Dempsey of the Upper Park Avenue Baptist Church: "I fight
narcotics pushers. One out of every ten of my people in Harlem is
an addict. How can you fight it when every pusher has a copy of
the Fourth Amendment in his pocket—the Search and Seizure
law? It retards justice in Harlem."

Anonymous patrolman: "We can't do anything right. If we
don't arrest the Negroes, the lieutenant is on our back. If we do,
the Negro leaders are on our back." Tall young Negro: "Ten years
ago, a policeman said I was the most likely candidate for Sing
Sing. Now I'm assistant Teaching Supervisor for the Board of
Education. Boy, would I like to meet him!"

The first thing the successful Negro does is disown Harlem. He
leaves for Westchester, for Long Island, for New Jersey—anywhere but the ghetto from which he sprang. A few stay, but the
sole goal of the majority is to leave. There are thousands of children in the slums between 110th Street and 155th, between Amsterdam Avenue and the East River, who have never left it—
never been to the country, never seen an apple tree, never been
on a train or a bus. Some don't even know they are Negroes.

The most grievous crime the white man has inflicted on the
Negro is that he has made him despise himself. Two hundred and
fifty years of slavery and a hundred years of second-class citizenship have taught the Negro to equate dark skin with the bottom

rung of the cultural ladder. Blindly he gropes for status. Status is a big shiny car; status is a bulging bankroll; status is a pale-skinned woman; status is a silk suit and a pair of custom-made shoes. Status is to be accepted socially by whites, even though the white friend segregates your drinking glass.

Day is the time of sorrow in Harlem. Day means many things, most of them unflattering. Daylight exposes the blind windows, the boarded up flats, the new unattainable housing developments, the dirty gutters, the smell of old cooking in dark hallways, the shiftless men with hands in pockets rocking with laughter on the street corners, the lack of work, the nervous depression of the morning hangover, the accusing eyes of wives and mothers, the serene narcotics pusher cruising slowly in his air-conditioned Cadillac, the battle for bread, the happy kisses of children who think that the whole world is like Harlem.

Sunlight is mean. It sneaks up over Queens and seeps through the holes in the bedroom window shade. It moves high and be-comes bold and brazen and it pours relentlessly against the walls of the concrete jungle. The heat renders the Negro as heat renders bacon. He oozes; he drips. He curses the sun which makes him squint; the sun which he needs so badly in winter when the landlord chisels on coal and the snow lies in rusty piles on the curb. Nothing in life seems to turn out right for the average Harlem Negro.

Nothing. Twenty per cent of all husbands leave home, never to be seen again. Negroes who have bachelor of science or master of arts degrees can become second-rate junior executives in the white world downtown, if they push hard enough for it. Mrs. Jacqueline Lowe's mother once told her: "Be twice as good as the white, and he'll accept you. Be three times as good and he might promote you."

What the Negro needs, more than integration, is pride in his race. He hasn't got it. It has been knocked out of him. The first thing a Negro child sees in an elementary school is a picture book with words. The book was devised by white men. The first picture shows a white couple in an automobile. Underneath, it says: "Mother and Father Go to the Country to See Grandma."

At once, the child is confused. The people he studies have different skin. He probably has a mother, and seldom sees his father. They have no automobile. And what is meant by "the country"? One fifth grader came home bursting with pride. "Know what, Momma?" he said happily. "Our ancestors were slaves. Teach told me." He hadn't known.

The smashing of the Negro child's skull against the anvil of the white world robs him of faith in himself and his people. With each passing year, the knowledge grows that he cannot possibly win. When he is sixteen or seventeen, he makes up his mind whether to seek refuge in booze, drugs, robbery and rape, or whether to resign himself to the servile status of the "good nigger," who can be trusted to run an elevator, park a car, or hold a small job in civil service.

If his skin is light enough, and his hair is unkinked, he might run away from Harlem, and "pass" as a white boy. If not, he can make love to a Negro girl who has a job, and live with her. Even among his own people, the colored boy is culturally a step lower than his sister. The women of Harlem have more hope in the future than their men.

They face the daylight. They will go out and shop, suckle their babies, mend old print dresses, scrub linoleum worn to the boards, cook, glance out the window to watch the youngsters at play between parked cars, hold the family together when there isn't a dollar coming in the door, and fight with animal tenacity to teach God and the goodness of life to the family. If she despairs, if she weeps, it is when she is alone in bed.

She's a special person. . . .

He sat in the dusty back room of his bookshop, a slender man of sixty-eight with a blue pendulous lower lip and the reactions of a cobra. L. H. Michaux is a minor leader in Harlem. He has a picture of Jesus Christ outside his shop and writes underneath: "White Man's God. This can't be Him because He has the wrong hair." Another sign says: "Repatriation Headquarters—Back to Africa Movement."

A big one says: "The Goddam White Man," and, in smaller letters underneath, "Read this book." Pickets paraded in front of the store with signs: "Lewis H. Michaux sold us out to the white man for $3,000." It seemed awkward for Michaux, a militant Negro, to be picketed by Negroes.

"Let them march," he said scornfully. "They bring more business." There are nineteen million Negroes in the United States. They have more leaders than their ears can bear. They range all the way from the positively passive Reverend Martin Luther King to the venemous segregationist, Malcolm X of the Muslims.

Somewhere between those magnetic poles are such organizations as the NAACP, CORE, the Urban League, Associated Community Teams, HARYOU, the Democratic Party, the Republican Party, the Communist Party, the People's Civic and Welfare Organization, the Y.M.C.A., the Civil Rights Groups, and the whites who feel they are achieving true brotherhood because they carry a banner in a demonstration. In 1963, everyone discovered the American Negro. Even the Negro.

In effect, he is leaderless. His organizations are spread like broken fingers. Each has some strength, but there is no fist. Michaux, for example, has such diffuse notions that he is difficult to comprehend.

"After being here nearly three hundred fifty years," he said, "there isn't really one black person in the U.S. When I hear Negroes asking for the rights of citizens, then I know that they are not citizens. If I go to Africa, I'll be a citizen automatically. My son is seven. If I take him to Africa, he can become a premier or a president."

Will Michaux go to Africa? Not a chance. "I've never been to school," he said. "I'm self-educated. Therefore, I'm outside the system. The Negroes here have nothing to offer. They can't make eyeglasses and they can't make sense." He smiled and shook his graying head. "I don't say that men are not created equal, but they don't remain that way.

"Integration is difficult. The Negro makes a good clerk, a good servant, but he has no shoe factory and no pants factory. The Puerto Rican came here recently, but he owns pants factories. He employs Negroes. I employ Negroes. Suppose a man comes here, he says 'Fire one of those Negroes and hire a white man.' I wouldn't do it.

"Man asked me is there any good white men. I said, 'Sure. I just ain't had the good luck to meet one.' "

No responsible Negro trusts the white man. Why should he? Would you trust the man who sold your ancestors into bondage, then freed you to enjoy second-class citizenship, underpaid you, overcharged you, forced you to ride in the back of the bus, made you live in a slum, abused you, exploited you, and then rubbed your woolly head for good luck? If the situation had been reversed, how long would white men submit to Negro domination?

There is a small office behind the Bethel African Methodist Episcopal Church on 132nd Street near Lenox. In it sat the Reverend Richard Hildebrand, president of the Harlem NAACP. He is big and dark, like an old oak in winter. Of the four hundred fifty thousand persons in Harlem, only eleven thousand are members of his group.

"For years," he said meditatively, almost as though he were thinking it out for the first time, "we in Harlem have addressed ourselves to problems in the South. No more. In recent months, we have turned to local problems." He clasped hands across his waist. The big head fell forward a little. "Equal job opportunities and desegregation of schools are high on our list. If it means that Negro children will have to be transferred to schools in white neighborhoods, it will have to be done."

It sounded strange coming from Pastor Hildebrand. It was almost as though the cautious NAACP had reversed its course in mid-flight; as though the friendly negotiator had suddenly bared his teeth. "We favor letting more Negroes into unions. It isn't so much a matter of segregation; it's ethical practice." He said that too many unions were known to be Irish, or Italian, Polish or Armenian. "They're going to have to change."

He's a man bigger than his body. "Let's forget bygones," as though much of Negro history cannot be altered, and is the worse for being remembered. "Let's move on from here. There has been talk of twenty-five per cent of the jobs for the Negro. I don't believe it. He needs lots of apprenticeship in crafts. He isn't ready for more than that. He needs a sort of crash program today, just to get him started."

Congressman Adam Clayton Powell is another leader. But he isn't seen in Harlem, except on Sundays. He talks Negro, lives white. Malcolm X,* a leader of the Muslims, forbids his followers to speak for publication. The Muslims are radical haters who want to keep the racial tension high. Their goal and the goal of the White Supremacy Councils of the South are identical; both favor segregation. The Muslims want the severance to be complete.

Dr. C. B. Powell owns the *Amsterdam News*. He and a few other intelligent men like Glester Hinds of the Y.M.C.A.; Dr. Schapp, superintendent of Harlem Schools; Dr. Godfrey Nurse; Dr. Kenneth Clark of Harlem Youth Opportunities Unlimited; Mr. Hildebrand and Mr. Dempsey; J. Raymond Jones, Democratic leader; and Roy Wingate of the Harlem Peace Corps are all men who understand that equality and acceptance at gun point are about as worthless as love at gun point. And just about as satisfying.

Dr. Powell is a physician. He doesn't practice any more because, after the white man made him a doctor, he denied this man the patients. So Powell was forced into roentgenology, and was relegated to an X-ray clinic in Harlem until he bought the *Amsterdam News*, biggest weekly in Harlem.

There is no rancor in him. He owns a big house in Briarcliff

* Since this was written, Malcolm X left the Black Muslims, and was later assassinated.

Manor, New York, and is the only Negro who lives there. His neighbors are white. He owns twenty-five acres, and has white tenants. Besides The *News*, he owns three funeral parlors, and real estate, and he has four servants, including a white gardener.

"Harlem," he says slowly, as though this is an old litany, "has been neglected, just as colored people have been neglected in Detroit and Chicago. They live in a dirty ghetto, underpaid, exploited, held down. Take here in Harlem. Practically all businesses arc white-owned. Negroes are trying to establish businesses right here among their own people and they can't make it. If they can't make it in Harlem, where can it be done?

"Even the apartments are white-owned. They charge one hundred twenty-five dollars a month for one room and a half in a slum. I don't expect to live to see true integration and true job distribution among races because my people do not have the education nor the skills, but if we get on the right track now . . .

"Now, I mean. Give us good basic jobs. Give us education and, in time, we'll be ready to assume the responsibility of high position. These people who expect an overnight change"—he shook his head sadly—"they're crazy."

Andrew A. Gainor is no leader. He's a small businessman with an appliance store at 225 West 116th Street. He is a strong, vital, hard-working Negro who learned about electricity and gas at a Navy school. His importance lies in his attitude of let's-do-it-ourselves. While others were talking for newspapers and television, this man started his own apprentice school in the field of gas and electricity. He cannot understand why he has drive, and others of his race have none.

"I got nine employees," he said. "We want young married men. They have more responsibility than the single ones. We'll train them. I'm ready to start them in the electrical and gas business. Others will have to start them in other fields. But for God's sake, man, let's stop talking and get started. Man I know named Doyle is ready to train men in radio and TV work. An attorney named Marion Jones is set to train people as domestics, as hotel workers, as restaurant waiters. It's a start.

"The boys in Harlem don't recognize their fathers, or even their fathers' work. They look to Momma for guidance, for a suit of clothes, for a dollar in the pocket. We got to get them out of this momma rut. They have to learn how to make a living." Gainor's lips curled a little. "They think of nothing but status. If you give them a job with a brief case, they'll work for peanuts. But they won't accept a job as a mechanic for a hundred and a quarter a week.

"Now you tell me. . . !"

Honesty is the key to Harlem's troubles. The whites who own
Harlem and the Negroes who live in it lie to each other. They
breathe love; seethe hate. Candor is impossible. You might try 179
West 137th Street. There's a little building labeled Associated
Community Teams Inc. Walk in, pass the receptionist, and try
the last door on the left. Then listen.

Roy Wingate sits with his back to the door. He has skin as
black as a good velvet collar. He thinks fast; he talks fast. He is
head of the Harlem Peace Corps, an educated man with energy.
Near the coffee table is a big handsome woman, Mrs. Jacqueline
Lowe, director of education. One look at the rich smile, and you
know whatever peace a Negro must make with himself was made
long ago by Mrs. Lowe. The slender man with the statistical
books on crossed knees is Madison Jones, director of research.

These people work together on the most vital problem in Harlem; raising the educational level of the masses; lifting the bottom rung so that, in time, it will match the bottom rung of white
society. It is the first domestic Peace Corps group, and it is
needed in three hundred other Harlems around the United States.
The illiterate and unemployed Negro is a liability to all taxpayers,
much more so than his Congolese cousin, who has been getting
Peace Corps attention all along.

Wingate looks at the ceiling. "Few people understand that Harlem is a matriarchal society," he says. "Few people. We're dominated by women. When the Negroes were slaves, the babies were
left for the mother to bring up. The father—sold, or sent off to the
fields. Marriage? There was no such thing. Children seldom saw
their fathers. They still seek only their mothers."

Jones sucks a lower lip against his teeth. "I've been checking
the figures again. In Harlem, we have 64,461 persons between the
ages of seven and twenty. Our total school enrollment is 60,237."
Mrs. Lowe presses a cigarette into a tray. "Dropouts are a big
problem," she says. "Soon as the average child passes the age of
compulsory attendance, he's out looking for a job."

"Even when the child stays in school," Jones says, checking
figures, "our ninth grade is two years behind the white school in
reading, three years behind in math." Jacqueline Lowe crosses her
legs, yanks her hem down, and laughs. "You don't have to go that
high," she says. "Our first grade students fail the Reading Readi-
ness Test because the tests are based on a national level and our
kids are living on a subcultural level."

Wingate nods. "Sometimes it's a problem just teaching the child
how to sit quietly." "That leads to a question," Jones says. "When
does a Negro first know that he is a Negro?" The smile dies on

Mrs. Lowe's face. "It's like being blamed for something you didn't
do. Can you tell a little colored boy that he cannot grow up to be
President of the United States? How do you say it?"

"Parents care," Jones says, putting his books on the coffee table.
"I'm sure they care. But of what help are they to the child? Can
illiterates help with homework? Can they assess a report card?"

"They care," Mrs. Lowe says, and the lopsided smile returns.
"They care. They show it by giving their children money, or toys.
They do things for them, not with them."

"There's more to it than that," Wingate says. "The man of the
family feels that if he brings in any money at all, he's done
enough. His wife finds it easier to get work than he does."
"Often," says Jones, "she earns more than he does." "According to
my figures," Mrs. Lowe says, "at least twenty per cent of all
Harlem marriages aren't working. The man has left."

'Well, Jackie," says Jones, "that's another problem." "No," Roy
Wingate says, "it's the same one. It means that one out of every
five marriages here has broken up, and that's not counting cases
where the husband has died, or only gets home to change his shirt
or get something to eat." "And," says Jones, "when the fatherless
child gets to school, he is again under the domination of a
woman."

"I've done a lot of guidance work in schools," Mrs. Lowe says,
"and I ask little ones who their heroes are. You know who? The
bookie, the dope pusher, the gambler, the thief. The first thing he
learns from Momma is that money is important. These people
have money."

"Teachers make mistakes," Jones says. "I know of cases where
a boy has ambition and he tells his teacher he's going to be an
engineer. The teacher says, 'Don't do it. A Negro doesn't stand a
chance.' " Wingate sighs. "O.K. That leads to another point.
Should we tell them the truth? What would you tell him?"

The conversation is at a stalemate. Tell the truth and watch
him wilt? Lie and make him beam with spurious hope? Which
way? Mrs. Lowe says, "He already knows that the money is in the
streets, not in stores or laboratories. School is doing time. He
must do time until he's sixteen.

"You want to know something funny?" Jones says. "I mean,
really funny. The TV horror programs are tame to Harlem children. Tame. They look at a program on drug addiction and they
bust out laughing. 'Lookit him,' they shout. 'He's takin' his fix all
wrong.' They grow up on crime. How are you going to point out
the pitfalls of lawlessness to a child who is old at ten?"

"The government wants to stop school dropouts," Mrs. Lowe

says. "It can start here. In high school, Negro dropouts average sixty to seventy-five per cent. Less than four out of ten remain in school." "It's a pity," Wingate says, "that we can't get more successful Negroes to speak to the children. They need an image bad. Boy, do they need an image."

"Progress," says Wingate solemnly, "has heavy feet." "Until recently," says Mrs. Lowe, "no bank would employ a Negro as a teller. Little did they know that any Negro would be so grateful to get such a position of honor that he would have died of starvation before he'd touch a nickel that wasn't his."

They talk school integration for a while. "We're so overcrowded now," says Mrs. Lowe, "that we wouldn't miss the ones who leave, and we couldn't accommodate the white ones coming back up." "Also," says Roy Wingate, "how about the colored child who gets to the white school and finds he's two years behind? You going to demote him? Or the whole class? How about his social life? Here, he makes friends. Are the white children going to invite him to their homes?"

"Worse than that," says Jones, "would the Negro boy have the nerve to invite his white friends to his slum tenement? How is he going to get around that little problem?" "Bad enough," Wingate says, "that the boy has to come home at night to the slum after seeing how other people live. But he certainly won't invite others to see the place."

Mrs. Lowe lights a cigarette. "If I were a white parent, I certainly wouldn't want my child transferred to a system which the Negroes admit is inferior. My solution is not to integrate the schools at all. We have to raise the level of education here first, then build better schools on the fringes of Harlem; schools which will attract both races."

Wingate nods. "We're asking for equality of opportunity. If it costs extra money, it should be spent. If two children were in a race, and one had one leg, you'd give that one a handicap. I personally have deep reservations about immediate integration. Who is ready for it?

"Only the middle-class Negro. The primary fight is to break the racial barriers today, but, when they're down, that's enough. I don't believe that the Negro should run across it. The Negro middle classes will not accept the Negro masses, so how can you expect the whites to do it?" He shakes his head. "We'll have true integration, but I don't believe my children will live to see it."

"There's a joke," Mrs. Lowe says, leaning back and puffing, "about the teacher asking each boy his nationality. When she came to the Negro boy, he looked around timidly and said, 'American?' " "If we could give the Black Man a pill," says Wingate, "a pill that would turn him completely white, would we have a problem? Answer: we would. Because, even if his skin is white, his cultural level is lower than his white brother's. Therefore, I must believe that there is more to segregation of the races than color."

"The responsible Negro leadership," says Jones, "and I like to number myself among them, is coming around to that way of thinking." Wingate smiles again. "The responsible leadership is also coming around to the point where he no longer believes that Martin Luther King's passive resistance will win the battle.

"Or, let me put it another way. They believe in Dr. King as long as he wins. If he stops winning, the Northern Negro will turn to violence. I was at a meeting and one leader told Malcolm X that the Hindus won freedom without fighting. 'Sure,' he said. 'There were a whole lot of Hindu sheep and just a few British wolves. We have a few sheep and a whole lot of wolves.' "

"There is another thought," says Jones. "You can't fight well unless you hate. Who fights with love?" "I met a union leader," says Wingate, "and he talked off the record. He said: 'I don't care what you say or how you legislate, you Negroes are not going to get union jobs. Know why? Because the Negro isn't worthy of the job. People tend to stand shoulder to shoulder with their own kind. When the layoffs come, the Negro goes first because none of his kind is in power to protect him.

" 'Why,' he said to me, 'you people don't even have a stake in business. You don't own your own businesses and you have no power. You may get a few jobs here and there in unions, but you won't keep them when the chips are down.' "

Jones laughs. "One thought always leads to another," he says. "Right now, we Negroes are asking for four hundred thousand additional jobs for our people. It's a noble thing, but it occurred to me that four hundred thousand white men are going to have to give up their jobs to make room for us." Wingate joins in the laughter. "I can't see them doing it." Mrs. Lowe stands. "We can talk all day," she says, "and get nothing done. I have to get back to work."

Show me a Negro who isn't neurotic, and I'll show you a Negro who isn't normal.

The Presidents

There is automatic majesty in the office of President of the United States. This is true even when the incumbent isn't worthy of it. The office itself, in the middle of the twentieth century, became the most powerful in the world. The man who occupies it is alone.

My interest in some of our recent Presidents has been as an observer. I had no desire to interview these men. I preferred to sit some distance away, and watch them at work and in their family life. I learned much more by looking and listening than by asking questions.

Once, after four days with President John F. Kennedy, he asked me when I planned to interview him. I showed him a notebook of 135 pages of tightly spaced notes. "I think," I said, "that I have all I need, Mr. President." He frowned, then smiled. I explained that I had interviewed everyone from his lovely wife to his Negro butler, and I could think of no more questions.

My impressions of Presidents are, as they must be, personal. I think that Dwight D. Eisenhower was too remote from the people and from his own staff to detect the pulse of the nation. Harry Truman, in my estimation, had a gift for making good decisions quickly. Franklin D. Roosevelt was a consummate politician in the finest sense of the word. I spent a little time with Herbert Hoover when he was very old. This most maligned man stole my affection without effort.

John F. Kennedy has been canonized because he was assassinated. *He had more potential greatness within him than any of the others, but the clock stopped suddenly and all the fine principles and nobility died with him. My impression is that, if he had been granted eight years instead of less than three, his achievements might have placed him in the company of Lincoln, Jefferson, Wilson and Washington.*

The Day Lincoln was Nominated

At noon today, Abraham Lincoln, a lawyer from Sangamon County, Illinois, was nominated for the office of President of the United States by the new Republican Party. He was a dark horse who appeared to be popular only with the ruffians in the gallery, all of whom demonstrated every time his name was mentioned. He won on the third ballot, after some of the most scurrilous horse trading ever seen on a convention floor.

The news was flashed by telegraph to th*e Springfield Journal.* Word received here late today is that the candidate had been out with a friend, looking to play a game of billiards, and had stopped in at the *Journal* office. When he heard that he had been named as the standard-bearer, Mr. Lincoln, a tall, smooth-shaven man of awkward pace, turned from the well-wishers and said:

"There is a lady over yonder on Eighth Street, who is deeply interested in this news; I will carry it to her."

There are some here who wonder whether the right man was picked for this crisis in history, just as there are others, mostly Westerners, who are certain that no one else could lead the Union in these times.

A short while ago, the Democrats met in convention at Charleston, South Carolina, and, because Stephen A. Douglas could not get the necessary two-thirds vote to win the nomination, he stood by and watched his party split into factions—North and South. This should guarantee a Republican victory in November.

At that parley, little Alexander Stephens, of Georgia, had said:

"We will be cutting each other's throats in a little while. In twelve months, we shall be in a war, the bloodiest in history."

And here in Illinois, the politicians who pleaded peace found their spokesman in Dick Yates, Republican candidate for Governor, who shouted:

"Let us hope that the South will not attempt to destroy this Union, but, if it should, flaming giants will spring from every cornfield in the state of Illinois."

The favorite at this convention was Senator William H. Seward of New York. At this time, he is at his home in Auburn, New York, writing his acceptance speech. On the first ballot, which was full of small totals for favorite sons, Mr. Seward had 173½ of the 465 total. Mr. Lincoln had 102. For nomination, Mr. Seward needed 310, and these were assured on the second ballot before the Senator left for Auburn. They had been promised by delegations who had to remain loyal to local favorites for one complimentary ballot.

The Seward campaign has been ably handled by Mr. Thurlow Weed, the New York boss. He has personally buttonholed just about every delegate at the Wigwam and, when he could not win a pledge of support without concessions, he has made them freely —sometimes promising the same post to two or three delegates.

In Springfield, friends told Mr. Lincoln about Mr. Weed, and tried to frighten him with stories of Weed's ruthless tactics. Lincoln was not scared. "Only events can make a President," he said. A loyal friend of Lincoln's said, "If all the ugly men in the country vote for Abe, he'll win."

There is a question of how much of the underhanded politics at this convention, executed in behalf of Mr. Lincoln, has been endorsed by him. He confounded the Seward Camp by writing a public note to a delegate in which he said:

"Seward is the best candidate we could have for the north of Illinois. And the very worst for the south of it."

This was condemnation in faint praise. Mr. Lincoln also sought the assistance of Mr. Mark Delahay, of Kansas, who is hardly of the respectable element in his party. He used Mr. Delahay to support him, and used others who have not smelled sweet since infancy. He has, on several occasions, denied aspirations to the presidency, and yet he said to Senator Lyman Trumbull, "The taste is in my mouth a little."

Mr. Lincoln sent Jesse K. Dubois and Judge David Davis here to the convention to represent his interest and to fight for the nomination. At the same time, he wrote to the Ohio delegation: "First, I think the Illinois delegation will be unanimous for me at the start; and no other delegation will."

Delahay asked Lincoln for money, and the Illinois lawyer de-

clined, then compromised. "If you shall be appointed a delegate
to Chicago," he wrote, "I will furnish one hundred dollars to bear
the expenses of the trip."

By the time the delegates began to arrive in Chicago last Monday, Mr. Lincoln was anxious to win. "I am a little too much of a
candidate to stay home," he wrote, "and not quite enough of a
candidate to go."

It was Mr. Lincoln and his men who had originally fought to
have Chicago as the convention city. This was shrewdly done to
exploit local Lincoln enthusiasm, and many of the big men of the
party grumbled about it because Chicago is a rutty city of planked
streets and raised sidewalks, a place of 110,000 citizens who
slaughter hogs and steers today, and who look to the prairies and
mountains of the Indian country for untold riches tomorrow.

On the opening day of the convention, the delegates were
pleased to see that the ladies of Chicago had dressed the Wigwam in patriotic colors, with paper streamers cascading from the
ceiling.

Mark Delahay had watched Thurlow Weed at work and had
become faint of heart. He wired Mr. Lincoln and asked if he
would accept second place on the party ticket. Mr. Lincoln had
replied that he would accept the vice-presidency if his friends
thought it wise.

A friend wired: "Things are working. Keep a good nerve. We
are laboring to make you the second choice of all the delegations
we can, where we can't make you first choice. We are dealing
tenderly with delegates, taking them in detail and making no fuss.
Be not too expectant, but rely on our discretion. Again I say,
brace your nerves for any result."

At the Tremont House, Mr. Lincoln's friends danced a little jig
the day the convention opened, and a reporter asked why.

"We are going to have Indiana for old Abe sure," one said. "By
the lord, we promised them everything they asked."

They promised everything to everybody. Caleb Smith was told
he would be Secretary of the Interior; Bill Dole wanted to be
Commissioner of Indian Affairs, and was promised it.

Pennsylvania had fifty-six votes, and they were all pledged to
Simon Cameron, a favorite son.

Dubois wired Mr. Lincoln that Pennsylvania could be had if
Cameron became Secretary of the Treasury. Lincoln replied: "I
authorize no bargains and will be bound by none."

Some said that Mr. Lincoln was being honest. Others said that
his friends understood this to be his public attitude, but that, in
private, he knew that bargains had to be struck in order for a

candidate to win votes. Either way, Cameron got his promise of a cabinet post, and Pennsylvania, in secret, waited with Indiana to ambush Senator Seward.

Mr. Davis, one of Mr. Lincoln's managers, said, "Lincoln ain't here, and don't know what we have to meet, so we will go ahead as if we had not heard from him, and he must ratify it."

Joseph Medill said it best: "Lincoln wanted that big Pennsylvania floor brought down on the scale." Another said: "We want the Presidency, and the Treasury is not a great stake to pay for it."

On the night before the convention opened, the program listed several speeches in behalf of Senator Seward. The Lincoln managers arranged for a delegate from Pennsylvania to take the floor, and talk Lincoln, and to hold the floor until the session died of fatigue.

When the temporary chairman rapped the gavel in the morning, hundreds of Seward adherents marched to the Wigwam singing, "Oh, Isn't He a Darling!" Ward Hill Lamon, who could sing a sad song with an old banjo, worked hard all night. He was signing forged names to convention passes so that the galleries would be filled with Lincoln bully boys.

These people, with their loud and dismal hooting, maintained a bedlam for The Rail Splitter. Some were sodden with whisky; some filled with religious fervor; some hoped for an appointment. No one knows how much they influenced the voting. One thing is certain. They were out of hand and could not be controlled by the Lincoln camp.

Norman B. Judd made a short nominating speech:

"I desire," he said solemnly, "on behalf of the delegation from Illinois, to put in nomination, as a candidate for President of the United States, Abraham Lincoln of Illinois." That was it. That was all. A reporter for a local newspaper wrote that, if all the hogs ever slaughtered were to squeal together, and be joined by a score of huge steam whistles, it would not equal the hosanna for Mr. Lincoln.

The first ballot was Seward: 173½; Lincoln 102; 189½ scattered. The second ballot, taken at once, was Seward 184½; Lincoln 181. This was the ambush. On the third count, Seward had 180; Lincoln had 231½. With victory in sight, the shrewd publisher Medill whispered to Carter of Ohio, "If you throw the Ohio delegation to Lincoln, Chase can have anything he wants."

Salmon P. Chase wanted a cabinet post. He got his promise. Carter asked the attention of the chair, and got it. He switched four Ohio votes to Abraham Lincoln. Other delegates, worried and indecisive, stood to ask a change of votes. When the tally clerk read the totals, Lincoln had 354. This was forty-four more than was needed for nomination.

Knapp sent a wire to Lincoln in Springfield. "Abe," it read, "we did it. Glory be to God!"

Lincoln's Last Friend

The laughter of a theater full of people filled the ears of President Abraham Lincoln when a large lead ball smashed through the back of his head, tore through his brain, and stopped behind the right eye. He did not hear the shot. In the midst of amusement, it was lights out.

The first man admitted to the State Box at Ford's Theater was Captain Charles A. Leale, Assistant Surgeon at the Army General Hospital, Armory Square, Washington, D.C. Dr. Leale was twenty-three, sandy haired, with wispy mustaches and sideburns. He was meticulous and dedicated, so proper as to be almost humorless. Sometimes, when he lost a patient, he was close to tears. He had only one hero in life—Abraham Lincoln. This devotion was so intense that Leale bought a theater ticket on April 14, 1865—not to see *Our American Cousin*, but to see his hero close up for the first time.

Now, by God's will, the young man was the first to know that the President could not live. He ordered soldiers to lift the patient from his rocker, to place him on the floor of the box, and to remove his frock coat and cut his shirt and undershirt from his body. Leale's heart hurt as he straddled Lincoln and, finding no pulse, bent over to breathe in and out of the President's mouth in the kiss of mercy. Then, probing with the hands which he had vowed would save life, Leale found the wound in the matted hair, removed a penny-sized clot—and Lincoln began to breathe.

Leale looked at Lincoln, grotesque and homely and now half nude, and he looked at Mrs. Lincoln, sitting on a couch wringing her hands. He said nothing. "Can he recover?" Mrs. Lincoln said. "Will you take charge of him? Oh, my dear husband!"

The play had stopped, the people were in bedlam, a swaying

mob outside the theater already blocked Tenth Street and an
intoxicated man who shouted, "I'm glad it happened!" was almost
torn apart. In the box, Laura Keene, star of the play, sat on the
floor with Lincoln's bloody head on her lap.

Leale pressed two extended fingers down the President's throat,
clearing the passage for breathing. Then he rocked over the body,
sliding strong fingers upward over the belly and under the ribs.
The heart action improved at once. Two doctors came in to assist
young Leale, and he whispered the diagnosis and prognosis in
one sentence: "His wound is mortal; it is impossible for him to
recover."

Looking down, Leale thought, His face is pale and in solemn
repose. His eyelids are closed, his face makes him appear to be in
communion with the Universal God he always loved. Leale
sighed. The boy again became the doctor and he turned to the
soldiers and snapped, "Remove him to safety." Someone suggested the White House. The doctor had a little rim of scorn in
his voice as he said, "He would die long before we reached there."

In the face of older, senior doctors, Leale ordered one to support Lincoln's right shoulder, another the left shoulder, and some
soldiers to hold the trunk and arms and legs. The party proceeded
backward from the box, with Leale holding Lincoln's head in his
kerchief and roaring, "Guards! Clear the passage!"

The man they carried, swaying slowly and sagging in the middle, had once said, "I do not consider that I have ever accomplished anything without God, and if it is His will that I must die
by the hand of an assassin, I must be resigned."

The moon was out, the long shadows cut black rectangles in the
frightened faces surging in the street. A captain preceded Leale,
swinging his saber and cursing: "Out of the way, you sons-of-
bitches!" The little party got to Petersen House, and Lincoln was
placed diagonally on a bed too small for him.

Leale was now removing clots every two minutes. This caused
blood to flow and prevented it from depressing the brain and
causing death. The doctor, in the presence of the great men of the
nation, ordered porous plasters to be applied to the front of Lincoln's body from collar bone to ankles. Leale worked to preserve
life when he knew that life could not be preserved. At midnight,
Surgeon General Joseph K. Barnes took charge of the case and
Leale was no longer important enough to be asked for advice. On
the far side of the bed there was a little space against the wall,
and Charles A. Leale sat there and held the President's hand. The
great men of the nation saw the young man, and wondered.

Frequently, Leale thought, recognition and reason return just before departure. I will hold his right hand firmly to let him in his blindness know, if possible, that he is in touch with humanity and has a friend.

Dr. Leale did. At 7:22 A.M., when the seventeenth President of the United States took a long heaving breath and died, Leale, the unknown last friend, was still holding his hand. The young doctor got up, listened to the Reverend Dr. Phineas Gurley say prayers for the dead, and walked out into the rain.

The Day Roosevelt Died

This was a sweet and bright morning. The sun was hot against the cheek in Warm Springs, Georgia. The tall ramrod pines stood in cool blue hummocks on the hills and a westerly breeze flattened the wood smoke in layers across the valley floors. Greedy bluejays feinted at frightened cardinals on the lawn of the cottage called The Little White House. The pickings were good. The lawn had been mowed.

A car came up the road. Behind it, a peacock feather of dust hung in the air. The car made good time. It was coming up from the Warm Springs Foundation, two miles below. It pulled to a stop in front of the neat bungalow and Commander Howard Bruenn got out. He pulled his medical bag from the front seat, nodded to a Secret Service man squinting in the sun, and stepped inside.

The time was nine ten. The day was April 12, 1945. Commander Bruenn stepped professionally through the living room and on into the pine-paneled bedroom. The President of the United States was in bed. His thin hair was sticking up. He lifted his head a little bit high as he picked a few papers from his breakfast tray. He had a hearty good morning for Dr. Bruenn and he told his valet, Prettyman, to remove the tray.

Bruenn saw what he wanted to see quickly. The presidential eyes remained pouched. The complexion was mottled under the superficial tan. There were small dark patches on the cheeks. The hands which removed the papers from the tray were not too sure of themselves. The mental attitude was bright.

It was a nice fresh morning out, Bruenn said. The President nodded. He ran spread fingers caressingly across his forehead. "I have a headache," he said. The doctor, whose specialty was cardiology, asked if the President had slept well. "It's a slight headache," the President said. "It isn't much." Bruenn asked if there were any other symptoms. "None," said President Franklin Delano Roosevelt.

Mr. Roosevelt had been at Warm Springs for two weeks. He was there to rest before opening the first session of the United Nations in San Francisco. He had slept late, had signed the bills which had to be signed, had answered the mail which must be answered, had read the dispatches from the Joint Chiefs of Staff, had absorbed the notes from Stephen Early, his secretary now in Washington, had briefed his Press Secretary, William Hassett, so that Mr. Hassett could inform the reporters from International News Service, Associated Press and United Press; he had driven down to Warm Springs to swim with the little victims of poliomyelitis who grinned at him and chanted "We want Rosey! We want Rosey!" He had conferred with President Osmena of the Philippines and, only last night, had sat talking with the Secretary of the Treasury, Mr. Morgenthau.

At eleven thirty last night, Mr. Prettyman had helped the President to undress, had swung the big dead legs onto the bed, and had pulled the bedclothes over the striped pajamas. The President had read a mystery under a night light. Now, as he chatted with Dr. Bruenn, the mystery was open on the night table. The new chapter was headed: Six Feet of Earth.

The doctor left. In the hall, Grace Tully was on the phone. She was Mr. Roosevelt's personal secretary. She was learning, from the White House, that the daily plane to Warm Springs had been forced down by bad weather and that the President's mail pouch would arrive by train in Atlanta at noon. She hung up, and passed the word to Mr. Hassett, who ordered a messenger to drive to Atlanta, seventy-six miles away.

Hassett went into the bedroom to tell the President. The Press Secretary suggested that, inasmuch as the mail was late and the President had an appointment to sit for a portrait, that he might want to relax and forego the regular work. Mr. Roosevelt shook his head no. "You might as well get the laundry out, Bill."

The laundry referred to congressional bills to be signed. As a matter of custom, the presidential signature is never blotted and, when a host of bills were signed, Hassett hung his "laundry" all over the room.

It was ten o'clock—eleven in New York and Washington—

when Mr. Roosevelt summoned his valet to help him out of bed. Dewey Long came into the bedroom. Mr. Long was the transportation officer and, before the President was assisted to the bath, he wanted to talk about the forthcoming trip to San Francisco.

"That reminds me," the President said. "I promised Grace I'd start work on the United Nations speech this morning." He frowned as he thought about it. Yesterday, he had finished the first draft of a Jefferson Day speech and a new and important one, designed to make brothers of men, was imminent. He needed a strong speech for the first session of the United Nations.

In a moment, the room was empty, except for the Negro valet and the President. Mr. Roosevelt did not like to be seen in his awkward moments. He trusted Prettyman and soon the legs were over the edge of the bed, the wheel chair was swung into position, and the valet lifted the President off the bed, turned him, and dropped him gently to the chair. Only the big picture of an old sailing ship, hanging on the wall, saw it. Only that and the brass ship's chronometer that ticked so loudly.

In the bathroom, Prettyman assisted Mr. Roosevelt with his morning toilette, and stood watching in silence as the brown-stained teeth were brushed, the face mopped with a warm damp cloth, the hair combed back in a loose pile on the great head.

Prettyman pulled the black sox on, drew the pale blue trousers up, clinched the zipper, and the President notched the belt. The shirt was white with soft collar, the tie was maroon. The shoes were drawn on, the laces bowed. Mr. Prettyman could always tell whether the President planned to do any walking by his attitude toward the ten-pound steel braces which had to be harnessed to his legs. This morning they were declined.

Outside, Michael F. Reilly talked to Dr. Bruenn. Mr. Reilly was a Secret Service man on permanent White House detail. He is a strong broad man with an Irish sense of humor overlaid with Irish premonitions.

Reilly asked the doctor about the President. Bruenn said that he had a slight headache. Both agreed that this was nothing because, when the President did not feel well, he never had to be coaxed to tell the symptoms. Mr. Reilly said that he hoped that the President could attend the staff barbecue in the late afternoon.

"The boys chipped in two fifty apiece for this thing," he said. "We have food and a little liquid refreshment. The mayor of Warm Springs will be there and we have a hillbilly band. You know how the boss goes for hillbilly music."

Bruenn was certain that the President would attend. He got into his car and said that he was going to have a swim in the big Warm Springs pool. "Me too," said Reilly. "I'll be down in a little while."

Outside the Little White House, the world moved eastward, spinning slowly. Mrs. Roosevelt phoned from the White House. She asked how the President felt. He had had a good breakfast, she was told. At eleven (noon in Washington) Vice-President Harry Truman let his gavel fall and the United States Senate came to order. On the agenda was a measure which concerned water rights between the United States and Mexico.

In Germany, Lieutenant General Simpson's 9th Army crossed the Elbe. This was the last natural barrier before Berlin. An hour before, some of those who had to die on this day died in the Italian harbor at Bari when a munitions ship exploded. There were 267 bodies. The current issue of *Das Reich* had a tragic quotation from Herr Josef Goebbels, the Reichsminister for Propaganda. "The war cannot last much longer," he said. "We have sunk very low."

Sister Kenny said that she was discouraged by the opposition in America to her way of treating poliomyelitis. Hundreds of Japanese died in Koriyama. A squadron of B-29's flew the longest round trip of the war—three thousand eight hundred miles—to bomb Koriyama's factories. Six hours earlier, the Soviet Union signed its first pact with Yugoslavia's Tito.

The weather in New York was warm and sunny and men in bars talked about the opening of the baseball season next week. A motion picture. *The Keys to the Kingdom,* was doing capacity business on Broadway. So were the plays *Oklahoma!* and *Life with Father.* In Okinawa, the army and navy gunners were thinking happily of other kinds of hits. They had downed 113 Japanese planes in one big shoot.

At noon, President Franklin Roosevelt was ready to be wheeled into the sitting room. He called Irinao Espencilla, his Filipino boy, and asked that lunch be served in the main room at one o'clock. Mr. Espencilla asked how many would be guests, and the President said that the painter and a few of the ladies would be present. Enough, he thought, to fill the bridge table. That would be four. Mr. Espencilla asked if he should give Daisy Bonner anything special as a menu. The President thought about it. No, he said, nothing special.

Prettyman pushed the chair into the sitting room. It was almost exactly noon. Mr. Roosevelt's spirits rose as he saw the ladies. He beamed a happy good morning to his cousin, Laura Delano, who was sitting in a corner of the room knitting. Another cousin, and also a spinster, sat in a nearby chair. This was Margaret Suckley, who was eager to watch the painting.

Near the front of the room stood Mrs. Elizabeth Shoumatoff. She was dark and attractive and, two years before, she had painted a wind-blown portrait of the President in his Navy cape. It had a quality of gallantry and determination which made it popular at once.

Mrs. Shoumatoff was a Russian-born American. She combined an almost photographic painting technique with an aura of character on canvas. This painting had been commissioned by Mrs. Winthrop Rutherford, an old and dear friend of the President, and Mrs. Shoumatoff had confided to her, the night before, that she was still worried, after four sittings, about the pose. She wasn't getting the ebullience she wanted.

Mr. Roosevelt was wheeled to one side of the canvas, so that he could look at the likeness of his head and shoulders. He nodded agreeably and was wheeled to a position in front of the big fireplace at the head of the room. The card table was placed adjacent to his knees. On it were placed an assortment of bills to be signed.

In front, a glass-paneled wall dimpled the sunlight. On the mantelpiece over the President's head, a ship's model reposed in a wood cradle. Some work would be done, the President said, while he was posing. He hoped that Mrs. Shoumatoff would not mind.

"Not at all," she said. Once she had the right light, the movement of his head and arms would not hurt her work. For the next hour, Mr. Roosevelt worked and chatted and lapsed into silences.

The painter asked for a variety of expressions. The President obliged while Mr. Hassett arranged his "laundry" over the bridge table. The pen hand whirled through the signature again and again and again, as though there would never be a last one. At one time, Mr. Roosevelt said, "Well, here's where I make another law," and signed a Credit Commodity Bill.

Mrs. Shoumatoff understood Mr. Roosevelt's long-time interest in stamps and she chose a time when he sat in silence and asked him about the new Florida Centennial. His face lit and she asked if he had anything to do with the designing of the new stamps.

"I most certainly did," he said.

Suddenly, and without reason, the conversation died. The lady looked at the President, studied a feature, went back to her canvas, and daubed with paint. Then she peered around the side of the easel, mixed more color, and made a few more strokes. Has-

sett told the President about the after-lunch arrival of the White
House mail and asked if the President wanted to work on it. Yes,
he said.

He lapsed into short responses. Mrs. Shoumatoff had a gloomy
thought. She was thinking of how bright and animated the President's face had been throughout last year's painting, of how his
words were punctuated with plans for the future. "Someday, I'm
going to——" "Next year we will——" "A few months from
now——"

Now the face was tired and thin and the words were terse and
carefully civil. She had posed him four days and not one phrase
had concerned the future. He looked like a man who needed a
long nap. All over the world, victory was close and he said not a
word about it. He was like a tired philosopher listening atten-
tively to the toll of a deep faraway bell.

At twelve forty-five, Mr. Roosevelt looked at his watch. "Now,"
he said, "we have about fifteen minutes more." He was exactly
right. She had fifteen minutes to go. So had he. The President
held his chin a little higher.

The Filipino boy brought in some salad with fruit pieces. He
placed them on the table. The knitting continued, the brush
strokes became swifter, the conversation seemed to die as the
noon breeze died.

In the bedroom, the brass chronometer ticked out the minutes.
The President sat staring at the glass-paneled wall. In the corner,
Miss Delano packed her needles and materials. Miss Suckley
watched the painting and was fascinated to see the features and
characteristic expression of her cousin come to life on the canvas.
Except, she thought, he looked suddenly old.

The President raised his hand to his forehead. "I have a terrific
headache," he said. Mrs. Shoumatoff did not hear him. She was
wiping brushes on a soiled cloth. She looked up in time to see the
leonine head lift up and lean against the back of the chair. The
eyes were closed. The skin was pale.

Miss Suckley screamed. Espencilla and Prettyman came in from
the kitchen. Arthur Prettyman, a Navy chief steward for almost
thirty years, studied the ashen face, the closed eyes, and nodded
to Espencilla. The women in the room seemed to be afraid to
approach the President.

The Negro and the Filipino wheeled the President back to the
bedroom and Prettyman lifted him from his chair for the final
time. Gently, he hefted 180 pounds of dead weight, swung the
feet onto the sheet, turned the face up on the pillow. Prettyman
was shaken. It did not seem right to see one arm hanging limply

off the bed. It did not seem right to see one eye partly open, in a long slow-motion wink. Not this man. Not this President.

Out front, James Beary stood on the lawn. He was the Secret Service Agent-in-Charge. The sun, high in the sky, poured warm gold over the world. Far off, he could hear a farmer's tractor start and then stop. Warm Springs wasn't always warm, but this, Mr. Beary felt, was a heavenly April for sure.

Mrs. Shoumatoff came out the front door. Her eyes were wide with fright. She swallowed twice and spoke. "Please call a doctor," she said. Ironically, Mr. Beary asked no questions. "A doctor?" he said, and he trotted to an outside phone and called Carver Cottage.

Agent Guy Spamen was on duty. Beary said, "Get a doctor up here right away." Spamen said it would be done at once. Normally, Dr. Bruenn would be at Carver Cottage, but he had decided to swim through his lunch period, and so had Agent Michael Reilly. Spamen hopped into his car and tore down the swinging undulating road to the Foundation. The time, as near as it can be ascertained, was 1:04 P.M.

Bruenn was resting on the side of the pool. His skin glistened with moisture. A water polo game was in mid-splash and Bruenn was laughing at the antics of Mr. Reilly and some of the patients as they lashed the water to a froth. Spamen came up to the doctor and said, "You're wanted at the cottage at once."

There is no record that the doctor asked who was ill. There is nothing to show that Spamen asked who was ill. There is nothing to show that Beary asked. The vital flow of communications seems to have died with Beary. It is possible that help could not have arrived any sooner, but the record shows, in any case, that Commander Bruenn walked to a dressing room, dried off, and dressed before leaving for the cottage. It was as though he had time.

In the pool, Michael Reilly watched the pantomime between the doctor and the agent and he swam over to the edge of the pool and said, "What's up?" Spamen shrugged. "They want Bruenn up at the Little White House." "Who is it?" Mr. Reilly was the first person to ask. Spamen said he didn't know.

When Commander Bruenn was ready, Spamen was behind the wheel. As they hurried up the little hills the short wave radio cut in with the voice of Beary. He was calling for Agent Charles Fredericks. Spamen thought that this was odd, because Fredericks was seldom called to the cottage unless the President was to be moved—in or out of a car.

It was close to one twenty-five when the doctor got out of the car. Mr. Beary looked at him gravely and said softly, "It's the

boss." Spamen heard it and swung the car around and headed
back to the pool to get Agent Reilly.

Inside, the doctor did not notice the women standing in a
group. They glanced at him beseechingly, but he hurried into the
bedroom without looking. Dr. Bruenn was asking Prettyman the
when, the how, the what, while he opened his bag.

The President snored in deep repose. The face was calm. The
lips were apart. Prettyman removed the pale blue jacket and
loosened the maroon tie. Dr. Bruenn unhooked a cuff link and
rolled a sleeve up. He was a fine doctor and his first job was to
find out what had happened to the patient. The second was to
do something about it.

The President had sustained a massive cerebral hemorrhage at
the rear of the brain. Dr. Bruenn did not know this. The only
testimony he had was the patient's own: that he had a slight
headache in the morning; and Mr. Prettyman's: that the President
had complained of a terrific headache and fainted.

A half hour after unconsciousness, blood pressure can be high
or, if the patient is in deep shock, it can be low. Manipulation of
the neck can show rigidity if the hemorrhage flanks the spinal
cord, or it can show suppleness. Eye reflexes can show dilation in
one eye, both eyes or, no dilation. The breathing can be of several
types, including the Cheyne-Stokes syndrome, which builds up to
rapid breathing, then cascades slowly downward to where the
patient doesn't appear to be breathing at all.

It was not an easy task. Commander Bruenn went about it
carefully and competently. He covered all of the tests, including
arm and leg reflexes. He came to a conclusion that President
Roosevelt had had a stroke. How big, how dangerous, how long,
no man knew.

Spamen got to the pool, jumped out, called Reilly, and said,
"It's the boss." The chill that came over Michael F. Reilly at that
moment would be difficult to exaggerate because, not only had he
protected Roosevelt as a Secret Service Agent should, but he also
loved the President. On recent automobile trips in the hills sur-
rounding Warm Springs, Reilly had noted, with uneasiness, that
the boss had often ordered the car stopped on a high rise and had
seemed to gaze off into the distance for too long a time.

Reilly hopped in beside Spamen and said, "Let's find Fox first."
George Fox was a lieutenant-commander in the Navy and had
been a Chief Pharmacist's Mate for years. Around the White
House, the President and the staff had used him as a friendly pill
roller for a long time.

In the sitting room, Grace Tully joined the others. This was a time for half-said sentences, half-finished prayers, for pacing, for hand wringing, for watching the closed bedroom door. Grace Tully, like Reilly, was a sentimentalist. She revealed now that, since Mrs. Shoumatoff had begun the painting, the President had engaged in an unusual amount of reminiscing. He talked at length about his childhood in Hyde Park, his mother, old friends, trips that he had made. The man who always looked ahead cheerfully suddenly looked backward.

She remembered now—of all times—that Mr. Roosevelt had made an unusual fuss because, on one occasion, he could not locate his burial instructions. Miss Tully did not know that he kept such things. After days of searching and half believing that they did not exist, they had been found in the White House in a small bedroom safe.

Grace Tully had read them. They had been dictated to Missy LeHand, his great secretary, on December 26, 1937:

> A plain white monument—no carving or decoration—to be placed over my grave, east and west as follows: length 8 feet, width 4 feet, height 3 feet. Whole to be set on marble base extending 2 feet out from monument all around—but said base to be no more than 6 inches from the ground. I hope that my dear wife will, on her death, be buried there also and that the monument contain no device or inscription except the following on the south side:
>
>
>
> FRANKLIN DELANO ROOSEVELT
> 1882   19——
> ANNA ELEANOR ROOSEVELT
> 1884   19——
>
>

The President had asked that the plot be located where the weather vane stands in the garden at Hyde Park, New York.

Miss Laura Delano could not bear the silence. She phoned the White House and got Mrs. Roosevelt. Franklin, she said, had fainted. Just fainted. There was a little conversation about it. The doctor, said Miss Delano, was in Franklin's bedroom right now.

It did not sound important to Mrs. Roosevelt. If it were, more than Miss Delano would be on the Warm Springs phone and there would be a good deal of White House activity before she was told. Still, to make certain, she got in touch with Admiral Ross McIntyre.

The admiral was her husband's personal physician and Franklin D. Roosevelt had made him surgeon-general of the

United States Navy. The admiral had traveled much with the President and knew more about his true state of health than the patient. He had not gone on the rest trip to Warm Springs, and had sent Commander Bruenn to substitute for him.

Ross McIntyre listened to the story of the fainting and said that it did not sound alarming. It was 2:45 P.M. in Washington and, if anything was wrong with the President, surely Dr. Bruenn would have phoned the admiral. McIntyre said that he would advise Mrs. Roosevelt to keep whatever appointments she had. She said that she had promised to speak at a Thrift Shop Benefit in the Hotel Sulgrave. Admiral McIntyre told her to keep the appointment.

A few minutes later, the admiral's phone rang again. It was Dr. Bruenn, standing in the hall of the cottage at Warm Springs. He had disturbing news. The admiral listened to the medical terminology flowing softly over the line.

He took a long breath. He told Dr. Bruenn to go back to the patient and to do whatever he could. The admiral would phone Dr. James E. Paullin in Atlanta and ask him to hurry to Warm Springs. One of the wonders of the telephone is that, within a few minutes, Dr. Paullin was getting into his old car and, while Secret Service Agents hurried out of Warm Springs to meet him on the highway, Paullin was hitting many of the second- and third-class roads in Georgia and made the seventy-six miles in exactly ninety minutes. Paullin was a heart specialist.

At three Commander Bruenn ordered the patient to be undressed. Prettyman and Charles Fredericks put President Roosevelt in pajamas, and made him as comfortable as possible. Commander Fox stood at the foot of the bed, ready to follow the orders of Commander Bruenn. Every face in the cottage, except Bruenn's, looked stricken.

William Hassett phoned Stephen Early at the White House and told him the news. Early said that under no circumstances must the illness leak to the press or radio. Hassett got off the phone and passed the word. Miss Hackmeister, weeping at the switchboard, had the most difficult job of all to keep her voice calm. When lights flashed on her switchboard, she dabbed her eyes, cleared her throat, and then plugged in to answer.

It was 3:23 P.M. when Dr. Paullin arrived. He was exactly the same age as the patient—sixty-three. There was this difference: the doctor would live for six more years. The patient would live seven minutes.

Paullin went into the bedroom and left the door ajar. Those outside could see him whisper to Bruenn. The men conferred. Dr.

Paullin unbuttoned the pajama top and listened to the arhythmic beat of the President's heart. He whispered to Bruenn.

Commander Bruenn hurried into the hall and ordered "Hacky" to get Admiral McIntyre on the phone. The connection was made quickly. The people in the sitting room watched mutely. Bruenn whispered. His face was pale. He was still whispering on the wire when Commander Fox yelled from the bedroom, "Bruenn! Doc Bruenn! Come quick!" The doctor asked Admiral McIntyre to wait on the line. He dropped the receiver and hurried past the dead-white faces into the bedroom.

He closed the door. Less than half a minute later, he came out again. Grace Tully and William Hassett and Michael Reilly glanced at each other. They were the Roman Catholics in the group and the look said: "Should we pray now?" Dr. Bruenn picked up the phone and whispered, "The end has come." Then he hung up, and went back to the bedroom. It was three thirty-five.

There was a howl. It was loud and high. It was the President's Scottie, Fala. He had been dozing in the sitting room. For no discernible reason he turned his head to the ceiling and howled and then ran through the room, out through the hall and crashed into the screen door.

Reilly walked quietly out into the kitchen and picked up the President's breakfast tray. The congealed remains of the food were on a plate. The Secret Service Agent took the food to a Warm Springs chemist and asked that it be analyzed for poison. There was none.

A trunk line on the switchboard lit up and Miss Hackmeister wiped her eyes, blew her nose, and plugged in. It was United Press Correspondent Merriman Smith. He was at the site of the barbecue. "We're all ready," he said. "What's holding you people up?" Hacky hung her head. "We'll be there," she said softly. "You know how these things happen."

In the cottage hall, Hassett was speaking to Stephen Early. "Don't say a word about this to the correspondents," Early said, "until we can reach Mrs. Roosevelt here. She's at a meeting." The time, in Washington, was four forty. A waiter at the Sulgrave answered a phone and asked Mrs. Roosevelt to come to the phone.

It was Mr. Early. "Please come home at once," he said. In her quavering voice, Mrs. Roosevelt said all right. She went back to the meeting room with firm step and excused herself. She excused herself to her table companion, Edith Galt Wilson, who had been part of a similar drama a quarter of a century earlier.

Mrs. Roosevelt had presence. The smile was still big as she bowed out of the room. The heart was leaden. She knew before she knew. Whenever fright hit her, Mrs. Roosevelt always appeared to be overly calm. The sign which no one ever appeared to notice was that she clenched her hands into fists and could not seem to open them.

She sat this way in the car and the fists were still clenched as she acknowledged the greetings of the White House doorman. She went up the elevator to her second-floor sitting room. Admiral McIntyre and Stephen Early stood inside the room. She listened calmly to the news she had already heard from her heart.

"Please ask Mr. Truman to come here," she said. Then, as an afterthought, she said that she had planned to fly to Warm Springs that night, and would both men accompany her. They said that they would.

It was 5 P.M. in Washington. In Warm Springs, Hassett was told by Early to make the announcement; that it would be made simultaneously in Washington. Mr. Hassett called Robert Nixon of International News Service; Merriman Smith of United Press; Harold Oliver of Associated Press.

Composing himself, William Hassett said: "Gentlemen, it is my sad duty to inform you that the President of the United States is dead. He died at three thirty-five o'clock this afternoon, Central Standard Time." The three reporters, who had literally lived with Franklin Roosevelt for long periods of time, were momentarily stunned. They looked at Hassett, looked at each other, fumbled for words, and broke for the telephones. A stone had been cast into a still pool.

Mrs. Roosevelt, again proceeding automatically, said to Admiral McIntyre, "I am more sorry for the people of the country and the world than I am for us." She asked for telegraph blanks. Sons James and Franklin and John were in the Far Pacific. Elliott was in England. Anna was at Bethesda Hospital with her son John. She sent identical telegrams. "Father slept away. He would expect you to carry on and finish your jobs. Bless you and all our love. Mother."

Harry Truman, at 5:04 P.M., stepped into a little room which Speaker Sam Rayburn called "my hideout." As the Vice-President stepped into the room, Rayburn said, "Steve Early phoned, Harry. He left an urgent message for you to go to the White House and enter by the front door." This was done to keep him away from the Executive Offices in the west wing.

The Vice-President hurried to the White House. He knew what this call was all about. Bishop Atwood had died and the President wanted the Vice-President to substitute for him as an honorary pallbearer. When he arrived, he was escorted upstairs to Mrs. Roosevelt's sitting room.

Mrs. Roosevelt stood and put her hand on Mr. Truman's shoulder. "The President is dead," she said. The Vice-President blinked behind his glasses. He was stunned. "What can I do to help you?" he said. Mrs. Roosevelt shook her head negatively. "What can we do to help you?" Both heard a sound and turned. In the doorway stood Secretary of State Edward Stettinius in tears.

The time was five twenty-five. On the radio, the music stopped. In buses and on subways and on the sidewalks, the ripples in the still pool widened. People looked shocked. Or laughed nervously. Some wept. In Chicago a barber listened to it on the radio. He was in the midst of shaving a customer. He folded his razor and sat.

In London, a frock-coated secretary knocked on a bedroom door and turned the knob at 10 Downing Street. "Sir," said the secretary, "President Roosevelt died a short time ago." The time was 11 P.M. Mr. Churchill sat motionless, staring at the rug. Then he said, "Get me the Palace." At Lloyd's, a director walked into the big room and tolled the Lutine Bell, which announces terrible disasters.

The brass chronometer in the plain bedroom at Warm Springs ticked louder than ever. The figure on the bed was not moved, and would not be moved until after Mrs. Roosevelt arrived late that night and had spent five minutes alone with him. In all New York firehouses, the sad "four-fives" were rung.

Time ticked on and the ripple widened. In Rio de Janeiro, a beggar with legs swollen like clubs saw an American woman approach. He pulled himself up painfully against a building wall, removed his ragged cap, and said, "Senora, I am desolated." In Moscow, huge red banners fringed with black were hoisted over the public buildings before dawn. People in Red Square looked and murmured, "Kak jhalko!" (What a pity!)

The sun was up in Shanghai and a rich Chinese merchant paused and read the oriental characters in front of a newspaper office. "But who killed him?" he said to the crowd. "Who would kill him?" At dawn, nuns in Rome led tiny orphan girls in prayer for the repose of the soul of Franklin Delano Roosevelt. A suntanned M.P. on Guam walked out into a field and jammed a bayoneted rifle into the ground, slung a helmet over the butt, and said: "We do this for all the soldiers."

A Day in the Life of
Dwight D. Eisenhower

7:15 A.M. The early sun butters the south side of the Executive Mansion. A crow stands on a branch of an old elm in tasteful black, cocking his head as bright-winged cardinals bank the turns on the lawn below. There is chill in the air, and wood smoke from old chimneys crayons the blue sky. An opaque dew clings to millions of blades of grass. The gatemen around the White House stand in the doorways to the sentry boxes, some sipping coffee, some staring at the first signs of daily life in the capital city.

The family elevator stops at the second floor. Colonel Robert L. Schulz, United States Army, gets off. The elevator remains there, with door open, waiting for the President of the United States. The colonel is tall, dark, balding and has a tic in the right eye which gives him a wise wink. He also has a silent sense of humor. As the President's military aide, Schulz looks out his window in the White House every morning at seven and murmurs, "Schulz, you came from nothing and look where you are now."

He sits, a little stiff in the blue-green Army uniform, in the second-floor corridor outside the President's bedroom. The wall lights are still on and Schulz picks up a morning newspaper and scans it.

Inside the door, Master Sergeant John Moaney, a handsome-looking man with skin the color of bittersweet chocolate, buttons his white jacket and approaches the presidential bedroom. He listens, hears nothing. He raps smartly on the door three times. Then he listens again. Inside, a muffled voice says, "Okay." Sergeant Moaney grins a little—he has never had to rap a second time—and he picks up a phone and orders breakfast for one. Then he hurries into the President's dressing room and his dark eyes make a final darting check of the day's wardrobe: light blue suit, pale blue shirt with long collar tabs, blue and red figured silk tie, undershirt and shorts, black socks, snowy handkerchiefs, a pair of brown, wing-tipped shoes.

Inside, Mr. President (as everyone calls him) has swung his legs over the side of the bed. He yawns, stretches, and rubs the skin behind the left ear. He stands, jams his feet into slippers, picks up his old brown robe, and pads off to the bath. The shower is warm. He is a man of fixed habits and he follows the same pattern every morning. He studies his face in the wall mirror and works up a lather in an old-fashioned mug. He shaves with a safety razor, moving down the pink cheeks, contorting as he works the sides of the mouth. The teeth are brushed, the halo of hair looks downy above the polished dome and, in a few moments, he is out in his dressing room bidding good morning to Sergeant Moaney and swinging a ten iron. He makes some practice swings, and sits.

The sergeant pulls the big drapes back and now the morning sun spangles the room. The President looks out at the Washington Monument and the Jefferson Memorial. Off to the side, the Potomac lies flat and fresh, a gray scar in the greenery. Breakfast, for the President, is also in a pattern: five stewed prunes, eight ounces of skim milk, a four-ounce steak, half a slice of toast, and two cups of Sanka.

Downstairs in the west wing of the Executive Mansion, a slender, graying woman smiles good morning to the Secret Service men in the corridors and enters the office next to the President's. This is Mrs. Ann Whitman, his personal secretary. A minute behind her is Miss Helen Weaver, young, blonde, and dedicated to her job. The two arrive about 7:20 A.M. and they leave at about 7 P.M. They work Saturdays and Mrs. Whitman "drops in for a few hours" on Sundays. At seven thirty in the morning they are typing some of last night's letters.

Farther to the west, in the wrinkled pile labeled the State Department, William J. Hopkins, White House executive clerk, is supervising the sorting of the morning mail. It averages two thousand five hundred letters per day. It has reached ten thousand. None of it gets to President Eisenhower firsthand. All of it is opened, scanned, and put into one of five piles: Whitman (personal mail); Goodpaster (the President's staff secretary); Persons (the President's liaison man with Congress); Hagerty (press secretary); Shanley (appointment secretary).

In the dressing room on the second floor, Moaney holds the trousers as the President steps into them; he holds the shirt, and he crouches before the feet as the shoes slip on. He helps with the cuff links and stands aside as the President twirls the tie into a knot and cinches it under his chin. A handkerchief goes into the breast pocket of the jacket, and Mr. Eisenhower slips it on. There is little conversation between the President and his valet. They have been working together since 1942, and they understand each other.

The master sergeant is a happy man. He is close to the man he respects more than any other, and Mrs. Moaney is employed as a maid in the same house. He and the President went through a war together, and Moaney never forgets it, and never mentions it.

Eight-o-five A.M. Down at the northwest gate, on Pennsylvania Avenue, two policemen stand in the doorway of a sentry box and watch the faces of those who are coming through. The tall pin oaks and the leafy elms etch blue shadows across the macadam driveway as the attractive girls and middle-aged men walk toward the press entrance to the Executive Mansion. The gates swing wide and a black Cadillac comes through, the policemen stopping it to look inside, front and back. The reporters come through the gate, so do the executives who form part of Ike's team, and the jaded cameramen—still, movie and TV.

The White House is coming alive. At eight-o-nine, the President steps out into the hall. He is ready for a day's work. His step is swift, slightly pigeoned, and the head is slightly down, as though addressing a golf ball.

Colonel Schulz is on his feet. The men exchange greetings and step diagonally across the hall and into the elevator. The car starts down to the ground floor. Schulz has problems, but he does not mention them until the President has spoken. The colonel is more than a military aide; he takes care of all the Eisenhower personal matters; bank balance, insurance premiums, payment of bills, gifts for relatives and friends, the presidential wardrobe.

Every morning, the colonel waits in the hall for the President, and every morning he walks him to the office. Whatever business transpires between these two must be accomplished in the one minute and twenty seconds it requires for the President to get from the bedroom to the office desk on the ground floor.

Mr. Eisenhower is affable this morning. He has slept well and he wears a lopsided grin. Sometimes he does not sleep straight through and, when this happens, he usually awakens around 2 A.M. After padding to the bathroom for a swallow of water, he goes back to bed and lies staring at the shadowy ceiling. He does not like sedation and takes it only when his mind refuses to shut down for the night.

"Warm out?" the Chief Executive says, as they leave the elevator.

"Yes, sir," Schulz says. "Sunny, too."

The President turns right, nods to the policemen on duty, and moves briskly toward the double white doors which separate the main mansion from the west wing. "Anything new?" he asks.

"Sir," the colonel says, "Manny Goldman phoned. [Manny Goldman of G.G.G. Clothes, in New York.] He suggests that you look over your wardrobe." This means that a few of the favorite suits should be retired.

They make a left turn, then a right around the little florist room in the White House. Inside, two men cut flowers for the scores of vases in the mansion rooms. "I'll check tonight," the President says, and now they walk under the open colonnaded terrace. The President squints in the morning sun and looks over the rose garden to where a little flag hangs limply over his putting green. "Good," the colonel says, but he doesn't really mean good because he and Mr. Goldman know that when the President likes a suit, he will sometimes order the same model three times as each one wears out.

At the end of the terrace, they nod to a policeman, make a left turn, and now the President of the United States is outside the French doors of his office. He stops. "Anything else, Bob?" The colonel stops. "No, sir." Then the colonel remembers something he wanted to say about the Eisenhower Trust Fund. This is an "irrevocable" trust fund, set up by the President when he was first elected, and before he assumed office. In it went most of his Army savings, plus the money he earned writing *Crusade in Europe*. Under its terms, he is not told how the money is being invested, or in what stocks or bonds. Thus, no conscious act of the President can affect his personal interests.

The colonel leaves. The President steps into his huge office. There are four entrances. Directly behind the desk is the French door leading out to the terrace and the lawn. Directly ahead of his desk is the door leading to the corridor where two Secret Service men and a policeman stand all day. To the left is the double door leading to the office of Bernard M. Shanley, appointment secretary. To the right is the door leading to the office of Mrs. Whitman and Miss Weaver.

He presses a buzzer. At once word flashes through the entire west wing that the President is in his office. It hits all of the recessed offices, and caroms around the corridors. Mrs. Helen Ganss, plump and pleasant, gets up from her desk and announces to Murry Snyder, assistant press secretary, "The President is in his office." Joseph Dodge, the President's personal adviser on foreign economic policy, sees Robert Clark, International News Service correspondent, in the big reception hall and says, "He's in." The secretary to Sherman Adams, the assistant to the President, opens Mr. Adams' office door a tiny bit and says, "The President is in." Policemen lounging near the several doors in this wing suddenly stand and face the exits. In the State Department, the Department of Defense, the Atomic Energy Commission, private phones buzz softly and voices say, "The President is now in his office."

And almost at once, the corridor outside the President's office is peopled with members of his team. Each one wants to see him at once. Each has a problem. Each one knows the unwritten rule: If you get in to see him, make it brief. Remember, we're waiting. They wait and they make small pleasantries and they stare at the gallery of amateur paintings on the wall.

At 8:19 A.M. Colonel A. J. Goodpaster, staff secretary, gets the nod to go in. This man is young, bright, and slightly harassed. He is on loan from the Army Engineers and he graduated second in his class at West Point. His job—if it can be defined—is to bring all the so-called "hot" problems of the State Department, the Atomic Energy Commission, and the Department of Defense to the attention of the President. He is also the intermediary presidential ear for the Central Intelligence Agency.

When he gets into the Eisenhower office, the President can almost tell, in advance, how "hot" the problem is by watching Goodpaster sit. If he sits in the chair by the side of the desk, directly facing the President, it is a very "hot" problem and Mr. Eisenhower often becomes impatient and reaches across the desk for the typewritten sheet from which the colonel is reading. On this particular morning, Goodpaster chooses the chair at the side of the desk and tells the President that the Atomic Energy Commission wants to discuss a plan for the dispersal of all atomic and nuclear weapons. The President listens and nods with understanding. "We are agreed on a plan," he says. "Get Lewis Strauss to work on this and see that he gets in to talk to me about it."

At eight-twenty-nine, Goodpaster leaves. As he walks through the double doors, executive clerk William Hopkins squeezes in. In his hand are the newest presidential appointments for signature. He also has three nominations for office which must be confirmed by the United States Senate. The President will not sign his own documents without reading them. It requires eleven minutes for Hopkins to get the signatures and be gone. At eight-forty-two Mr. Eisenhower rings for Mrs. Whitman.

She comes in from his right side and, besides notebook and pencils, she has an accumulation of newly arrived personal mail, plus some letters ready for signature. Sometimes Mrs. Whitman answers routine requests without dictation. In these matters, she knows the President's thoughts and she knows his style. Now, they exchange good mornings. The President is not verbose, hardly jovial.

Nothing, to his way of thinking, is as important as his job and so he wastes little time on the amenities. He dictates overlong letters and does it precisely, enunciating the commas, the periods, and indicating the new paragraphs. In this he is the tiger type, pacing up and down behind his chair, studying the landscape outside, turning to watch Mrs. Whitman's dancing pencil, rubbing that spot behind the ear.

At eight-fifty-seven, Mrs. Whitman thanks the President and gathers her gear as Gerald D. Morgan, special counsel to the President, comes in from the Shanley side of the office. Mr. Morgan reads all bills pending or passed in Congress, and part of his job is to read, symbolically speaking, the fine print in the lease. The President also reads all bills and last night, for example, sat in his upstairs study reading all the amendments to an agricultural measure. Now, Mr. Morgan has two bills for signature, one for veto. Tersely, he reacquaints the President with each measure. Fortunately for Eisenhower, he is able, without strain, to drop one important subject for another and to concentrate on each one to the fullest. Mr. Morgan is gone in four minutes.

In the west wing lobby, Senator William Knowland of California comes in, big, blond, and grim. He walks down the pastel green corridor toward the President's office. Behind him by twenty seconds is the man with the caterpillar eyebrows: Representative Joseph Martin of Massachusetts. And behind him is Senator Styles Bridges of New Hampshire. Last one in is Senator Leverett Saltonstall of Massachusetts, who smiles at one and all.

This is a Republican Party meeting and the congressional leaders have been called to a morning meeting because the President is not satisfied with the pace of the Congress. In an election year, negation strangles congressmen on both sides of the aisle and they are prone to worry more about what bills not to be caught voting against than what to be seen voting for.

The President is a prodder. He sets high minimum goals for the Congress and he gets angry when he sees the House or Senate loafing. He has been taken out of the Army, but someone forgot to take the Army out of him. He is punctual, precise, and a slave driver. He works every day, and he expects no less from his party cousins.

In the hall, the members of the team who have been waiting for a moment and a word give up. Murray Snyder, young, dark, obliging and almost humorless, returns to the office of the assistant press secretary. The retreat is general. Sherman Adams, the assist-

ant to the President, takes his finely honed mind back to his desk.
So does press secretary James Hagerty and special assistant Meyer
Kestenbaum.

It is a few minutes after nine and this type of meeting always
lasts until ten. Outside the press room, the newsreel and television
men set their tripods in the sun. They will catch the party leaders
on their way out, and will ask a lot of questions and will record
grammatically desiccated replies. In the press room, the White
House correspondents sit single-cheeked on tables, or sit in phone
booths talking with their city desks. Like soldiers, these men
spend most of their time waiting for something to happen.

The President sees them only once a week, on Wednesdays at
10:30 A.M. Hagerty sees them at least twice a day, to give them
the routine news of the White House and, now and then, some
very hot news. The press secretary plays no favorites, and will not
make an announcement until the three wire services are present.
In this way, the reporters are protected from the nightmare of
being beaten to choice news.

In the President's office, the congressional party leaders shake
hands and sit on grouped chairs or on the settee against the wall
to his right. They not only listen to him; they study him as well.
He is aware of this, but since his recovery from the Denver heart
attack, he feels better than he has in years because the matter of
taking care of himself is now compulsory and he knows that he is
well rested, that his skin glows pink, the bottom lip flutters a little
and the almost invisible eyebrows rise until they form wrinkles on
his forehead. His hands are on the armrests of his chair and he
propels the chair seventy degrees to the right, and an equal distance to the left. Sometimes he rolls a pencil under the palm of his
hand across a blotter.

He gets down to business at hand and tells these men that this
session of Congress is now in the late hours and they have much
work to do. If he feels that a pending bill is a bad bill, he tells
them now so that they pass it at their peril. He will veto it.
Dwight David Eisenhower is the boss, and in private conversation
is referred to as such. In his attitudes toward the men who work
on his team—and this includes the members of the Cabinet—he is
not a martinet, nor is he suppliant. He is a firm father who listens
intently, with head cocked, and then makes his own decision. It
matters little how eloquently the members of the team argue or
plead for a reversal; Mr. Eisenhower believes that he has a mandate from the people to be President of the United States and he
is the President of the United States. Healthy or sick, he is tem-
peramentally unfitted to lend himself to a regency. He trusts his

subordinates and this, in addition to his stubbornness, represents a virtue and a vice.

Dwight D. Eisenhower sees himself as the all-high arbiter rather than the boss. He sees himself as thinking in terms of all the people rather than the good of the Republican Party. This too is a virtue and a vice because there are highly placed men in the Republican Party who do not feel that the President is a Republican.

They sense his aloofness, his armor-plated dignity, and some mutter: "Don't worry, we'll make a Republican out of Ike yet." His trust of subordinates is so complete that, when one is caught in flagrant error, his personal shock and anger keep abreast with his blood pressure on the rise. His stubbornness reaches a point where, having made up his mind on an issue, he is loath to listen to further arguments to the contrary. One thing is certain: no man can pressure Eisenhower into altering a decision.

He has spent almost all his life as an Army officer. He is accustomed to listening to the separate pleas of underlings, then, when his mind is made up, issuing an order with the knowledge that all hands will obey it. He is irritated by those who continue to disagree after the event. Also, he has a self-confessed weakness in the field of mathematics and economics. "A general," he says, "is accustomed to requisitioning what he wants, not computing the cost."

He has an affection for all the men on the team, from Sergeant Moaney up to the Secretary of State, John Foster Dulles, and with the affection goes a loyalty resistant to petty indictments. Still, all of the men who work with him are held at arm's length. The President has no after-hours cronies in the crowd. The person closest to being an Eisenhower buddy is Treasury Secretary George Humphrey, and Mr. Humphrey has never been known to lean his elbow on the presidential shoulder.

At 9:55 A.M. the doors open and the congressmen spill out into the corridor. Some are still saying good-by when Major General Wilton "Jerry" Persons, deputy assistant to the President, walks in and leans on the President's desk for a quick, whispered conversation. General Persons is second in command in the White House to Sherman Adams, who is second only to the President. Persons' primary job is congressional liaison, and thus whatever agreements were reached at the conference just concluded are important to him.

Outside, Senator Knowland and House Minority Leader Martin sit behind Jim Hagerty's desk. The reporters stand close, tongues and pencils at the ready. This is a daily game of question and evasion. The reporters try to get news. The congressmen try not to give any.

Inside, the President buzzes for Bernard Shanley and they go over the daily appointment calendar together. The appointments are two: the legislative leaders' meeting, which is now over, and Herbert Hoover, Jr., at lunch. On some days, there are five appointments, seldom more. Since the September, 1955, heart attack, the ceremonial appointments have been stopped. It is no longer necessary that the President pose for pictures with a retiring admiral or executive. He no longer dons Indian headdresses for the newsreels, and the man who wants to present the homemade wicker rocker no longer gets in to see the President, even when accompanied by his congressman.

But the gain, to the President, amounts to nothing. He now has more time to see his secretaries, his assistants. There are four hundred persons in the White House and in the old State Department across the street who work directly for the President of the United States. In addition, there are fifty-five agencies, commissions, and boards which are responsible to him for their work. All executive groups, from the Defense Department down to the Department of the Interior, turn to him for daily guidance. The President must be (1) a work horse; (2) equipped with an elastic mentality which can stretch from one type of problem to another in a trice; (3) patient with his team; (4) able to shrug off all problems of state at night so that he will be fit to assume new burdens in the morning.

Eisenhower comes close to the ideal. He likes hard work; he can switch from a conversation on nominees for ambassador to Peru over to a discussion on medium-range missiles without giving either matter less than his best; he lacks patience with his men, at times, but the presidential explosions are much more rare than they used to be. He is still prone to bring his problems home for study, but he is learning to leave all but the most urgent ones in the office. If any great changes can be noted, it is that he does a more efficient day's work now than before the attack.

Recently, Mrs. Eisenhower glanced at one of the new appointment lists and phoned Mrs. Whitman at once. "I've been looking at the President's appointments," she said happily. "He isn't going to be busy and I have something for him to do."

Mrs. Whitman gulped and said that she would put the President on the phone. Ike listened, then said, "Look, hon . . ." and tried to explain that, while the official list may be lean, the day's callers are multitudinous. Mrs. Eisenhower is still certain that, husbandlike, he was just trying to evade a marital chore.

Shortly after ten, Hagerty sits with the President discussing the day's news, and what can be revealed to the press. This seldom requires more than four to six minutes. Hagerty returns to his big office on the north side of the White House and dictates plain, unglossed announcements. He will read these aloud and hand out copies of them to the press at ten thirty.

If the day is Tuesday, Hagerty has a longer conference with the President because of the weekly press conference in the Indian Treaty Room of the old State Department each Wednesday. At this meeting, the President appears before the newsreel cameras and the 180 to 200 accredited members of the White House correspondents' group to answer news questions. On Tuesday evening, Jim Hagerty sits at home and, as a one-time reporter for *The New York Times,* tries to anticipate every question which may be asked. In the morning he goes over these questions with his staff and asks for suggestions. At nine forty-five A.M. he reports to the President's office with Snyder, General Persons, and Colonel Goodpaster, and they brief the Chief Executive on matters which may be brought up at the press conference. Of course it is impossible, even for a reporter, to anticipate all the questions, and, now and then, Ike is hit with what is called "a curve." Hagerty no longer worries about his boss, though, because the President has learned to play editorial ping-pong fairly well.

A Secret Service man is talking to a policeman outside the Eisenhower office at eleven-o-four when Colonel Goodpaster rushes inside. He has a sheet of paper in his hand and he sits in front of the desk opposite the President. The President holds still, without swinging the chair, as he listens. Then he thinks for a moment and makes an answer. Goodpaster nods, tries to fashion a farewell smile, and races out.

At eleven twenty Ike is alone for a moment. This is so unusual that he looks around to make sure. He picks up a phone, sets it back on the cradle. He gets up, walks out toward the right, and into Mrs. Whitman's office. Both stenographers look startled. The President smiles apologetically. "Got any work for me?" They shake their heads mutely and he goes back into the office.

He is barely back in his plush cage when Sherman Adams comes in. As top assistant, Mr. Adams is the only man who is sometimes too busy to see the President. He speaks swiftly and his problems range all the way from statecraft to ward-heel politics. He speaks. He listens. He is gone.

At eleven thirty the president leaves his office by the French door for a job he doesn't like. He is going swimming. He does this every day at this time on orders from his doctor, Major General

Howard McC. Snyder. Dr. Snyder wants him to exercise before lunch, and no sport involves the use of so many muscles as swimming. The doctor also wants the President to break his work day with a nap, and this is the time for it.

He walks over to the pool built in Franklin D. Roosevelt's tenure, about a hundred feet from his office, under the colonnades. Like a good but unwilling patient, he walks into the little dressing room at the right, removes his clothing and dons a pair of swim trunks. The air in the building is heated to eighty-two degrees; the pool water is heated to ninety-two degrees. The water looks flat and blue and he can count the tiles along the bottom.

The President is not permitted to use the diving board. He looks at the water, grins at the two Army sergeants standing nearby, and slips down into the warm water. He swims alone, kicking easily and making his strokes slowly. He crosses back and forth, and floats awhile. Sometimes a shadow falls across the room and he looks up to see the old doctor standing in the doorway. General Snyder is seventy-five, oldest Army medical officer on active duty. He is there, not to banter with the President, but to watch his exertions. He watches how heavily the President breathes and how long it takes for his respiration to return to normal. He also watches skin tone, color of lips and fingernails.

At noon, the swimmer climbs out and, dripping, walks to the rubbing room. He peels the trunks off and dries himself vigorously. Then comes a little bending exercise. After that, he lies face down on the table and submits to a light rubdown at the hands of Sergeants Spanko and Sidmore.

He dresses again, thanks the sergeants, and says, "I think I'll go home." At twelve ten he walks back to the main part of the Executive Mansion, making the swing around the little florist room, walking through the main corridor, and taking the elevator upstairs.

On the second floor—actually the third—he walks across to his bedroom, and inside. Sergeant Moaney has the bedclothes turned down. The President would like to drop on the bed, clothed, but the doctor has told him to undress and get between the sheets, and he does. The sun is high and bright and he lies there, trying to doze, and failing. The hands on the blanket do not fidget. He has good control. Sometimes the eyes remain closed; sometimes he stares at the ceiling and thinks.

At twelve forty-five, Sergeant Moaney raps on the door, "Okay," the President says, and flips the bedclothes down and gets out of bed. The sergeant helps him to get into his clothes. This man dresses and undresses six times each day and it can be a chore. He washes in the bathroom, and leaves for lunch. The guest today is Under Secretary of State Herbert Hoover, Jr., who, in a very real sense, grew up in this mansion.

The President used to have from two to ten guests at breakfast, and from a half dozen to twenty at lunch. Now, usually, he breakfasts alone with Mrs. Eisenhower or with his mother-in-law, Mrs. Doud. The business lunches were discouraged by General Snyder because Mr. Eisenhower concentrates so deeply on the table conversation that he has a tendency to bolt his food.

Still, his luncheons with Hoover or with Dulles or Wilson can be classified as business, and, as such, they constitute part of the work. They require a little more than an hour—roughly 12:50 to 2 P.M.—and this is the quiet hour in the west wing. Here and there, a typewriter clatters, but, in the main, the wing is silent. The reporters leave for lunch. One by one, they walk up the long macadam drive toward Pennsylvania Avenue and, at the gate, the policemen check them out.

One man who may still be in the office is Bernard Shanley. The appointment secretary is a good-looking, graying man from New Jersey. Perhaps his most important job is not making appointments. Hundreds of congressmen would like to stop in for a moment to say hello to the President, or bring a constituent in to say hello, and Mr. Shanley must find new ways of saying no without offending the gentlemen.

He works in the finest surroundings. His office is large and bright and has a deep rug underfoot. Near the door to the President's office is a big fireplace with the American flag and the President's flag on brass standards. Over the fireplace is a full-length portrait of Ike in a blue suit. One of Shanley's jobs is to clock the exact moment the President leaves his office. At the end of each day, this list is typed and passed around.

At two the team is back from lunch and the west wing hums. Adams is at his desk. So are Hagerty, Persons, Goodpaster, Snyder and the rest. Some are already waiting in the corridor outside the office. At two-o-nine Mr. Eisenhower steps in from the south walk to his office and, at once, the buzzers ring in the main offices and the word is passed that the President is again at his desk.

He sits and rings for Mrs. Whitman. Now he is jovial, light of heart and instead of formal dictation, he says, "Here's what I want to say" and he permits her to compose it. The only other thing he permits her to do on her own initiative is to remind him, on cold days, to please wear his hat and coat when he steps outside. He is anti-hat, anti-telephone, anti-television (unless he is before the camera), also anti-swimming.

When Mrs. Whitman leaves, two men come in. One is Dr.
Gabriel Hauge, presidential adviser on economics. The other is
Dr. Arthur Burns, chairman of the Council of Economic Advisors.
These men seldom carry a problem. They bring informal reports
of economic health and illness abroad and at home.
Three years of hard study, as President, has made Mr. Eisenhower a fundamentalist in economics and agriculture. He does
not aspire to be an expert, but many hours of study have given
him a comprehension of both subjects. Hauge and Burns sit with
the President, and give him the latest figures on the cost of living
in the United States, and they will relate it to employment, scale
of wages, price of steel, and so forth.

At three forty-five Hagerty is in again to discuss his afternoon
press conference. They talk over what went on at the luncheon
with Under Secretary Hoover and, if any of it can be released to
the nation, the how and how much is hacked out now. Also, if
anything in the field of economics is newsworthy, this too is discussed fully. If none of it can be told, Jim Hagerty will browse
through the offices of Adams and Goodpaster and others trying to
find news for reporters who have morning editions which must be
fed.

As he leaves, the Secretary of State comes in, and there is a
genuine fondness in the face of the President as he stands to shake
hands with John Foster Dulles. He respects this man for his will-
ingness to go anywhere in the world at any time to try to promote
peace, and he will sit and listen to this great shaggy man make his
informal reports for long periods of time without interruption.

Still, the President is restless at four fifteen, when Dillon Anderson, special assistant to the President on national security affairs,
comes in. He has a new progress report on the early warning
radar system which will stretch across the top of Canada and
through the Yukon. Ike listens, asks a few questions, and seems
pleased. At four twenty-five he says good-by to Mr. Anderson,
and now he knows that he owns the clock. The day is officially
done. He has no more appointments, official or unofficial.

Now he may make a phone call or two. He asks Mr. Shanley to
get the Secretary of the Treasury for him and in fifteen seconds
George Humphrey is on the phone. He calls Mrs. Whitman in and
asks her to clean up his desk work. There are some letters to sign,
a few late ones to be read and digested. Sherman Adams peeks in
to ask a question and disappears behind the door like a wise turtle
in a white shell. The President buzzes for "Bern" and asks about
his appointments for tomorrow.

At 5:03 P.M. the word scatters through the wing that the Presi-

dent is out on the lawn making short chip shots. The dark flag on
the green snaps in the late afternoon breeze and the President
addresses each ball as seriously as though he had bet his salary on
sinking it. He makes a neat backswing, pulls down vigorously, and
straightens up to watch the ball settle on the green.

Fifteen minutes of this and he is back in the office. He calls Mrs.
Whitman, and he picks up a big manila envelopeful of homework. "I'm going home," he says. "Good night." Now, as he steps
through the door and out onto the south walk, everyone knows
that the President has left for the night. The word passes in quick
ripples and one of the men who gets it is General Snyder, whose
office is on the ground floor of the White House.

So, as the President walks back to the main part of the
mansion, the old Army Doc is standing in his own doorway,
watching. Mr. Eisenhower has to pass Snyder, and the physician
again has a critical eye on his patient. "Let me see the way
he lifts his heels and the way he carries his head," General
Snyder says, "and I will tell you how much the day has taken out
of him."

The President sees the doctor standing in the doorway. The
boyish grin spreads over the Eisenhower face. They wave. Sometimes Snyder thinks he sees something in the skin tone, or the
muscular attitude, and he says, "I think I'll run upstairs with you."
They get to the elevator together. This permits the doctor to ob-
serve his patient closely without appearing to be clinical.

"I have no objection to the President's doing a day's work," the
doctor says. "He's fit. My objection is that he tends to do two and
a half days' work each day. He charges into his duties as though
they were something which had to be defeated quickly. My job is
to keep breaking the tempo of his day."

Upstairs, they sit in the big oval study next door to the President's bedroom and chat for a few minutes. When General Snyder
leaves, Ike will go through his bedroom, through the little dressing
room, to Mrs. Eisenhower's room. He is, of course, devoted to his
wife and he will kiss her and ask what kind of a day she has had.
If Mrs. Eisenhower's mother is in from Denver, the three will sit
and talk for a while, and it is at this time that the President
unwinds.

If he is in a mood for reading, he will glance at one of four
newspapers, or perhaps at all of them: *The New York Times*, the
New York Herald Tribune, the *Washington Post*, and the *Wall
Street Journal*. His blue eyes skitter down one column and up the
next. He is expert at finding the things he wants to read. He is
even more expert at avoiding the stories which irritate him.

At six he tells Mrs. Eisenhower, "Hon, I'm going to put on my paint clothes." He goes back into his bedroom, removes his suit, and dons old slacks and an old shirt. He walks across the hall to a place he calls his paint room, and there he mixes his oils, and, alone, begins to paint, or, perhaps, works on a partly finished painting. He has finished several portraits of his two favorites: George Washington and Abraham Lincoln. He cocks his head, glances critically at his work through his rimmed glasses, and applies each stroke with care.

At seven, if there is no formal dinner scheduled, he will come back across the hall refreshed, and Sergeant Moaney will help him to clean up and dress for dinner. If his grandchildren pay him a visit, he will ignore the adults and lead the little ones to the top floor of the White House. There he will take them to a solarium, and will broil a steak on a charcoal grill for himself and the children.

Otherwise, dinner will be served at 7:30 P.M. in the upstairs hall. This is not a dining room, but presidential families who have lived on this floor toward the western edge of the mansion have fitted the hall up to look like a combination dining room and drawing room. The President and the First Lady often dine alone. At times, they eat from trays, she in silence, he looking at a television set.

Sometimes, Ike will have a drink of Chivas Regal Scotch, with water. He might even have two. As a drinker, he's a "nurser" and can sip one drink for an hour or more. Once, at a stag dinner, he nursed a single drink all evening long and, although the servants brought trays of drinks for the guests, the gentlemen kept refusing out of deference to the President. They were all ready to say good night at 11:10 P.M. when Mr. Eisenhower said he thought he would have a second Chivas Regal. He was an astonished host when, out of the blue, all eighteen of his guests suddenly ordered a second drink.

He is fond of his mother-in-law and, if Mrs. Doud is visiting, Ike will hurry through his homework and then phone downstairs to get a motion picture ready. At eight forty they will start downstairs to the private theater and, if the President has his way, the picture will be a Western, in color. He also likes fast-moving mysteries and broad comedies. Some years ago he saw a comedy called *Angels in the Outfield*, starring Paul Douglas, and there is a feeling among the members of the staff that he hasn't stopped laughing yet.

It was about a baseball manager who was always losing his temper (and ball games) and who was promised by an angel that, if he would control his emotions, winged cherubs would field all the difficult plays in the outfield. President Eisenhower asked for the same picture a few weeks after seeing it for the first time. Then he asked for it again. And again. Last year, in Key West, the staff groaned when the President announced happily, "Guess what we're going to see tonight? *Angels in the Outfield.*" That was the eighth time.

Mrs. Eisenhower likes television and is acquainted with most of the network shows. In the living quarters on the second floor there are five or six sets, some of them color. But, if she is watching TV, and he doesn't want to watch, he will read. Here again his taste goes to Westerns. He is also a student of history, although this does not relax him as much as the you-take-the-pass-and-I'll-head-'em-off-at-the-gulch novels.

On the other evenings, the President will play bridge. This is one of his favorite amusements. Should an old crony like General Alfred Gruenther be in Washington, they will play until the late hours, and the high-level needling is like a tonic to Ike. The President is a better fisherman than a bridge player, and a better cook than a fisherman. The world knows him as a golfer, and, on sunny Wednesday afternoons, he is usually at the Burning Tree golf course.

Most of the early night hours are taken up with study. Ike will not permit others to tell him what is in an important bill, or the contents of a 250-page report from a commission or board. He must read it himself, and, quite often, he will spend weeks reading, annotating, and studying one report.

When he is ready to make a decision, Mr. Hagerty stands behind his desk at a morning press conference and says: "The President announces that he has accepted the Hoover Report and finds himself in agreement with most of the recommendations." The press and television marvel that the President has made up his mind so quickly and so succinctly. Privately, they often feel that the report was read by one of the numerous secretaries, and that the President read a two-or-three-page digest of the problem, and based his decision on it.

On one of the days I was at the White House, Mr. Eisenhower spent the entire evening reading the amendments to a bad bill. He knew that it was a bad bill; he knew that, if it was passed by the Congress he would veto it, but he had to study every clause and every line so that, when he called the congressional leaders in for a conference, he would be able to defend, item by item, the portending veto.

At 10:20 P.M. he leaves the downstairs theater with his ladies,

head down, listening to their comments. He nods to the Secret
Service men in the corridors and takes the elevator to the second-
floor apartment. Outside the partition, he finds James Hagerty and
Secretary Humphrey chatting. The President excuses himself and
sits with the two men.

They talk about state matters for a few minutes. None of them
realizes that this nightly chat has become a ritual. Hagerty has
been saying good night to President Eisenhower for over three
years. It is not required as part of his duties as press secretary, nor
has anyone asked Secretary Humphrey to appear outside the presidential quarters at this hour. Still, the three men manage to meet
at this hour, and they close the conference in the same way: by
walking with the President to his bedroom; the room where President Harry Truman built a small balcony.

There, Mr. Eisenhower stands in the doorway for a final word,
and all three men say good night. The time is now ten forty and,
when there is no state function, no private stag dinner for industrialist friends, the President retires at this minute. This is not
according to plan, but rather according to subconscious rut.
Hagerty's acidulous New Yorkerish tone is still caroming in the
corridor with "Good night, Mr. President" as the door closes, and
the two visitors go home to whatever family life is left at this
hour.

They think that the President sleeps in that room. They are
mistaken. Master Sergeant Moaney stands inside the room. As the
President undresses, sitting on the edge of the bed, Moaney takes
the clothes and hangs them in closets, or places them in hampers
for laundering. President Eisenhower says little. The clothes are
removed swiftly, with purpose. The pajamas go on in the dressing
room, and the robe.

The President goes into the bathroom, closes the door, and takes
care of his nightly ablutions. He washes, brushes his teeth, rinses
his mouth, and takes a few swallows of water. In the big bedroom,
Sergeant Moaney lays out the clothes for tomorrow morning. He
places a tan suit with tiny stripes, a white shirt, a solid brown tie,
brown sox, and brown calfskin shoes on the bed.

At 10:55 P.M. the President comes out of the bathroom rubbing
his chin. He says good night to the sergeant. Moaney bows, and
leaves by the hall door. The President looks around the room, and
extinguishes the lights. A little illumination pervades the room
from the tall lights in the south driveway. Mr. Eisenhower goes to
the night table, picks up a small plastic case full of nitroglycerin
tablets and a glass of water.

In the gloom, he carries them to a closet. In it is a doorway. He walks through it, closing it behind him, and he is now in Mrs. Eisenhower's room. She sits at her dressing table, as gracious and lovely and feminine as any First Lady in the nation's history, and they chat for a few moments. It isn't much of a private life, but they cherish it like newlyweds.

When she finishes brushing her hair, President Eisenhower slips into his side of a big double bed. He clicks the switch off the last light, says a short prayer that all will go well with the nation and with him, and he is breathing deeply and easily while Mrs. Eisenhower is still watching the street lights flicker across the ceiling.

John Fitzgerald Kennedy

Suite 9335 of the Los Angeles Biltmore was cool. The hall was hot and, in its dimness, photographers and reporters leaned against the walls. They were waiting. A stocky man at the door laid his hand gently on the chest of anyone who tried to enter.

Inside, there was a private office. A thin stenographer in a red, white and blue dress worked at a desk. Three men stood whispering. One of them moved to an inner door with some words scrawled on a piece of paper.

The news this morning had been bad. There was talk of defection from Senator Kennedy and talk of coalition to stop Senator Kennedy. Votes were switching and no one knew for certain whether Senator John F. Kennedy was holding his seven hundred votes, or losing.

The door opened from the inside and the man handed the sheet over. "New Jersey is switching to Kennedy," he whispered, and the man inside nodded, accepted the paper, and closed the door. He walked across the carpet of the big sitting room, which was complete with fireplace, settee, and color portrait of Senator Kennedy on the mantel, to two men who were whispering.

One was Pierre Salinger, press secretary. The other was Charles Roach, also of the press staff. They studied the paper and smiled. New Jersey, which had pledged forty votes to Governor Robert Meyner, had just announced that it would switch its vote after the first ballot to $31\frac{1}{2}$ to Senator Kennedy, $3\frac{1}{2}$ to Mr. Stevenson, 5 to Governor Meyner.

This was a lift. The paper was given to David Powers, a Bostonian who had been with Senator Kennedy in all of his campaigns. Mr. Powers, who walks and talks like a man perpetually in church, took the paper and walked to a gold door. He rapped on it with his fingernails. The door opened and Robert Kennedy looked out. The paper went in.

It was noon hour of Zero Day for Senator Kennedy. He and the whole Kennedy family had been working for years to boost him toward the White House and, as the Senator said at noon, "We make it in two ballots or we are dead."

"Has Jack had lunch?" Mr. Salinger said. Mr. Roach shook his head. "He ordered a chicken sandwich and a container of milk. It hasn't come up."

Behind the chair was a Wollensak tape recorder. To the left, a big television set sat staring out of a blind eye. On an end table, two dozen red roses sprayed from a silver vase like Fourth of July rockets in flight.

A tall, dark, good-looking woman came out of the little gold room in stocking feet. "Where's the lunch?" she said. Someone whispered that it was on the way up. She was the Senator's sister, Mrs. Peter Lawford. As she went back, a waiter brought the sandwich and the milk. It disappeared inside.

Senator Kennedy sat inside, chewing and sipping, listening to his brother Bob evaluate the morning situation. In the big sitting room, Mr. Roach was on the settee, doodling with a pen and dialing numbers.

"Hello. This is Chuck. Governor Sanford of North Carolina is going to make a second speech for the Senator. He needs some tickets for the arena. You got any? Who? They don't have to be on the floor. They don't have any votes. This man is desperate for tickets. Okay, I'll take one." (Terry Sanford is actually the Democratic nominee for Governor.)

Dave Powers tiptoed over. "What about the luncheon Jack was supposed to attend? Has anybody canceled it?" Evelyn, the thin secretary, came in to say that the Hawaiian delegation was here. "Shall I let them in?" Mr. Powers passed the word through the gold door. Mr. Salinger left and another man came in. "They have a camera," he said.

The Hawaiians came in. Most of them appeared to be happy Orientals. Their women wore togalike garments of burnt orange and white. In a moment, Senator Kennedy was present. He is medium tall, his hair is thick and brown, his smile is lame and ready, and he wears clothes well.

He moved around the sitting room quickly, giving his name as he extended his hand or, if he recognized the name, shouting it in a happy whoop and shaking hands warmly. Some of the Hawaiian delegates wore Stevenson buttons and one said:

"We don't have anything against you, Jack, but Stevenson is better known around the world than you, and we need someone who is well known. Very well known."

The Kennedys have a facility for rebutting politely and at once. "I think I'm pretty well known," the Senator said. "If you have followed my travels, through Africa and elsewhere, you know that I've been around. In any case, a man who is elected President of the United States becomes well known immediately."

The Hawaiians nodded appreciatively. They were not convinced, but they had happy eyes for this man. "I would like to say," the Senator said, "that if you have any questions to ask, I'll be happy to answer them. I realize that no souls will be saved after nine o'clock tonight, so permit me to do it now."

They asked him about McCarthyism and he said he didn't think that it was an issue. Maybe not, a man said, but we'd like to know your position on it. Senator Kennedy has a habit of slapping hands together to punctuate key words in sentences.

"At the last convention," he said, "Governor Stevenson asked me to nominate him and I doubt that he would have done that if he did not think I was in accord with his views."

He lowered his head for a moment, and traced a pattern in the rug with a brown shoe. "I think the issue today is, who is strong enough to win and, having won, will be strong enough to present the cause of the United States forcefully—forthrightly."

A Hawaiian woman with a becoming streak of white in her hair threw a flower lei around his neck and hugged him. "I couldn't be in better hands," the Senator said, and winked over her shoulder. She grinned and said, "But you didn't give me the kiss that goes with it." He bent forward and tapped her cheek with his lips.

Senator Kennedy doesn't handle affection gracefully. He hides his embarrassment with laughter. This time he was saved by a telephone bell. When he left to answer it, his brother came into the room and said, "I'm Bob Kennedy." He shook hands affably, a younger, smaller, more intense edition of Jack. "I spent my honeymoon in Hawaii," he said.

Jack returned to the room to say farewell to each delegate. When the door closed behind them, he took a comb from his jacket and flicked it through his thick hair twice.

"Let's go to that luncheon," he said. "That luncheon" was a garden party affair tendered at the Sheraton West by Mr. Reynolds of the Reynolds Metal Company.

The Senator nodded to me to join him and it required four

minutes to get out into the hall. Every time he moves, an entourage of silent men moves in behind him. The Senator always walks
in front, and always sits in the front of his rented limousine with
the chauffeur.

He passed an elderly cleaning woman and she pressed herself
against the wall as he moved toward her. Her eyes were shining.
"God bless you," she murmured, and he came out of his reverie
and looked at her, then reached for her hand. He got into a
Biltmore elevator and his men followed until the Senator was
pressed against the back wall.

On the street, the moving mobs spotted him and paused to look.
At every turn, a man or woman jumped out of the crowd to say,
"I'd like to shake your hand." The sun was white and hot, and it
burned through the shoulders of a summer suit and caromed off
the sidewalk into the Senator's squint.

Senator Kennedy got into the car and someone said that this
lunch was for the delegates of five states where the Reynolds
people had plants. He nodded and began to tap the top of the
dashboard with his fingernails. Idly, almost vaguely, he watched
the traffic, saw the store fronts, nodded to traffic policemen, and
thought about the big night of decision, which was now only a
few hours away.

At the hotel, a tall young man with a familiar wrinkled grin
grabbed the Senator's hand as he got out of the car. This was
Franklin D. Roosevelt, Jr. They tried to thread their way through
the sidewalk crowd. Ahead were a dozen photographers, crouch-
ing, aiming, firing the bright silent winks, and moving forward to
try again.

Senator Kennedy shrugged his shoulder, adjusted his tie with a
pat, turned the candidate's smile on, and began the handshaking
routine. In the garden, some girls got out of the swimming pool to
take a good look.

The party moved with agonizing slowness. Hands were thrust
at Senator Kennedy like friendly spears from affable natives. He
grasped them one and all, gave two or three pumps, and moved to
the next. He was averaging twenty greetings a minute.

Liz Whitney, dark and handsome, waved from the perimeter of
the crowd. "Your dad here?" she said. He turned, waved, and said
no. Young Roosevelt put a heavy arm across the candidate's shoulders and helped him through the grove of palm trees, the low-
hanging banana leaves, the well-dressed men in silk suits, pressing
tighter around him.

The garden was arrayed in big tables under huge colored umbrellas. Governor Lindsay Almond of Virginia, short, white-

haired, and a disciple of Senator Lyndon Johnson, shook hands with Senator Kennedy and managed a smile for the photographers. Senator Kennedy moved from table to table. He had a sweet neutral word for everyone and he has learned to beam a solid grin when a stranger announces that he hopes someone else gets the nomination.

The candidate was introduced to Mr. Reynolds and he sat with him as a waiter brought a plate of beef stroganoff with noodles and fresh garden peas. The Senator did not say that he had eaten his lunch. He picked up a fork, and began to blend the beef with the noodles. He lifted a forkful to his face and almost made it. A beautiful woman came from behind and thrust her face close to his. He dropped the fork and shook hands.

He tried it again, and one of the entourage whispered in Senator Kennedy's ear. At once, he arose and excused himself. There was an important phone call inside. Two men showed the way, and again in the hotel crowds formed and he had to shake hands and move at a limp. The Senator was shown behind the glass partition. There he conversed, with his hand around the transmitter.

On the way back, he passed through the dining room and waved. Then he stopped. At a table across the room, Senator Kennedy saw Chester Bowles of Connecticut having lunch. He broke from his entourage and went to Mr. Bowles. The two men moved to an empty table, where they sat whispering.

The photographers shot at least four hundred pictures in the thirty minutes the Senator spent at the garden party. At 2:25 P.M., he decided to leave. The word was passed and, out front, three policemen surrounded the Senator's rented car. The chauffeur yelled to a Kennedy man on the curb: "Where are we going? Back to the Biltmore?" The man on the curb shrugged.

It was not until two forty-four that Senator Kennedy reached his car. I was sitting in the back seat. He looked at me, smiled, and shook his head. Ed Morgan of the ABC network got in. The cameramen stood on the curb ready to make the final picture, and Senator Kennedy said wearily to one man, "Please wave to me so that I can wave back." The man did. Senator Kennedy did.

That was the last wave. He turned to the chauffeur and said, "The hideout." The car swung away, and the people waved from the sidewalk and the sun slanted in the right side of the car and caught Senator Kennedy's face. This was to be his last public move. The last wave of the hand. The last handshake. The final smile.

He was tired. I asked him a question and he looked at me

blankly, as though he didn't comprehend. I tried to get a smile from him by telling him that I had gone to the wrong hotel—the Beverly Hilton—to cover the Virginia caucus and, when I asked the desk clerk where I could find the Virginia caucus, he stared at me and said, "How does she spell her last name?"

Senator Kennedy chuckled. "You're kidding," he said. I said I wasn't. He went back to tapping the top of the dashboard. Mr. Morgan asked the Senator if Senator Humphrey might be considered for Vice-President if Senator Kennedy was nominated. "You think Humphrey is dead for the second spot?" Mr. Morgan said.

"Oh, yes," Senator Kennedy said. "He turned away from us. He said he was fed up with our tactics." I asked him how many votes he expected to get on the first ballot.

"You can't count votes without counting switches," he said. "Some of the delegations wait until the ballot is over, then switch. When the switches are over, we ought to have about seven hundred eighty."

Suddenly, the fatigue hit. The tension was still with him, but the fatigue hit hard and the eyes squinted against the hot sun so that he was staring through his long lashes at the road ahead. The hills of Hollywood came into view, chocolate globs of ice cream speckled with flecks of mint homes, and the Senator asked me not to reveal his hideaway. I said I wouldn't.

"I'm going to stay at this little apartment and rest," he said. "You'll be watching television," I said. "You can't kid me." He rubbed his sensitive fingers across his brow.

"I'll watch later," he said. "I'll take it easy until tonight." He turned to the chauffeur. "Take Jim back to the Biltmore," he said. "Then come back, I won't need you, but just come back in case."

I asked if he would appear at the convention later if he was nominated. No, he said. No, he would stay at the apartment and rest. The car pulled up a side street and Jack Kennedy got out and shook hands.

"Good luck," I said. "I mean it." He climbed back up onto the famous smile. "Thanks," he said. The door slammed and I watched him walk, head bowed and alone, into the apartment. The chauffeur picked up the car telephone and swung the wheel with his other hand.

"Station five?" he said. "Station five? I just delivered the Senator at the hideaway." He listened for a moment. "Yes," he said. "He's going to stay there."

The door was ajar. I was talking to Evelyn Lincoln, the President's personal secretary. From the other side of the door, a man's voice called, "Jim? Jim? Come on in." My appointment with President Kennedy was not due until the next morning. Mrs. Lincoln pushed the connecting door open and John F. Kennedy, too young-looking, too vigorous, too handsome, got up from behind his desk and came around to the door to shake hands with Mrs. Bishop and me.

I tried to beg off. "Come on," he said and he motioned to two beige couches flanking a fireplace in his office. We sat. He pulled up a rocker with the legend USS *Kitty Hawk* on the backrest, and sat. He knew why I was in the White House. I was there to do a personal close-up of him and his family for the magazine *Good Housekeeping*. He leaned forward, elbows on knees, the brown suit freshly pressed, and he put on the big Kennedy grin.

"A magazine article?" he asked in mock shock. "Couldn't you make a book out of it?" I thought about it. "Maybe," I said. "It would depend upon how much you and Mrs. Kennedy will sacrifice your privacy." He reached a hand out and patted a knee. "I read some of your other books," he said.

We talked about *The Day Lincoln Was Shot*. It was a minute-by-minute account of the sixteenth President's final day. Mr. Kennedy's voice softened. "I remember," he said. "There were about fifty-odd things that happened that day that, if they had not happened in the correct sequence . . ."

"Lincoln would not have been shot," I said. He lowered his head a moment, as though thinking. When he brought it back up, the big smile was on again. "Are they taking good care of you here?" he said. They were. I had interviewed his secretaries, the presidential assistants, the servants, and was en route to talk to Mrs. Kennedy and Caroline and John-John.

I asked the President why he called his little boy John-John. He said he didn't want him to be called Jack. He didn't like Johnny either.

So he called him John-John and the President had a favorite trick he used with his son, and he used it to make the little one laugh. Whenever he saw John-John, he called him over and said, "Tell me a secret." John-John would whisper in his father's ear "bzzzz-zzz-bzzzz." The President would lean backward, shock on his face, and say, "You don't tell me?" and the little boy would fall down laughing.

Mr. Kennedy may not go down in history as the greatest President, nor the poorest. No one can dispute the fact that he was the hardest-working Chief of State we ever had.

I have written stories about Dwight D. Eisenhower, Herbert Hoover and Harry S Truman, and I have researched the lives and events of others. But President Kennedy worked at his job from 7:20 A.M. until 11:30 P.M., every day, seven days a week.

I asked him why.

"A man," he said, "must have goals. There is not sufficient time, even in two terms, to achieve these goals. Almost all Presidents leave office feeling that their work is unfinished. I have a lot to do, and so little time in which to do it."

His Negro valet, George H. Thomas, a dark cherub of a man, awakened the President every morning shortly after seven. Thomas always knocked on the Kennedy door lightly, so that he would awaken the President, but not disturb Mrs. Kennedy. He would listen for a cough, the whispered "All right, George." The President would slip his feet into slippers, put a robe on over his short nightshirt, and come out into the second bedroom.

George Thomas always gave him four newspapers. The President devoured these in fifteen minutes, while fresh clothes were being laid out by Thomas, and the bath drawn.

Devoured is the word. Mr. Kennedy read vertically. He could spot a two-paragraph story on page twenty-three regarding the storage of corn, or a remark of the Soviet Foreign Minister, and he would call the West Wing of the White House and ask to see the Secretary of Agriculture, or the Secretary of State, at eight thirty. Many of his appointments of the day were based upon the news he digested before breakfast.

He liked four-and-a-half-minute eggs, and orange juice, and toast. The children were in upon him before he could finish coffee. Caroline, who, at six, is beginning to develop a little reserve, and John, who skids around the turns of the second floor of the White House, thinks nothing of running down the great hall in the nude holding a flag aloft, arrived like racing desperadoes.

The President enjoyed being President, but he loved being a father. No matter how stiff the state occasion, he always found time for his children because he realized that, psychologically, they would spend their formative years in the White House.

He was pleased beyond measure when he found that neither of the children understood the term President of the United States. They knew that this was his title, but they didn't know what it meant and they had no notion that he was more important than other men.

On the third floor, there was a little private school. Caroline and ten other boys and girls attend first grade there. There, Miss Grimes, a Long Island girl, taught kindergarten. There, Caroline had a paper on which she had printed her name twenty-five times in huge block letters.

The other students were not the children of Cabinet members, but rather children of old Kennedy friends from Georgetown. Each of these youngsters brought lunch. Mrs. Kennedy insisted that Caroline carry a lunch box like the others, and eat with them in class.

Mrs. Kennedy had an adamant, and misunderstood, notion that she and the President were entitled to a private life. She used to drive the children out to Glen Ora Farms, to watch the animals. She used to walk with them in Lafayette Park, across the street from the White House.

She did not relish cameramen taking zoom-lens photos of her with her children, or water skiing, or on a yacht. In fact, it was a victory for the President that she agreed to make the trip with him to Texas.

The glamour of the presidency escaped Mrs. Kennedy. "I have learned to live with it," she told me. "I used to feel badly because I enjoy a family life; and I appreciate old friends. I do not like politicians."

She smiled almost apologetically. "I have met a lot of them, but I can't say I like them." Why? "Well, as far as I am concerned, they are all self-seeking people—egotists."

On the day I spoke to the President, it was obvious that he planned to run for a second term, and it was equally obvious that he did not think it would be a soft campaign. His views on civil rights had made him a thorn in the side of the tender South, and he felt that he had to go South—was impelled to go South—to explain and re-explain his position. He needed Southern votes, and he was going to need them sorely next year.

So he planned trips to Florida, and made whistle stops in small places so that he might win support. The trip to Texas was important to him because he had to have those November, 1964, votes. He asked his wife to go, because she had a popularity of her own—a good vote-getting popularity—and he liked to announce, as he did on the last day of his life, that he was sometimes known as Jacqueline Kennedy's husband.

In the days I spent in the White House—Mr. Kennedy's final days, as it now develops—he was always cheerful, energetic, and he led his Secret Service men as a comet leads its starry trail. He swam in the White House pool twice a day and, when Mrs. Kennedy was away, he swam with Caroline and John-John. When they played on the south lawn, with their trampoline and seesaws, he would hear the shrieks from his oval office, and would leave his desk to stand in the doorway and clap his hands three times.

The children knew the signal, and would come running. In the evening, when there were no state dinners, the children were fed at six. John-John sat in a high chair and wore a plastic bib. Under the high chair was a plastic mat. They ate in the private dining room on the second floor of the White House, within the eight-room span in which our first families live.

There are 132 rooms in the White House, but the Kennedys, the Eisenhowers and the others used only eight. At night, President Kennedy had dinner with his wife. He never brought problems of state to the mansion.

"Once," Mrs. Kennedy said, "just once—the other day—I asked my husband at lunchtime how matters were going." She laughed and held her hand before her face. "He held his hand up and ticked off ten separate things which he said had gone wrong, and he said, 'The day is only half over.' "

In the afternoon, his eyes felt blurry while he was reading, and President Kennedy told Mrs. Lincoln that he wanted to see an ophthalmologist named Roche. Mrs. Lincoln phoned the Secret Service.

Jerry Behn, chief of the White House detail, sent a car with two men to Dr. Roche's office. They examined the premises, the doctor, the waiting room, and then, by radio, called Behn to pronounce the premises "sanitized."

Behn phoned Mrs. Lincoln. "Please tell the President that we are ready any time he is," he said. The President was given the news, stepped out the back door, tucking his tie inside his jacket— a characteristic gesture—and got into the second of three cars which took him everywhere. Secret Service men were in all three.

When they arrived at the doctor's office, the Secret Service men got out first, scanning the sidewalk, the halls, the rooftops, the upper-floor windows on both sides of the street.

Then they opened the back door of the Presidential limousine, and John F. Kennedy got out to go to the doctor's office and find out that there was nothing wrong with his eyes, they were fatigued from too much reading.

The Secret Service accompanied him everywhere—even to St. Matthew's Procathedral for Mass. If the President saw a big crowd in the street, he changed the church and attended Holy Trinity in Georgetown, his parish when he was a Congressman.

I asked President Kennedy if he prayed outside of church. "Oh, yes," he said. "I get on my knees every night before I go to bed. Funny, I don't say a prayer in the morning. Just at night."

It was like reserving the final minutes of consciousness for God.

Newspapers

Old reporters are maudlin over dead newspapers. They attribute to them virtues they never had. They exaggerate the wisdom of stupid editors. The mundane and sordid events of an earlier decade are given music and lyrics. The cheap little stories become page-one newsbeats. There is a glow to everything that happened long ago, a glow which increases in proportion to the dimming of the aging reporter's vision.

He despises today and all the todays marching toward him. He mocks the schools of journalism as though they were factories turning out computer reporters. He is suspicious of young city editors, and he cannot abide copy boys with college degrees. He no longer solicits the easy affability of politicians; the Old Reporter stands off and waits for them to solicit him.

He is certain that he thinks better, and more swiftly, than in the old days. On the other hand, his notes are more meticulous because he no longer trusts himself to remember names and numbers and streets. His lapses are longer and his temper shorter, his bottom is broader and his outlook is narrower, but he denies these truths as office politics. Often, his face looks like a bubbling rarebit, but he fancies himself as a dandy with delicious sins lying ahead, as well as behind him.

Once, when I was a working stiff, I knew him well. I knew him and his newspapers too. Now, as I approach the years which will transmute me into him, I'm beginning to admire the codger and the era of his greatness. I am beginning to see that he was right all the time.

The Tabloid

It was a hot summer morning and the trucks rolled weakly over the cobbles of Varick Street. A pushcart peddler with sweat on his chin tried to sell two-cent ices in front of the *Evening Graphic*, but there was no one on the street. The city dozed and the spires shimmered. In the side streets, hydrants spun silver sequins against the pale skin of tenement house youngsters.

Two fans buzzed in the editorial department of the *Graphic*, but the editors couldn't keep themselves cool. There was a shaded lamp over the city desk and Bill Plummer sheaved the galleys in his big bony hand and took them into the office of the managing editor. He walked like an old man before he was old—head low, shoulders hunched, big feet barely off the floor.

Plummer was a competent city editor who worked in growls. He went to the back of the building and knocked on the door of the office. A voice said, "Come in." Plummer went inside to the desk set diagonally across the back window. He set the sheaf on the desk blotter. "It's pretty quiet," he said.

Emile Gauvreau picked up the sheaf and ran through the lead paragraphs. Daddy Browning had left Atlantic City. President Hoover had opened the Pan-American Congress. The Detroit Purple Gang was trying to move into New York. Mayor James Walker was planning a trip to Europe. Ruth Snyder had made a new appeal for executive clemency.

A dull day. The *Graphic* couldn't stand a dull day. It lived in a shriek. The news had to be more exciting than this. Gauvreau went through the galleys again. His front page had been living on 120-point caps and 144-point wooden type so long that anything less would read like an apologetic whisper.

Mr. Gauvreau was a little man with a limp. He had black hair with a loose forelock and a face with a semipermanent impish grin. He had, at one time, been the staidest of editors on the staidest of newspapers—the *Hartford Courant*. Now, he and Mr. Phillip Payne of the *Daily Mirror* were fighting for top ranking as the fathers of tabloid journalism. The difference between them was that Payne played the sensational game as though his life would be forfeit if he lost—in time, he was proved to be right —whereas Gauvreau played it in the manner of an intellectual shooting craps in an East Side alley to prove that the laws of probability are sheer nonsense.

"We have to do better than this," said Gauvreau. Plummer stood leaning on the outside of the desk. He shrugged. Gauvreau swung his swivel chair so that he faced the back window. The sun came through and the shadow of the fire escape steps made cool dark bars on the pane.

"Can you think of anything?" Gauvreau said. Plummer deepened his normal frown. "Campbell says the Detroit Purple Gang is moving into New York. We can get a district man to have the police commissioner declare war on them." Gauvreau shook his head slowly.

"The commissioner couldn't declare war on his wife," he said softly. "The Dutchman is running beer all over town. That crazy Legs Diamond is looking for trouble with Big Frenchy and Owney, and the commissioner doesn't lift a finger. No, Bill. We have to do better than that."

The city editor and the managing editor lapsed into the silence of high-speed thought. Plummer turned the galleys around so that he could read them and he filtered them through his hands slowly, trying to get an idea.

Gauvreau chuckled. "I've got it," he said. "Send Meff in here." Plummer took his galleys and left, closing the door behind him. He looked along the desks of the rewrite battery and beckoned to Arthur Mefford. "The boss wants to see you," he said.

Mefford had his jacket on the back of his chair. He reached for it, and changed his mind. Instead, he opened his shirt collar a little more and pulled the knot of the tie down onto his chest. Mefford was a good all-around reporter. He enjoyed the game. It was his life and it eased the tensions which kept his soul strung too tight.

He walked into Gauvreau's office with the ease of a fellow conspirator. His thin dark hair glistened with perspiration. Gauvreau opened the bottom drawer of his desk. He wore a small grin.

"Arthur," he said, reaching down. "You were in the war." Mefford nodded. "You handled a gun?" he asked, putting one on his desk blotter. Arthur Mefford straightened up from his leaning position.

"Sure," he said. "Many times." Gauvreau looked along the back of the Smith & Wesson. It was loaded. He pushed it across the blotter toward the reporter.

"You got a good eye?" Mefford swallowed. "I think so," he said. "What's on your mind?"

The managing editor pointed to his back window.

"Meff," he said, "I want you to go downstairs and out the back way and up that fire escape. When you get outside my window here, fire a shot diagonally upward so that you hit the ceiling."

Mefford shook his head, more in sorrow than insubordination. "I could get locked up for a trick like that," he said. Gauvreau rose. He limped around the corners of the desk to lay a friendly hand on Mefford's shoulder.

"No one is going to arrest you," he said. "I'm behind you, Arthur. Just do as I say."

The reporter appeared to be reluctant. Gauvreau stood looking up at his good man. "All I ask," he said gravely, "is that you keep remembering that I'll be sitting at my desk. Aim up. Up, Arthur."

"How about the police?" Mefford said. "Somebody may phone in."

"Somebody will," Gauvreau said. He tapped his chest. "Me."

"Oh," Mefford said, as though everything was now clear. The editor placed the gun in Mefford's hands. He explained the assignment again. "And Meff," he said in conclusion, "don't say anything about this to the gang in the office."

The gun went into a trouser pocket and a hand patted the bulge down.

"Okay," said Mefford. "I'll do it for you."

Gauvreau acknowledged the tribute with a mock bow. He limped back behind his desk, got a big sheet of paper. He printed a few words on it. He called for a make-up editor and asked him to have the words printed in 144-point caps at once, and brought to his desk.

The wonderful aspect of his relationship with his city room was that all hands were in rapport. All of them had sensational savvy. The boss had only to give any one of them a glimpse of a story, a mere peek, and he would understand the entire yarn and could see the lead in five-column 18-point ulc before it was written. All of them knew how to take a small elastic truth and stretch it to a tremendous thing without breaking it.

Gauvreau called the art department and asked Arthur Ridley to come in. Ridley was a thin man with a ruddy wart of a nose and blue eyes the size of BB's.

"Get a good photographer out in back in ten minutes, Art. Have him shoot a picture of my fire escape from the street. I want you to get a print fast, and ink in a drawing—a sort of black silhouette —of a man with a gun at the top. See the window?" Ridley glanced and nodded. "He's aiming the gun in the window. I want a dotted line from the street up the fire escape, showing how he approached."

"Just a figure?"

"A figure. And, Art—I want to make the one-star with this. Leave me room for three lines of one-forty-four-point with a few leads."

Ridley sketched on a sheet of paper. "Like this?" he said, showing it. Gauvreau studied it for a moment. "Yes," he said. "That's it, Art. But I also want the dotted line. Don't forget that."

The art director left. He closed the door and the sound of the slight slam blended in with the bang slam of a bullet leaving a gun, tearing through a window, and embedding itself in the editor's ceiling.

A little plaster sifted down and Gauvreau shook it out of his black hair absent-mindedly. Plummer came running and so did a couple of men from the sports department. In the midst of the excitement, the make-up man came in with the headline.

Mefford came back, panting and disheveled. Gauvreau ordered everyone back to work. Mefford waited until they were alone, and handed the gun back. The boss blew into the barrel, found a shell in his drawer, and replaced the one which had been fired. He put the gun back into the bottom drawer.

"You did a good job, Art," he said. "Ridley is drawing up a composite of the fire escape with a skulking figure on it firing into this office."

"I'm not going to get into any trouble?" said Mefford.

"Not a chance," the boss said. "Now go out and write the story for me and lay it on heavy." "What story?" the reporter said.

"Sorry," Gauvreau said. "I forgot to tell you the story. Here's a proof of the headline. You read it and start your lead while I phone police headquarters."

Mefford read the triple bank head. It read:

GANGLAND TRIES

TO INTIMIDATE

GRAPHIC

The Night Editor and the Murderer

It was nine o'clock and the one-star was going to bed. The fans hummed in the city room. Two intellectual rewrites played chess. Bald Charlie was dummying a new page three. He was the night editor. He was a quiet man who wore outrageous plaid shirts because his wife ordered him to wear them. She was a Lucy Stoner.

Opposite Bald Charlie sat Frankie. He had slick black hair and he was Charlie's assistant. Frankie was quiet, too. He could stay madder longer than anybody. Someone asked Frankie how old Charlie was and he said, "I don't know, but when he dies I understand they are going to saw the top of his head off and count the rings."

At 9:05 P.M., a stranger walked into the city room. His face was scratched. He was about thirty, and built like a rangy halfback. He asked for the Fish and Game Editor. Frankie pointed. The stranger walked over to the Fish and Game Editor, a handsome man with snowy hair.

The stranger talked while the outdoor columnist typed. He said that he had never had any fun in life. He had never been anywhere; never done anything. Just read the Fish and Game Column and worked nights in a garage. He liked the Fish and Game Column and so, tonight, when he shot his wife, Mamie, he thought he would repay the columnist by giving him the scoop.

The columnist slowed his typing. Then he stopped. The stranger saw the disbelief. So he drew a gun from his pocket. He wasn't aiming it. Just showing. The columnist became very calm. "My boy," he said, pointing to the city desk, "the indoor sports department is over there."

The stranger was hurt. He backed away, and then he reported to Frankie that he had shot his wife and wanted to tell that nice man who writes the Fish and Game Column, but the man didn't want the scoop. Frankie was always nervous and exact. He wrote everything on copy paper. When a reporter passed by and said hello, Frankie would write hello on the paper.

Frankie asked a lot of questions. Bald Charlie was having trouble dummying in page three. A flash had come in that Mary Pickford had just married Buddy Rogers and he wanted to use a stock cut, but he wanted one with curls. That's the way she had looked the last time Charlie had gone to a movie.

The stranger talked quietly. He had suspected for a long time that his wife was the friendly kind. Tonight, instead of going to the garage to work, he had gone to a saloon to think. When he was done thinking, he had gone home and found Mamie with a friend. He had hauled off and shot Mamie twice, but not until she had furrowed his face with her fingernails. Her friend hurried off, leaving his shoes and necktie.

He laid the gun on Frankie's blotter. He said he had tied Mamie up and stuffed her in a trunk, and he had some piano wire left over from the job. He dropped that on the blotter, too. He added a bloody kerchief, which he had used to mop his face.

Bald Charlie found the one-column cut of Mary Pickford. It was two-and-a-half inches deep and he told the engraving department to cut her neck off, but not to touch the curls. The engraving department asked Bald Charlie what the heck he was smoking lately, and would he save them a drag.

He looked across the desk at Frankie and then he looked up at the sad-faced murderer. He looked at the revolver, and the wire, and then, without embarrassment, he studied the scratches on the face of The Stranger.

At that moment, he delivered himself of journalism's most imperishable line, "What do you say, Frank?" he said softly. "Think there's anything to this?"

The City Editor

The city editor is a man with no feelings, no friends. His staff of reporters is never as good as he would like, seldom as bad as he fears. A good one seldom thinks. He worries. He worries about the city; he worries about politics, church, corruption, the opposition press, drinking, ulcers, deadlines and, somewhere at the bottom of the list, his family.

There must be an old city editor. I've never seen one, but then, I don't know all of them. The ones I knew: Frank Carson, Edward Mahar, Harvey Deuell, Harry Reutlinger, George Clarke, Harry Nichols, Paul Schoenstein, George McDonald, Warden Woolard, Gene Farrell were all pretty young and were burdened with hearts and consciences—the liabilities of the craft. Worse yet, they had friends.

The city editor makes me think of the driver of the twenty-mule Boraxo team. He cracks the whip over his reporters because they are his eyes and his ears and, through them, he sees the city. His rewrite men are on the far side of his desk and, through their typewriters, they give him what he wants when he wants it.

He sits behind a double desk. His assistant sits opposite. Between them are several telephones. They have direct wires to police headquarters, to the courthouse, to the prosecutor's office and the mayor's office.

The city editor knows approximately what time the big trial of today will recess, who the witnesses are expected to be and, quite often, what they will testify. He knows who is on the skids at the police headquarters and who can do no wrong. He knows things about the mayor's private life that Mrs. Mayor doesn't know.

He knows the policies and the politics of his publisher and, although the city editor may not subscribe to them, he will defend them, in print, to the death.

From the moment a story breaks the city editor is on top of it. When a third alarm comes in, for example, it is only one of many stories on which he is working, but he will usually, at this moment, do these things:

(1) Detail a good man to cover it; (2) ask the picture editor to assign a photographer; (3) tell the make-up man to leave some place up front for the fire; (4) pick up the phone and tell his editor that there is a big fire going; (5) ask an artist to draw a street map showing the site of the fire; (6) call the reporter at the nearest hospital and tell him to be alert for victims and injured firemen; (7) order the rewrite man who will rap the story out to phone the fire marshal's office to find out if this one is incendiary; (8) ask the morgue for clippings on recent big fires.

While he is doing this, the phones are ringing. The court reporter is waiting to ask the city editor how much material he wants on today's trial; another wants to know if he can take tomorrow off; the publisher's sister wants to ask him why he cannot assign a reporter to a ladies' luncheon for the suppression of horror comics, etc.

No matter how good he is, the city editor never stops worrying.

His moment of truth comes each day when a boy comes in with the opposition newspapers. He continues to shout his orders as his eyes search page one for a good story which he hasn't got.

When he doesn't see it, he begins to breathe. The weight lifts from his chest. "Get my wife," he says to the assistant. "Tell her I'll be home for dinner. . . ."

Penance at Dawn

The last of the star reporters was Red Dolan. After him came the age of the editorial specialist. Red was not the best reporter I knew. He was the most colorful. He could cover anything from an assassination to an assignation. Mr. D. was big and he had orange hair and he never wore a hat. He listened with his head cocked and his hands clasped behind his back, like a cop.

In the days when a good rewrite man was getting sixty dollars a week, Red was getting two hundred. Sometimes—as on the occasion when he lived with rumrunners and wrote about them—Red started Congressional investigations. If a lovesick counter girl in the five-and-ten committed suicide, Dolan was the man who knew where to look for her secret diary.

Red was a bachelor. His gravest fault was that he was chronically late. I never knew him to get to an assignment on time; I never knew him to be in the office on time.

This went on for years. One day the boss called him over and made a little speech. The words were tough. "You've been late once too often, Red. Beginning tomorrow morning, you're on ship news. That's all."

The city editor laid his pencil down. "Your assigment," he said slowly, "is to go down New York Bay at five A.M. aboard a Coast Guard Cutter and meet the ships. Meet them, Red. Don't be a minute late, because the Coast Guard won't wait for anybody."

Red was unhappy. He went next door to Suerkin's and downed a brace of drinks and announced that he was going to quit. He didn't. He sat up all night to make sure that he wasn't late. At 4:50 A.M. he was at the Battery looking at the gray faces of reporters.

All hands shivered and stomped into a little salon aboard the cutter.

Out in the Narrows, at Quarantine Station, the *Ile de France* swung at anchor. She was big and she got bigger as they approached. Red swallowed his pride and asked the others how a man covered a story like this. They told him all one had to do was to climb aboard, look over the passenger list for notables, and interview them.

Dolan almost wept. He could stand humiliation, but not drudgery. He climbed aboard, looked over the passenger list with the others, and saw only two names of interest. One was Gloria Swanson. The other was Joseph Kennedy. Swanson, Red knew, was a movie star. Kennedy was some sort of tycoon.

As the ship hoisted anchor and moved up the Hudson, Red asked silly questions of Miss Swanson. Then he went to Kennedy's suite and went through his tycoon questions. It is ironic that the punctual and precise Kennedy liked the unpunctual and careless Dolan at once. Red, in fact, dropped the pencil and, over rare refreshments, began to regale Kennedy with a few choice stories. They parted on the pier and vowed undying friendship.

Back at the office, Red leaned over Jack Miley's desk and said, "Tell me, who is this Joe Kennedy? The guy offered me a job writing for movies at three hundred a week and, obviously, he has lost a few buttons."

"Kennedy," said Miley, "happens to be head of United Artists." Red skidded into a phone booth and called United Artists. The operator said that Mr. Kennedy had just arrived from the ship to pick up some mail. Dolan demanded to talk to him. Kennedy said that yes, he was serious about that offer. Red thanked him and hung up. Then he went over to the city editor and whispered something naughty in his ear.

We never saw Red again. He signed a contract and went to Hollywood. He was late arriving at his office every day.

One day he was visiting Washington, like a reporter emeritus, and he was laughing with the boys when he fell over dead.

Red's sister ordered the body cremated and she invited a few old friends to an apartment in New York for a farewell. She had an urn on a marble mantelpiece. Some of the reporters had to down several drinks just to look at the urn. No one had ever seen Red in a vase. When the party was mellow, Red's sister called the city editor over and tipped the urn. It was empty.

"Isn't that just like Red?" she said sadly. "Late again . . ."

The Tender Thief

The Flash was the slowest man on the paper. He was the cashier. On Fridays, he sat like an owl in his cage, passing out the pay checks. On other days he visited the editorial department, marveling at the speed and excitement of the occupants, digging into big wastebaskets for cut-up editions of afternoon newspapers, a whispering, self-effacing little Santa of about fifty.

Once, to make conversation, I asked him if intelligence was the most important thing for a man to have. "No," he said softly, almost shyly. "A good heart is more important than a good head. Me, I would rather understand mercy than genius."

I was a young reporter. I knew everything about everything. I felt sorry for The Flash. He knew nothing of life except how to add figures in a ledger. The Flash was a stupid man.

If, as cashier, he was fired, who would hire this whispering nothing? Still, in my wisdom, I liked him because, when any of us ran short of money on Thursday, The Flash would honor a phony voucher for five or ten dollars. The voucher said: "For expenses covering murder in Brooklyn—to be accounted for."

On Friday, The Flash would deduct the money from the pay. It did not occur to me that this represented extra work for him.

It was on a hot summer day that the boss came out of his office with a velvet box. All of us had chipped in to buy The Flash a gold watch. The cashier was standing near the city desk. The boss motioned for us to follow him.

He walked up behind The Flash and tapped him on the shoulder. The Flash jumped eight inches off the floor and he looked so frightened that everybody laughed. The boss said, "As a member in good standing of the Thursday before Friday Club, I wish to present to you this slight token of the esteem of every man in the place."

The Flash looked at the open case and the glittering watch. His yellow jowls shook and then the tears came and everybody laughed. He tried to talk, but he couldn't.

Three weeks later the accountants were in and word filtered down to the editorial department that The Flash's accounts were $23,000 short. Everybody said, "Well, whaddya know?"

The boss editor heard about it and he hurried upstairs where the publisher was grilling The Flash. The cashier confessed he had been betting on horses, and he had taken the money in fives and tens over a period of years. He was ready to make a formal confession and he was sorry he had betrayed the nice people on the paper.

The boss editor asked the publisher if he was going to have The Flash arrested. The publisher said certainly. The boss argued loud, long and bitterly. "This," he said pointing to The Flash, "is a silly, stupid man. He'll do a couple of years in prison and nobody will ever employ him again. You'll never get your money back.

"Keep him on the payroll. Take it out of his salary at ten dollars a week for the next four or five years. Then, if you don't think he's worth keeping, fire him."

The Flash kept his job. His punishment lay in the fact that all of us knew; and he knew that we knew. He had done many favors for all of us.

But when he needed a friend, only one of us understood the quality of mercy.

The Newspaper

What is a newspaper?

A newspaper is lumber made malleable. It is ink made into words and pictures. It is conceived, born, grows up and dies of old age in a day. Yesterday's newspaper is used to wrap today's fish. Or to start a log fire, which brings it back to its origin.

Most of all, a newspaper is current information. It is the bridge between a home and the rest of the world. It tells of people and events swiftly and in detail. It listens to the threats of a dictator, the crack of a bat against a baseball, the anguish of a lost child, and recipes for making cookies.

Newspapers, like people, come in many sizes and many personalities. Some are fat and sedentary; others are lean and hysterical. And, like people, some are reliable and some are not. There are newspapers which scream for attention and there are others, on the same newsstand, which whisper the news. All newspapers reflect the character of their owners.

A good newspaper must show a profit. All newspaper owners know this. That is why they establish good character in their papers, and maintain it. The other road, they know, leads to bankruptcy.

Character is an indefinable quality best understood by women. They live by it. They can detect it in merchandise, in people, in publications. They, more than their husbands, understand the newspaper they buy. Men usually read the front-page news, the sports section, and their favorite features. Women leaf through a newspaper slowly, carefully, concentrating more on local news than international, assessing the advertisements, relishing the woman's page with its club meetings, lawn parties and gossip, and reading the obituary notices.

Good character in a newspaper is not enough. It must be enterprising and have strong civic purposes. It must use its editorial page not so much to condemn as to propose, not so much to revile powerful enemies as to have the strength to support them if they are worthy of support.

The average newspaper contains 150,000 words or more of information. This is the daily equivalent of two novels. It is never perfect, never completely accurate. It is as near perfect as a chain of human minds—leading from editor to city desk to composing room—can make it.

A good newspaper maintains a balance of 60 per cent news to 40 per cent advertising. When wages go up, and the price of newsprint is hiked, the ratios slip closer together. Sometimes, in a poorly managed newspaper, the ratios pass each other going in opposite directions.

In large cities, readers do not always favor the best newspaper. If they did, only one would sell. Readers seek their own information level; some like it cold and desiccated; others prefer liveliness and spice; the ignorant buy venom.

A newspaper is private enterprise for the public good. It relies on many minds to fill it every day, in addition to machines which chatter incessantly about news coming from Rome, from Bangkok, from Tokyo and Topeka.

A boy on a bicycle can take all of these things, roll them up, and toss them onto a front porch while chewing gum and preparing a good excuse for a poor report card. A blind newsdealer can sell all this information for a small coin without ever seeing it.

In some countries, the newspapers are the instruments of the government. Perhaps the best thing which can be said about newspapers in the United States is that they are in chronic disagreement with each other.

This is what is meant by a free press. A newspaper is always a little more than the sum total of its parts. It is also a friend who can be dropped, or picked up at will.

What is a newspaper?

Heywood Broun

The kid walked leaning against the wind. It pulled his cheeks back into a wintry smile and it tore at his heavy coat and the peaked cap. The street was empty. The shops slept with their shades drawn. It was Christmas morning.

The kid rubbed the back of his mitten across his nose. He turned into the Gazette Building, walked up the squeaky stairs, and unlocked the door marked "Editorial Department."

The room was big and square. The front windows were dirty. On a rewrite desk was a curled-up cheese sandwich, and sludge in a coffee container. On the floor were yesterday's newspapers. They had been alive and exciting twelve hours ago. Now they were dead. There were galleys, polished spikes, telephones, typewriters, page dummies, even a slug of metal here and there.

The boy beamed happily on the debris and the silence. He had to work Christmas morning and he cherished it because he was a newspaperman and he would never want to be anything else. Let the city desk send him out for coffee twenty times a day; let the rewrite men bawl "Boy!" until his ears hurt; let the copy desk give him that withering, pitying glance of the truly erudite—none of it mattered. He loved this place.

No world of money and influence in all the tomorrows could keep him from the excitement of this one. He was still thinking when he heard a staccato chatter from the telegraph room. He listened. No one was in the office. The kid did not understand dots and dashes, but he knew that when a machine chattered, a story was coming through.

Many a time, he had stood behind one of the telegraphs and watched the operator adjust an empty can of tobacco under the key so that the dots and dashes came through just loud enough to please him. Then he ran a sheet of copy paper into an old typewriter, listened, and began to type. The boy had seen the staccato sounds run through the operator's head and come out through his finger tips as letters and words.

The boy was thinking of this when a second machine began to clatter. He became worried. He rushed into the telegraph room. No one was there. Must be, he thought, that there is a big fire somewhere. Or maybe an important bulletin. Something is going on and we're not covered.

He stood looking at the machines and he was helpless. He understood none of their music. He wrung his hands and wondered if he should call the city editor at home. While he was worrying, a third machine started. Soon, it was joined by a fourth and now only the sports key was silent.

The noise frightened the kid and he turned to run to the phone. It was then that the first telegrapher arrived.

He was hanging his coat when he saw the kid. "Ah," he said, "a Merry Christmas to you, Master Heywood Broun." The youngster grabbed his arm.

"Something awful is happening," he said, pleadingly. "Hurry up. The machines are going crazy. They're all going at once. Maybe there's a war, or the President has been shot. Come on. Listen."

The telegrapher took his time. He draped his muffler over his coat, and put his fedora over the muffler. He rubbed his cold fingers together, pulled at his red nose, and walked behind the boy.

He listened. Then he smiled.

"It's a bigger story than you thought," he said to the kid. "It's the greatest story of them all. The machines are saying: 'A child is born. A child is born. A child is born. . . .'"

The Characters

The tears of the writer are shed for himself. He never tires of telling how lonely his work is; he must disarm his subjects to get material and he must do it as though he were inside a confessional; then he must read his notes and, in isolation, reduce the mass of information into a readable story.

This is a fairly accurate accounting, but the hardship is overemphasized. The writer selects his profession; it does not select him. He is usually an introverted egotist who desires to impose his views on great masses of people. The loneliness, glanced at from another side, really means that he does not want to share his creation with anyone else.

Writing has never been fun for me, but then, it has never been a painful work either. I have spent thirty-five years at it, pruning and paring words until they come fairly close to what I want them to say. I have disciplined myself so that I write but once, never rewriting, polishing, or trimming. The best practice, I found, was in writing short articles. It is not easy to present a quick portrait of a person.

A pianist might call this section Finger Exercises. In it you will find glimpses of such different personalities as Aaron Burr, Billy Rose, and Robert Wagner—certainly diverse.

In some cases, I have tried to depict but one phase of his character. In others, I have given a fuller portrait.

The McKeon Court-Martial

He reported in to Barracks 761 at 5:30 A.M. This was a late start for a drill instructor at Parris Island, but this was Sunday. He walked into the white U-shaped building slowly, leaning a little against the wet east wind, and limping.

Matthew C. McKeon was a caricature of a drill instructor on April 8, 1956—tall, skinny, with a pair of pale blue eyes under a yellow shoebrush of hair; a man in faded suntans leaning on a broomstick, a man of many disappointments and a lipless smile. This is no Gung-Ho Marine. No hero. This is a pro. He trains unremittingly for battle and, when he gets in one, his goals are two; to win and to live. He volunteers for nothing, and, although he has seventeen battle stars, he doesn't show them.

He has eleven years in the Navy and the Marine Corps and, like a cop, he's bucking for a pension. Right now, as staff sergeant, he brings home sixty-eight dollars a week with allowances and allotments. The bungalow rent off the base is fifty-five dollars; lighting and water are almost ten. There is the girl he grew up with in Massachusetts, Betty Wood McKeon; and there are Becky, five years old and shyly silent, and John, ten months old and crawling around in diapers gleefully trying to stop a floor fan with his pudgy fingers. That's all, except for the third one due soon.

Sergeant McKeon and all the other D.I.s on Parris Island, a big green pear halfway between Charleston and Savannah, work 126 hours a week. On their days off, they work only until 5:30 P.M. On other days, they quit when the boots hit the sack. A boot is a new recruit. He enlists—that is, 52,000 do each year—because he wants to be a gyrene; he longs to plant the flag on Suribachi; he aches to stand officially on the street in his home town in dress blues and white gloves and watch the girls watch him; he is a mannerly boy with long hair and a caved-in chest who has seen too many motion pictures.

The D.I. at Parris Island is given ten weeks in which to make a fighting man of the boot. Seventy days. One thousand six hundred and eighty hours. When that time ends, the boot must be a ramrod United States Marine; he must be clean, healthy, know that his best friend is his rifle; he must be sure that, in battle, the man on his left and the one on his right will not break and run, no matter how sticky matters get, because they too are Marines.

He must know that he is a member of a corps which trains, not for parades, but for wars; he must appreciate discipline so well that he will execute an order—any order—by reflex, as a knee jumps because it is tapped with a rubber hammer. He ends boot training quieter, more self-assured, and he is so full of the word "sir" that he unconsciously says it to his mother.

To do this, the D.I. must be tough. The commissioned officers have little to do with the matter. They rank the D.I., and they supervise, but the vertebrae and marrow of the corps is the drill instructor, the mean, lean man with the venom in his eyes. Everyone from the commandant, General Pate, on down knows that the D.I.s do lots of things which are not in the rulebook. They call slow-witted boots into their offices at "thumping time" and beat them up, smash their faces and bellies. They order the goof-ups out in the simmering sun to run back and forth with a rifle over their heads. This is further refined by removing the boot's belt before he starts. He can be ordered to throw his rifle into the mud, clean it until it is spotless, throw it into the mud again, and do this four or five times. A mild punishment is a swift face-slapping.

Matt McKeon didn't believe in any of these things. He had been a boot at Parris Island in 1948, and he had been beaten. It didn't help him and he invented his own system. If the boots goof up, work them to death. If that doesn't work, take their privileges away and give them discipline, discipline, discipline. If that doesn't work, scare them to death. McKeon had seen youngsters caught smoking ordered to extinguish the cigarette, wad it up, lay it on the tongue, chew for a while, and then swallow. He had a better idea. Or so he thought.

On Sunday, April 8, 1956, the Sarge was discouraged. He had finished drill instructors' school two months before, and, as a junior to Sergeant E. H. Huff, had been given Platoon 71 to run through the Parris Island concrete mixer. Seventy-one was his first platoon and, in thirty-five days, they had broken his heart. There were seventy-eight men in that platoon—men? They averaged seventeen and a half years and most of them, white and Negro, looked as though they had just concluded an all-night rock and roll session—and, of the three men who dominated their lives, they feared D.I. Huff, they kidded with junior D.I. Scarborough, and they laughed junior D.I. McKeon off as a sarge who talked tough but who wouldn't muss a boot's hair.

Even on the rifle range, when they had failed and the range guards had to wave the red signal—Maggie's drawers—signifying no hits, McKeon had walked up and down the line saying, "Don't worry, fellas. You'll get the hang of it."

McKeon wanted 71 to be the best platoon on this ever-loving oleander island. But the boots, if left at ease for a moment, fell to laughing and wrestling and dozing in the grass. At the thirty-fifth day of boot camp, half the training was over and platoon 71 was what D.I.s refer to scornfully as a herd.

On April 8, the sarge got the kids out of bed. Then he went to six thirty Mass, celebrated by Father Cook, and was eating at seven fifteen. The Protestant boys would be going off to services at ten and there was time to kill around the barracks. He walked out in front, had a cigarette, stared at the 500-yard rifle ranges on the far side of the street, and wondered what he could do to make his kids—good, happy-go-lucky kids—understand that this business of training was serious. Right now, some of them were in the back doing laundry and he had told them four times that he did not want to see laundry done on Sunday.

He told them to go back for seconds at mess only to get more meat, or more proteins, but never to take second helpings on starches, or desserts. He had watched them, before his eyes, go back for seconds and for thirds on pies and puddings. He had failed, even as a militaristic mother. McKeon doused the butt. Inside, he looked in at the recruits around the racks (beds) and went through a double door to the D.I.s' room. There, he read a religious pamphlet, used the lavatory, and dropped on an iron bed to doze.

Later in the morning, Sergeant Scarborough came in. With him was Sergeant King, a D.I. with another platoon.

"You got anything to drink?" Scarborough said. McKeon sat up, digging for a cigarette. "I got nothing here, Gunny," he said.

McKeon is a fair drinker. His favorite is beer, which he calls a Cherry Valley highball. He seldom drinks whisky, unless, as at weddings and wakes, it is on the house. When he drinks beer in a tavern, his big feet begin to shuffle and he drops nickel after nickel in the jukebox. Then he likes to dance and, after a few brews, he loves everybody and is at peace with the world.

"You want a drink, Mack?"

"No, I'm sleepy. Lately, I'm dead, Gunny. I fall asleep watching the fights." Scarborough smiled. "Take me up the road a ways. I got a bottle." McKeon looked at Scarborough. He knew that it was against the rules. But it was Sunday morning and Huff would not be around, so who could get hurt having a slug? He looked at King. He drew his legs over the edge of the cot. "Okay," he said. "Okay."

He and Scarborough went out to the curb and got into the

McKeon car. They drove up to the red brick administration building. "Stop," said Scarborough. He got out. "I'll turn around," said Matt. He drove on up to the corner, swung the two-toned job around, and came back. Scarborough was waiting with a paper bag in his hand.

When they got back, the three sergeants shut the door of the D.I. room. There was a half bottle of vodka in the bag—about fifteen ounces. McKeon had a drink. Scarborough had a drink. King had a drink. The time was 11:15 A.M. They talked about their herds. Then they each took a second drink.

McKeon said he didn't like it straight, so he chased it with a bottle of Coke. A drink is about an ounce and half of liquor and in fifteen ounces there are nine drinks. This made three drinks each, but McKeon had two and, not owning the bottle, he was careful not to hit it hard. Scarborough asked him to have another, and Mack said maybe later. The bottle was set behind the left rear leg of a table against the wall. The table was close to the D.I. door and to the immediate left. A curious man would have to stoop to see it. McKeon went out into the barracks room and the platoon was kidding around. At once he ordered a field day, which meant that the seventy-four boots who were present would have to start cleaning the barracks walls, radiators, rifle racks, beds, huge wooden floor, window sills, and lavatory (head) until they gleamed.

What saddened the boots was that all of these items were already gleaming. Besides, this was Sunday. The sarge watched them work. It didn't make him feel good. The thing that would make him feel good was something they couldn't seem to give him—a first-class platoon. So he watched, and he remembered that his older brothers Jim and Ned had been boots and both had come out of the war as Marine sergeants, and he wondered what the earlier D.I.s had on the ball that he didn't.

He looked at the innocence of these youngsters, and he asked himself if it would do any good to scare them to death. He decided against it. Take a kid like Leake. You scare Leake to death and maybe you'd ruin him as a Marine. Leake was a Negro, and God had given him an awkward body and a head full of trust without reason. The sarge felt sorry for Leake. When he stood, he seemed to come undone in sections, and some of the other boots called him Stepin Fetchit. When he sat, his hips came up to his ribs. Leake loved the sarge. Leake would do anything for the sarge. All the sarge had for Leake was pity.

The sun came out. At one o'clock the temperature was fifty-eight. The sarge ordered 71 out for drill and, when he gave them a cigarette break, they fell to pushing each other and laughing. One boy was tripped and dumped to the grass. McKeon said nothing. He stood pounding a bony fist into a bony hand, and then, resignedly, he shouted, "Okay. We'll have another field day." The boots groaned, and, back in building 761, they broke out the yellow soap again. And the scrub pails. And the lye. And they looked at the gleaming deck and wondered how many washings before the wood became porous.

Recruit Leader Lagone, a conscientious boot, got to his knees and started scrubbing. The little kid whom everybody protected, Jerry Thomas, wiped off a grin and started to clean radiators. Big Norman Wood, Negro, ordered all his beautiful muscles to synchronize, and he flew from window to window, washing, drying, polishing, washing, drying, polishing. What could you do with them? They didn't complain. No matter what you hit them with, they didn't complain. How then could you make them stand up and take this training seriously?

Matt McKeon went over to the N.C.O. club. He ordered a glass of beer, swapped small chatter with other Junior D.I.s—most of whom were pleased with their platoons—and, after two or three sips, found that he could not take it. He went back to barracks. Matthew McKeon did a lot of thinking. The more he thought about his platoon, the closer he drew to cracking up. They weren't trying. Whether they tried or not, he, McKeon, had to make good. This was his first platoon. He had to make good. Either he'd break them, or they'd break him. They had gone to a movie last night, so he couldn't take a movie away from them. Anyway, what kind of sissy punishment was that? He had to hurt their pride some way —if they had any. He had to hit them or hurt them or scare them—something.

At six thirty the sarge called Recruit Leader Lagone in. The boy stood to attention in the doorway. "Come in," said McKeon softly. A few other boots stood in the doorway. He reached under the table and picked up the bottle of vodka.

"Have a drink, Lagone?"

The boy was shocked. "No, sir."

'That's right, Lagone. You will not have a drink because you are not a man. Only men can drink, right, Lagone?" There was still vodka in the bottom of the bottle and McKeon swished it around in circles against the sides. He edged over to Recruit McPherson and threatened to slap him because the platoon lacked discipline.

"When you finish boot camp," he said to Lagone, "then you'll be a man, hah? Then you can have a drink." McKeon tipped the bottle and drained it. He was going to tell the young man that, at supper, he had watched him—of all the boots—go back for a second dessert. But he didn't. The sarge was going to tell him that the other D.I.'s laughed at 71 and called it a herd, but he didn't. He was going to tell him that both of them knew that Senior D.I. Huff was so overworked that he threw his swagger stick away because he was afraid that the next time a boot disobeyed him, he'd beat the kid with it. But he didn't.

Instead, he said, "Lagone, you go back and tell those beasts that we're going on a night march tonight. Yeah, tonight. You know where we're going, Lagone? We're going out behind the rifle butts." He pointed. "Out there is a swamp and Ribbon Creek. We're going to march in that creek and we're going to march until I get tired of watching you. And when you go back to the racks, tell those idiots that those who don't drown will be eaten by sharks."

Lagone said, "Yes, sir," and backed out of the room.

In the early evening, McKeon stood in front of the barracks, squinting in the sun. He knew nothing of psychology, but he had the first bud of a thought that it was not the youngsters who had to make good in seventy days—but rather, Matthew McKeon. It was not McKeon who was running the herd; the herd was running McKeon. He began to think that, even if he got tough—not tough-talking, but truly tough—it was too late in any case. In thirty-five days, he had to have a smartly turned out platoon of United States Marines. The commissioned officers did not care how it was done, so long as it was done. They knew of the beatings, the swamp marches at night. It was part of a secret, silent system. He stood waiting in front of the barracks, knowing that tonight they would bend to his will, or they would break him. That's why he didn't regret threatening Lagone. It would help if Lagone remembered to tell the kids that the sergeant planned to take them all out to Ribbon Creek tonight, and those who couldn't swim would drown, and those who could would be eaten by sharks. He had told these things to Lagone. But in doing so, the sarge was the childish one because the young men of the platoon knew that drill instructors are not paid by the Corps to drown anybody, nor to conjure sharks in a marshy creek. Platoon 71 knew these things, and so they turned out smartly, tumbling out of Barracks 761 on the double, the tall, the short, the white, the Negroes, the bright, the stupid. Seventy-four boots lined up in nine squads.

McKeon, weary and beaten, threw his head up and snapped: "Count . . . off!" And the bass and treble and cracked voices went through the time-honored arithmetic of one to four. When they had finished, and he could find no fault with it, he leaned on the broomstick and said:

"Lay-y-y-uft, face!" They swung, almost in concert. "For-warr-r-r-d march!" He limped beside them, keeping the count for a moment until they cleared Baker range on the right. "Hup, two, three, four! Hup, two, three, four. Hup, hup, hup . . ." Then he ordered route step and swung them to the right, across Wake Boulevard and over the grass of the rifle range. Once he heard them whispering, and he shouted, "No talking in ranks!" A boot squeaked, "Mother hears everything!" and some of the boys giggled.

What McKeon proposed to do was more of a mean trick than a frightening thing. The ranges run flat and grassy over five hundred yards toward an artificial embankment, which absorbs spent ammunition. Behind these butts is a spongy lawn of heavy crab grass, running a hundred yards to Ribbon Creek. The sarge had seen this creek many times, from the butts, and he knew the D.I.'s had, many times before, marched goof-up kids in the water along the banks, soiled their boots and muddied their uniforms and rifles, and returned them to barracks ordering them to have everything impeccable in the morning.

Of the 25,000 recruits who report to Parris Island each year, a good percentage of them arrive in zoot suits with long hair, dirty fingernails and crusty bodies. Some must be shoved into the showers.

Fifteen per cent of boots flunk swimming—although all of them get ten hours of swimming lessons—because they do not like water. It takes more than a shaved head, a green uniform, and a rifle to make a Marine. It takes obedience, knowledge, pride of self and pride of Corps, in that order.

Platoon 71 marched out of the warm bath of lights around the rifle barracks area into the night at the left of Baker range. There was a little rim of light around the edge of the world and, as they marched, they could see each other in silhouette. They marched four thousand five hundred feet, and they did it in twenty minutes. They got behind the butts, turned right, then diagonally left through the crab grass. Ribbon Creek was not out of bounds. As they marched toward it through the crab grass, the ground was springy underfoot. After a hundred yards, there is a loamy bank which drops about two feet, and then there is a flat table of marsh grass which runs out toward the creek for sixty feet. Beyond that is the gray snake of the creek, twisting silently through the swale on its way to the sea. The sarge proposed to march his platoon on the flat table of marsh grass. At low tide, there was no water here; just a mass of cracked chocolate pudding. At high tide, there is between two feet and three and a half feet of water on this table. The creek itself is farther out and is four feet deep when the tide is out; eleven feet three inches deep when it is full.

Ribbon Creek was at full tide exactly two hours before Platoon

71 arrived. The grassy table was still covered with three feet of water. McKeon had limped back and forth along his platoon, and he was more disgusted than before. Some of the boots didn't know how to follow a man in front in the dark. A few wandered far out of line and the sarge, in anger, had shoved them back. Now, in the dark, he stood on the little two-foot sandy bank overlooking the table, and he barked: "Follow me!" In this he was more merciful than other D.I.'s, who had ordered boots into the water without getting themselves wet. McKeon, who would later have to shave the mud from boots and from uniform with a knife, jumped off the bank first. The temperature was fifty-eight degrees. The water reached just below his belt. The boots followed him, skidding in pairs down the bank and into the cold water. They made no complaint. If this was what the sarge wanted, why okay.

McKeon hugged the inside of the table and moved upstream. The water, moving downstream at two knots, pulled against his thighs and the mud on the bottom grabbed his feet with viscous affection. Behind him, the platoon began to make nervous jokes. One youngster found a twisted stick and threw it into the air and shrieked, "Ooh, look! a snake!" Another one, far in the rear, yelled, "Hey, Sarge. Something just swam between my legs!"

They moved upstream, slowly, laboriously. The sarge, humorless, explained to those who would listen that, in battle, a good soldier never tries to ford a stream unless his entire unit is ordered to do it. "Out in the middle, a man is a good target even in the dark. Always stick close to shore, like we're doing, and always keep moving. Don't ever stand still." Someone yelled, "Hey, Sarge, let's swim to the other side."

In the dark, his heart sank. This was supposed to be a disciplinary march, not a picnic. He moved on a little farther, then ordered the head of the column to turn left—which would take it farther off the bank, and then left again, which would turn it south and back to where it had started. All of them could still feel the grass underfoot, and so they knew that they were still on the table, not in the creek proper. But McKeon noticed, as he turned south, that the water was up to his chest.

He was not worried about his command, which could be in no deeper water than he, but he was worried about one man—the Negro kid, Leake. Leake was a character. He knew nothing. He learned nothing. He had a weird bony figure and he was afraid of everything in the world, but he loved everybody and everybody felt the genuineness of his affection. Now, of all times, McKeon couldn't get Leake out of his mind. So he stepped out of line, watching some of the men move by him in slow motion, and he

yelled down the line, "Where are the nonswimmers?" Floating to
him on the gusts, he heard voices say, "Here!" "Here!" . . . "Here!"
"Where's Leake?" he asked. And Leake, flanked by two tall white
boys who were holding him erect, said, "Here, sir. Right here."
"Are you scared, Leake?" This was a silly question, because Leake
was always scared. "Yes, sir"

The sarge looked at the other men in the dark. "Take care of
Leake," he said. "Put him in the back." His solicitude of Leake
may have taken two minutes of his time. Perhaps three. But, by
the time he got back to the head of the column, the men were in
panic. As he looked along the rim of the horizon, McKeon saw at a
glance what had happened. Platoon 71 had broken up into separate groups. Some were in close to the bank. One group, the head
of the column, was near him. Beyond them, a group of youngsters
had wandered out into Ribbon Creek proper and, as the D.I. held
his chin close to the water to get the benefit of the little light, he
could see bobbing heads out there.

He cupped his hands and yelled, "Everybody out of the water."
There was no panic in his voice, and none in his heart. He was
angry because they had goofed again. He had said "follow me"
and, if they had, they would be on the table and could feel the
grass on the bottom at all times. In making the 180-degree turn,
some had wandered out to deep water. He heard childish voices
yell for help. All around him were his boots. Most of them were
scrambling for shore, and, once the herd began to panic, their
brains were scrambled.

McKeon lifted himself on his toes and began to swim. He swam
straight for the dark corks bobbing out there. He hadn't gone
more than ten feet when he felt something soft in front and he
grabbed a boy and towed him in to shallow water and went back
again. He spotted the same group out there. They were not yelling, but he could hear them coughing and struggling. The sarge
was never a great swimmer. Back home in Leicester, Massachusetts, his sister Anne had had to rescue him three times from the
local pond when they were children. The Marines had made a
passable breast-stroker of him, and now he swam as fast as possible toward his men.

Before he reached the group, McKeon felt someone grab him
and, whoever it was, grabbed good and hard—both arms around
neck, both legs around his legs. They went down, and the sarge
fought savagely to break the hold. They came up and McKeon
grabbed his man around the head and tried to pull him around to
the front. He thought it was Private Wood, a tall reticent Negro,
and he tried to yell at him to take it easy, but nothing came out of

his mouth but water. They went down again with McKeon yelling, "Keep your head. I'll get you in."

Wood—if it was Wood—said nothing. He grabbed tight and they went far down. The sarge felt tired. Suddenly, while under water, Wood relaxed his grip. His arms opened and McKeon kicked his way to the surface. He heard ringing noises and his eyeballs seemed to press outward. He gulped air and his lungs spat salt. When he got his breath, he looked around and the waters were flat and quiet. There was no one out there at all. McKeon trod water until he got some strength, and then he swam slowly back to the table, stood up weakly, and staggered back toward the bank. Two boys stood on the table, in water, looking at him. "God," the sergeant said softly, "they were only kids." The living kids said nothing.

A Spanish-speaking boot, Martinez, waded close to the sarge and said, "I'll go out and dive for them." McKeon felt dizzy. He felt that he wasn't thinking right at the moment. "Never mind," he said. "Never mind doing that. We lost Wood. Oh God, what have I done?" Privates Moran and Martinez helped the sarge across the table and up the mouth of a tiny creek and out onto the spongy crab grass. They were standing, dripping and shivering, when they saw a car pull around behind the rifle butts and turn the upper brights on the scene. From all around, boys yelled, "Put out the lights. You're blinding us." The driver swung the car away and parked. The platoon staggered out of the water. Someone yelled, "Fall in!" But they didn't. A few fell down and lay there gasping and choking. The rest staggered toward the butts. Technical Sergeant Taylor, commander of the guard, was waiting. He's a big man and he ranks McKeon.

"Who's the drill instructor?" he snapped. "Who's in charge here?" McKeon looked up at him. "I am," he said. "I'm in charge." Another car came around the butts and pulled up. Captain Patrick, Officer of the Day, jumped out. McKeon croaked, "Fall in! Fall in, men!" And there was pleading in his voice, rather than peremptory command, because he wanted a quick count. Nobody fell in. "Get them back to the barracks," Sergeant Taylor said. "I'll take charge here."

The wet boots, sixty-seven of them, shuffled off in little groups, between the butts of range Baker and range Charlie. McKeon had no command. He saw the last of what he had fought for—discipline—slide out between his muddy fingers on the way back to Barracks 761.

He shuffled along with Private Moran. Over and over, he kept saying, "I know we lost four or five. I know it." "Take it easy, Sergeant. We didn't lose anybody. They're all out of the water."

McKeon shivered and he felt numb. When he got to the squad bay, the kids were milling around the racks, trying to peel their clothes off.

McKeon looked at them and he wanted to cry, but no tears would come. He just stared at them, and they glanced at him. He kept swallowing and his clothes made small puddles on the floor which he had ordered scrubbed again and again. Captain Patrick was coming in. Taylor was with him. The captain pointed to Matt. "Arrest that man," he said. McKeon paid no attention. He walked out through the double doors and into the D.I. room. Patrick appeared with two military policemen. "Watch this man and keep him inside," he said. "He's under arrest." The sarge sat on his rack and changed his clothes. "Captain," he said quietly, "you'd better call Sergeant Huff. He better know about this."

This too was Marine training. He was not worried half so much over what Captain Patrick might do as he was about the reaction of his immediate superior. The captain said, "Get a report on how many men are missing." One man was sitting on the far bank of the creek and would not be rescued until dawn when the planes and helicopters and boats cut the gray surface of Ribbon Creek in frosty foam. Six boots, given in trust by parents to the United States Government, floated beneath the surface, their faces in repose, hair lifting and falling, as they made slow time to the sea.

Huff arrived. He looked around. "How's everything going, Mack?" McKeon looked up and shook his head slowly. Huff went on trying to look like a man who will not permit anyone to hate his sergeant. McKeon remembered the empty vodka bottle behind the leg of the little table. He knew that, if they ever found this, they'd say that he was drunk. So he got up slowly, looked through the open door, and saw no one. He stopped, lifted the bottle and carried it as casually as possible into the lavatory which adjoined his office. He set it down behind the toilet and came out. A military policeman walked by him, went inside, and said, "I'll take that." He beckoned McKeon. "Let's go, Sergeant."

The sarge is out of the brig now. A lot of the zip is gone and he spends too much time in reverie. The tough drill instructor has a new job. He's a clerk to a priest. Every morning, Matthew McKeon salutes Commander Maurus Cook, USNR, and assists at Mass, or drives the priest to the infirmary for visits to the sick, or runs errands. Three times a day he must report to the provost marshal. He tells where he has been, what he has done, and what he proposes to do with his time that evening.

The evenings are alike. He drives off the base, through the

marshland, to a little bungalow in Port Royal. It sits like a piano crate under big oaks dripping with Spanish moss. The rooms are small, the furniture unexciting. The Sarge helps his wife with the supper and he helps with the children. To Rebecca, he is the only man in the world who can get a splinter out of a foot without hurting. To John, he is the man who holds a guy up, throws him in the air, catches him without ever missing, and blows tickling sounds in his ear. To Betty, he is a good husband, the father of the baby she expects.

On the base as Parris Island, he is the hard-luck D.I. Everybody knows the story and, all over the island, Marines shake their heads and say "Poor Mack." When they see him driving the padre, they yell from the sidewalks, "Anything new, Mack?" He shakes his head. One ranking officer said, "In a way, McKeon is the best thing that has happened to us in thirty years. He made us revise our thinking about a lot of things. Four generals have already been transferred. The explosions haven't died out yet." To Matthew C. McKeon, the issues are simple and he states them simply, "I did wrong and I should be punished."

To him, the drowning of six recruits is translatable into six huge mortal sins. The names and faces of the six are scarred across his memory for all time and he remembers them in his prayers, at Mass, and as a communion intention: Tom Hardeman, twenty; Don O'Shea, eighteen; Leroy Thompson, eighteen; Norman Wood, seventeen; Charley Reilly, eighteen; Jerry Thomas, seventeen.

No matter what the seven judges of the court-martial say, in finality, to Matt McKeon—and they can say ten years—he is the conscience-bound Christian who will pay and pay and pay without remission. In cases of this type, punishment is sometimes courted. It's an easier way out. At night, McKeon tries hard to find things to do around the house. Betty, dark and pretty, never talks about the night of April eighth unless her man brings it up. She grew up in Leicester, Massachusetts, with this boy and they went to high school together. She thinks of him as the best junior drill instructor the Marine Corps ever had. She is certain that, if justice is done, Matty will be acquitted and restored to rank and pay. Her faith is complete. She chatters brightly about things they will both do after the court-martial as though the trial is a formality to endorse her husband. It is only when the six dead ones are mentioned that she flips the switch on her mechanical smile and she begins to finger the edge of her apron. She knows that Matty intended no wrong and she wishes they were alive so that they would stop clouding the happiness of her babies.

There is no comprehension in Sergeant McKeon's mind that the entire nation now knows about the night march and has taken sides for him and against him. He knows that there is a continuing excitement on Parris Island. He understands this. And he understands vaguely that a New York State Supreme Court Justice named James B.M. McNally has organized a committee to see that Matty gets a fair shake in court, and has retained Emile Zola Berman, a trial lawyer, to protect him in the military clinches, but he knows not why. Nor can he understand why anyone would want to help him because, if another sergeant did what Matt did, McKeon would scorn him as a disgrace to the Corps. What he does understand—and will not discuss, even with Betty—is that his night march has started a high-level fight about the U.S. Marines' system of training boots. It is either too tough for youngsters, or it isn't tough enough. The nation, one gathers from letters pouring into the Pentagon, is split. Parents especially complain that their sons often experienced more danger to life and limb in the two boot camps at Parris Island and San Diego than in battle at Peleliu or Seoul. The Marine Corps itself is not split. They think that the present ten-week boot camp is weak and soft. The men spit and say, "We don't want any den mothers."

The Corps prides itself on being the elite fighting outfit of the world—200,000 finely honed men trained to kill and to survive—and anything which tends to humanize the boot is, in their estimation, sabotage in the Corps. When McKeon was studying to be a D.I., he heard the drill instructor's credo many times: "Let's be damned sure that no man's ghost will ever say, 'If your training program had only done its job.' " Matty has another way of saying it: "When I was in a machine gun platoon in Korea, it was a nice feeling when the going was rough to know that the guys on our right and the guys on our left had the same training we had and would not break and run." Ten hours before the night march, the sarge had said, "There are men in this platoon who would not make the grade in Korea."

Since the drowning of the six, the Marine Corps has, in secrecy, sent 27,000 questionnaires to Leathernecks on duty and in the Reserve and, granting them the privilege of not signing their statements, asked whether the training program was too tough, too soft, or just right. The replies stand in bales in the office of the Inspector General, Major General David Shoup, winner of the Medal of Honor. They have not been cross-indexed as this is being written, but the answers would indicate that the training program should be toughened. This is the opinion of men whose proudest boast has been: "We never abandon our wounded."

Maybe. But the brass abandoned McKeon overnight. First, the Marines withheld the news of the drowning. Then when they found that six kids under water cannot be written off as a statistic, they jumped into print emphasizing that the sergeant was drunk, even though the evidence seemed to indicate that he was not. Later, the Corps retreated on this and made the charge "drinking on duty," not drunk on duty. Within a matter of a few days, they had 450 pages of testimony from every possible interested party on Parris Island, and yet no general officer, or public relations officer, tried to correct the "tipsy sergeant" charge. They searched Sergeant McKeon's school records to find a rap to pin against him and the record said that his schooling and aptitude were "excellent to outstanding."

In May, 1956, the Marine Corps commandant, General Randolph Pate, issued a statement to Congress in which he said: "I know you will appreciate how deeply shocked I was, and still am, at what went on in the drill instructors' quarters of Platoon 71 during the hours that preceded the fatal march." If General Pate remains in a state of shock every time he gets the word that a Marine has been caught with booze on the premises, he must be in a state of agitation most of the time because Marines have been caught sneaking a fast belt on many occasions and, if my memory is intact, the common penalty for a first offender was the removal of a stripe. In truth, up until *l'affaire* McKeon, noncommissioned officers at Parris Island drank beer at noon mess.

The General further said: "I consider that my first military and moral obligation in this case is to take every lawful step available to me to insure that all three of these sergeants are tried and punished to the fullest extent allowed by our uniform code of military justice." It is presumed that the seven judges who will hold the court-martial can read. Each one is a military career man, who must continue to live in and with the Navy Department after this trial is over. General Pate is their top boss. The words "and punished to the fullest extent allowed" are poorly chosen because they indicate that Sergeants McKeon, Scarborough and King are adjudged guilty before trial. The General, it seemed, was not only eager to plead the sergeant guilty, but the whole Corps as well. "In a very real sense," he said, "the Marine Corps is on trial for the tragedy of Ribbon Creek just as surely as is Sergeant McKeon." A Corps which left its dead in windrows on Iwo Jima cannot be on trial in an accidental death. What is on trial is the drill instructor system, and Pate, in common with all other officers, condones it. Now, all of them want to hang McKeon for using the system weakly. It is possible that the sarge is guilty and deserves such

punishment. Still, no one has even heard a worm scream as he is
impaled on a big hook. This particular worm squirms in silence.

The McKeon family is without pretension. Their men are big.
Their women are pretty. Their children are many. Originally, the
McKeons and the Trainors came from Ireland and many of them
worked hard in the textile mills of Worcester, Massachusetts. They
feared God, knew the value of a dollar, and were unafraid of hard
work. Plain people. Clannish. Hard luck brings them together
more quickly than good. Alice Trainor McKeon ruled the roost.
She married young and, after the death of her husband, married
James Edward McKeon, an easy-going man who, at seventy, has
diabetes and a perpetual tear trembling on the lower lid of his
right eye. Alice set her hopes, not in Jim, but in a family of boys
and girls who would, she hoped, do better in life than she had.

To insure this, she not only had the children—nine altogether—
but she took a job in a Worcester mill and left for work at five on
winter mornings when the temperature sometimes paused at nineteen below zero. With the exception of her beloved Matty, who is
accused of drinking and causing the death by drowning of six
Marines, Alice has achieved her goal. Eight of the nine are still
living. All are doing well. Now she is nearing seventy and she sits
in her living room at 176 Mayfield Street, and she is as plain as the
settees and chairs around her. Her hands are white and bony and
the blue veins throb beneath the skin. Mrs. McKeon had a great
deal of pride, but it is all gone now. The first news she heard
about Matty was the day after it happened. An enterprising young
reporter came to her door and said, "Mrs. McKeon, there's been
an accident at Parris Island and Matthew is the only survivor. Can
I have a picture of him?" She gave the picture. And she thanked
God that her boy had been spared. She got on the phone with her
daughters and told them that it was the extra prayer that did it.

Every night, this woman with the dark face, the worried eyes,
the straight hair, gets on her knees and says prayers for the safe-
keeping of her children—as do millions of mothers everywhere.
But she always said an extra prayer for Matt, "because Matt is the
only one still in service." Now there had been some sort of accident and Matt had been spared, praise be to God.

It wasn't until evening that she saw a newspaper. There was
Matt's picture, but the headline read "Tipsy Sergeant Drowns Six
Recruits." Alice McKeon was in the hospital the next day, with an
oxygen mask over her face. Her heart was involved in more ways
than one. Now she is home. We sat talking and she tried to talk
and, at the same time, stare at the hands in her lap so that no one

would know that she was crying again. What could she say? Her testimony comes from the heart of a mother and is, therefore, worthless. "Matt was a good boy. Always good. He was a good baby too. Always laughing. He liked sports—baseball, hockey and I don't know what else—but anybody can tell you that he would never lie. Never. Matthew would tell the truth, no matter what. The worst thing I ever remember him doing was the time he stepped on a fire cracker—a cap, they call it—in class and the sister sent him home and I had to go to the convent with him to straighten it out." Now she says special prayers for six boys who died. "For the repose of their souls."

Nothing will ever be right for her again. She went to Parris Island with Dad, and they brought Matthew to her like a criminal, between two armed guards. And this is a scene she sees late at night when sleep will not come, just as her Matt, at times, sees heads bobbing like corks. The Irish have a saying that, in large families, God saves one for mother. In the case of the McKeons it was Mary, the oldest. She didn't marry. Jim, thirty-three, was a Marine sergeant in World War II, and he still has the haircut to prove it. He's blond, tall, lean, more nearly the father of the family than the father. All of the McKeons seek Jim's advice because Jim always "Had a head on his shoulders" and he's cautious. He's married, father of two, a schoolteacher.

Anne is next in age, a blonde attractive woman of thirty-two. She was a lieutenant in the WAC in wartime, is a registered nurse, married to Thomas Costello, a New York attorney specializing in negligence claims, mother of four. Anne's husband will be part of the defense counsel at the court-martial. The Costellos live at City Island, New York. Matthew was born a year after Anne. Edward, the tallest and quietest, is thirty. He works for the telephone company. He, too, was a Marine sergeant and, like Jim and Matt, experienced the roughness of Parris Island boot camp without a murmur. "Do as they tell you," Jim said, "and they can't find fault."

Ellen is twenty-nine, pretty and poised. She was a schoolteacher, but is now Mrs. Blanchard, mother of three boys. Francis X. McKeon is twenty-seven, short, compact, the personality kid of the McKeons. He's called "Frannie" and "Dutch." Francis is the one who failed to make the Marine Corps. He wears glasses and, when the doctor asked him to read the small letters on the chart, Frannie had trouble finding the chart. So he enlisted in the Army instead. All McKeons, including Anne, enlisted. There were no draftees in the family.

Worcester, and particularly the suburb of Leicester, cannot believe that Matty McKeon has done anything wrong and the people await the court-martial with eager belligerence because they are certain that what happened was that the sarge did something in good faith and some of the youngsters wandered into deep water and drowned. This, according to their thinking, is an act of God and nothing else. Matthew, they argue, was the instrument of His will. When the vodka is mentioned, the people who know him become a little flushed, and their inward anger makes them overly polite. Bill Crosby, bartender at the Tower House, stands behind a knotty-pine bar in a white nylon shirt, and he speaks for all on the subject of McKeon drinking because Matty and his neighborhood friends hung out in Tower House.

"Most of the time," says Crosby, a man of dark wavy hair who chooses words after considerable thought, "he brought his wife with him." Mr. Crosby jerked a thumb over his shoulder. "They used to eat in the back. Matt was a beer drinker. He never had a drink of hard liquor in here." He studied the hand that held the bar rag. "This could be a nice business if they were all like Matt. There wasn't a bit of trouble in that boy. He comes from the Cherry Valley section and he always said, 'Gimme a Cherry Valley highball.' That meant a glass of beer. Once, when he and his wife were celebrating something, they stayed late and, after the fourth beer, Matt gave his car keys to a friend at the bar. He was that kind of a boy." He thought for a moment. "If I were you, I'd ask about him in every bar. Then you'll know the truth." I did. It's nice research, if you can get it. Many of the bartenders did not know McKeon. At the big drive-in bar called Deer Lodge, I met Jack Hennessy, a hearty man in a duck-billed hunting cap, who is a clerk to the board of selectmen in Leicester. Mr. Hennessy was having a beer before reporting home from work to a wife and seven children. "I know Matty," he said, "as well as I know my own kids. He wasn't a drinker no matter what standard you use. Best of all, he liked the jukebox. Matty would spend forty cents on beer and a dollar sixty on the hit tunes. When Matt was here, the blasted machine never shut up. His feet never stopped moving. If Betty was with him, he'd dance the legs off her. Nobody ever saw Matty hit the hard stuff. That's why, when we read about vodka" —he shrugged and laughed—"Matt McKeon? Vodka? It sounds like a joke."

Some of it valid. Most of it prejudiced. The McDermott brothers own a grocery store in Leicester. There are big Teddy and little Matty, old-timers in town and they know everybody. They knew the McKeons away back when Mom was working in the mill and, although they do not mention it, they remember when the

McKeons owed them as much as sixty dollars come payday. It's an old-fashioned store with a two-step front porch, a tobacco clock on the rear wall, a stove in the middle of the floor and bottles of Dazzle starch lining the shelves. "Matty?" they say in concert. "If you knew Leicester, you'd give Matty McKeon the highest recommendation of anybody in town. He was never anything more than a happy-go-lucky kid. He was at his best with children, going fishing with them, teaching them how to throw a ball or buck a line in football. He was a big kid himself."

Anne Costello was driving me through the old neighborhood. We stopped against a tall hedge in a hilly lane and Delia Thompson came out, stout, aging, pushing her glasses higher on the bridge of her nose. "I want to get in touch with your mother," she said in a tone of bereavement. "How can you say the things you want to say? Fussin' and hollerin' and cryin' does you no good. No good at all." Then her gloomy thoughts about Matty were broken by a big smile. "I have seventeen grandchildren, you know." The woman talked about the grandchildren, and then Mrs. Thompson got back to Sergeant McKeon. "When I first read about Matt, I couldn't believe it was our Matt. Why, Anne, you know that Matty was too lazy to march anybody at night." She thought for a moment. "Especially a Sunday night. If he had been someone who was fresh and bossy—but Matt? My goodness! Not Matt."

The nun who taught Matthew in St. Peter's school has molasses skin and a big chunk of soul in her eyes. Her testimony is as valid as that of the bartender. She knew McKeon at one stage; the bartender knew him at another. "When I read what they say about Matthew," she says, sitting primly in the convent, "I become angry. I feel like getting on the radio or television and telling the truth about him. He was a youngster who was always devoted to God and his country. He was loved by all children from the first grade on, and little ones aren't easily fooled. It would not be truthful if I said he was a student. He wasn't. He would obey; he always did as he was told, but he never tried to get near the top of his class. The things I know about him I can tell you briefly: he never did a mean thing to another child. Very few people attended the Holy Name Hour on Thursday nights, but I could look among the few old ladies in church and there would be Matthew McKeon."

The big white curtains in the convent billowed inward. "Long after he left school, Matthew continued to write to me. I even received letters from him during World War II. When he started to keep company with Betty Wood, he came to me and said, 'Sister, I've got a girl and I'm serious about her. If I bring her here would you tell me what you think?' "

He graduated from St. Peter's school, and he went to Leicester High School. He played left field for the Cubs, and, on at least one occasion, he got three for three. He played in the line on the Leicester High School football team. In 1942, McKeon's sophomore year, he was sixteen and he couldn't bear not being in the war, so be begged his mother and father to sign him into the U.S. Navy, and they did. He was aboard the carrier *Essex* when it was hit by a Kamikaze. In 1946, he was out of service, working at Reed and Prince's screw plant back home. He didn't like it.

"If you work twenty years here," he said to his brother Jim, "what happens? You got twenty years to go. That's not for me."

In 1948, he signed up for the U.S. Marines, and he spent a long time aboard the heavy cruiser *Columbus*. At Chelsea Naval Station, in Massachusetts, he was coming down the gangway one afternoon and saw a fellow Marine being clobbered by sailors. McKeon didn't pause to ask questions. He got into the fight, came out with a broken jaw. In 1950, he married his Betty, and his fellow Marines, as a gift, gave him a black Labrador retriever named Chelsea.

In boot camp, at Parris Island, he took the tongue lashings and the dismal duties and the swamp marches as a matter of course. "In twenty years," he wrote his mother, "I'll still be a young man and I'll have a pension. I'm in the Marines for life." The other boots, averaging seventeen and eighteen years of age, looked upon a World War II veteran as a sage. They called him "Pop."

The record shows that he never shirked a duty, never went over the hill, never showed fear. He was in Korea and he has seventeen battle stars and a good conduct medal. Testimony. It's part of a portrait of a man.

Somebody lied. There are nicer ways of saying it. But this is not a time for sweetness. Somebody bent the facts a little, and bent them cleverly. Sergeant Matthew McKeon and a small clique of officers in the Marine Corps are standing on something the size of a pinhead called righteousness and they are trying to shove the sarge off, and he's trying to shove them off. There is no longer room for both. One side has to go, and I have never seen a group of officers surrender to a sergeant whether he is right or wrong. Both sides fight hard for a nebulous thing called honor and pride. The Marines have had it for almost two centuries. McKeon has had it for thirty-one years, but he fights hard for the pride and honor of his wife, his two babies, his mother, and the Corps which, behind the scene, seems determined to degrade him.

Major McLeod, the provost marshal, asked McKeon if he drank any vodka. "Yes, sir," he said. "Two or three, sir." The publicity released by the command at Parris Island said McKeon drank "an unknown quantity of vodka."

The sergeant was asked why he took Platoon 71 on a night march and he answered that he was trying to teach discipline as he had been taught. The press release said the night march was "punitive," or punishment, "and was not authorized." At once, millions of people saw Sergeant McKeon as a drunken beast, a mean man who tortured blindly obedient kids until they died in a creek. The official charges read that he is charged with "the possession and/or use of alcoholic beverages. . . . In barracks housing single enlisted personnel." In itself, this is a grave enough charge, and, if McKeon is proved guilty of it, he should be punished. But why wasn't he charged with intoxication?

Again the clique of officers—men standing far back in the dark and not identifiable—made a blunder because two other sergeants were charged with drinking the vodka with McKeon on that day of April 8, 1956, and one of the others owned the bottle. Since that time, both men have been court-martialed and, for this serious offense of possessing and using alcoholic beverages in an enlisted men's barracks, both suffered a reduction in rank of one stripe, and sentence was suspended. In sum, they were censured. Nothing more.

If this is true, then why did the commandant of the Corps, General Pate, announce publicly that he wanted to see these sergeants punished to the full extent of the law—a loud hint to subordinate officers serving on the courts-martial to hit them with the book? It would be awkward for the Marine Corps, if, when McKeon is tried, he is given a greater sentence on the charge of possession and/or using liquor than the men with whom he drank as an invited guest. It wasn't McKeon's bottle. He didn't bring it to the post. And, if these sergeants were court-martialed on the original charge of drinking with McKeon on the death day, why wasn't it broadly publicized? Why did the public information office of the Corps wait until close to the time of McKeon's court-martial to announce that another sergeant, totally unrelated to the McKeon case, was found guilty of being intoxicated on duty and was given a year at hard labor?

When I was at Parris Island, a young officer, who knew I was about to see McKeon and his counsel, took me aside and said, "I want you to promise one thing: if they say anything important to you about McKeon, come back and tell us and give us a chance to answer it." Who is us?

And—come to think of it—whatever happened to all those drill instructors and plain buck privates who shouted that they were going to testify in his behalf and tell of other D.I.s who, without authorization, led platoons into the creeks around Parris Island? They were all talking loudly and courageously and suddenly there was an earsplitting silence. No one was talking.

The defense counsel was dismayed to learn that a contagious form of poor memory had afflicted many men all over the island. Emile Zola Berman, chief civilian counsel to McKeon, was so worried about this that he flew to Washington and asked General Pate to please issue an order to all hands at Parris Island announcing that anyone who testified in the sergeant's behalf would not be punished now or later. The commandant said, at that time, that he would think about it. And why, when the original announcement of the tragedy was drawn up, wasn't it announced that Major McLeod had asked for a Bogen test (an examination of blood to determine the amount of alcohol in the blood stream) and that the examining doctor did not want to perform the test, said so in the presence of McKeon and the M.P.s who accompanied him, and had to consult a book to find out how such a test would be accomplished.

It is not known if the doctor used alcohol to swab the arm before puncturing it with the needle, but, if he did, the test may be invalid because some of the rubbing alcohol is bound to get inside the needle.

Among the whys I'd like to hear answered is why the Corps announced that McKeon, on the death march, was carrying "a stick" when everyone in the platoon knew that it was a broomstick used as a cane and not something used for beating recruits? To my knowledge, the Marines did not say that, before the march, the sergeant was in such pain that he limped, used a broomstick as a crutch, reported sick and was told to rest for twenty-four hours and to report back for full duty. This happened while he was working more than 120 hours each week trying to make Marines out of seventy-eight laughing youngsters.

Nothing that happens in the Marine Corps in peace or war is too big for the attention of General Pate and yet, when the McKeon case broke, he did not constitute this court-martial himself, but instead, washed his hands of the affair by dropping the mess into the lap of his boss, Secretary of the Navy Thomas, who thereupon constituted the court-martial and named the officers who will try the sergeant. Why? Was McKeon too big for Pate? No. Not by a million gung-ho's. But it is possible that, in McKeon, General Pate saw his entire rough-tough boot-training program being challenged, and so, in a back-bending display of fairness, he took the matter out of the hands of the Marine Corps.

Still, in turning the matter over to Secretary Thomas, the general may have committed the blunder of his life; that is, assuming that he really wants to see the sergeant punished to the full extent of military law. Thomas knew that he could constitute a court numbering anywhere between five and twelve members and, for some reason which has not been explained, the Secretary of the Navy chose seven. This does not seem to be of consequence until you learn that, to convict Sergeant McKeon of any of the four charges under which he will be tried, or all of them, a two-thirds majority of the court must concur. Thus, the prosecutor will need five votes to convict.

The defense needs three votes for an acquittal. If there were six men on the court, the prosecution would need but four votes and the defense would still require three. Had Mr. Thomas appointed twelve members, any eight might have convicted McKeon and, to win an acquittal, defense counsel would need five votes, instead of the three now necessary to set the sarge free.

There has been talk that, to erase this blunder, the Secretary would "reconstitute the court" because some members were due to be transferred out of Parris Island anyway. If this is done, and the court is augmented by additional members, then it is obvious that someone among the "us" crowd is conscious of the mathematical blunder.

The sergeant will be tried on four charges: (1) use of liquor in barracks; (2) oppression of Platoon 71 by "leading" it into the mud and water of Ribbon Creek; (3) "unlawfully" killing six men through negligence and oppression; (4) drinking liquor in the presence of Recruit David H. McPherson. He can, I believe, be convicted on counts one and four without much trouble. The penalty for these is small. Counts two and three are arguable and the interest of the country will focus on whether he "oppressed" his boots by leading them into a creek, where some were drowned.

The composition of a court-martial is different from a civilian trial. For example, the seven members of the court are not judges. They are, in effect, an elite jury. They will hear the evidence, ask questions when counsel has concluded direct or cross-examination and, when they are ready to deliberate a verdict, the jury will remain in the courtroom; all others will leave.

The presiding member of the court is Colonel Edward L. Hutchinson of the 2nd Marine Division at Camp Lejeune. Assisting him, and with equal votes, are Marines Lieutenant Colonel Nicholas A. Sisak, Lieutenant Colonel Robert D. Shaffer, Lieutenant Colonel Walter Gall, Major Edwin T. Carlton, Major John G. Demas and a Navy doctor, Lieutenant Commander Hampton

Hubbard. The law officer of the court will be Captain Irving N. Klein, U.S. Navy. He will be the real judge. He will counsel the court, and will rule on the admissibility of evidence. Klein is not permitted to deliberate a verdict or to advise the court on the weighing of evidence. When the officers deliberate a verdict, he too leaves.

The prosecution will be handled by two able officers: Major Charles K. Sevier and Captain Frederick M. Haden. These men are called trial counsel. For weeks they have been questioning witnesses and lining up the case against Sergeant McKeon. The naïve ones in the Marine Corps make a to-do of hating the trial counsel because, in any drama, it simplifies matters for those of small mentality if there is a villain and a hero sharply defined. Sevier and Haden, men of honor and accomplishment, were selected for the job of prosecuting because (1) they have considerable experience in courts-martial; (2) they will do their best to convict McKeon, just as the defense will do its best to acquit the sergeant.

The defense outranks the prosecution, as it must in all such cases. The chief prosecutor is a major. The chief of defense counsel is Lieutenant Colonel Alaric W. Valentin, a small and cheerful bomb who once taught military law at Quantico. Assisting him will be Major John de Barr, dark and handsome, a man with four pounds of hair on his chest and not an ounce of fuzz on his head. De Barr represented this country as a member of the United Nations truce team in the Middle East. The third man is First Lieutenant Jeremiah C. Collins, a Georgetown University lawyer. He has a wife and a daughter, Joan, and he will go home to them in Newark, New York, out of uniform—after McKeon's court-martial.

There are two special defense lawyers—both civilians. The first, Emile Zola Berman, called "Zuke," probably will steal the show. He is an able New York counselor, much sought after in negligence cases for his brilliance and his tenacity. He will work without fee.

The second is Thomas Costello, McKeon's brother-in-law, also a negligence trial lawyer and highly regarded in New York. Sitting in the box with McKeon at the trial will be his co-defendant, the D.I. system. The little clique of distance-darkened officers says that this is not so, that the sarge is the sole defendant, but they fail to realize that the reason this court-martial became a minor league Dreyfus affair is that Sergeant Matthew McKeon is no longer an unknown, unsung noncom who sinned: he is, rather, a symbol of what the Marine Corps calls the ideal drill instructor.

The drill instructor *is* the Marine Corps. It is his savage dedication to his job which makes the Corps the toughest fighting outfit, man for man, in the world. He is especially trained to transmute jelly into concrete. He must be able to do everything that he orders the raw boot to do, and he must be prepared to do it better. He must be impatiently patient, a mother, a father, an ulcerous boss, a parlor psychiatrist, a sadistic superintendent of an orphanage, a big bleeding-hearted brother, and most of all, the Marine that the poor boot would like to be. The D.I. cadre is what saves the Corps every time a war comes along. War means expansion; expansion means hundreds of thousands of new men; the corps doesn't want mere men, it wants Marines.

If a D.I. turns out Marines, instead of neurotics, he has done his job. To do it, he has to work against the clock, teaching men more than they should be able to absorb in a short time. To do this, he has got to spot the goof-ups early because the goof-ups can infect a whole platoon. When he spots them, he gets them aside and warns them that they will learn, and learn quickly, or be invited to a thumping class. A thumping class is held in the evening. The D.I. invites the deliberate dope to his room, locks the door, and beats him until he is a whimpering wreck. The cold fact is that the D.I. in so doing is protecting his job because he is either a good D.I. who turns out smart, savvy platoons or he is a softie who cries in his beer and is reassigned to latrine duty.

The officers in Parris Island and at San Diego are hypocrites if they say that thumping is not part of training. It is against the rules, just as a Sunday night march in the swamps is against the rules but, barring accidental drownings, the thumping is much more cruel than the night march.

Not every career Marine can become a D.I. It requires a special, carefully screened personality. For instance, when McKeon was graduated from D.I. school in early spring, his personality was evaluated in this way: His teacher was given several choices to grade the student D.I.s in each category. Under motivation, the paper says: Strong drive and desire for D.I. duty. Better than average drive for D.I. duty. Average drive for D.I. duty. Weak drive for D.I. duty. Absent drive—strong desire not to be D.I. The instructor marked the first on the list. The next category said: Motivation appears sound and healthy. Indifferent— neither particularly healthy nor pathological. Pathologically motivated (e.g., sadistic, psychopathic orientation). The instructor marked the first choice on the list. Under hostility factors, the sheet is marked: Average hostility, appropriately displayed and controlled. More than average amount of hostility, occasional loss of control or inappropriate display, but not severe. Extremely hostile, with poor control, inappropriate display. Clear paranoid character traits, not well compensated. Less than average amount of hostility, passive trends. Excessive use of hostility repression. The instructor marked the first line again.

In the final category, "service accomplishment," the sheet was marked: Unusually high achievement (e.g., in earning rank, commendations, combat or otherwise): Better than average achievement. Has accomplished at level of average Marine. Below average achievement. Conspicuously poor service achievement. The instructor marked the second line.

The average over-all mark for all D.I.s is 80 per cent. McKeon started in a class of ninety tough Marines which was whittled to fifty-five, and he came in fourteenth with a mark of better than 84.50. It is easier to become a good second lieutenant in the Corps than it is to become a good D.I. The drill instructor is perpetually suspended between lazy boots and spying officers. The aspiring drill instructor, as part of the course, must listen to a between-the-lines lecture. The heading of this lecture is "Maltreatment." The subheadings read: "History of Abuse at P.I." (Parris Island), "Fear of Brass—Officers Will Back D.I.s." The first paragraph of the lecture digest says that "many drill instructors have a fear that the brass is out to get them." This must indeed be awkward and unwarranted if the officers are always backing up the D.I.s. It goes on to say that they develop this unreasonable fear through hearing of investigations. The lecturer is told to "stress fact the CG [commanding general] and BCOs [battalion commanding officers] recognize that errors in judgment are possible, also that every effort is made to help a D.I. in difficulties or trouble, but that it is impossible to whitewash maltreatment."

The lecture notes go on to ask what is maltreatment, and then answer by saying "unnecessary rough physical or mental treatment." The grammar is poor, but the sense is good. If the contemplated action on the part of the drill instructor will "hurt" the recruit, don't do it, says the lecture. If you don't know what the word "hurt" means, the sheet says, "do it to yourself; if it hurts, it's hurt." This is followed by a warning not to make the training "soft—far from it." At this point, sergeants lose judgment.

Under the try-it-yourself system, everything hurts. The D.I. who tries scrubbing barracks will find that it hurts. The same applies to reciting parts of the rulebook with head-in-stove (a common form of punishment); it is also true of having to run around a marching platoon with M-1 rifle over head, of being confined to barracks when others are at the movies, of thumping, policing the grounds, standing to attention for fifteen minutes in a sizzling sun, being deprived of a liberty pass, night marching in mud and water, drawing extra duty, having to reclean a clean rifle, being chewed out by a superior and many other "hurts."

The lecturer is always careful to warn the D.I. against the methods he knows must be employed. The officer makes certain that he never knows what methods the D.I.s are using. If a boot is hurt, the drill instructor is punished. If the D.I. abides by the lecturer's admonitions, he cannot make Marines of boots in seventy days, and he is sacked.

Parris Island lies halfway between the finger of Savannah and the elbow of Charleston, and has the graciousness of neither. It is a place of curving roads, breeze-swept palms riffling like a deck of cards in a lonely gambler's hands, Spanish moss hanging like drying fish nets, and thousands of unhappy young men. They are making a major adjustment in life. They are becoming United States Marines. They all whisper the scuttlebutt about what is going to happen to Sergeant Matthew C. McKeon.

The town of Beaufort, five miles to the west, is beginning to show a little sparkle as the press of the nation arrives to cover the big story. The Golden Eagle Hotel, where a spittoon is still a challenge to a marksman, is unique with its lobby organ which calls everyone to dinner in dismal tones, and its stuffed animal heads on the walls. One of the major topics of conversation is the existence of a few—and very rare—copies of the proceedings of the court of inquiry, which heard a lot of testimony last April about the drowning of six recruits in Ribbon Creek. Some anonymous benefactor hid one in my brief case. It is not a dull document and, to my knowledge, it has not been revealed to the people. It comes to a fat four hundred-odd pages and the preface was written by Major General J. C. Burger, who was the commandant at Parris Island when the tragic night march occurred on April 8.

The general has since been transferred, as a mark of disfavor, under the old and witless military axiom that the top man is responsible for the actions of all under his command. It is possible that the sergeant's action may prevent the two-star general from ever becoming a three-star general. The general writes: "The local marshes have never been, and are not now, a source of danger to human life, limb or health. They are constantly used by fishermen and hunters, and there has not, to my knowledge, been a death or injury attributable to the marshes in this area." He advised against declaring it out of bounds, which, I infer, means that it was never out of bounds. Staff Sergeant E. H. Huff testified that he had heard of platoons being marched into the swamps, although he had not seen one.

Colonel William B. McKean testified that he knew of a platoon which was on night compass marches and lost its way in the swamp. Eleven others testified that they had never heard of marsh marches. The general concluded that Sergeant McKeon ordered the march because of a "zealous but unreasoning desire to prevent future conduct considered in breach of discipline among recruits of Platoon 71. . . . That the immediate purpose of the march was to inflict fear and physical discomfort upon members of the platoon as a result of former conduct . . . that the march was undertaken without intent to kill or inflict grievous bodily harm to anyone."

The testimony of Private Edward Leonard epitomized what the twenty-six boots told the court. He was polite, but he was adamant too. One thing was apparent. He was not going to hang McKeon.

Q. Describe what happened as the platoon started into the water. A. Well, sir, we started toward the water and Sergeant McKeon was the first one in. We went in the water and we started parallel toward the shore. When the entire platoon was in, we started to form a circle. [Note: the word circle seems confusing. Leonard apparently means that, after McKeon led his platoon in the water, he walked upstream thirty yards, lecturing, then turned downstream. Thus the head of the platoon met the rear of the platoon, giving an illusion of a circle of marching men in water.] Q. How deep was the water over there, approximately? A. Up to about my waist, sir. Q. How was this instruction given while you were in the water? A. He was just walking along and we were all following him, sir. Q. What happened as the platoon walked along the bank? A. We walked up along the bank and we started a circle and we were all grouped around in some sort of a group. Some of the boys wandered out into deeper water. Sergeant McKeon did not give them an order to march into deep water. Q. How deep was the water, approximately? A. Up to about our chests, sir. Q. What happened then? A. Well, sir, some of the boys couldn't hold on. I guess the current got them. A few of them started to be carried away. Q. Did you have reason to notice Private Thompson about this time? A. I'm not sure which it was, sir. I was ten feet from him before he went down. Q. What was this person doing? A. He was trying to stay above the water, sir. Q. Why do you say it was Private Thompson or Private Wood? A. That's the only two colored boys that were at the head of the line that were big. Q.

Did you fail to reach him or did you reach him? A. Yes, sir. I had my clothes on and my boondockers and just couldn't reach him in time. Q. When was the last time you saw this person? A. Well, I was within about ten feet of him and I seen him sink under water and I kept swimming towards him, but that's the last I saw of him. Q. Did you see Sergeant McKeon do anything? A. I seen him trying to reach the men that were yelling for help, sir. Q. Would you say that he led the people behind him into deep water? A. No, sir. I wouldn't.

The court of inquiry informed the witness that he was privileged to make any further statement related to the subject matter. Private Leonard thought for a moment, then said: "I think that Sergeant McKeon did—he was only trying to help us and teach us further training that we should know if we ever got into combat. I don't think that he ever intended for any of the boys to be hurt. I think that it was an unfortunate accident, sir. And that's about all I have to say, sir."

Private David H. McPherson on drinking: Q. During the time that you were in the room did you see any evidence that Sergeant McKeon might have been drinking? A. Yes, sir. Q. What did you see? A. Sir, I saw Sergeant McKeon take one drink, sir. Q. What kind of bottle? A. A vodka bottle, sir. Q. Could you see the label on the bottle? A. Yes, sir. Q. How much liquid was in the bottle when he took the drink, approximately? A. Approximately three to four inches, sir. Q. And approximately how much was left afterwards? A. Approximately the same, sir. Q. Did you smell alcohol on Sergeant McKeon's breath? A. No, sir. Q. How did Sergeant McKeon act? Did he act normally? A. Sir, he did act normally and very seriously. Q. In your opinion, was Sergeant McKeon drunk? A. No, sir.

Parris Island is a place of constant adjustment; a place where thousands of men work hard so that they may be sent somewhere else; a place where the sun slants white off oily water; a place of drill grounds and outdoor movies and night baseball games and tenacious insects; a place for griping and scuttlebutt and a two-star flag; a place that looks almost pretty if viewed from the near side of a frosty Martini in a drape-darkened club; and ugly if viewed through the windage sight of an M-1 rifle; a place to broil a sentry at 2 P.M. with a summer sirocco coming up out of Savannah; a place where, in winter, the wind at 2 A.M. can flatten the eyeballs of a sentry and slam the lids on top.

There, without collusion, the boots decided to vindicate the sergeant, just as the officers, with collusion, decided to condemn him.

There is a long super-ranch house here and it is called bachelor officers' quarters, or BOQ. It sits behind stunted palms and lacy willows and, all day long, furtive men glance at the door, look up and down the street and then step inside. These men are witnesses for the defense in the court-martial of Staff Sergeant Matthew C. McKeon and their hearts are honest and true but there is fear in their feet. These are the career drill instructors—the D.I.s who want to testify in behalf of McKeon.

Some of them hold snappy little overseas caps in their hands, and they fold these caps nervously, and refold them, and ask in low growls, "What will they do to us if we testify? Maybe the officers don't want us to testify." It's a thought. Maybe, when this court-martial is done, the D.I.s who told the truth will be marked men, dogged with lousy duty until they quit. Maybe, on the other hand, Major General Litzenberger and his staff will appreciate an accurate airing of the Drill Instructor System. Maybe they would like to know what goes on at this training command. Or, if they are sophisticated, they already know and do not want anyone else to know.

On this quiet day, I sat with two D.I.s in a room. The senior was in suntans; the junior was in green fatigues. They were ashamed to ask that their names not be used, but they had to mention it because each one has almost a decade of service in the Marine Corps and each has a wife and family and each wants to remain in service for as long as the Corps will permit. They fidgeted and said that they had no okay to talk to anybody and they didn't want to hurt their careers but, at the same time, they wanted me to know what the new system of boot training is like since the six recruits were drowned in Ribbon Creek.

"We have a herd," said Sergeant Suntan. "You know what a herd is. Out of about sixty men, the sarge and I can knock off at least fifteen names of boys who do not want to learn to be Marines."

"Excuse me," said Sergeant Fatigue. "I asked several of these boys why they enlisted, and you know what they said? They all said the same thing: 'Sarge, I don't know. I just don't know.'" Since the accident at Ribbon Creek, the training system used in boot camp has changed. It has softened until now it is a spongy mess which nauseates drill instructors.

None of the new pamper-the-platoon orders are to be found in writing. None of the old ones were committed to paper either. They come down the chain of command verbally. The last man to repeat them is the first lieutenant in charge of the company, who tells them to the D.I. Take Platoon X, the one the sergeants were talking about. It has almost finished boot training and Sergeant Suntan lowers his head when he talks about his men. "Soon, they will be going home on leave and when I think of those stupid—birds standing on the corner in their home towns, wearing the uniform of United States Marines, my belly knots up and I feel sick." "I felt like belting some of those boys," says Sergeant Fatigue. "After a number of weeks, wouldn't you think a boy would understand simple things like what is left face and what is right face? Honest, now." "How about the one who told us he had ten years of education?" Suntan says. "We got him in the D.I. room one night and he wasn't sure who George Washington was and when we asked him who was President of the United States, he pipes up Truman. I asked who Eisenhower was and he says a general." "I don't know," says Fatigue, "I still don't think that's as bad as the kid who—only seventeen, mind you—admitted he has been tried for arson and burglary. And how about them letters from mothers asking us to hang onto their boys for a little while longer because they couldn't do nothing with them at home?" Suntan smiles. "They didn't do so bad on the rifle range, though. I was surprised. I mean surprised. Only eight flunked out."

What are the new soft rules? Well, there are no more night disciplinary marches, for one thing. If a platoon refuses to understand the discipline and complete dedication of the Marine Corps, a D.I. is now allowed to give the men "extra instruction." No more locker box drill. Until McKeon, dumb boots were ordered to shoulder heavy locker boxes and shift them from one shoulder to the other like rifles. That's out, under the new rules. It's considered to be hazing. "Let's face it," Sergeant Fatigue says. "We can't punish a boot any more. We're ordered to teach discipline, but how can you teach 'em discipline when they read in the papers that the D.I. can't do anything to enforce discipline? Tell me, mister. Can a mother teach discipline to her babies if they know that she cannot punish them for disobedience?"

There are six hundred drill instructors on this island. In a single voice, they wail the passing of the tough boot training they once had. As an index to the new pamper-the-platoon policy, they point to the fact that visitors are now allowed on the island at any time of any day. Anyone can come through the main gate and ask to see a son, a brother, or a husband. If the boot isn't on an assignment, he must be excused to see his parents. Signs have been set up, shouting "Welcome Visitor." Picnic grounds are set aside under shady trees, where a youngster can cry his heart out about the hell he must undergo in this Godforsaken place. The command has even set up a snack bar. The boot knows that his D.I.

has warned him off between-meal snacks, but, when he is with his visitors he can load up on Cokes and cakes and instead of getting leaner and harder, week by week, he becomes softer and fatter, like the system.

Until now, this was an island of seventeen thousand men who admired only each other. Now they are split. And split badly. The boots, the noncommissioned officers and a few captains and majors are determined to stick by Staff Sergeant Matt McKeon. A smaller group, led by ranking officers, would like to disown the sarge as a Marine to save the entire Corps from being investigated. The split is clean and deep and it will not heal for a long time.

A few days ago, Lieutenant Colonel Robert A. Thompson, battalion commander, said he never heard of night marches and would not permit one in his group. In glancing at the accused in this general court-martial, he seemed to be coldly outraged. Yesterday, Sergeant McKeon's immediate boss, Senior Drill Instructor Edward Huff, took the stand to say that it has been a Parris Island practice to take goofy recruits on night marches into the swamps. He even led with his chin by saying that he had threatened a platoon: "If you don't snap out of your hockey, I will march you into the swamps." (Hockey, translated from the gyrene patois, is a naughty word.) Sergeant Huff was asked what he thought of Junior D.I. McKeon and, after a moment, he said, "He done his work, he done it well, and he never seemed to complain." When Huff was asked how much McKeon worked, he said, "By my figuring, he worked a hundred thirty-two hours a week. A good man."

Where does the truth lie? In Colonel Thompson's words? In Sergeant Huff's? I don't know. Further, it is none of my business, but it is very much the business of the seven high officers who sit as members of the general court-martial. Whom will they believe? Most of the commissioned officers, on the witness stand, admit nothing and volunteer nothing unless they are jockeyed into a corner. Captain Charles E. Patrick, a graying man with a dimple in his chin, was Officer of the Day when Platoon 71 came out of Ribbon Creek minus six men. He told about driving down the rifle ranges and, in the yellow funnel of his own headlights, seeing young recruits, half dressed, all soaked and shivering, and some carrying others.

On cross-examination, he admitted the area at Ribbon Creek is not out of bounds for Marines except during daylight hours when rifle bullets are pinging down the range. The most interesting witness of the day was Thomas Grabowski, the first member of Platoon 71 to take the stand. He is tall and boyish, and all of eighteen. He comes from Kearny, New Jersey, and is religious.

Grabowski was put on the stand as one of Major Charles K. Sevier's prosecution witnesses, but he stayed to become a defense witness. When he first came into the Marine Corps, Grabowski was called a crybaby by McKeon, because, when his work was criticized, he burst into tears. Now he sits tall and cold and self-assured, and he will not be mousetrapped into diluting his testimony. He told the story of the fateful day tersely from reveille to church to chow to smoke break to field day to chow and letter-writing.

By the time the prosecution and the defense got around to needling the kid, I expected that he might waver, or crack. But it was obvious that the months of life as a Marine had put a little iron in his nerve. He was determined to tell the truth, as he saw the truth, without trying to help the sergeant or hurt him.

Grabowski was coming back from a novena at 6 P.M. with a few other boys when the sarge walked up in the dark to ask where they had been. "That," said Grabowski, "was when I smelled liquor on his breath." No amount of cross-questioning could shake him on what he smelled. "Later," the Marine said, "he took us out. Somebody said for a swim. He asked about the nonswimmers— when we got into the water, he told us to stay in the shadows, that an enemy could see you if you moved out—you know, he was trying to teach us about war. We were in water about up to our chests. When he turned us around and started back, maybe we turned out too far. I stepped off the bank and I went down in the deep part of the creek. Other fellows, to my right, went down. The bank just disappeared from under our feet."

Grabowski became reflective. He had the presence (the first witness to do so) to study an aerial photo of Ribbon Creek and to boldly mark off where Platoon 71 entered the water, where McKeon led them, where the turn was made, where the panic was started by the frantic scream of one unknown Marine, and where they piled out of the water onto the bank. The court officers studied it for a long time.

"We thought it was a lark," Grabowski said softly. "We knew that McKeon was serious; that he was trying to teach us discipline." "Would you say that Platoon 71 had good discipline?" defense attorney E. Z. Berman asked in cross-examination. "No, sir." Berman, who knows that part of the charges against the sergeant specifies that he—and presumably his platoon—was not acquainted with the creek area behind the rifle ranges, asked Grabowski if he had ever been down there before. The lawyer, who is shrewd and polite and who has a whining rising voice, hit pay dirt this time. The witness said that, oh yes, he knew the area because, after Platoon 71 had had a week of rifle practice, they had to go down to the rifle pits to set and pull targets for other platoons. Sixty yards behind the pits, in plain view, is Ribbon Creek.

The court was jammed with off-duty Marines and ladies in bright cottons who metronomed their Japanese fans while looking and listening. "What kind of a drill instructor was Sergeant Mc-Keon?" "A good one," Private Grabowski said sharply. "He had a lot of patience with us." "Had you ever heard of other platoons being taken out into the boondocks?" "Yes, sir. I heard it mainside. From what other Marines told me, it was the usual thing."

The court-martial is one thing: It can be seen and heard and assessed. But the bitter fight going on between the Marine Corps brass and Sergeant McKeon behind a door marked "Trial Counsel" is a bigger battle and for the first time it will come out into the open. The sarge says he needs two hundred witnesses to prove his case. The prosecution, which fights for the high command, denies McKeon's right to call that many and, in fact, has refused so far to summon the first seventeen defense witnesses. This is oppression of a new kind. Under courts-martial law, all witnesses must be summoned by the prosecutor, who is called trial counsel. This is Major Charles Sevier. Although he has reporters and stenographers and typists working on the testimony of the court-martial as already adduced, it was a long time before he was able to produce a page of transcript from his own witnesses. I met him in the hall of the courtroom and asked him about it. The major smiled. He had been out to the beach, he said, and he was going back. He was stopping in to pick up about ten minutes of transcribed testimony for Emile Zola Berman. And Berman was getting this little bit only because he asked for it.

McKeon's court defense resumes when Marine Private Melvin Barber of New York returns to the stand for cross-examination by the sarge's counsel. Barber, a six-foot eighteen-year-old and a survivor of the disciplinary march into Ribbon Creek has already testified that some of the platoon thought it was a lark. He has said there was "a lot of kidding" on the "death march" until, in the swirling waters of the creek, the men "panicked" and tried to save each other.

"I am going to fight hard," Berman said, "to bring as much proof to bear as possible. The paramount issue in the case is whether the type of march McKeon led is a standard practice here."

Major Sevier contends that it was not. His witnesses never

heard of a night march into the swamp, and beginning with Colonel Robert A. Thompson of this base, they deplore such things. But, counteracting the colonel's words come telegrams from scores of ex-Marines who are willing to come down to Parris Island and swear that such things did take place and were fairly common.

"Was in Platoon 273, first recruit Battalion, in 1951," wires Daniel Marlow of 6852 Coral Way, Miami, Florida. "Under drill instructor Staff Sergeant Robert A. Olsen. Forced marches in Ribbon Creek area at night was routine for all platoons. Will testify at own expense or give affidavit." There are lots of these, and the sarge, if he must go to prison, would like to prove first that he is not a sadistic drunkard. But he cannot have witnesses unless Major Sevier agrees to call them. And Sevier's contention is that the expense of this court-martial is running too high right now.

The defense counsel has not cost the government a dime. Berman is a volunteer. So is Howard Lester. Expenses for transportation for witnesses and stenographic work is running high, but ex-Marines are sending in small checks to help. McKeon wants all checks returned, with thanks, to the senders. His rationale is that he is guilty of causing the deaths of six young men, and the quicker the court-martial is over, the quicker he can start paying for it.

McKeon thought he would get a break when law officer Irving N. Klein ruled that his counsel could examine the questionnaires sent out to Marines and ex-Marines asking their opinion of boot training. This questionnaire was an act of questionable intelligence on the part of Headquarters, Marine Corps, because, in effect, it asks ex-Marines to sit as a jury of 27,250. There were four pages of questions. The one omitted is: "Did you ever participate in a night march in swamps or creeks at Parris Island?" When an assortment of the replies were examined by Emile Zola Berman, he saw that someone had stamped, across the bottom: "For official use only." This means that he cannot use the material at the court-martial. Among the questions asked were if the signer had observed commissioned officers supervising a platoon during training hours. This is important because, since I have been here, I've watched many platoons and have seen no commissioned officers. This is noncom country. Commissioned officers play golf, or sit in air-conditioned offices.

There were questions about the drill instructors too. Did they use dirty, filthy, vulgar language? Was there "hazing" such as wearing buckets over heads, repeating vulgar expressions regarding one's self or marching on elbows and toes. It was asked if any human rights had been abridged, like attendance at church or the reading of personal mail. There were questions about striking, beating and kicking.

The Marine Corps' greatest living hero is coming here to testify for Sergeant Matthew C. McKeon. He is Lieutenant General Lewis B. Puller, retired, and the only man, living or dead, to be awarded five Navy Crosses. "Chesty" Puller will come to this base to stand beside the sarge and take the stand to testify that, unless the Corps endorses its tough drill instructors, the Marines will not be combat-ready and, if they aren't combat-ready, it isn't much of a Marine Corps.

This is the most interesting development of the court-martial.

This pits brass against brass for the first time. Commandant General Randolph McCall Pate is on a contrary tack, apologizing to the Congress and the American public for McKeon and the Drill Instructor System. The four-star general announced that, in a "very real sense," the Marine Corps is on trial with McKeon. Now a three-star general volunteers to come here—sticking his retired neck away out—to defend the tough drill instructor, to swear that, while he doesn't condone cruelty, the Corps expects the D.I. to make boys into tough Marines, ready to fight anywhere at a moment's notice.

Puller went through boot camp himself in 1918. He was too late to see service in World War I, but he went up through the ranks, step by step. He is a little man—not more than five feet eight inches tall. To make the grade, he had to be tougher than anyone twice his size and it paid off at the battle of Peleliu, where Colonel Puller's regiment ran into the caves and killed ten thousand Japanese and captured one. This one was sent back to headquarters with a sign on his chest. It read: "Herewith one Japanese prisoner with apologies, Puller." The High Command sent him home as "battle happy." He was a colonel then. He went to Korea and led the Marines there as a general. He got almost to the border of China before General MacArthur called him back.

Major Charles Sevier rested the case against the sarge in a blaze of fireworks which may figure in an appeal, if McKeon should be convicted. Emile Zola Berman at once asked for a postponement so that he can conduct urgent official business in New York. The business could hardly be more official—the eighth birthday of Berman's daughter. She had sent a card to him on which was scrawled: "Do you think, Daddy, that you could come to see me on my birthday?" Like Puller, this ex-Air Force Colonel is tough up to a point. Berman will be at the birthday party.

For the prosecution, the last witness was the big witness. He is

Colonel David W. Silvey, assistant Chief of Staff at Parris Island
in charge of plans and operations. The Colonel is short, compact,
as terse as a sling shot. He swore that no night marches are scheduled in basic training here. He also read an order prohibiting
marches into Elliott's Beach tidal waters. Through this, Major
Sevier hoped to get across the idea that McKeon, in marching
Platoon 71 into the boondocks of Ribbon Creek, was, in effect,
defying written orders. An argument started between Sevier and
Berman about this. The major was trying to confine the issue to
the colonel's exact words. Berman was trying to show that the
average drill instructor was paid, not for listening to orders about
Elliott's Beach, which is a mile away from Ribbon Creek, but to
use his discretion and to turn out a smart platoon without bother-
ing the commissioned officers for permission.

Q. The D.I.'s job is to teach and maintain discipline? A. Yes. Q.
Does he have latitude and discretion, Colonel? A. Within certain
limits, yes. Q. Has it come to your attention, Colonel, since you
came here in 1953, that there have been unauthorized marches
into the swamps? A. I know of only one report since I've been
here.

Berman read parts of a statement made by General Pate in
May. He asked the colonel if he agreed with the general. Silvey
smiled broadly. "I certainly agree with any policy that General
Pate lays down."

Morale is low. The best way to gauge it is to look at the spit-and-
polish drill instructors. Until McKeon was court-martialed, the
D.I.s strutted like barrel-chested gods on this island. Now, many
of them need a shave. Their boots are dull. Their tropical tans are
wrinkled. At night, they drink in silence. They stand around the
Noncommissioned Officers Club whispering and nodding to each
other.

A hard-looking man with wavy hair and a mustard mustache is
cleaning the ash trays in this press room, across the hall from the
courtroom. He and his men pick up wrinkled papers and empty
garbage pails and clean the men's room. His name is Staff
Sergeant Robert J. Rawlins. He wears the Silver Star. In Korea, he
jumped out of a crippled tank and cut a steel tow rope out of the
tank treads while Chinese artillery zeroed in on him and a captain
who helped. They saved the tank. Rawlins got his Silver Star, and
he picked the shrapnel out of his legs and back and neck with his
fingernails. Now he has been sentenced to eight months at hard
labor, loss of all pay and allowances (there are a wife and two
children in Jacksonville, Florida), and a bad conduct discharge
from the Marine Corps. Why? He slapped a couple of recruits for
being stupid. He was given a one-day general court-martial. The

hero goes home with a prison record. He's bitter because no one gave him the word that the Corps decided to go soft on boot training after McKeon was arrested April eighth. Rawlins was arrested April tenth. Everything here happened before or since McKeon.

Under their breaths, the six hundred D.I.s say that it was a proud outfit before April eighth. Now everybody is a space cadet. Diffident and indifferent.

Staff Sergeant Tom Rice is Private First Class Rice. He lost his temper and shook a recruit silly. He's licked and ready to quit. No more Marine Corps for him. "What the lesson plan allowed you to do," he says, "and what you did to a platoon were two different things. The officers knew everything that was going on. There were no secrets. The boots were turned over to us—the D.I.s—and they gave us ten weeks to make basic Marines out of boobs. We did it. Now the officers prefer charges against us and handcuff us. I'm through."

Scores of D.I.s are serving time quietly, waiting to get out.

Before McKeon, the routine was hard, but not cruel. The recruits arrived at Yemassee, South Carolina, on a train. On the platform stood a military policeman in scarlet and gold helmet, white gloves and lanyard. The kids with the long hair and the weird clothes were still admiring him when he barked: "Get off that train. Run. Don't walk." This is the start of what the Corps calls a "fear and shock" stage. The boot must be immersed in it and kept that way until he graduates from basic training. After that, pride and esprit de corps will make him a good Marine.

The boots rode thirty miles to the big "toll" gate at Parris Island. There, an M.P. boarded the bus and exchanged deadpan words with the original M.P. "Just got the word that a drill instructor in the Third Battalion strangled another boot last night. The command wants them to stop strangling." At the receiving station, the boots were taken inside, screamed at, formed into platoons of seventy-five men, formed outside, and met their three D.I.s—a senior and two juniors. In hot weather they were given a tin helmet, a cartridge belt and two canteens of water. Their welcome to the platoon consisted of orders to keep their mouths shut, eyes and ears open, and not to speak unless spoken to. The first and last word out of your mouths, at all times, will be "yes, sir."

They were formed into four ranks. The longest-striding D.I. got in front and led off at high speed without ever looking back. The other D.I.s got in back and booted the boots with the side of their shoes, yelling, "Close up, maggots. They kill recruits down here."

At hygienic station, they were stripped nude, examined for lice and venereal disease and given a haircut. Some wept as the electric razor mowed across their scalps. Next came a soapy shower. Many had to be shown by D.I.s how to wash the recesses of the human body. Uniforms were never handed to a boot. They were flung at his face and he had to catch them. While he was catching, the D.I.s kept yelling: "Keep moving, hurry up. On the double, you scum." A boot could not wear Marine emblems on cap and shoulders until he graduated from boot training. He rolled his civilian clothing and sent it home by railway express. At the PX, he bought a razor, toothbrush, creams and lotions.

On the way to battalion barracks, the boots had nothing but shaved heads and scared faces. Their trouser legs were rolled up so that the fit of their boots could be seen. This also showed more experienced boots that these were the newest "idiots."

In the morning came examinations of eyes, ears, hearts, and an examination by the "talking doctor." This is Marine for psychiatrist. Then a meeting with the chaplain of the boot's particular faith and a lecture by the company commanding officer.

Married D.I.s often spent the first week sleeping in the squad bays with the boots until they passed the idiot stage. A D.I. would get them to bed by 10 P.M., then clean his own gear, take a shower, write his reports, and get to bed at 1 A.M. He was up at 4:45 A.M. and he had to shine because he must be the Marine the boot hoped to be. At 5:30 A.M. the D.I., sparkling like Sergeant Quirt on a date, would stand in the bay and roar: "Hit the deck. Reveille. On your feet. Fall out of them racks." The boots stood in front of their beds with their blankets and sheets on their arms. The reason? One is to make sure that, when they make the bed, they start from the mattress up.

At morning calisthenics, the D.I. tried to locate the weaklings. Not the lazy ones. Just those who could not hope to make the grade as Marines. These were weeded out. How does he do it? He looks for changes in skin color and for pain wrinkles around the eyes.

The D.I. publicly humiliates the homesick and the crybabies because, for them, there is no easy way. He warns the lazy ones, the wise guys and the sea lawyers. If none of this works, he works them over. He slaps them with the back of his hand; he leans them against a wall locker and shakes them until the noise is deafening. Sometimes he loses his temper and punches them in the stomach. "Fear and shock." When a kid begins to obey, or tries hard, the D.I. calls him into the D.I. room alone and says, "Know what, kid? I think you can make it. You're going to become a U.S. Marine." The youngster treads air for days.

When he graduated, the boot went home on leave. He was neat, clean, smart, slightly silent, and very polite.

What is it like now? It's different. It's soft. At Yemassee, the M.P. calls, "Come over here, men, your bus is waiting." If the boot isn't drilling or in class, he can smoke. Special troop handlers walk the men slowly to the hygienic station. They talk in ranks. Nobody's hair is cut to the bone; a half inch remains in front. They lie on benches to be fitted for boots. No one shouts at them. Their trousers are rolled down. The boot gets his Marine Corps emblems at once. There is no fear and shock. A little discipline. No field days (scrubbing barracks) except on Thursdays for Friday inspection. No slapping, no slamming against lockers.

An off-duty D.I. is not permitted to see his platoon after 4 P.M. There is talk of putting radios in the squad bays. Where they used to walk, they now get buses. The D.I. must take them to movies and night ball games whether they've earned these or not. No abusive language is permitted. Boots may be called "Marines, recruits, or men." They even have something called "the recruit of the day." A boot is picked each day from each of six battalions and, for the day, he is orderly to General Greene or his office aide. The boot wears tropical uniform, with white barracks cap, gold marine emblems, a white M.P. lanyard and holster, and a red armband which says "recruit of the day." When he's not busy, he has a double-dip chocolate soda with whipped cream and a cherry.

The vodka belonged to a buddy. Staff Sergeant Elwyn Scarborough, first witness for the defense in the court-martial of Staff Sergeant Matthew C. McKeon, testified that it was his bottle; that it was half full when he brought it to McKeon, and that Scarborough, McKeon and Sergeant King each had about "two drinks" out of it before it was stashed under a desk. Thus the drunk charge in this dramatic trial was finally laid to rest.

On Saturday, April 7, Scarborough said, he went to an afternoon battalion party near the Able rifle range. He is a man with eighteen years' service in the Marine Corps and wears a weathered face. He took a fifth of Hiram Walker's vodka with him. There was beer and chow, and Scarborough nipped at his private bottle and had fun. McKeon was not present. Scarborough left the party at about six thirty. The bottle, now half empty, was wrapped carefully in a brown paper bag and placed in Scarborough's quarters in building 700. The next morning, Sunday, he went down to building 761 to see McKeon about his herd. Platoon 71 was low on discipline and lousy on the rifle range. Scarborough was a range officer. They talked about it and a Sergeant Muckler came in and said that 71 was out in the back "laying on the grass."

McKeon, who had been listening to abuse about his charges, got up from his desk and went out back with Scarborough and saw some of the recruits laughing and frolicking on the lawn. He sent them inside and ordered a "field day"—a thorough clean-up of barracks. The sergeants went back into the Drill Instructors' room, and Scarborough said, "Want a drink?" "We don't keep any here," said McKeon. "I have some if you want to get it with me." They drove in McKeon's car. Scarborough carried the bottle back into building 761. The time was about noon on Sunday. The vodka was Scarborough's property so he took the first slug. Then it went to McKeon, who got a bottle of Coke from a machine as a chaser. Sergeant King, another junior D.I., came into the room and he had a drink. A little later, the bottle went around a second time. Now there were about two inches of liquor in the bottle. Scarborough wrapped it in the bag and placed it behind the leg of a table. It was twelve fifty.

"Did you see any recruit in that room at any time?" asked defense lawyer Emile Zola Berman. Private McPherson has already testified that, sometime during that day, he saw McKeon take a drink. "No. Not as I recall." "Was the door to the barracks always closed?" "Yes, sir." "Then what happened?" "McKeon said to me, 'Ain't you going to take your bottle?' " I said, 'I'll come back later and pick it up.' "

Both got into McKeon's car and went for platoon mail. Then they went to the staff NCO Club, where, the spectators at the court-martial learned with surprise, beer and liquor could be purchased at lunch hour by any of the six hundred drill instructors on the island. "What did you do?" "I saw a friend. He waved at me so I went to the bar." "What did Sergeant McKeon do?" "He had lunch and took his mail." "When did you next see the sergeant?" "At the court of inquiry a few days later."

After Navy Captain Klein's ruling, Warrant Officer Leslie E. Volle, of Camp Lejeune, testified that he spent ten days charting Ribbon Creek for depths and for holes. He found no holes. He went on to explain a huge topographical map of Ribbon Creek, the depths of water at various tides, and the strength of the current.

At noon recess, Sergeant McKeon showed his first sign of disgust when he told of a visit by a New York lawyer who tried to get him to sign a Hollywood contract to film the court-martial and the death march for $1,000. The movies want to memorialize what he tries to forget.

"The main points of the prosecution's case," Berman said, "are so weak and confusing that I think I can shorten this court-martial considerably. I may be finished with the defense of Sergeant McKeon in two or three days," he said. "It won't run much beyond that."

The sarge, who has been mentally hanging by his thumbs since April 8, will hang only a week more. Then he will know what the seven-man military court has in store for him. Two years in prison? A year? Six months? Freedom? The last one is doubtful. Drill instructors do not win acquittals for drowning recruits, no matter what the motive of the march into the swamps.

Most of a morning was spent arguing motions to dismiss charges. Berman is convinced that the Marine Corps, through Major Charles Sevier, did not present a strong case against the sarge so far as negligence and oppression are concerned. When he presented written briefs to Navy Captain Klein, the defense counsel did not ask for dismissal of charges one and four—which involve drinking in barracks and drinking in the presence of a recruit. However, on the important charges: Oppressing a platoon by marching it into a creek; culpable negligence in the drowning of six men—Berman claims that the Government has not proved its point.

The sarge, who sits straight and soldierly in court every day, gets the jangles every time he thinks of being on the witness stand. He has already been advised that he has no problem except to tell the truth. He will admit to the few drinks of vodka, but his defense will be that if the boys in his platoon had followed him in the marshes, they would not have been in water over their heads and none would have drowned.

After that, the defense will call Lieutenant General "Chesty" Puller. He will not testify to anything that McKeon did, because he does not know McKeon and did not witness any of the acts with which the sarge is charged. But he will draw a bead on the current crop of generals, who want to soften the boot training here and in San Diego, who want to keep recruits happy, and who send bleeding-heart letters to parents about how well their boys are doing in boot camp.

"They were good boys," the sarge said today of all the recruits of Platoon 71. Staff Sergeant Matthew McKeon said this of the dead and the living, and he paused, and studied his clasping and unclasping hands before him on the witness stand at his court-martial. The judges waited until he found his voice again. "They were good boys, but they used the buddy-buddy system and I didn't want them to leave here with no discipline. I put them in the shock and fear stage when we first got them," he said, as defense counsel Emile Zola Berman sat and gave the accused his head. "No violence. Just kept them moving. They had good morale when we got them. But they were always slacking off. The drill instructors didn't see enough of them. In the morning, we had to take them to the range and the range officer had them all day until four thirty. Then I'd take them back to the barracks to wash 'em up and have mail call. Then chow. Then the swimming pool and some instructor would have them until eight thirty. Then I'd get 'em back and I'd try to have them in the racks (beds) by nine thirty, because they had to get up so early." He swallowed. "When they fell out, if the kid in front was slow, the one in back, instead of running over him, would slow up too. They'd all slow up. It was a lot of little things like that. Nothing big. A lot of little things. Sometimes I'd get them into the racks and they were supposed to be in there flat at attention. They'd start kidding around and I'd fall them out of bed and make them hit the deck and do pushups. Then back to the rack. Then out of bed again. This would work for maybe a day. Then they'd start slacking off again. Sergeant Scarborough was the range officer and he said it was the worst platoon he ever saw. Then Sergeant Huff started to complain. What they needed most of all was a foundation of discipline. I wouldn't care if they left this island with nothing else than discipline. That's the foundation. If you haven't got discipline, maybe you can make a good technician out of a man, but underneath, he hasn't got the proper foundation and when the time comes that he's needed alongside of his men—he just hasn't got it."

The sergeant said that he slept in barracks with his platoon on the night before the swamp march. He got up at five and had the recruits out of the racks by five thirty. The Catholic Mass detail left at six thirty, McKeon with them. At five after seven he left Mass, even though it wasn't quite over, and he went back and took the non-Catholics to chow.

"After breakfast, I shot the breeze with a couple of drill instructors." Along about ten, he called Private Lagone, recruit platoon leader, and said, "I don't want to see any dirty gear tomorrow. I saw some dirty laundry last week and I don't want to see it again." McKeon ordered the men to finish washing their laundry now. Lagone said the men had done it yesterday. McKeon said he had seen some dirty laundry in bags on this Sunday morning.

The sarge walked out of the D.I. room and down a hall and looked out at the back lawn. "Some boys were sitting on the steps writing letters. Everything looked normal."

McKeon felt a bad throbbing pain in his left leg and went back to the D.I. room and hit the rack. "I dozed off. The next thing I remember is hearing Sergeant Scarborough. I turned around. We talked about the platoon. "Who came in?" "Sergeant Muckler came in and he said, 'Whose platoon is that out on the back lawn?' I said it couldn't be mine and he kind of laughed. So I got up and looked out the back window and they were mine all right." The sergeant shook his head slowly. "Some were laying out on their backs. Some were on the grass on their elbows. They were laying all over the place." "Is there anything wrong with that?" asked Berman. "Sir," said McKeon, "that's a cardinal sin." The sarge ordered the men indoors on the double. This was his first platoon and he was now in trouble because his boss, Sergeant Huff, had condemned them as a "herd"; Sergeant Scarborough had said they were the worst he had ever seen, and Scarborough has eighteen years of service; now Muckler was kidding him about them and McKeon began to look like a poor drill instructor.

He called Private Butler in. Butler was assistant section leader. McKeon, who had confessed earlier on the witness stand that he had sometimes slapped men because of disobedience, did not slap Butler. He dressed the boy down for permitting this thing to happen. "I was going to give the men an up-and-down show with the rifle, but sometimes, when you make them raise and lower rifles in barracks, it knocks the dope off." "The dope?" "The rifle readings for windage and so forth."

The court was still laughing when Colonel Edward Hutchinson, the president of the seven-member group, ordered a recess.

The sarge stepped off the witness stand after 102 minutes of cross-examination and, while the press corps here thinks that he did very well and that Major Charles Sevier, the prosecutor, "took it easy," Staff Sergeant Matthew C. McKeon pleaded guilty to two charges: (1) drinking in barracks; (2) unlawfully killing six men through negligence. McKeon admitted to Major Sevier that he had drunk vodka in a barracks room. And, for the first time, he admitted that he led the seventy-eight men of Platoon 71 into Ribbon Creek with no more knowledge of what he was doing than a casual look at the water. This is self-admitted negligence.

Charge Three, Specification One, says that McKeon "unlawfully killed Thomas C. Hardeman, Donald F. O'Shea, Charles F. Reilly, Jerry L. Thomas, Leroy Thompson and Norman A. Wood, by leading them into the waters of Ribbon Creek in the dark without proper precautions . . . and without first familiarizing himself with the hazardous condition of the creek."

Let's listen to the testimony on that point, as the sarge sits straight and secure in the witness chair. Major Sevier stands twenty feet away, gesturing softly with a pencil as he works his man over. The major is a bullethead with the jawline of an English bulldog. "Had you ever entered Ribbon Creek before?" "No, sir. I never had." "You never made any reconnaissance that night?" "Before I stepped off the bank, I looked at it. It didn't look dangerous to me, sir." "How far did you walk into that stream?" (Thinking) "Two or three steps. I didn't hit water at first." "You turned right?" "Yes, sir. I went up about twenty-five or thirty feet. I didn't actually count them." "You made a turn and went downstream?" "Yes, sir." "Was all of your platoon in the water then?" "Yes, sir, I think so, sir." "You had a double line of men—about seventy-five—and the line measured about sixty feet up and down the stream and all those men were in?"

The sarge was silent. He thought for a moment. Then he said, "You're right, sir. Under normal conditions, there should have been forty inches between ranks. These were not normal times, sir." "Did you lead them into deep water?" "To be frank with you, sir, if I thought that one of those kids would drown, I'd have never taken them in. I never led them in water beyond my own chest."

If the seven judges of the military court take McKeon's words as an admission to Charge Three, Specification One, he could be sentenced to about a year at hard labor at the retraining command, Camp Allen, Virginia. With any sentence of over six months goes an automatic bad conduct discharge, plus forfeiture of rank and pay.

McKeon got on the stand at 8:38 A.M. and was finished with cross-examination by 10:30, with a ten-minute recess. He was polite, almost submissive. His spine never touched the back of the witness chair.

The court recessed at that time to greet the Marine commandant, General Randolph Pate, who had arrived at the jet complex outside Parris Island and who would testify briefly on the United States Marine training program. The publicity on this court-martial is now so overwhelming that the commandant himself has chosen to become a witness.

It was a real time of trial for McKeon, and he bore up well, but Major Sevier, who smiles throughout bayonet drill, scored now and then. "Did the men slack off?" "Yes, sir." "Don't you think it was the drill instructor slacking off?" "No, sir." "How many times did you slap these men?" "I don't remember exactly." "It must have been a great number of times if you can't even count?" "I can count." "But not that high? Did you set an example of discipline by bringing a bottle of vodka in and drinking?" "I grant you, sir—that that is not a good example of discipline." "When you entered the staff NCO club you had the intent to drink?" "Yes, sir. I wanted a can of beer." "Had your drinks affected you?" (With scorn and slowly) "No . . . sir. . . ." "It was the mark of manhood to show a recruit how to drink in barracks?" "It was a poor gesture, sir. I told you that." "Didn't you tell McPherson that the platoon wouldn't fall out until the movie started so that nobody would see you taking them on a night march?" "No, sir. That never entered my mind."

Before the sarge stepped off the witness stand, Colonel Edward Hutchinson, president of the court, had a question or two to ask about disciplinary action. He wanted to know how the sergeant would define it. McKeon said that he read about it in books and it was punishment, usually meted out by the commanding officer.

"Is it punishment?" the colonel asked gently. "I would say so. Yes, sir." "You think that there is a difference between teaching discipline and disciplinary action?" "Yes, Colonel." "Do you think that your commanding officer held you responsible for teaching discipline?" "Yes, sir." "Do you think he held you responsible for disciplinary action?" "No, sir."

In the final chapter of this movie court-martial, the United States Marines are coming, charging over the hill out of the sunset to the rescue of one of their own—Staff Sergeant Matthew C. McKeon, whose status has apparently changed from prisoner to hero. Lieutenant General Lewis Puller said that he joins General Pate in regretting "that this man was ever arrested."

He makes a commanding witness. When Puller left the stand, the spectators stood in respect and almost cheered him on his way. Women looked at McKeon, chest caved in, military bearing almost gone, and they wiped their eyes. Corporals and sergeants in the hall watched the pouter pigeon strut out of the school building, his riding crop swinging at his side, and they stood to attention and saluted and a few were misty-eyed.

Two former drill instructors had just finished testifying that they too had marched their platoons into the marshes on occasion, when Puller was called.

He traced his career for Emile Zola Berman. Then as a military expert, Puller was led into the McKeon story.

He observed that the mission of the United States Marine Corps —the object of all training—is "success in battle." He said that boot training is to prepare young Marines so that they will be successful in the next war, and that Napoleon stated a long time ago that the most important element in military training is discipline. Without it, an army is a mob.

This was important to McKeon because much of his defense

hinges on his claim that he took Platoon 71 out into Ribbon Creek to "teach them discipline and morale," not to punish them. The prosecution claims he was punishing them because he could not handle the men.

Berman recited some of the facts of this night march, and asked General Puller if, in his opinion, this constituted oppression. "In my opinion," the general said, causing two loud speakers on the left to screech, "it is not." Berman called Puller's attention to the fact that McKeon led his men into the swamp, and that he remained at their head throughout. "Any kind of a commander or leader is not worth his salt," the General said, "if he doesn't lead his troops." Berman then proceeded to recite a long hypothetical question about unscheduled night marches and asked Puller if he thought that it was right or wrong for the drill instructor to undertake one. "The reason that the American troops made out so poorly in the Korean war," the General snapped, "was the lack of night training. If we are going to win the next war, we had better devote fifty per cent of our training to night practice." What McKeon did, said Puller, is "good military practice."

Major Charles Sevier, who is now fighting a retreating action, had to cross-examine a legend. And no matter how carefully he framed his questions, General Puller kept testifying for the defense. On the matter of restricting the authority of drill instructors: "When I was on Parris Island as a recruit and a drill instructor in 1918, the drill instructors had practically unlimited authority." On the matter of going by the book: "I would train my troops in the way I thought they should be trained, regardless of what the directives said." On the matter of night marches: "The trouble with the American today is that he is so used to electric light that he is practically night blind." On McKeon's tragedy: "I would say that this night march was and is a deplorable accident. There was a case, recently, of an Army man who acted as coxswain on a Liberty boat off the Florida Keys. Seventeen men were drowned. Nothing got in the papers about it and the man wasn't even arrested. From what I have read in this morning's newspapers, General Randolph McCall Pate agrees and regrets that the man [Sergeant McKeon] was ever arrested."

At 11:30 A.M. Mr. Berman stood and announced that the defense rested. In three days and three hours, he had concluded a swift and hard-hitting defense.

The sarge waits. The tick of the clock is slow. By sundown, he will know whether he must bid Betty good-by a few days before their third baby is born, and go off to prison in Virginia, or whether he will be free after three weeks of court-martial.

McKeon, as noted, expects punishment. He courts it. Even though he maintains that his intentions were of the best, six young men are dead as a result of the sarge's discipline. Six who approached manhood will never reach it. Six sets of parents, reasonably content, are bereft. They sit at home dry-eyed, reading about McKeon. Some of them wish the worst for him. It is doubtful, however, that anyone condemns McKeon as mercilessly as he condemns himself.

In the years ahead, the mention of the name McKeon will conjure a lot of pictures in my mind. I will always remember the permanently sad, contrite face of Staff Sergeant Matthew C. McKeon, and I will remember how, when General Randolph McCall Pate slapped him on the back and walked away, the sarge turned to me and mumbled, "I just wanted to tell him how sorry I am, but I never got to say it." I will remember, too, the night that he confided to me that guilty or not guilty, he is going to quit the Marine Corps because, if he is acquitted, too many officers will have the ax out for him.

There is the picture of palm trees shimmering in the sun and the smell of flowers on fat oleander bushes. Tall swale grass undulating in a hot breeze and nineteen platoons marching on the drill grounds while little D.I.s in campaign hats swing alongside like collies flanking sheep. The sweet dark smile of Betty McKeon and the outrageous promises of Mrs. Thomas Costello to God if only He would set her brother free. The philosophical dignity of Captain Irving Nichols Klein as "judge" of the court-martial was balanced by the pugnacious face of Major Charles Sevier as prosecutor. The heat, the perpetual hum of fans, the pastel-green quonset huts, the slippery face of a sentry sweating out an early post. The guts of Sergeant Leland Blanding to get up and say, "I too marched platoons into the boondocks," after the prosecutor twice warned him that anything he said might be used against him. The search for analytic truth by Jim McKeon, the older brother. The food at the Gold Eagle Hotel and the night of the big excitement there when all the guests ran out on the porch to see a boat going through the drawbridge. A sign: "Colored folks, get your sandwiches here," at the back door of a small shop. The local dogs, who sleep all night in ditches in front of their homes; the speedboat races in the Beaufort River; the Spanish moss dripping like thick molasses from branches; the fire-engine red of the setting sun. The archaic typewriters in the press room; the good coffee the Marines sell at five cents a slug; the skinhead haircuts everywhere; the scores of court-martialed D.I.s, all busted down to nothing, all asking reporters, "How does it look for Mack? He's a good man. Don't let them hurt him."

The courtroom brilliance of Emile Zola Berman, who knew that the race haters were watching him because he is a Jew and who won them all with his charm. The fine knowledge of law shown by Berman's assistant, Howard Lester, which was noted by "Judge" Irving Klein. The courage of General Pate in trying to reverse a tide he had started; the competence and heart displayed by Lieutenant Colonel Alaric Valentin and Major John de Barr. The chill which the higher officers put on Commander Maurus Cook, Catholic chaplain, because he took McKeon out of the brig and made him a clerk. The homely friendliness of Mr. and Mrs. "Sammy" Samuel of the Gold Eagle, who will not give you a key to your room because "this is a family hotel." The roar out of Lieutenant General Lewis Puller, when he said that he and General Pate regretted that McKeon ever had been arrested. The singsong cadence count of Southern D.I.s.

The pajama-type sports shirts of the press; the kidding one writer got because he always wore a jacket. The competence of Press Information Officer Captain Wood, who was promoted to major in the middle of the court-martial. The smell of curry in the evening. The Scotches downed by the men who judge McKeon. Brigadier General Sam Marshall walking out into the boondocks to find out how deep it is.

The TV men on the lawn in front of this little schoolhouse, waiting under the trees like bird watchers. The change in millions of people who started by hoping that McKeon would be hit with the book, and who ended by hoping that the Corps would set him free.

"I ask you not to send him to the brig," defense counsel said to Staff Sergeant Matthew C. McKeon's judges, "and I ask you not to take him out of service." Emile Zola Berman won a light verdict for the sarge. He was found guilty of drinking, and the negligence count. No others. Now he wanted a light sentence. If the judges gave McKeon a maximum sentence on the count of drinking in barracks and the count of negligence in leading six men to their deaths, he could serve three years at hard labor and he could lose rank and pay too. No one expects that. "If there is one time in his life when he belongs with his wife," Berman said, "that time is now." He cited McKeon's perfect record as a Marine, as a family man, as a religious man. "He has already served forty-five days in the brig," Berman said pleadingly. "I cannot see how a jail sentence will help."

The judges were gentle with the sarge. They could have been rough. Out of four charges, they said "guilty" on two, "not guilty" on the others. The moment of the reading of the verdict was a dramatic one.

Sergeant McKeon had been getting edgy. He was at Father Cook's house all afternoon while the military court deliberated. He tried to prove that he wasn't edgy. He laughed. He stood. He paced back and forth. He patted Betty on the shoulder. He maintains that win or lose he will quit the Corps. We were shooting the breeze together. I went into an argument with him about how the Corps had not let him down, but that he was now going to let the Corps down. The sarge half listened. He didn't seem to be impressed. When I finished, I felt like a flag-waver. He smiled. "I'll think about it," he said.

After thinking about it overnight, he told Jim Kilgallen that he will stay in the Marines. "If they'll have me," he said. I asked why the sudden change. He grinned. "You talked me into it," he said. "I'm no quitter."

All day yesterday, time ticked. His brothers, Jim and Ned, and Anne and Tom Costello made small talk and kidded each other. They looked at watches and they talked about home and they talked about children and they talked about that wonderful Emile Zola Berman. The sarge and Betty went to the chapel and prayed and came out and Matt looked at his watch.

The judges started to deliberate at 12:39 P.M. The seven of them argued in an air-conditioned room in the Administration Building on this base. The reporters kept a deathwatch in the press room and, one by one, they looked at their watches and went out for sandwiches. Time clicked. Some women were at the soft drink machine in front of the court and they talked about the swimming pool and who was at it and how you can't watch the children close enough; they'd drive you right out of your mind. Either eating hot dogs or falling in the water. It was four fifteen.

In Bachelor Officers Quarters, Defense Counsel Berman dozed. His bare toes kept twitching. The sun came through the blinds and made dark bars across his face. The phone rang. He jumped. "That a verdict?" "No," a voice said. "A man wants to know what McKeon had for lunch."

The second hand moves swiftly. At five o'clock it was the "happy hour" in the officers' club and everyone was there, because only on Friday in this hour all drinks are twenty-five cents. They talked about the verdict. They talked about the sarge. They talked about his pregnant wife. They talked about the handsome Major Charles Sevier. Two M.P.s with arm bands sat in the court shooting the breeze. They watched the school clock. It was six ten. "Chow," one said. The other nodded sleepily. "Chow," he murmured. "Good old ever-lovin' cotton-pickin' chow."

The sarge was back at six twenty. Now he was pacing. He stood and put his tie on. Major John de Barr stood behind him. They did an Alphonse and Gaston act trying to give the mirror to each other. Betty McKeon sat lumpily, out of shape and sagging, in a corner. She was watching her man's back. She was thinking.

At six thirty, Colonel Edward Hutchinson, president of the court, sent word in that the court would convene shortly after seven. Reporters raced for typewriters. Bulletins were rapped out. High-ranking officers began to show up. Phones jangled all over the island. "They're coming in," the word went. "They're coming in."

At seven time was still ticking slowly. The courtroom was jammed. The faces were expressionless. Everybody had waited three weeks for this. Major Sevier sat on the small of his back and glanced at the clock. Captain Irving Klein sat on his high dais. He looked angry. He glared at one and all. A man with a movie camera made a few feet of film and was ordered out of the court. He said he didn't know. Berman came in. An hour before, he had told me, "They won't hit him hard. These are real Marines, my friend."

McKeon sat in front of me. Betty sat three rows behind me. Anne Costello was still praying as she sat. At seven twenty-three someone yelled, "Everybody rise." The court came in. The colonels and majors looked grim. Some had sheaves of papers in their hands. They sat. Colonel Hutchinson, father of two Marines, sat slowly and flicked his microphone open. "The court will come to order," he said. Everybody sat. Major Sevier said, "Let the court show that all the interested parties to this action are present." Klein nodded to Hutchinson to proceed. The people in the court stopped breathing. Captain Klein said:

"Will counsel for the accused, and the accused please rise?"

Without a word, the sarge and Berman stood. Klein nodded. "Advance." They walked over to a position directly before the judge. Colonel Hutchinson took a paper and read from it. He shook his dark head, reading slowly, pronouncing each word as though it were being burned in the floor. McKeon and Berman stood to attention. McKeon heard isolated words like "guilty" and "not guilty," but he told me later he did not understand what they meant or which charges the colonel was talking about.

"It is my duty to inform you," the colonel said, "that the court in closed session and on secret written ballot, two thirds of the court concurring at the time each ballot was taken, find you:

"On Count One, Specification One, guilty. [Drinking in barracks.] On Charge Two and the specification thereunder, not guilty. [Oppressing a platoon by marching them into a creek.] On Charge Three, guilty with the exception that the word culpable preceding negligence shall be changed to simple. [This was negligence in not reconnoitering the creek before leading the platoon in it.] On Charge Four and the specification thereunder, not guilty." [This was drinking in the presence of a recruit.]

It was over.

The clock said seven forty. The spectators began to breathe. Some began to think. There was a buzz. He had not been hit hard. That was the word. The most he would get was a year. The probability was that McKeon would end up, after an appeal, with six months or less and a fine. The sergeants in the hall were worried about something else. "Will he get a B.C.D.?" This is a bad conduct discharge. No one knew at the time.

Captain Klein spoke. "It is now seven forty-five," he said. "Or rather, nineteen forty-five. I would propose that the presentencing procedure be postponed until nine tomorrow morning." Colonel Hutchinson nodded. Sentence will come in the morning. He looked tired. The court recessed.

I reached across the press rail and grabbed McKeon's hand. He didn't know whether to be happy or not. He still did not understand the verdict. Major Sevier grabbed Berman's hand. Captain Klein began to beam. Betty McKeon hurried to the hall. Matty hugged her. Both began to cry at once.

"It's all right," he kept whispering. "It's all right. No strain."

Everybody began shaking hands with everybody else. There was no shouting. Someone pointed to Berman. The big bad New York lawyer was weeping. He tried to laugh through it. "I stood to attention, didn't I? Didn't I stand to attention in front of those judges?"

Anne McKeon Costello was crying. Jim McKeon, the oldest and the worrier, said, "Now tell me something. Exactly what does this mean?"

The sarge felt that he had been kicked in the pants. That was obvious. He walked up and down outside the courtroom with his brother-in-law, Thomas Costello, and he kept shaking his head. "Well," he said with a very faint smile, "I'll be physically free in nine months. I'll never be mentally free. I'll be saying the names of those six dead kids, over and over, the rest of my life."

His wife stood leaning against a porch post. She was watching him closely, her eyes squinted against the late sun. Her man drew nine months. She's just finishing a term of those proportions, although hers was a happy sentence. She did not approach him. Just stood watching, knowing all the signs as every wife knows them. Letting him cool a little before she came closer.

Emile Zola Berman, who had won a victory, looked like a man who had lost. He paced up and down inside the screen door, head down, shoulders hunched. "No comment," he said. "No comment from me, and nothing from the sergeant." He wasn't thinking about Sergeant Robert Rawlings, the Korean hero who started serving eight months yesterday for merely slapping recruits. He didn't drown anybody.

Reporters were racing up and down the halls, and bells were ringing in the press room. Fifteen phones were in use and some men were roaring that they couldn't even get a dial tone. Two reporters hurried out in the alley to get to McKeon. They stuck their hands out. "It wasn't so bad, Mack," they said. "This is only the start. This sentence will never stand up when it comes before the Board of Review." He got eight months.

Colonel Edward L. Hutchinson said that McKeon will get a bad conduct discharge, which will deprive McKeon of a lot of GI rights. It may sound bad. But it isn't. The parents of any of the six who drowned would be willing for their boys to draw that sentence if they were only alive to take it.

McKeon and his brother-in-law walked away from the reporters. "Hey," the sarge said turning around. "I want to thank you guys for being so nice to me. Honest to God, and listen—would you please say thanks to all the people who sent the letters and the telegrams and phoned—all the people who said prayers for me? I don't know where to go to thank them, and you guys can do it in your column. Especially thank the people in the Valley. They'll understand." The "people in the Valley" are the folks of the sarge's home town.

Major Charles B. Sevier thinks that McKeon will not start serving his sentence for at least six weeks, which means that the sarge will be at Mrs. McKeon's side next week when she expects her third child. The court-martial record is heavy, and, when it is all typed, it will be jammed into many large manila envelopes and sent by Marine plane to Navy Secretary Charles Thomas, in Washington. It is he who must decide what is to be done with the sarge. He will probably convene a board of review, composed of law officers, who will go over every word of testimony. They have the power to reduce a sentence. They haven't the power to enhance it.

Private Matthew C. McKeon may go to Camp Allen, Virginia, to the retraining camp, to start serving his sentence. If the forty-five days he has already served are taken off his sentence, he may do about six months with good behavior. In that case, he would be home with Betty and the children around April 1. Then he will start hunting for a job. He told me that he is going to need one bad, and he would like to work in or around Boston or Worcester.

The McKeon court-martial is over. Except for the bad conduct discharge, I think that the sarge got off lightly indeed. The courts hand out too many BCDs and the result is an enormous waste of the taxpayers' money plus the throwing of combat experience into the trash heap. For example, McKeon's eleven years of training in the U.S. Navy and the Marine Corps has cost the United States $25,000 in salary alone, not counting what it cost to clothe him and feed him and to keep him in good health. Somewhere, yesterday, a kid enlisted in the Corps, and you exchanged that youngster for McKeon. My feeling is that perhaps punishments should be heavier, and that courts should be restricted in handing out BCDs and dishonorable discharges. Remember, the sarge had no record. He was never arrested. He didn't have a blemish against his name until the night he marched Platoon 71 into Ribbon Creek.

The sarge's rating as a drill instructor was higher than average; his gunnery marks were higher than average; he had combat ribbons from aboard the carrier *Essex* and from the Marine Corps in Korea. He was a career Marine who was in for life. He did not aspire to be an officer; he wanted to be a D.I. and nothing else.

Parris Island goes back to its routine. The hoopla of the most dramatic court-martial in history is over. The typewriters sit silent. Emile Zola Berman and his assistant, Howard Lester, are on a plane homeward bound. Major Sevier goes back to his tank battalion at Camp Lejeune. Major John de Barr and Lieutenant Colonel Alaric Valentin, of the defense corps, go back to the humdrum life of fine Marines in peacetime.

Captain Irving N. Klein, the law officer, returns to Washington, having been as impartial a judge as this reporter has ever seen. Colonel Hutchinson, president of the court, is back at work in Camp Lejeune.

The sarge is at his little bungalow in Port Royal, South Carolina. There is no more adulation. No more stacks of letters. Just quiet. The phone that was put in temporarily by Father Maurus Cook will be yanked out. Betty is tired. There are letters to write to Matty's mother in Worcester, a baby to be born.

McKeon has nothing to say. He's a Marine.*

---

* McKeon was stripped of stripes, back pay and privileges. He was sent to Cherry Point, North Carolina, as a rear-rank buck private. Within one year, he was voted Marine-of-the-Month. He served his time. Then he quit and went home.

Robert Wagner

The cold white marble corridor of New York City Hall is the mausoleum of politicians. One hundred and two ambitious mayors have died there. They leave—discredited, disgusted, disgraced, disenchanted and, sometimes, dispossessed. Few have escaped oblivion. And yet, the Quiet Man who now walks the corridors uses the walls for burying his political enemies.

His name is Robert Ferdinand Wagner. He is a plump dandy, five feet seven inches tall, fifty-four years old, a man with a mechanical smile, poached eyes, and the gravelly voice of a native. "Nobody loves him," a politician said, "except on election day." Wagner is a Democrat who is concluding his third four-year term.

Beyond that, it is easier to relate what he isn't than what he is. He is not a playboy, not a drunkard, not a charmer, not an orator, not a spotlight seeker, not bossy, never loses his temper, never says anything spectacular, and yet, in the past four years, he has beaten Tammany Hall into impotence and has become the political proprietor of New York City and the Democratic leader of New York State.

Robert F. Kennedy could not have run for the U.S. Senate without Mayor Wagner's approving nod. He understood this, and he pleaded for the nod. Congressman Buckley refused to truckle to Wagner, and was smashed. Carmine De Sapio, Tammany boss, fought Mayor Wagner and lost the city and his own post. Politicians great and small have assessed the mayor as the "nothing" son of the late Senator Robert Wagner, the man who wrote the Labor Relations Act. Almost all of them are politically dead.

This man, who now emerges on the national scene as a Democratic Party leader, is an admixture of strengths and weaknesses. His strength is that he is always on the side of the right; he is conscientious to the point of pain. As a mayor, he is also a workhorse and, except for a few vacations each year, works from eight thirty in the morning until midnight every day. He also makes himself available to all of the eight million New Yorkers who wish to speak to him. His weakness is that he is a procrastinator; he requires too much time to make up his mind. At times, he appears to be slow-witted and humorless.

His mind is sharp, but he permits himself to be bogged in detail. In the privacy of his home at Gracie Mansion, Wagner flashes a good sense of humor. His current joke is about a man who was walking along Broadway complaining about New York aloud:

"Lousy city . . . the subways are crowded and smelly; the streets are dirty; people get mugged in the parks; kids knife each other; the traffic is so congested that you can't drive a car; the air is polluted . . ." At this point, an elderly woman listens, and says, "Sir, if you don't like New York, why don't you go down to City Hall and complain to the mayor?" The man draws himself up in dignity and says, "Madam, I am the mayor."

Wagner spends three and a half billion dollars of New York's money every year. This is a bigger budget than most nations have. From the city, he takes $50,000 a year, an ancient house, a Cadillac sedan, and a cook and butler. For a time, he aspired to his father's seat in the United States Senate. In 1952, he couldn't even win the nomination. In 1956, his party endorsed him and Wagner lost to Jacob Javits.

Now his ambition is to be Mayor of New York longer than anyone else. He will run for a fourth term next year. If he wins, Wagner will achieve what no other metropolitan hero has done. And, unless he changes his political sights, he will run for the same office again and again. After all, next to the Presidency of the United States and the Governorship of New York, the Mayoralty of New York is the third most important post in the country.

Personally, Wagner is a sentimentalist who is ashamed of it. The mayor and the man are different beings. Bob Wagner revered his father, and still does. He makes pals of his sons. Bobbie, twenty, is a senior at Harvard College. Duncan, sixteen, is at Kent Hills Preparatory School in Maine.

Most of all, he loved Susan, his wife. Last year, when the doctors told him she would die of cancer, he sat alone, pounding a fist on his knee and rhythmically repeating, "Why her? How is it the crooks and murderers live on, the thieves thrive, and my Susan has to go? Why?"

She was a blonde, gracious woman, as pretty as the Pogany portrait which captures the mayor's eye every night over the fireplace. She died on March 2, 1964, and, for once, the imperturbable little man lost his composure. He not only wept, but he could not go back to Gracie Mansion. He slept at the Carlyle Hotel for months.

Then his sons came back from school and said, "Let's go home." He went. Now he faces the multitudes in City Hall loneliness

every day, and the silent rooms of Gracie Mansion every night.
When he awakens each morning, Mayor Wagner reaches for his
Susan. "I must learn to stop doing that," he says apologetically.

De Witt Clinton finished City Hall in 1812. Three years later,
City Hall finished him. Once, this classic building was imposing.
Now it rests inside a craggy volcano of skyscrapers, the poplar
trees reaching listlessly for a thin bar of sunlight.

The corridors are crowded with petitioners. They arrive with
the morning light. They lounge all day, waiting for a word with
Mayor Robert Wagner. They leave with the sun. There are
cameras and cables and microphones and reporters and photographers. There are policemen and politicians and party hacks and
publicity hounds. There are Union Leaders, Race Leaders,
Women's Club Leaders, Corporation executives, Commissioners,
Dinner Chairmen, Builders, Planners, Economic Experts, and
People.

At eleven the mayor arrives in a black Cadillac. He walks
swiftly to the little office in the northwest corner of the ground
floor. There is a small desk, a fireplace flanked by American standards, a few chairs, and an appointment calendar framed on the
desk.

The mayor wears a plain gray suit, a striped tie, and glistening
black shoes. His assistants come in one at a time. Leslie Slote,
Acting Executive Secretary, watches the mayor light a cigarette
and says: "The boys will be in in a minute. You're proclaiming
C.Y.O. week. It's a picture and a proclamation. No speech."

Wagner sets the cigarette on a tray, greets the C.Y.O. group,
waits for the television and still cameramen to get ready, and
adjusts his breast pocket handkerchief and his smile. The newspapermen say, "One more, Mr. Mayor." "That's got it." The
group leaves. He picks up the cigarette and glances at the calendar. "What's next?" he says. "The Girl Scouts?" It's the Girl Scouts.

He averages four minutes per ceremony. Between them, Mrs.
Bernice McCray, his personal secretary, hurries in with letters to
be read or signed. She has three assistant secretaries. Slote handles
press relations. Frank Doyle is in charge of personnel. Paul
Bragdon is assistant in political and civic matters. Julius Edelstein
is Executive Assistant to the Mayor, in charge of Planning and
Policy.

Each one has a large stake in Wagner's future. Each one is
bright and jaded. When their advice is poor, the mayor gives them
his left ear—the bad one. He's a good listener. He speaks softly. In
anger, he frowns and stares at the object of his disapproval. Even

when he is one hour behind the appointment schedule—which is every day—Wagner will not permit his chauffeur to drive over the speed limit, or use a horn to pass a car.

At eleven fifty-five he walks upstairs to the Board of Estimate Chamber to proclaim United Nations Day. Visiting diplomats give him a standing ovation. Wagner faces the crowded chamber, bows, smiles, nods to the Department of Sanitation Band sitting under a portrait of Thomas Jefferson, reads the proclamation, and leaves.

On the main floor, Slote is asking another assistant, "Is he appearing at the Puerto Rican rally tonight?" "No." "Better ask him. He makes promises on street corners and doesn't tell us." "No, he's appearing at the Latin-American rally." "Yeah? Maybe that's it."

At twelve eleven, the mayor is back in his office, signing mail. He makes a phone call to Deputy Mayor Cavanaugh. The deputy mayor's unmarried sister Barbara has been Wagner's companion at functions which require couples. The mayor's friends are aware that, since the death of Mrs. Wagner, Miss Cavanaugh is the only female with whom he feels "relaxed."

At twelve thirty-two, Wagner hurries down the white steps of City Hall, trailing a herringbone topcoat, gets into the rear seat, snaps his fingers and says, "Come on. Come on." The others pile in front and on jump seats. En route to the Garment Center, Wagner reads a speech silently. He memorizes the best phrases. An assistant puffs like a fish on sand. The mayor grins. "It doesn't wear me out," he says. "I like the job. Where is this thing?" "Thirty-eighth and Seventh."

Cross-town traffic is choked. The car cannot move. Someone suggests that trucks should be made to deliver by night. "No," Wagner says. "It won't work. The truck drivers are family men. They're entitled to be home with their wives and children at night."

He looks at his watch. He's late again. The mayor gets out of the car and walks to the rally. On the sidewalks, men pushing racks of clothing and women walking with children recognize him. Some say hello. Others merely stare at his back. He walks fast, nodding and smiling.

At the rally, he climbs steps to the top of a blue Plymouth, takes a microphone, and addresses fifteen hundred citizens who stand behind carpenter's horses. Afterward, he autographs bits of paper for twenty minutes. A police sergeant tries to free the mayor. Wagner frowns. "No, no," he says. "Let them come to me."

He is forty minutes late for a television program at NBC. The day has just begun.

At one thirty-five, Mayor Robert Wagner is walking through a hall at the National Broadcasting Company. His appointment is to answer questions from first-time voters, on a youth forum. He sits under lights for a little make-up, and strides swiftly to a studio where he sits smiling, waiting for the tapes to start.

He answers the questions with the usual neutrality. He agrees with the youngsters who pose the questions, and permits them to make the speeches, nodding agreeably. Wagner is in a perpetual state of rationalization. He sometimes sees good where there isn't any. Often, he not only forgives his enemies, but gives them jobs. Forgives, but not forgets.

He is so unassuming that he doesn't even have a special license plate on his car. At baseball and football games, he will not sit in a box seat, nor take a bow. And yet, Wagner is now so important that even the newspapers which oppose him assign two men to cover his activities. The reporters have an organization called The Inner Circle, which lampoons all politicians at an annual dinner-show.

The event occurs in March. Because Mrs. Wagner died at that time, The Inner Circle did an unprecedented thing. It postponed the dinner until June, then opened the show with a song: "Hello, Bob, Hello—You're Still Tops with Us."

In the afternoon, he appointed a lady to head New York's Anti-Poverty Campaign, posed with NAACP leaders; appeared at two luncheons without lunching; promised to appear at three dinners that night, and got into Gracie Mansion, the mayor's official home, for two hours between four and six. Even this time was used for work.

The Latin-American mayors and their wives were present for a cocktail party. On the second floor, representatives of the Police and Fire Departments waited with Council President Paul Screvane to negotiate new wages. A reporter from an "opposition" paper sat in an anteroom waiting for a political interview.

Henry Schmidt, the mayor's fat German butler, runs the mansion. It isn't a mansion, really. It's a white manor house which stands on the edge of the East River at 89th Street. It was sold by a Mr. Gracie for $2,500 in 1797. The floors creak under broadloom. On the porches, new paint flakes off old. Only the kitchen and the landscaped lawns appear to be worth salvaging.

The butler probably knows more about Mayor Wagner than anyone except his two sons. He awakens Wagner at seven forty-five each morning and, in deference to rising blood pressure, serves lamb chops instead of bacon and eggs. The mayor turns on a bedroom radio at once to listen to the newscasts.

He bathes, shaves and dresses as he listens. Mail is brought up from City Hall and he reads and signs. There are two phones, no switchboard. One is a direct line from City Hall; the other is unlisted. At nine he is downstairs, ready for confidential appointments.

No matter where he turns, there is a reminder of his Susan. In the living room is a huge oil painting of her over the fireplace. In the sitting room is a silver-framed photo on an end table. Around the house are inscribed photos of kings and queens and princes and prime ministers, but the likenesses of the late Mrs. Wagner have only one rival in the gallery—a photo of the mayor's father on a grand piano.

He leaves, and the policeman at the sentry box salutes as the black car eases out of the driveway. With him in the car is Sergeant Bill Wichart, a jut-jawed policeman who is one of three bodyguards. Each man works twenty-four hours, then takes two days off.

Mayor Wagner will return around midnight. He will walk into the mansion with the morning newspapers under his arm. He goes upstairs to the big square bedroom in the northwest corner. Alone, he hides from his loneliness. A white portable television is moved to the foot of the double bed. The newspapers are dropped on the spare pillow.

The beige counterpane has been turned down by Henry. Two white phones are silent on the night table. They guard a package of Marlboro cigarettes. There are pictures of Bobbie and Duncan, but pictures are mute. There is a sofa and two wing chairs.

He reads and looks at the late movie, especially if it's a Western. On the third floor is a big attic. It speaks louder of sentimentality and loneliness than the bedroom. In the darkness is a box of footballs, a plastic Christmas tree, a set of electric trains, a closet with Susan's clothing, a military campaign hat, two tennis racquets, some plaques and awards, and children's games.

Robert Wagner hides his feelings. I prodded him. "When I wake up in the morning, I expect my wife to be around—you know, to talk about things. For the minute, I forget she isn't here. It hurts. The rest of the day, it doesn't bother me at all. I get it again late at night when I walk into that bedroom."

He meets more people every day than the President of the United States. Still, Robert Wagner is the man nobody knows. . . .

Billy Rose

The last of the exquisite baronial mansions is at 56 East 93rd Street, New York. It is a rare jewel, squeezed between apartment houses. Its halls echo to the delicately slippered feet of Billy Rose. It's his. The solemn faces that look down from the wall may be signed by Goya and Gainsborough and Rembrandt, and they are cherished by the lonely storyteller who walks the halls.

Mr. Rose is called a showman. He produced *Jumbo* and *Carmen Jones* and the Aquacade and many other spectacles. He isn't really a showman. He has also been called a dollar machine, but he isn't that either. He's a picture framer. If the picture has real beauty—whether it's a painting or a show or a live girl—Billy Rose will tack a frame around it and hang it somewhere for everybody to see.

Few men have more appreciation for true beauty, and few men started with less of it. Billy Rose was born Rosenbloom on the East Side. He never knew a time when his father brought twenty-five dollars a week home. The Rosenblooms were poor among the poor. They moved frequently to save a month's rent, and there were times when Billy and his two younger sisters were sent to bed without a meal.

The flat on Allen Street was full of people who commiserated with one another. Still, there was a clannish loyalty, almost a joy, in poverty and the neighbors shared the happiness of birth and marriage, and wept with grief at illness and death. It was and is a place of Yiddish lamentation and philosophy—most of all, of neighbors.

In their nothingness these people had everything. The beach was a fire escape; Delmonico's was the icebox in the kitchen; love was a stout mother pouring foreign diminutives in a child's ear; the mountains were a climb to a tar-paper roof; God was in the shadows behind a flickering Menorah; wealth was a fifteen-dollar cloth coat; friendship was a gruff voice saying, "So what's new?"

The map says that it is six miles from Allen Street to East 93rd. The map lies. It is a million miles and it costs a dollar a mile. Billy Rose made it because he was born running. He made it because he had to do something better. He wanted money too—he doesn't knock it—but he had to shine brightly at something.

He was still a boy when he was champion stenographer. He worked for Bernard M. Baruch and the War Industries Board in 1918. Billy was earning two hundred dollars a week when his father was still trying to make twenty-five. Whenever he reached a point where he thought the job could not be done better, Billy Rose quit and tried something else.

The body was small—he looked like a dissipated jockey—but the mind was big and the ambition was enormous. He wrote songs: "It's Only a Paper Moon," "Me and My Shadow," "The Night Is Young and You're So Beautiful," "Without a Song." He wrote others too, and these brought in $50,000 a year in royalties.

When Mr. Rose felt that he was writing lyrics about as well as anyone in the business, he dropped it. He took his money into the night club business. He opened the Casino de Paree, the first New York theater-restaurant. He followed with the Casa Mañana, and The Diamond Horseshoe. His places made money, and he kept the money because he had bigger plans and Mr. Rose does not believe in partners.

He owns 100 per cent of everything he touches. The feet of his wives touched the cold marble in the foyer. If it is done often enough, it will chill the heart. Mr. Rose married, in turn, Fannie Brice, Eleanor Holm and Joyce Matthews.

Billy did more than love them. He adored them and spoiled them and, in time, the chill was on them. Miss Brice was Baby Snooks. Miss Holm was a great swimmer. Joyce Matthews had a beauty with inner lighting. The best way to lose anything is to hold it too tight. He lost them one at a time.

He produced shows and he banked $250,000 a year.

He wrote a newspaper column called Pitching Horseshoes, and he bought Broadway theaters—the Ziegfeld and the National. When Billy gambled at Monte Carlo, and found that he couldn't beat the roulette wheel, he tried to buy the place. The French wouldn't sell.

Instead, he bought the mansion on East 93rd Street. It's a big marble mansion, and the butler can hear the dainty feet of Mr. Rose clicking from a long way off.

I walked into the lobby of the mansion. There was a sweep of white tile with black edging. A butler took my hat and coat in silence. There was an elevator to the right. It took me to a big smoking room. Billy Rose, better looking at sixty than at fifty, met me at the elevator.

The center halls are spacious. The stairway curves like a pretty hip. Everywhere there are old masters hanging on the walls, each face looking brightly or grimly down the centuries. An alabaster sphinx rests on a footstool. Logs flicker discreetly in a fireplace. A sterling cigarette box gleams under a table lamp.

There is a small office with a desk, a blackboard, and a Dow-Jones ticker. Here Billy Rose sits from nine thirty until two thirty buying and selling blue chip stocks. His Wall Street business amounts to more than a million dollars a year and he divides it among Hutton, Ungeleiter and Dreyfus.

The little loner chalks symbols on his blackboard, feeds the ticker tape through graceful hands, and phones his orders to buy or sell. On his desk is a big television offer to put on a network show. Billy Rose thinks he will decline it. NBC doesn't understand that Rose would have to run the show alone. They have a clause in the contract about "good taste." Who knows what that is?

He bought the Ziegfeld Theater sixteen years ago for $630,000. Billy, as always, paid cash and paid in full. He has been offered $3,000,000 for the dream theater, but he doesn't want it. The land alone, he reasons, is worth two hundred dollars a square foot and he has fifteen thousand feet of it. He bought the old National Theater and renamed it the Billy Rose Theater.

Monuments are important to a poor youngster. He can stop anything in the big house except the clocks. At sixty, Billy has riches and esteem and powerful friends. Somewhere along the line he lost four women: his mother and three wives. He walks the halls alone, listening to the echo of shoe on marble.

In a corner, he has his own barbershop. It has a chair, a lot of equipment, a striped barber pole that lights and turns, an electric horse, a massage table and barbells. How frequently can a man get a haircut?

In several rooms there is an electric coffeemaker plugged and ready. He likes coffee. There are electric chafing dishes with chicken livers and cocktail frankfurters so that, if Mr. Rose feels hungry at three in the morning, something is always ready.

The Spartan spark is in the bedroom. It is big, but against a wall is an old iron bedstead used by one of Napoleon's generals. It is small and light. There is room for one. Outside, in a wall, is a built-in refrigerator. Down one flight there is a poolroom with a full-sized pool table overhung with two big orange globes.

Billy likes to shoot pool and he can run six or eight balls. There is an ornate card table, a black lacquered snack bar and, outside the room, a chilled wine cellar fronted by a bank vault door.

When he tires of the mansion, Billy goes to Tavern Island. This is a small body of land off Darien, Connecticut. He bought it outright, including the big house on it. He has servants there, but no friends.

A few weeks ago, he wrote a will. In it, he left something for each of the old retainers. He left something for his two sisters and for his last wife, Joyce Matthews, and her child. There is nothing in it for Eleanor Holm because as Billy says, "She's already been taken care of. We're the best of friends and she has nothing to worry about."

Most of his millions—perhaps ten when the estate is liquidated—will go to the Billy Rose Foundation. It will beautify "the gifted in the performing arts." If a good actress needs to have teeth straightened or scars covered, the foundation will do it, in secrecy.

I asked him if he had ever gone hungry over a period of time. The intelligent face smiled faintly. "Once between jobs, I lived on two five-cent packages of salted peanuts a day for several weeks. They are the cheapest and the most nourishing."

Father John Kelly

The man in Misericordia Hospital looked tired. His big ugly hands traced a silent pattern on the bedspread. His eyes searched the ceiling. Johnny Kelly was moving off stage.

Once upon a long ago, he was a rough, tough kid. The voice was loud and Brooklyn in timbre. Johnny Kelly could play ball, defend himself with his fists, argue ably on subjects about which he knew little, and swim. One day he was swimming at Coney Island and a big wave picked him up, spun him, and jammed him headfirst into the sand.

The kid was fourteen. He was in a spasm when they dug him out. After that, John Bernard Kelly was a quiet boy. He went for long walks alone. He meditated. At seventeen, he insisted that he had a girl friend. Everyone knew that John Bernard Kelly had never been seen with a girl.

He studied for the priesthood at Dunwoodie, in Yonkers. One of the priests who taught Johnny was Father Duffy. It was Father Duffy who saw the big rough kid for what he was: a poet.

After his ordination, the young priest developed spasms. They averaged six a week. The doctors found no evidence of epilepsy. No evidence of brain damage. It was Monsignor Lavelle, Pastor of

St. Patrick's Cathedral, who broke the bad news to Father Kelly.
He took the young priest to a baseball game.

The white-haired monsignor squinted out toward short. "He
couldn't play that position if they left him alone in the park," the
monsignor said softly. "He'd make a great right fielder, but that's
the way it goes. They keep putting people into the wrong jobs.

"Now take yourself, Johnny. You're not going to get a church. I
wish there was a nicer way of saying it, but there it is. We can't
use a priest who might become ill in the middle of Mass. You
understand that?"

Father Kelly clasped his hands between his knees and bowed
his head. He understood. The monsignor nodded. "All right. As
long as I draw the breath of life, John, there will always be a room
with your name on it at the Cathedral. I don't want you ever to
forget it. His Eminence has thought about your particular problem and he has decided to organize a Catholic Writers Guild.
You're head of it."

The spasms lessened a little in the middle years. Three a week.
The Writers Guild bought an old brownstone building on West
71st Street. For years, the priest could eat nothing except melba
toast and honey. Still, when he met writers, his big fists would
curl, his jaw would come out, and he would demand to know why
more of them were not writing about his girl friend—the Blessed
Mother.

He was at his best when writers were discouraged. His cure was
to roar with rage, the long arms flailing, the voice demanding how
a writer with all this talent could afford to sit and brood like a
schoolgirl. Father Kelly used this rough therapy on me when I
didn't have two dimes and no editor wanted anything I might
write.

Last year, when he passed seventy, Father Kelly's spasms had
almost disappeared. He sat long hours alone in the brownstone
house among the dusty books. He sat alone.

He wrote doggerel and he wrote about his girl friend. When the
book was finished, it was called *Heaven Is a Circus*. No publisher
begged for it. In a final humiliation, Father Kelly borrowed
money and published it himself.

The man in Misericordia Hospital looked tired. His big ugly
hands traced a silent pattern on the bedspread. His eyes searched
the ceiling. Johnny Kelly was moving off stage.

Alone. He looked up once, and he mumbled, "I know who you
are," but he didn't. He had an appointment . . .

Mr. Foot-and-a-Half

The yard master in Jersey City posted the assignment sheet. The engineers read it and no one was surprised that Foot-and-a-Half drew the best train. He was an engineer's engineer and he had put many years on the Pennsylvania Railroad trying to combine speed with safety. The best train was not the New York-Chicago Flyer. It was the night newspaper train.

The Express, in 1905, made many stops, all the way from Trenton to Gary, Indiana. The newspaper train made none, except for water. It left the Exchange Place yards at 2 A.M.—that's when the morning presses began to run—and it carried six baggage cars and nothing else. It ran to Harrisburg on the Philadelphia division and it made the 190 miles in about three hours.

Foot-and-a-Half had lost all the toes on one foot before the turn of the century. He never talked about it, and no one ever called him Foot-and-a-Half to his face. No one ever told him he was the best. He knew it.

The only fear he had was of sleep. He said that more engineers were killed while dozing than through mistakes in block signals. If he felt fatigued before a run, he would notify the yard master that he did not feel well, and Foot-and-a-Half would be docked a day's pay rather than pull a train out while tired.

He eased the Newspaper Special out of the yards, the big tower lights staring at his gleaming steam locomotive. He crossed switches and looked back at his coaches, loaded with bundles of newspapers.

At Rahway, his fireman was reading the green-over-green signals ahead and yelling them around the throbbing boiler to Foot-and-a-Half.

When the train approached a station, the men in the cars picked out the fat bundles of newspapers intended for that town, rolled them to the edge of the open doors and stood with a foot on them. Two hundred feet before the station, the feet kicked the bundles. They hit the ground, bounced high, skidded and rolled to a stop in front of the station door.

The Newspaper Special eased into the Harrisburg yards on time, panting, the rods clanking loosely, the steam boxes sighing. Foot-

and-a-Half pulled to a stop on the minute because he knew his train and he knew himself.

One night in 1905 he was westbound out of New Brunswick on track three and he was moving fast because the *Morning Herald* had held him up four minutes. It is downgrade to Princeton Junction and Foot-and-a-Half hit ninety. Five miles ahead, a long freight was on track two crawling in the same direction. The freight had tower orders to cross track three onto four, then move from four onto a siding and wait.

Foot-and-a-Half got a block signal orange-over-green. He ran through it. A mile further, he hit a red-over-red signal. Stop. He and his train went through it like a flaming comet. Ahead, half the freight was across the tracks.

The Newspaper Special raced around a high sandy bank and dead ahead was the freight. The flyer went through it like a steak knife through a worm. The freight cars began to pile up in slow motion. The Newspaper Special went on for three hundred yards. Then it tilted slowly. Then it crashed into the ditch. There was a sound like a heavy door slamming somewhere, then silence. Foot-and-a-Half and his fireman were killed instantly.

No one ever solved it. But the ghost of Foot-and-a-Half begs me: "Say anything, but don't say that I fell asleep. . . ."

Horatio Alger

One of the worst combinations to beset a man is to have a strong conscience teamed with a weak will. This type succumbs to all the attractive sins, and then beats himself to death with feelings of guilt. He never wins, unless he lives long enough to grow old and sanctimonious.

Horatio Alger is an example. He wrote stories for boys. I grew up reading his books. They always opened with a poor but honest youngster shivering in the cold as he tried to sell his newspapers so that his mother would be able to afford thin soup for supper. They ended with the triumph of virtue over greed; the kid grew up to become rich and righteous and he always married the most beautiful girl in town.

Horatio Alger wasn't anything like his books. He was born in January, 1834, in Revere, Massachusetts. His father was Dr. Horatio Alger, a stainless steel puritan and a minister. The father watched every other breath of his son, determined that the boy should become a Unitarian minister and a saint on earth. The neighborhood called the youngster "Holy Horatio."

His father was pulling hard in one direction and the devil was yanking the kid on an opposite course. Horatio studied at Harvard Divinity School and tried to marry the first jezebel he met. His dad stopped that. Horatio wrote stories for the press, and the doctor tried to stop that too. In 1860, the young man ran off to Paris.

He was twenty-six, and there was no one to watch him. Horatio fell into indiscretions at night and spent his mornings pounding his chest and begging God for forgiveness. This went on until Horatio was certain that he was losing his mind. In 1864, when the Civil War was big news, Alger was ordained a minister in Brewster, Massachusetts.

He lasted two years. If his life in Paris was bad, this one was worse. He couldn't stand preaching the wages of sin, on the one hand, and thinking of how lovely those sins could be, on the other. This was hypocrisy. Alger fled to New York.

He wrote books. Here again Alger was frustrated, because he longed to be a fine novelist. Instead, his works became cheap paperbacks, selling for five cents. He returned to Paris. There he fell into a love affair that left him temporarily insane. He returned to the prison of the conscience in a hospital bed.

Still, his books sold in the millions. He went back to New York and did some charitable work in the Newsboys' Lodging House. He never married, but he informally adopted a Chinese orphan named Wing. He made friends with the gamins of the city and wrote about them.

He wrote *Ragged Dick, Pluck and Luck, Tattered Tom, From Canal Boy to President, Bertha's Christmas Vision, Frank's Campaign or What a Boy Can Do,* and many others. In all, he authored 119 books.

Alger earned a huge fortune. He spent it faster than it came in. He gave it to the poor boys and he gave it to women who were not poor. He loved the big city and he hated privation, so that even in New York he felt a sense of frustration. He could never reconcile himself to the world as he saw it, and he could not make peace with himself or with God.

In 1896, he left New York, broke. His sister had a home in Natick, Massachusetts. She said he would be welcome. Alger went to her and, as small royalty checks came in, he tried to repay her.

He lasted three years, a lonely graying figure who walked the sand dunes in a heavy cape, the winter winds tearing at his face and the howl assailing his ears with the sound of punishment to come.

In 1899, Horatio Alger died. He was sixty-five, and sick of himself.

Benedict Arnold

The druggist walked out of his store in New Haven and went off to war. He didn't look like a hero. He was thirty-four, had black hair and dark skin and eyes as pale as the blue in a Ming vase. He had thick arms and a big chest and enormous pride. The druggist left a wife and three sons: seven, six and three.

That's the way Benedict Arnold did things. He acted on impulse, and stuck with his impulses. He was born on January 14, 1741, and if there was one thing that drove him to his wit's end, it was his mother. She said no to everything he wanted to do. He ran away from home twice. Mother brought him back. Mrs. Arnold was hyperreligious. Benedict didn't believe in God. She supervised his thinking. He rebelled. He wanted most of all to be trusted to think for himself.

He was a captain in the Connecticut militia and he went off with his men in April, 1775. Within a month, he and Ethan Allen took Fort Ticonderoga. Another thirty days and Arnold captured Fort St. John. He was one of the first heroes of the revolution and, ninety days after he had left the drugstore, he quit the army and returned to New Haven. It was another whim. Another impulse.

He learned that the Continental Congress was investigating him. When he got home, he found that the drugstore was failing, and that his wife had died on June 19, 1775. Benedict Arnold was sickened. However, he received a promotion to colonel and eight hundred dollars and he returned to battle.

George Washington admired the Colonel as a fighting man. There was nothing cowardly about Arnold. He fought battles against superior British forces, and led the attacks. One of his horses was shot nine times before the animal and rider fell.

In 1776, Arnold was made a brigadier and led a brigade up the Kennebec into Canada under hardships. He fought blizzards, ice and starvation before he met the British.

His decimated battalions were beaten by the British at Quebec, but the British now knew him and feared him. In the summer of 1776, Benedict Arnold built a fleet of small ships and fought a losing battle so fiercely on Lake Champlain that the British General Carleton had to retire and rearrange his plans to join Howe and Burgoyne in the capture of New York.

In February, 1777, Congress appointed five men, junior to Arnold, as major generals. They ignored Arnold, so he quit again. Even General Washington was angered at the slight to Benedict Arnold. Congress said it was sorry, but that Connecticut already had two major generals.

The commander-in-chief prevailed upon Arnold to return to battle, and he did. He fought two frenzied battles and Congress made Arnold a major general, but junior to the five promoted men. This rankled in the man who had so much pride.

In April, 1779, Arnold was commander at Philadelphia and he married Miss Margaret Shippen, a flirt. Miss Shippen loved uniforms and regal living. In a short time, Benedict Arnold was deeply in debt and jealously watching his wife. In December he was court-martialed for using his post for private gain. He received a reprimand.

In the summer of 1779, General Arnold began a correspondence with Sir Henry Clinton. He was ready to betray the colonies. He asked money, recognition, and a commission in the British Army. All summer and autumn he spelled out information about Washington's troop movements, supplies, ammunition, plans, and the strength of the French fleet sailing to America.

The following summer, George Washington gave him command of West Point. Arnold wrote to Sir Henry that he would betray the fort. He wanted $100,000 if he succeeded, $50,000 and a British commission if he didn't. The terms were settled with Major John André, who made the mistake of leaving West Point in disguise, and with the plans of West Point in his stocking. The gallant major was captured and hanged.

Benedict Arnold fled to the British. He fought the colonists up and down the seaboard, and burned New London to the ground. In December, 1781, he and Margaret took their last look at New York as they sailed for England. He had been unappreciated.

Arnold expected to be a hero in London. He saw nothing but lips curled in scorn. The British gave him $31,575 and some land in Canada. He died at sixty, broke.

Neither side ever forgave him. . . .

Karl Marx

The father of communism died seventy-five years ago. His name was Karl Marx and he regarded himself as an economic messiah come to save the people of the world from the greed of the few. Capitalism, he said, is pregnant with the world of communism.

He was a sick and angry man. The back of his neck was lumpy with carbuncles and much of his time was spent in illness. He was born in Germany of a middle-class Jewish family who became Christians. He deserted them and deserted both faiths. Herr Marx grew up to be one of the world's foremost exponents of the rationale—he wanted to be able to understand and explain everything by reason. He had faith in nothing.

Marx was born in Trier on May 5, 1818. He studied law at Bonn and attended the University of Berlin. He was intelligent, truculent, impatient. He worked passionately, indefatigably, for a world economic revolution. One of the things he believed was that the workers of the world were being exploited by the capitalists.

Somehow, between fights with illness and entrenched wealth, he fell in love with Jenny, daughter of the Baron von Westphalen. Everyone, it seemed, opposed the marriage. Marx married Jenny and wrote to a friend: "I can assure you without any sentimentality that I am in love from head to foot and in all seriousness."

He was a poor husband. Most of his honeymoon was spent in the libraries. Much of the rest of his life was spent being expelled from Germany, France and Belgium, and seeking sanctuary in England. Marx spent more time with his disciple, Friedrich Engels, than he did with Jenny.

The first requisite for friendship with Marx was complete abasement and subordination. Engels, the codeviser of modern communism, wrote much of what is credited to Marx, but he has made the pages of history only as a postscript to his friend. Engels supported Marx when Karl would not seek a job, and he kept the rent paid when Karl was ill.

These two men shook the world. It is still shaking. Their major works are dull and complex: *The Communist Manifesto* and *Das Kapital*. Marx and Engels exploited a brilliant thesis, which was that the wealth of the world moves progressively into fewer hands (capitalists) who, in turn, squeeze the multitudinous workers (proletariat) by paying them less than they are worth. From this, Marx concluded that all history is a struggle between classes of people.

In 1851, Jenny died after fighting cancer for years. The father of communism was so sick with pleurisy that he could not attend the funeral of his wife. He lived two more years.

Today, according to estimates, about 1,131,000,000 people live under communism. They worship Marx, but they do not practice what he preached.

Neither their politics nor their economics are Marxian. Communists live under monolithic socialism—a diluted form of Fascism. Perhaps that is why the men in the Kremlin ordered no observation of the seventy-fifth anniversary of Karl Marx's death. They owe him nothing but two confusing books.

Ed Sullivan

The room was dark. In the room, a skinny man threaded film. Another sat on a couch looking at the blank screen. At a mahogany desk, Ed Sullivan, a man with a face that has been slept in, sat waiting.

"It's a great idea," the agent said from the deep couch.

"We'll see," Sullivan said. He chewed on a lozenge. The screen came to life. A blurry picture of a man in a gray hat showed. It cleared up. The sound wasn't in right.

"He gives three comics a minute to make a contestant laugh," the agent said.

"We'll see," Mr. Sullivan said.

From the screen, an aging face masked a swift mind and tongue. The features of Walter Winchell smiled at Ed Sullivan. The man in the dark room did not smile back. His big Lincolnesque lips twisted around the mint.

Winchell—on a kinescope from his television show—said that he selected a contestant from his audience and he would give three top comedians, Henny Youngman, Dave Barry, and Jerry Lester, a minute each to make the contestant laugh. As long as the contestant did not laugh, he would be paid at the rate of a dollar per second.

The comedians had to work fast, leaning into the face of the contestant, rattling jokes, witticisms and one-liners off his ear. After 115 seconds, the contestant threw his head up and roared, Dave Barry walked off the screen, palms up in triumph.

The man in the dark room watched two more contestants. One was a man-and-woman team. The woman tried hard, but she broke up and went limp laughing. The film ended. Lights went on in the room. Sullivan shook his head in sorrow.

"No," he said slowly. "It goes against everything I have learned about show business. You pay comics to make people laugh and then you want to pay people not to laugh at the comics. That isn't my show."

The agent smiled courageously.

"Winchell did very well with it," he said. "The people laughed," he said timidly, "because the contestant was trying so hard not to laugh."

Sullivan sucked on the lozenge and shook his head. He nodded to his secretary to fold the screen. The agent swapped pleasantries. He left on a cordial note.

Another came in. This one had a trained dog and horse act he wanted to sell to the Ed Sullivan show.

Mr. Sullivan said no. He said that he once had Frankie Laine on his Sunday night television show with a horse in an old corral. The singer had sung five bars of "I Believe" when the steed forgot his manners. The curtains closed abruptly and Mr. Laine began to die in a pitiful whimper. Sullivan waved the singer down to the footlights, had the curtains closed behind him. The audience gave Laine an ovation.

No horses. Then Sullivan watched a kinescope of a young man doing a juggling act on the Dorsey Show, and that closed the daily search for new acts for that day.

Sullivan made a phone call to his coproducer, Marlo Lewis, a bright and handsome man who is also an executive producer of the Columbia Broadcasting System. They talked about the role of the Lord Mayor of Dublin, who will appear on the show.

He hung up. His granddaughter Carla climbed laboriously onto his lap. She tried to tell Ed Sullivan that her brother Bobby had drawn a ball-point pen across her forehead and down her nose, but the words wouldn't come. All she could remember, at eighteen months, was "Gopca"—Grandpa.

Mr. Sullivan called Bobby to him. Age fifty-five counseled age three, that mannerly men do not draw pictures on their baby sister's faces with ball-point pens.

Age three did not have sufficient command of words to explain to age fifty-five that mannerly men sometimes become nauseated at all the attention paid to baby sisters just because they have angelic faces and eyes like dark dinner plates What Bobby never got to say was that a little warpaint might improve a face like that.

Ed Sullivan stood. He wore tan wing-tip shoes, brown slacks, a two-button worsted shirt. His body is thin and small and hunched. The head is huge and hanging, and the eyes look up hurt, like those of a penitent spaniel.

At heart he is a perpetual Port Chester High School sophomore, playing to win, but ready to shake the hand of the winner if the winner has not violated the Frank Merrill code.

By all the rules of the theater, this man is a cipher. He cannot act. He cannot sing. He cannot dance. He cannot tell a joke. Sometimes he utters a sentence as though it was for life.

The late Fred Allen said that Ed Sullivan was a pointer. "You can teach a dog to point," he snapped, "by rubbing meat on the target." The *New York Journal-American* columnist, Jack O'Brien, referred to Ed Sullivan as the "Toast of the Tomb." Milton Berle, musing on Sullivan, said sadly: "They're trying to figure just what he is."

What he is is a producer. Like Florenz Ziegfeld. Like Sam Goldwyn. By any standard, a good one.

Once he introduced a soprano with the words: "It is my pleasure to prevent the next singer . . ."

When Michigan State won the Big Ten Championship, Mr. Sullivan had them on his stage and kept referring to the team as the boys from the "University of Michigan." They did not complain. The football players went home and sent Sullivan a huge birthday cake—and on it his name was misspelled.

He is dismissed as The Great Stone Face, the Cardiff Giant, The Sleepwalker, the Miltown Maestro, Smiley, and they say that when he tries to smile, he looks like someone trying to swallow a quince whole.

This dyspeptic little man earns $8,150 a week. On January 13, 1958, the American Research Bureau estimated that 68,275,000 persons watched him rock on his heels and play with the knot in his tie—more people than have ever watched a regularly scheduled show. In Chicago, the jaded agents of the press voted Sullivan the Man of the Year.

He has outclassed all of his talented detractors. They are gone. He is here and on the top. In his ninth year he can point to the fact that his show has been in the top five of television longer than any other. By some extra turn of the wheel, Ed Sullivan, once a sports writer, is now the King of Television.

The show format is not original. Most neighborhood theaters used it in the 1920s. A man comes out of the wings, introduces an act and says: "Now let's hear it for good old Lem Foogie of Wet Moccasin—" and disappears.

At the end of the act, he appears in time to lead the applause and shake hands with the performer. The only difference between the local master of ceremonies and Ed Sullivan is that Sully lacks polish.

He recites the formula in seventeen words:

"Open big, have a good comedy act, put in something for the children, keep the show clean."

That's it. Nothing more. It could be the format of the Perry Como Show. Or the Steve Allen Show. Or Ernie Kovacs. A poor man's Omnibus; a rich man's Talent Scouts, vaudeville on an ulcer diet.

Still, there are those 68,275,000 people. And those are sensible citizens. On an average Sunday, about 40,000,000 Americans will devote an hour to Ed Sullivan, about half the number who devote equal time on the same day to God.

Therefore, one is led inexorably to the conclusion that this man is too easily dismissed; the big cipher must have an X in front of it, an X which denotes the unknown side of Ed Sullivan, the side which millions of people feel by instinct.

Sullivan came back into his office. He had swallowed the lozenge. At his desk, he toyed lightly with the keys of a gold-plated typewriter given to him by Jewish War Veterans. He wasn't typing. The man was thinking.

Outside stood Mr. Rudolf Bing, waiting to see him. Mr. Bing is the aging director of the Metropolitan Opera Company. He is a gentleman, an intellectual.

Ed Sullivan stopped thinking. "Send Mr. Bing in," he said.

Both knew that this would be a painful interview. Early in the season, Sullivan had tried opera on his show and had agreed to stage it three more times. Maria Callas had been first guest, and the Trendex ratings proved that Sullivan—culture and all—had dropped fourteen points. The people did not care for opera.

Now he would like to forget his commitments to the Metropolitan Opera Company. Or, at least, change the appearances from straight opera to concert appearances.

Mr. Bing wanted Sullivan to honor the commitments. He was nervous. He eased the final two inches of his torso onto the outer two inches of the couch. He smiled bravely and his words had the slight and sweet sound of a Bavarian mountaineer who has mastered English while working as an usher at the Paramount.

Sullivan told Bing to stop worrying. The matter could be worked out. Instead of three more operatic appearances, he would use two. Could they try concert work? Please, Mr. Bing said. No. Please give opera a chance.

"I have seen two or three bad shows of yours," he said without guile. "But this is none of my damned business. You control the show and it is always in the top two or three."

He tried to recoup with a gaiety.

"The only thing I criticize is your ventriloquists. I laugh two times. Three times. But when I see them seven times, that it is too much.

"Use two, Ed. Cancel the last one. Then we are out of it."

Mr. Sullivan offered a cigarette. Mr. Bing did not want it. A moment later, he was smoking. It's a neurotic business.

Mr. Bing left. A woman came in. She had a trim figure and lines of gentility and compassion on her face. In one hand was a small shot of milk. In the other was an orange pill. This was Sylvia Weinstein Sullivan, the heart, and quite possibly the soul, of the household.

"I took my pill," Mr. Sullivan said belligerently. "An hour ago."

"I know," Mrs. Sullivan said softly. "This is another one."

"Every hour?" the husband said. "No ulcer is that bad."

"What did the doctor say?"

Ed Sullivan took the pill and popped it into his mouth. He swallowed the thick milk like a man who is squishing a mouth rinse between his teeth.

"Pictures," he said. "He took pictures. Barium test and pictures. After all, Sylvia, this isn't new. I've had this duodenal since I was a kid. Maybe before."

She nodded.

When the milk was down, Robbie came in. He pointed to Bojangles, the French poodle. Robbie tried to explain that Bojangles growled at him, but he couldn't think of the word growled. Carla came in running and half falling. She fell on "Boj" and he didn't even growl. He kissed her.

The man gets out of bed at the crack of 11 A.M. He wanders around the five-room suite on the eleventh floor of the Hotel Delmonico, scratching and wondering. He makes his own breakfast.

It is always the same: oatmeal and a glass of milk. To eat it, he sits on a high stool in a narrow kitchen. He chews like a man determined not to complain.

"A man with an ulcer has half a life," he says. "He's only half living."

In the case of Ed Sullivan, it is less than half because, many years ago, his nose was broken twice in football games and he has no sense of smell. Later, his sense of taste began to die.

Now, he cannot even taste the mush he eats. For him, dinner often consists of a plate of mashed potatoes drowned in soft boiled eggs.

The phone rings. He props it against his ear and spoons the oatmeal.

"What? Oh, let's cut out the police motorcycle escort. Yeah. Uh-huh. That's all I need is to arrive in Chicago and be met by a Cadillac. Nothing doing. Right. No, I'm not worried about that. They'll introduce themselves and I'll make little notes. . . . Sure thing."

He hangs up. Mrs. Sullivan stands in the doorway. She looks dejected.

"Can't you eat without the telephone?"

"I'm imitating my doctor."

"Oh stop."

"No. He eats and talks into a telephone and examines patients at the same time. He hasn't got an ulcer."

The ulcer, like an old volcano, is active at the moment. It is situated in the duodenum and, when it erupts, it locks the stomach exit in a closed position. When this happens, Ed Sullivan sticks two tubes through his nostrils and down into his esophagus. Then he pumps out his stomach.

Surgery might have given Sullivan a resection job years ago. But he was afraid of the knife, and still is, although he professes to believe that this is not so.

"If worse comes to worse," he argues, "we can always resort to the knife. But if we don't have to—why do it?"

The chronic ulcer patient is often sensitive to emotional stress. Sullivan is the epitome of the ulcer man. He has a driving ambition to be famous and appreciated; he is hypersensitive to criticism; he feels, subconsciously, that it is not manly to show emotion—tears, laughter, anger—so he represses these. He wants to be in control of himself at all times.

He has an inordinate admiration for champions—whether they are fighters or golfers or writers or actors, typists, pilots, singers, jugglers, tycoons, admirals or pool sharks—and he wants to be one.

He is a perfectionist and, when everything goes wrong for him, as it often does, his voice moves up a solitary notch and comes through his nose in a whine. He makes no other concession to irritation.

"Take Winchell," he says. "He'd have had an ulcer long ago, but he can let off steam. When he gets mad, he just talks and talks and talks and he never stops talking." Sullivan stirs a little bicarbonate of soda in a glass. "Now, if I could only do that . . ."

Winchell is an old enemy. There are others who disenchant Ed Sullivan from time to time—Arthur Godfrey, Westbrook Pegler, Harriet Van Horne, Frank Sinatra, Jack O'Brien—but the Winchell animosity, like the ulcer, is so old that it is now almost honorable.

Sullivan was ashamed, last autumn, to be caught admiring the Winchell television show, but he liked it and it was against his code to lie about it.

"A heck of a show," he says, nodding gravely. "But the deck was stacked against him and they never gave him a fair chance."

The enmity dates back to 1928, when both worked on a dying tabloid. Winchell, as a gossip columnist, was the only attraction the paper had. Sullivan was sports editor.

The managing editor worked Winchell over like a sadistic child with a new puppy. Ed Sullivan appealed to a vice-president to order the editor to stop. The editor heard about it and almost took Sullivan apart. He said that he learned about Sullivan's intercession from Winchell. That did it.

Walter Winchell doesn't like Sullivan because, when Winchell left the tabloid, Sullivan was the second man to take Winchell's old column and use his three-dot system of retailing gossip. Louis Sobol was the first.

On the rare occasions when Sullivan finds himself in the same restaurant with Winchell, he orders a table facing his old adversary and he sits and stares and stares and stares. Sooner or later, Winchell is called to take a long distance message and that closes the eye fight.

Sullivan has not liked Godfrey since the day that the Virginia millionaire took off in his private plane at Teterboro, New Jersey, made a wild left turn, and barely cleared the control tower as the men inside hit the deck. Ed Sullivan interviewed the men in the tower, and wrote a column about it, telling how many children they had, and indicting Arthur Godfrey for recklessness.

Since then, whenever Godfrey fires someone—Julius La Rosa, Marion Marlowe—Sullivan hires them at a heavy fee to appear on his show. In this, he claims to be objective. "If Godfrey is ever fired," he says, "I'll hire him too."

At the moment, Sullivan and Sinatra are friends. A few years ago, when Sullivan paid Sam Goldwyn $32,000 for some film in which Frankie appeared, the crooner demanded extra compensation from Ed Sullivan.

He was turned down, and he became so angry that he took big advertisements in trade papers saying: "To Ed Sullivan. You are sick, Ed. Sick, sick, sick."

The thing that stings Sullivan the deepest is criticism which he regards as "unfair." This embraces almost all criticism, of course. He can see justice in grabbing Godfrey's castoffs and making bigger attractions of them, but he cannot see justice in a television columnist referring to Sullivan as a no-talent, stage-struck columnist.

When he reads these criticisms, Sullivan sits in cramping pain. He turns to his typewriter and begins to peck a letter to the offending columnist. He often pecks until the late hours, chewing pills and working his jaws. Then, in exhaustion, he goes into the front bedroom, undresses quietly, and slips into the big Hollywood bed he shares with Sylvia, and tries to sleep.

In the morning, he gets up, reads the letter again, and sometimes works it into a ball and drops it in the wastebasket. Sometimes, he mails it.

What makes him maddest, in that externally serene manner of his, is when the columnists wonder out loud how a big television show can afford such an obviously lousy master of ceremonies.

Being a master of ceremonies, Sullivan insists, is the smallest part of his job. Few people seem to understand, he feels, that he is the owner of the Ed Sullivan Show. He is responsible for it, from start to finish. He not only M.C.s it, but he often travels 175,000 miles per year scouting for new talent for it. He is also the coproducer of the show.

In addition, he is responsible for the $50,000 that is paid out to talent and to behind-the-scene specialists each week. He even okays the sets, changes the jokes, set the pace and routine of the show, and tells the ladies how much décolletage they will be permitted to wear.

Getting out in front of the cameras and introducing acts is the final fillip, as far as he is concerned. That part is easy, and to prove it, he does it with no teleprompter.

He did it once too often when Gene Fullmer won the middleweight championship of the world and appeared on the Sullivan Show.

The fighter came onstage, and Sullivan's mind went blank. He went through the cerebral files from A to Z. Nothing. So he danced around the fighter, feinting and jabbing and throwing his arms around the champion's neck, and saying:

"Well, Gene . . . how's it feel, Eugene old kid? . . . Tough fight? . . . Let's hear it for good old Gene, ladies and gentlemen, the new middleweight champion of the world! . . . What a fight! . . . What a fighter!"

As bad as this is, Sullivan doesn't feel that it is as funny as the night Rosemary Clooney asked Lauritz Melchior for his autograph and then, in awe of the opera star, said: "Thank you, Mr. Tibbett."

The Sullivans are, by choice, somewhat aloof and lonely. They are not seen at the glittering parties on Park and Fifth Avenues. They do not attend the smart cocktail soirées. They skip many of the Broadway openings, although tickets lie on Ed Sullivan's desk.

A beautiful Lincoln is given to them each year, and they use taxicabs.

The Sullivans are, by choice, lonely. They will not try to impress anyone. They use the services of a hotel maid, rather than hire one.

A man in Ed Sullivan's position can use forty to fifty suits of clothes. He has twelve. Two of them are new.

Sylvia Sullivan has a beautiful dark ranch mink coat. This and a handful of smart gowns are Mrs. Sullivan's only ostentation.

Ed has an obsession about "phonies," and sulks in Irish obstinacy if he is asked to do something or say something which he does not regard as genuine.

Sylvia sits in her living room, overlapped hands curling on a knee, and her thick dark hair frames the mood on her face. She has been married to this man, whom millions idolize, almost twenty-seven years. She knows him, as all women know their men. She loves him to the point of self-effacement, but she is not deluded.

"Ed likes to do everything for himself. He doesn't want help. We don't socialize because we're not the dinner-party type. I think that if Ed wants to take a nap at seven P.M. and eat at ten he should be able to do it."

She smiles small, and shrugs.

"Nothing infuriates him more than to *have* to be at a certain place at a certain time. And it's poison for him to know he has to go to somebody's house for dinner.

The few close friends remain constant: Joe Moore, Ben Sokolows, Walter and Rose Shirley, of a real estate development called Shirley Acres; Charlene and Dave Marx, of a children's toy company; Mildred Winston, an artist; Dorothy Shubarat, interior decorator; Jerry and Betty Brady, of the American Totalizator Company; Cherey and General Ephraim Jeffe; Nervyn Schenck, of M-G-M, and, until her death, Mrs. Bugs Baer.

The more you study the Sullivans, the more the word "average" comes to mind. Maybe it should read adamantly average, because this couple seems to be determined not to be lured into anything suggesting a posh life.

The Sullivans even argue like average couples. In 1929 and early 1930, they fought so much that they used to stage farewell dinners to each other. The good-bys, after a spat, were sad and lingering.

The estrangement always lasted about three weeks, at which time Ed would phone Sylvia—not to make up—but to propose one more farewell dinner. They were married April 28, 1930, by a Roman Catholic priest. Sylvia, Jewish, agreed to bring up the children, if any, as Catholics.

The fights are more subdued now, because Ed, at fifty-five, is an aging tiger.

But Sylvia, who dreads to relinquish the good old days, insists that "Ed has a terrific temper. He asks me to hand him his glasses —or some small thing—and if I don't do it promptly he gets the glasses and one word leads to another.

"Once the fight starts, he's very good at remembering all the little things I didn't do for him years ago."

The best spat in recent years occurred over a charity drive. Sylvia took a fifty-dollar chance on a car and a trip to Europe. The night before the drawing the dialogue went like this:

Sylvia: I have a feeling I'm going to win.

Ed: Win what?

Sylvia: The car and the trip to Europe. It's tomorrow.

Ed: You can't win.

Sylvia (voice rising): Why not?

Ed (elaborate ulcerous smile): Because, Darling, the committee asked you to pick the winning ticket.

Sylvia: What has that got to do with it? I paid fifty dollars of my own money and bought my own ticket. If I win, I'm going.

Ed (popping pill between clenched teeth): Has it also occurred to you that my cousin is running this particular raffle? The raffle is staged by the Sullivans, a Sullivan picks the winning ticket, and it turns out that a Sullivan wins the trip to Europe.

Sylvia (angry at losing fifty dollars): It wouldn't make a bit of difference to me who is running it or who is picking the winner.

My fifty dollars is in this thing and I'm making that trip to Europe.

And so on, far into the night. In a sense, it was a waste of a good family fight because, the following day, someone else won.

The Sullivans have one child: Betty. She is dark and bright and is Ed Sullivan's number one fan. And vice versa.

He is not demonstrative in his affection. A cheek-to-cheek kiss and a brief hug is overdoing it, as far as father is concerned.

It is a tribute to the Sullivan life—his rough policy—that Betty was raised unspoiled. It is also a tribute to Sylvia, who taught the child her catechism and sent her off to Mass and the sacraments, while at the same time trying to avoid being crushed by the father-daughter mutual admiration society.

Betty was sent to the University of California at Los Angeles. There, in the Class of '52, she met Robert Precht, Jr. Today, they live in Scarsdale, New York. Precht is 26, blond, handsome and independent. He has a job as assistant to the producer of the Ed Sullivan Show.

Precht wants no favors from his father-in-law and, as nothing would please Sullivan more than "helping the kids," this adds to his tensions.

"I want to break away, professionally, from my father-in-law," says the young man.

He admires Sullivan, but he doesn't want to create a shadow in the rays of a star.

Precht majored in international relations, served a hitch in the Navy, is the father of Bobby, three, and Carla, two. He and Betty expect another baby.

The future is important to the Prechts, and young Bob's goal is to be a television producer of a Public Affairs show. His smile uncovers big square teeth.

"Of course nobody will trust me with such a program now. Just give me a little time."

Twenty-two years ago, Ed Sullivan starred at Loew's State, in New York, in a review called *Dawn Patrol*. He introduced acts, tried hard to smile, and got offstage as quickly as possible.

In the dressing room, a boy waited. He was fifteen and he looked like someone whom a good meal could cripple.

"I shine shoes and run errands," the boy said in a whispering voice.

Sullivan asked him if he would wait for a newspaper column and deliver it to *The News*. The boy said sure. He has been doing it ever since.

His name is Carmine Charles Santullo. He is thirty-seven, and he is as devoted to Ed Sullivan as some are to a favorite saint. He is Sullivan's secretary, although he never studied stenography or typing.

He sits at a desk across the room from Ed, the face dark and solemn, the mind always trying to anticipate the wishes of another mind, the thin body wrapped in a plain V-neck sweater and a pair of slacks.

Santullo's father had a shoe repair shop on East 128th Street. He had five brothers and two sisters. The shop did not bring in enough money to furnish pasta for all, and Carmine was not too proud to go down to the theater district to shine shoes.

Sullivan saw the intense, almost spiritual quality of the boy. The kid talked in soft bursts, like a convict who doesn't want to be seen moving his lips.

He was hired at $35.00 a week. Today he earns better than $150 a week and he is still Sullivan's right arm.

Carmine has never called Sullivan anything but "Mr. Sullivan." Whether the boss is at home or making a public appearance, Santullo knows where he is every minute of every hour.

Example: "It's three thirty here. That means it's two thirty in Chicago. He left there at one forty-five their time so he must be about over Detroit now. Mrs. Sullivan is going to leave for Idlewild in two minutes."

Santullo, among many other duties, sends the rough draft of the two newspaper columns which Sullivan still writes each week, to the boss's desk. Ed looks over the items, pencils certain ones out of existence, and writes his column from the remainder.

For this, *The News* pays him barely enough to cover Santullo's salary: $150 a week.

The remaining person in the Sullivan office is a newcomer. Her name is Mrs. Jean Sweeney, and she has been there only six years. She is young and pretty and was introduced to Sullivan at a country club. After five minutes, he said to her:

"Would you like to be my assistant secretary?"

She thought he was a flirt. He wasn't.

Sometimes a man is more clearly seen by looking at his father. You can look at Ed Sullivan all day and what you will see is a sad, serious fiftyish man sitting on the lid of his emotions.

But if you spend a moment or two studying Edward's hero—Peter Arthur Sullivan—the son begins to come alive with meaning and you understand that Peter is Ed's Babe Ruth, Bobby Jones, Jack Dempsey, George Washington and model.

Peter Sullivan, now long gone, came from Amsterdam, New

York. He was a short, strong boy and he found it easy to get jobs. He married Elizabeth Smith and it was she who tempered the times of terrible wrath when they came.

Peter was loaded with principle and courage. Once, when the Sullivans were living in Port Chester, New York, a rooster was stolen from the back yard.

That night, when Peter Sullivan heard about it, he merely stared at his growing sons in disbelief, and then stalked out, hopped a fence into the next yard, walked into a neighbor's kitchen, grabbed the rooster by both legs, glanced at the eating family, and growled:

"If any of you ever so much as lay a hand on anything of mine again, I'll break all of you in half."

He walked out.

Ed still aspires to have that kind of physical courage. He hasn't got it. He has moral courage, lots of it. No one can speak disparagingly of another race or another faith in Sullivan's presence.

No one can "shove" him. Sullivan is unafraid, even politically. He contributed to the campaign of Adlai Stevenson and made no secret of it.

Peter raised a good-sized family on a small salary. He worked as a political appointee. Ed is certain that Peter is up there praying for him, watching over him.

Not long ago, Ed Sullivan wrote:

"My television show dropped into my lap by accident. It is my deepest belief that this resulted from prayer—not so much my own—but the prayers of priests and nuns I have known. And certainly the prayers and intercession of those close to me who have died."

In spite of his strong spiritual side, Ed Sullivan is not an outstanding Catholic layman. He is charitable—his favorites are the Marist Sisters of Framingham Center, Massachusetts; The New York Catholic Charities; the Heart Fund, and Sister Kenny—but he does not wear his Catholicism on his sleeve. Often, when he is gray with pain, he will attend Mass because he thinks he should "set a good example."

Like most theatrical performers, he seldom gets to bed before three in the morning. When he gets to Mass, it is almost always ten at St. Patrick's Cathedral. Sylvia does about as well in her faith. When the high Jewish holidays are impending, she visits her sister and attends temple services. Every night of the year, Sylvia stands at the bedroom window to pray.

The major influences on Ed Sullivan were: (1) Peter, (2) his mother and his church, (3) Sir Walter Scott, (4) high school sports, where the credo is "Play hard and play to win, but play clean."

In his sophomore year at Port Chester High, Ed Sullivan tried a part-time job as school correspondent for the *Port Chester Item.*

Within a few weeks, the boy found that he was "important." He was no longer just another halfback; he was read and quoted by students, by faculty, by parents, and he was praised, condemned, reviled and adored. Only the players heard the coach's words. When Ed spoke on a typewriter, he was read by thousands.

This is of small consequence to any except introvert-hams. These usually feel tremendous emotion, but are powerless to express it.

Young Ed was an introvert-ham. His greatest pleasure was in traveling to Bridgeport on Saturdays and watching the vaudeville acts; marveling at the people who had the nerve to stand in a little white spotlight and dance, or sing, or make jokes. All of them had the courage to risk mass displeasure. Ed loved the stage.

He quit high school, worked in factories, got a job as a catcher of a semiprofessional baseball team, returned to the *Port Chester Item* as sports editor. Salary: $12.00. Later, Ed got an offer on the *Hartford Post* and he was tendered a big farewell party before he left home.

In a week or two, he had lost the job and he thought about the triumphal farewell party and knew that, once again, he could not go back home. He sat in a rooming house in Hartford, wondering what to do next. Defeat and humiliation were for weaklings

He was lucky. While brooding, Ed got a letter from the sports editor of the *New York Evening Mail,* asking if he would like a job covering school sports in the big town. Would he!

Sullivan went to New York via Port Chester, just to pause long enough to pass the word that he had already made the big time; he was going to work on one of the big newspapers of the world.

After a couple of years on *The Mail,* where the Great Stone Face distinguished himself by referring to tennis star Helen Wills as "Little Miss Poker Face," he got a job as sports editor of the brassy new tabloid: *The Evening Graphic.* Here he met the punchinellos of the press: Emile Gauvreau, managing editor; Walter Winchell, Broadway; Louis Sobol, entertainment; Lew Grogan, composographs; William Plummer, city editor.

In time, the public tired of boudoir raids and gang killings, and *The Graphic,* which anticipated every news event except its own demise, died. What talent there was on the paper fled to the comfort of better pay checks on other papers: Sobol to the *Journal-*

American; Winchell to *The Daily Mirror;* Gauvreau to *The Mirror;* and Sullivan to *The News.*

The column wasn't enough. It was widely read; it was passed under the searching eyes of eighteen million persons every day, but it wasn't enough. It would have been enough for the average egomaniac.

But Sullivan—like Winchell—wanted to be known and respected by everyone. After the first few years, Ed Sullivan knew that he was not going to make himself a national figure with three dots and a dash of Winchell.

A Broadway columnist is a man who writes love letters on a mirror. He is paid to inflict his opinions on others. Some columnists find it necessary to inflict themselves, as well as their opinions, on the people.

In this stage, the columnist becomes a personality. He feels that he can make people, or break them. He reaches upward toward punditry while, in the same paragraph, he crouches in the gutter of innuendo.

The Broadway columnist is the living proof that there is but one side to a question. His words are whips. They crack loudly from coast to coast and, when he isn't writing his column, he's defending it. Long before his time, he is jaded, tired, old. The ultimate triumph is always won by a blank sheet of paper.

Sullivan was aware of these things. He knew that, in time, he would not have the column; the column would have him. Night after night, he sat in the Delmonico poring over the offerings of press agents who tipped him off to juicy bits, or who sent quips and attributed them to their clients. Smiley felt that he had missed his goal. The column wasn't enough.

He had unreasoning ambition, and an ulcer. When the Second World War came, Ed was forty. He earned about $500 a week. It wasn't much for a big man. About $\frac{3}{100}$th of a cent per reader. And more important than the low salary was the lack of prestige.

Sometimes he fronted for his newspaper by playing master of ceremonies for its promotion schemes. One of these was the annual Harvest Moon Ball. In this, he had a chance to stand in the tiny blue spotlight and to feel the rapt attention of twenty thousand people. Ed Sullivan liked it. Whatever gnawing hunger pained his stomach, this fed it. This soothed it.

Added to the promotion stunts, he appeared now and then with a vaudeville troupe. And, during the war, Sullivan was a prime mover in staging shows for the wounded. He was beyond fatigue.

When the war was over, the columnist was stunned to find out how quickly a whole people can forget the maimed. Few stars wanted to travel to Staten Island to do a show at Halloran Hospital. Few organizations cared.

One of the few was the Isaac Gimbel Post of American Legion. Because this group continued to help the helpless long after the echoes of the last shot had died, Sullivan M.C.'d their annual fund-raising show year after year. Peter Sullivan would have applauded that.

In 1947, Ed got his big break. Like most big ones, this one was disguised as a small one. He was staging the Harvest Moon Ball, which was being carried on a New York television station. One of the watchers was Worthington Miner, of CBS. Mr. Miner was a producer. Later, he would stage a show called Studio One. At the moment he was looking at Sullivan and saying: "He seems relaxed and likable. He has none of the brashness of the hardened performer."

The next morning, Mr. Miner put those words in memo form. The Columbia Broadcasting System had a new show for Sunday night called Toast of the Town. It was to be a necklace of vaudeville acts hung on a string to be supplied by a master of ceremonies. Several well-known personalities had been considered, but Sullivan got the job.

Ed was delighted, and petrified with fright. He kept telling himself that, at forty-six, a reporter's future is in back of him. "Where am I headed for?" he kept saying to Sylvia. "The copy desk? Working in a morgue digging up old clippings?"

He masked the fright—just as he did the hope—behind an elaborate façade of cool stone features and halting words.

The budget for the show was $1,250 a week. This would pay for all talent, for the master of ceremonies, plus a producer. How was it to be done for these soggy peanuts? That would be up to Sullivan.

He leaned on his friends in the theatrical business, and some stars agreed to appear on the show for scale—for minimum— wage. On the first show were Martin and Lewis; Monica Lewis, a singer; Kathryn Lee, ballet dancer; Eugene List, a pianist who had entertained President Truman and Josef Stalin at the recent Potsdam Conference; Ruby Goldstein, who was about to referee the Louis-Walcott fight; and Rodgers and Hammerstein, talking about and playing a bit of Oklahoma!

The enduring format had been established: Six acts, a bit of sports, a chunk of culture, a topical personality. The reaction to Sullivan was less than enthusiastic. The television critics took a look and began to hone their typewriters. The fans took a look, and the kindest letters came from a lady who wrote: "Believe me, it takes a real man to get up there with a silver plate in his head." Some congratulated Sullivan on his triumph over Bell's palsy.

Ed began to write vicious letters to the critics. In the early days, he mailed them. Some of the humorless newspapermen expressed a desire to break Ed's nose a third time.

In the case of Sullivan, nothing is ever so bad that it cannot get worse. He was putting on shows for pennies, and telling himself, in a whisper of desperation, that it was now or never, and then *The News* rose up to ask him what he was doing on CBS when they had just opened their own station, WPIX.

Sullivan blew up. He reminded *The News* that, when he first heard of the CBS offer, he had gone to WPIX and told them that he was available. *The News* television people acted as though he wanted to be a leprosarium. The editors now insisted that it was a matter of personal loyalty to the paper. The critics said that Sullivan was setting television back about six months—which was all the way. The people said they felt truly sorry for him.

The animosity of his newspaper to the new career crippled Ed in another direction. It was the custom of columnists to browbeat theatrical personalities into appearances on a show for minimum wages by writing something nice about them in the column. If the star refused, he was assailed in the column. Sullivan was robbed of this economic device by his editors, who made it explicit that they would publish no plugs for his show in his column.

From an advertising agency he got Marlo Lewis as producer of Toast of the Town. Lewis, a handsome man who brings his own padding to a suit of clothes, knew nothing of television. But then, according to the critics, Toast of the Town wasn't television anyway.

The two men, with John Wray, an excellent choreographer, dreamed the show into being each Sunday. Lots of television people used to tune in just to see how long the immobile punching bag could take it.

He was discouraged; he was desperate; he was frightened: he was angry. But Sullivan knew that, at age forty-eight, there was no road back. It lay ahead, or there was no road. He went to Philadelphia for Emerson, a sponsor.

From the railroad station to the factory, people stared at him and waved and yelled: "Hello, Ed." "Keep slugging, boy!" "Hey, Sullivan! How about two passes?"

Sullivan turned to Sylvia. The lower lip hung loose and pendulous. "The people know me," he whispered. "Look at them. They know me! They know who I am! Sylvia, for God's sake they like the show!"

His throat tightened and he couldn't speak and he waved at the crowds and the people waved back and sent up the first surflike roar of affection he had ever heard.

That was in 1948. Immediately after the little triumph, Sullivan's sponsor quit on him, and so did the network. The word spread up and down Madison Avenue that Columbia Broadcasting System was offering Toast of the Town with or without Ed Sullivan.

One of the things Ed Sullivan lacks is quitting pride. Some have it. Some do not. This is a spurious form of snobbery which impels a man to resign when he knows he is not wanted.

The Columbia Broadcasting System made it plain to the world of television that Sullivan was old and through. He stood by, working twice as hard on his show, not daring to take a dollar out of the budget for himself or for his producer.

He got Martin and Lewis to appear for $250; Lena Horne was paid $75.00. *Billboard*, a trade magazine, said that Sullivan was using his column to slug artists into appearing on his show.

Sullivan was angered. His blue eyes looked like little blueberries in apple turnovers as he showed up at *Billboard*'s office with his show budget, his payments to artists, under his arms. He proved that CBS gave him only $1,250 for the one-hour show, and that neither Sullivan nor Marlo Lewis had taken a dime in pay for their work.

The American Guild of Vaudeville Artists summoned the M.C. to appear on the same charge. Dewey Barto, an old friend and father of Nancy Walker, actress, was on the board.

Sullivan, harassed and on the ropes, opened his books for the committee and argued that he had paid out every cent of the budget for talent and, if the pay scale was too low, it was not the Sullivans of the world who made it so, but rather the American Guild of Vaudeville Artists, who did not demand more from the tightfisted titans of television, like CBS. He proved, beyond argument, that the most money he ever had left over from a show was $180, which he used the following week to buy better acts.

In Detroit, The Ford Motor Company was shopping for a television show for the Mercury Division. The car should have been selling to people who were buying Buicks and Oldsmobiles, and Ford was about ready to push Mercury.

The advertising department liked Toast of the Town because (1) it was a cheap buy; (2) it was getting to New York and

Boston and Philadelphia and would soon be in Baltimore and
Washington; (3) it was entertaining and seemed to have everything from jugglers to ventriloquists; (4) it was a family show
with early Sunday evening time; (5) it could be had without
that painful-looking man named Sullivan.

The prayers of Peter, in Heaven, must have been fervent. The
General Sales Manager of Mercury was Joseph Bayne. This man
was a one-time radio executive who had worked with Major Edward Bowes and his Amateur Hour.

The Major enjoyed remarkable success in spite of the fact that
he was known to knee the English language and rabbit punch his
own syntax. America had learned to love the Major.

"The thing about the two of them," said Bayne to the Mercury
people who were opposed to Sullivan, "is their genuineness and
truthfulness. We'll buy Sullivan for thirteen weeks."

That was that. Ed was safe for three months. No longer. He had
exactly ninety days in which to show the Ford Company that he
could sell Mercurys; he had the same length of time in which to
show CBS that they had made a grievous mistake in betraying
him; meanwhile, he had to find a way of placating his bosses at
The News, who had taken to writing menacing notes which
opened: "When are you coming back to us?"

All this and no compensation too. Sullivan almost implored the
people to like his show. He tried to smile when he couldn't think
of anything to smile about. The ulcer spasms returned and each
morning the glamour man pumped out his stomach.

The show began to catch on. The viewers began to like Sullivan.
Why? No one knows. It may be that they felt the same sympathy
toward the animated Blarney Stone as one feels toward an Uncle
Charley who has asthma. Or the reason may be found in something that Bing Crosby once said: "The way I sing, everybody
who listens feels that he can sing as good. So they sing with me."
Maybe the people felt that they could do as good a job as Sullivan
as an M.C.

The show moved upward. The National Broadcasting Company
stopped laughing at Toast of the Town. The president of NBC
once said that the reason Sullivan never lost his appeal is that he
never had any. It is a sad commentary on great intellects that this
particular president is now gone, and Sullivan is bigger than
ever.

The moment NBC began to take Sullivan seriously, his troubles
multiplied. The executives of the rival network felt that Sullivan
had to be killed—televisionally speaking. They began to pour
money into the show opposite Toast of the Town. They tried the

Colgate Comedy Hour and, for a while, it looked as though Sullivan could be killed.

The people, however, are strange animals. They laughed at the Comedy Hour, but the faces were always different, and they wanted to see some familiar faces; even stone ones. So they went back to Ed. NBC tried Jimmy Durante, Berle, Sinatra, Judy Holliday, Bop Hope. Ed beat them. NBC gritted its teeth and hired two torpedoes from the coast: Dean Martin and Jerry Lewis. Sullivan lost to them for a while, and then drew abreast of them.

This is like the New York Yankees being shut out by the girls' team of the Florence Crittenton Home. Ed did so well, in fact, that CBS negotiated a new contract with him in the summer of 1950. Instead of $1,250 a week for everything and everybody, the network boosted the ante to $6,000 for the first year, $7,000 for the second, and $8,000 for the remaining three. The network suggested that, out of this, Ed ought to take $2,000 for himself. Further, he won the right to be introduced on the show as a columnist from *The News,* which, he hoped, would keep his editors pacified.

The Sullivans went off on a vacation. The one place Ed wanted to see was Ireland. In particular, a place called Bantry Bay. That is where his grandparents came from. When Sylvia and Ed arrived, Sullivan felt a warm glow of family pride and said to the woman serving tea:

"My family came from around here."

"Indeed?"

"Yes," said Ed. "I'm the first of the clan to get back."

"Is that so?" the woman said frostily. "Well, it took ye a dom long time."

Everything in life took Sullivan a dom long time. But, at the age of fifty-five, he has touched all the bases, made all the goals he set for himself. He is an enormous success, and is a good moral force in an industry which tends to demean itself.

The date on which success hooked arms with Ed Sullivan is November 23, 1954. By that time, the show had become a "standard"—millions of people were in the "habit" of tuning in on Sullivan whether the show was good or bad. He still lost an occasional Sunday fight to NBC, but not many.

The network wanted to negotiate a new contract with Ed. So, ironically, did NBC. This turned out to be the last of the harrowing TV episodes in Ed's life. NBC made a good offer. Sullivan brought it to CBS. Jack Van Valkenburg hedged. He got Sullivan aside, and asked him why he needed a producer like Marlo Lewis. Someone got Lewis aside and said that, if he played it smart, he could produce Toast of the Town himself, and rotate several masters of ceremony—without Sullivan. A network lawyer said: "What is Sullivan? Just an inept M.C."

A legalistic war was on. CBS returned to Sullivan $125,000 of his salary which it had been holding in escrow. This forced Ed to pay full taxes on it at once. NBC said that Smiley would be appreciated on their network. They would even name the show after him.

Sullivan appealed to a lawyer named Arnold Grant for help. Mr. Grant took Sullivan to Music Corporation of America, theatrical agents, and Sonny Werblin became Ed's handholder. For a while, the little man with the big ambition looked like the bouncing ball in the old-time movie tunes.

When Columbia Broadcasting System surrenders, everything drops including its corporate trousers. CBS gave Ed Sullivan a twenty-year contract. The name of the program was changed to The Ed Sullivan Show. The weekly budget is $50,000; half for talent, half for producers, directors, band, ushers, and theater. Sullivan's salary: $8,000 a week.

Of this, half goes into an escrow fund, to be paid to him in his declining years, if any. This leaves $4,000. Several hundred more goes for taxes and fees. Sullivan has $1,500 per week take-home pay. This is $250 more than the whole show cost nine years ago.

The contract says that this is to continue for seven years. After, CBS must pay Ed Sullivan $100,000 a year for the next thirteen years whether he works or not. He seems secure up until age seventy-three.

With all of the money coming in, the Sullivans remain comparatively poor. Sylvia is the bookkeeper. She takes charge of all folding money, and makes all disbursements. When she and Ed ride a taxi to Pavillon for dinner, she sits without protest as her husband pays the fifty-five cents and gives the driver a quarter tip.

Their only valuable possession, besides Sylvia's mink coat and a Renoir painting Ed bought for her birthday, is a place called Kettletown Farm, near Southbury, Connecticut. The Sullivans had never owned a house, never lived in one. To get a down payment, Ed had to go to his friends at CBS and borrow $25,000. The place is antique American, about 185 acres. The house is early spinning wheel. There are some cows. So far, $150,000 has been paid into Kettletown; $100,000 is owed on mortgages. The reason his bank account remains small (according to Sullivan) is that he likes to shoot craps. The dice are hot for everyone but Ed.

Most of the weekday work now is on the phone—arguing with agents about fees for stars—or watching kinescopes of acts he

may want to book, or flying to Japan or to Paris or Rome to look at
personalities who may be worth importing.

Today, Sullivan still lacks a good sense of perspective. He is the
long-term king of television, the most enduring thing on camera.
And yet he still winces at the newspaper critics, and he would
rather tick off his "firsts" (first with television biographies; first to
introduce celebrities from the audience; first with Sadlers Wells
Ballet; first with scenes from unreleased motion pictures; first with
opera) than to discuss his own superhuman, almost miraculous
rise to the top.

Aaron Burr

It was cool for a summer morning and the barge came across the
Hudson in long rhythmic sweeps of the oars, like a dark beetle in
a lily pond. The early sun stared across the woods of Manhattan
and tossed gold against the dark rocks of the Jersey Palisades. The
barge grated against sand at Weehawken and four men got out.
Today, two great men would die—one swiftly, one slowly.

The date was July 11, 1804. Aaron Burr, who had just completed a term as Vice-President of the United States, had challenged Alexander Hamilton, former Secretary of the Treasury, to a
duel.

The enmity of the men dated back to 1791, when Burr defeated
Hamilton's father-in-law, General Philip Schuyler, for the U.S.
Senate. Nine years later, Burr and Thomas Jefferson were dead-
locked in electoral votes for the Presidency. The deadlock lasted
through twenty-five ballots. At that point, Hamilton switched his
influence to Jefferson.

Burr did not forget it. He and Hamilton felt their prestige decline after that, and Hamilton founded a newspaper so that he
would continue to have political influence. Burr decided to run for
governor of New York. He had the half-support of the Federalists
until Hamilton wrote: "He is a dangerous man of whom I could
detail a still more despicable opinion."

In effect, Hamilton had deprived Burr of the presidency and
now the governorship. It was the ultimate defeat. Burr issued a
challenge.

Hamilton did not want to accept. He could not summon the
courage to face Burr at ten paces and pull a trigger. He had
stepped on this man politically, and had killed him, but he could

not grind his heel on the quivering remains. The challenge was accepted with reluctance and, so that the laws of New York would not be violated, the men agreed to meet at Weehawken.

Burr was waiting when Hamilton arrived. They exchanged formal greeting. The seconds conferred, counted off ten full paces, and tossed a coin for honors of position and honors of giving the word to fire.

Both went to Hamilton's second. The duelists loaded the matched pistols and then stood on the lines marking ten full paces. Mr. Hamilton's second said: "I shall ask the gentlemen if they are ready. If the answer is yes, I shall say 'Pree-sent!' The gentlemen will thereupon lower the pistols from a vertical position, take aim, and fire."

The sun was sharp upon them when the word was given. Hamilton's second said, "Pree-sent!" and both men looked at each other in silence and the pistols were lowered. Hamilton did not fire. He waited. Burr pulled the trigger and a sound like a pop of a paper bag hit the cliffs and echoed across the water.

Hamilton grunted, and clutched his stomach. The handsome little man folded forward into the sand. Burr stepped forward, an expression of sympathy on his face, and his mouth opened to say something, but his second said that, if they waited longer, they would be identified.

Burr left. A surgeon came up and ministered to Hamilton's wound. He spent thirty hours in agony and died.

Burr left his home in Richmond Hill and became an outcast. He bought a tract of land in Louisiana and, some said, tried to start his own empire. President Jefferson had him arrested for treason and Burr was acquitted by a jury, but not by the public, and he fled to England.

He lived a cheap life on borrowed money, and, when his daughter tried to join him, her ship sank in a storm. In advanced age, Burr came back to America and practiced law in Port Richmond. He stopped breathing on September 14, 1836, but he really died that morning at Weehawken. . . .

William Hartack

He fights time and so he sits uneasily in luxury. The house on Deer Run, in Miami Springs, is bright and sexy, with deep pile white rugs and lavender seminudes on the wall of the bar and gay chairs designed by the man who has no patience. His name is

William Hartack and, for the fourth time, he is Jockey of the Year.

Most jockeys look like boys with the heads of old men, but Mr. Hartack has blue eyes, a thick pelt of dark shiny hair, a small iron body and features that 150 girls find attractive enough to make him worth a try. Most of the girls who make a pilgrimage to Deer Run are beautiful and wear pants as tight as an extra layer of skin.

The sports writers do not like William. They call him tough and insolent. He is. He is a perfectionist who gets on a horse to fight the clock and he has no time for tact. They say that he is not a picture rider. He isn't. On a hard run, his hips should be level with his head. Instead, Hartack bounces, his arms flap, and he switches the whip from one hand to the other by passing it through his teeth.

He isn't a picture rider, but he rides more winners than anybody else. He has been in about ten thousand races and has won about twenty-seven hundred. This year he won more than three hundred, and that beats Gomez and Shoemaker, the runners-up. A few years ago, his mounts won $3,000,000 in one season. At the age of twenty-seven, he earns somewhere around $200,000 a year, owns the house on Deer Run, a Cadillac and a Jaguar, a big wardrobe, a farm, some municipal bonds, and is going to build a motel near the Miami Airport.

I spoke to him about girls. He looked down at his hands. He doesn't smile easily. "I like kids," he said. "Someday I'll get married." He let it go at that. He didn't mention his charities: the boys' baseball teams, the bowling teams, the den mother feeling he has for youngsters.

When he dismounts from a loser, the trainer and the owner wait for him. "What happened?" they say. Tact tells a jockey to excuse the horse and the trainer by saying that the horse was bumped, or dirt was kicked in his face, or he lugged in at the wrong time. Hartack stands for the brutal truth. "The reason we lost," he says, "is that the horse didn't have it." Outfits like Calumet and Frank Merrill do not use Hartack. Once, in the tack room, he said to a trainer, "Why don't you put me on slow horses?"

He doesn't like racing writers either. "I don't know five men in the sports field who tell the truth," he says, "because they don't know the truth." He keeps a bale of bad notices about himself. When he feels himself getting into an uncomfortably good mood, he opens the clippings and starts reading about how awful he is.

"When these writers approach me," he says, "they don't stand a chance."

His mother was killed in a car accident when he was five. His father worked hard loading, by hand, in the coal mines of Pennsylvania. Today he has his father on a beautiful farm. There is a story—and that's all it is—that if he catches his father working, he stops his allowance. There is a sister Evelyn, twenty-nine, and married, and a sister Maxine, twenty, engaged.

I asked him if he had a special pride in anything he has ever done. "Yes," he said. The grin came up and he wiped it off. "I once entered a jumping race at Monmouth and won it. The horse was Mielaison. It's good I won it, I guess, or else I'd still be trying."

Most jockeys believe that horses are stupid animals. Hartack disagrees. "Some are. Some have racing intelligence. There was one named Pet Bully. He wasn't great, but he could pace himself and that's intelligent. If he found himself out in front, he would slow down: when he felt another horse closing in from behind, Pet Bully would open up."

Once he was in Chicago on a horse named Mighty Moment. Hartack was sitting easy in third place when the bridle came off in his hands. The bit came out. "The whole thing fell in my lap. Some other jocks went by and I yelled, 'Look. No hands.'

"Mighty Moment finished five lengths behind the winner. One race later, he ended fifteen lengths in back.

"The trainer said to me, 'What do you think is the matter?' I said, 'Run him without a bridle!' "

When William Hartack loses—which is three quarters of the time—he is mad. Not moody. Mad. "I'm mad at one of three things," he says. "Me. The horse. Or the trainer. If the trainer does his work properly, and the horse does his part, I must do mine."

He is sensitive. He is unpopular. He is unreasonable. He is tough. He is honest. He is a champion. . . .

Jack Paar

The bellmen recognized him in the lobby of the Beverly Hilton. They nodded and smiled. He removed the cigar from his mouth and smiled. No words were spoken. The man wanted to remain at the big Hollywood hotel in a status called incognito. He looked like Jack Paar. He was as nervous as Jack Paar. He was Jack Paar.

So he signed the register: Mr. Primrose Magoo, and then swung the register around so that the assistant manager could look at the name. "Yes, sir," he said. He hit the bell. "Boy, please take Mr. Primrose Magoo to his suite." Paar smiled apologetically.

"It's just that I don't want the phone ringing all the time," he said. The assistant manager smiled understandingly. Paar smiled. "You know," he said, "the phones, the autographs—all I want is peace and quiet." The assistant manager watched him walk to the elevator behind the boy and the luggage.

Jack Paar looked over the rooms. They were beautiful. Good clear view of 20th Century-Fox's oil well. Nice furniture. Cheerful decor. The boy raised the blinds, turned on the air conditioning, switched the bathroom light on, put the baggage on the racks, and held out his hand. Paar tipped him.

Then he picked up the phone. "In case anyone calls me," he said, "I'm Primrose Magoo." There was a silence. "You're who, Mr. Magoo?"

"Magoo. Magoo. I'm not Jack Paar to anybody."

"Of course, Mr. Magoo," the operator said sweetly. "The listing just came in. It says Primrose Magoo. Why should anyone who wants you ask for Mr. Paar?"

"Never mind," he said. "Just give me long distance." He got the operator and called the National Broadcasting Company in New York. "Mitzi," he said to his assistant, "I'm at the Beverly Hilton in Los Angeles. Yes. It's me. In case you want me, just ask for Mr. Primrose Magoo. What? Primrose, dammit. Like the flower. Magoo. You don't have to know how to spell it, dear. Just ask for it and I'll pick up the phone. Anything new. . . ?"

Mr. Paar, who is as sensitive as Miss America with a chin pimple, sat. No phone calls. No autograph hounds. No knocking on the door. Nothing. "This," he said to himself, "is great. Simply great." He phoned a few members of the cast in other rooms. "In case you want me, just call Primrose Magoo. What? I wish you were that funny on the program, pal."

He sat. Nothing. He fidgeted a little. Nothing. He tried a newspaper. Nothing. He went into the bathroom and tried the faucets. The hot water ran hot, the cold ran cold. He examined the closets. On the hat shelf was a Bible autographed by Cecil B. DeMille. He looked out the window and rocked on his heels. Nothing. The oil was still there.

Paar decided to call Mrs. Paar back home. A good idea. He picked up the phone and panicked. What was the home phone number? How ridiculous not to remember. It was Deerfield something or other. How many numbers could little old Bronxville have? He put the phone back on the cradle.

It was unlisted. Oh well. He picked up the phone again. "Honey," he said. "Get me information in Bronxville, New York. Yes, Bronxville." He waited and spun the cigar slowly in his mouth. "Hello, Bronxville information? Good. This is Jack Paar. I'm out in California and I can't remember my home phone number. Can you—

"Oh, come on. I know it's unlisted. It's my number. Excuse me? You listen to the program? Well, that makes everything easy. Recognize the voice? I'm Jack Paar. Sure. I just want to call home and—what? You can't. Now look here, Miss. It happens to be my phone and I pay the bills and I want that number. Why don't you ring Mrs. Paar and ask her if she wants to speak to her lawful husband?

"This is too much. Tell you what you do, Miss. Now don't hang up. I know that rules are rules. I can even tell you what the number used to be before I changed it. Once it was Deerfield 7-7187; once it was Deerfield 7-9299. Excuse me? No, dear. That's what I want you to do. If I remembered, would I be on my knees begging?

"All right. Okay. If you want to make sure that this is Jack Paar speaking, call me back right away at the Beverly Hilton Hotel in Beverly Hills, California. Just call right back. Call collect. I'll pay for it. Then you'll be sure.

"What dear? Oh no. Just ask for Primrose Magoo."

John Barrymore

It was hot. At noon, there was no shady side to 44th Street. A policeman's horse stood with hanging head outside The Lambs. Up on Sixth Avenue, Joseph Urban rehearsed his newest extravaganza at the Hippodrome. The Texas Guinan Club was closed for the month of August. Eva Tanguay's name was up in lights at the Palace. " 'I don't care,' " she sang. " 'I don't care . . .' "

A cab pulled to a stop in front of The Lambs. A man hopped out, tossing a bill to the driver. He wore a curving homburg and he paused in front of the horse to raise it politely. "Don't whinny," he said softly. "I couldn't stand it today."

The man went into the actors' club. At the reception desk, the attendant grinned and said hello. On the rack of members beside him, he raised the name of John Barrymore to the "In" position. No one could ever mistake that classic profile, that pale, handsome face with the wounded eyes.

The actor removed his hat and tossed it into the cloakroom. He went on through the archway, into the hardwood dining room, and on through another arch to the billiard room. He nodded to Joe Penner and Victor Moore and Jack Pearl, who were arguing with George Shelton about whether the New York Giants were starting to fall apart.

Two overhead fans flicked big blades at the dead air. Mr. Barrymore stepped up to the bar. He turned stern eyes on the white-jacketed bartender. "This is no time for levity, Joe," he said. "Just bring three of the most sparkling gins at your command and put them in something like a water pail. I'm a nervous man."

"Yes, sir," the bartender said. He poured three hookers and drained them carefully into a big goblet. The glass was placed in front of the Great One. He touched it and permitted himself a small smile.

"No man ever died in a saloon," he said. "Men are killed in the hospitals which come after saloons." "Did you?" the bartender said. Barrymore nodded. "This morning," he said. "Part of a graduating class at Bellevue. The most undistinguished bums I've ever met."

He started to lift the glass. The hand shook. The glass was set back on the bar. Barrymore seemed to be repelled by a big campaign button worn by the bartender. It held a photo of Alfred E. Smith, but, when the bartender turned the photo disappeared and it said "Vote Democratic."

This disturbed Barrymore. His nervousness increased. A mist was on his noble brow. He turned to look away. An old actor stood under the fan, sipping a prohibition beer. Barrymore was finding it difficult to breathe. He watched the old actor and he was horrified to find that the glue on the front of the man's toupee had become unstuck.

The overhead fan lifted the front of the wig a little, held it aloft for a second, and dropped it. Then it lifted again, held, and fell. "Oh, my God," Barrymore murmured. "Oh, my God." He lifted the glass with both hands, and tried to reach his trembling lips, and failed. The glass went back on the bar.

His fingers drummed the mahogany. Dan Healy told a joke and the roar of laughter assaulted the Barrymore ears in waves of surf. He turned his face in the opposite direction and saw a man hoisting firkins of shaved ice across the bar. "Nice quiet place," Barrymore said. "Oh, my God . . ."

The man with the ice turned to look at the star. Barrymore was stunned to see that only one eye turned. The other continued to stare across the room. He held his hand out, and watched it tremble. "This," he said murmurously, "is no day for glass eyes. This is hardly a day for real ones."

The man with the ice smiled. "Too noisy?" he said. Barrymore looked at the rebel eye and said, "I need more than fifty per cent of anybody's attention," and walked out. He picked up his homburg in the cloakroom, mopped the perspiration off his forehead, and set the hat rakishly, flicking the long blond locks back under the brim.

"Check me out," he said to the attendant, who removed Barrymore's name from the "In" file. "I'm always being checked out or in, off or on, up or down, stop or go. Mostly stop."

He was palsied with fright when he hit the hot sidewalk in front of The Lambs. The horse was gone. For a moment, he wondered whether the animal had left, or whether both his eyeballs had turned to glass. At that moment, the rehearsal at the Hippodrome ended, and forty midgets marched past Barrymore in police uniforms.

He hailed a taxi "Where to?" the driver said. Barrymore sank in the back seat. "Back to Bellevue," he whispered. . . .

Will Durant

The bar at the Castellana Hilton was dark and cool and the waiters glided in silence. The handsome heretic smiled absent-mindedly into the orange whirlpool of tea. His love sat beside him and, in the depths of the cup of tea, fifty years did not seem very long ago. It wasn't, at least not to a man who thinks in terms of millennia.

It is nearly fifty years since Will Durant married Ariel Alexander—a marriage, according to all the religious and ethnical precepts, which should not have lasted fifty days. Now, Dr. Will Durant is almost seventy-eight years old; Ariel is sixty-five. He has pink baby skin and white hair and a snowy mustache. She is dark and vivacious, a woman with very short hair, a plain print dress, and the animated face of an orphan seeing the circus for the first time.

Within my ken, there is no marriage like this one. Dr. Durant is the author of *The Story of Philosophy, Transition,* and seven volumes of a ten-volume work called *The Story of Civilization.* Mrs. Durant's family were Jewish refugees from Poland. He grew up in Kearney, New Jersey, of a Catholic family. His sister recently celebrated her golden anniversary as a nun at St. Michael's in Jersey City. Ariel Alexander lived in Harlem.

He broke with his church. He finished an eight-year course at St. Peter's in Jersey City in seven years, as he puts it wryly, "I came in second, in a class of two." He taught in a small school in New York at twenty-five, and Ariel was a student, thirteen. The young man fell in love with the child. She was fifteen when he obtained the consent of her parents to marry her in a judge's chambers in New York. He had to resign his teaching job.

She didn't have carfare, so she put on her roller skates, and her skinny legs flashed all the way from Harlem to downtown New York. En route, she fell. She arrived with torn stockings, her hair was disheveled and her face bruised, the skates hung around her neck. The judge spent an hour begging Dr. Durant not to "rob the cradle." He might have saved his breath.

We sat in the Castellana Hilton, in Madrid, talking about it. My wife, Kelly, made notes. Dr. Durant is here to write the prologue to a motion picture called *The Fall of the Roman Empire.* He works in longhand; Ariel "types my stuff, tears it down, and I rewrite it. Then she tears it down and it is ready."

When the doctor fell in love, he forgot the use of the personal pronoun. All of his great books, "we" wrote. It is apparent to anyone who listens that these two human trees not only grew side by side, their roots fused. They are one person.

He speaks slowly, as scholars should. She speaks in animated bursts, and he stops in midsentence in deference to her. "I am his old shoe," she says, "hanging on for fifty years. He loves me because I love him to distraction. My ears," she says, "are open to the world. His head is buried in the past. In a way, I'm his headache too. I always ask 'why.' "

They have a married daughter and two grandchildren and they live in California. Volume eight of "their" *Story of Civilization: The Age of Louis XIV,* was about to be published. "We know each other's thoughts and moods," she says; "and when to shut up. Once, in a public group, I wouldn't shut up and he kept passing plates of nuts to me. I ate them and still kept talking."

Only once did she become serious. "He was my teacher and my master fifty years ago. He wrote on my blank mind. He is still my teacher and my master." The doctor shook his head no. He

changed the subject and recalled how much trouble he had been
to Sister Cecilia in Kearney when he was a little boy. Many years
later, she invited him to a church celebration. He wrote and asked
if she was sure she would want a "heretic" to be present.

The nun said yes. So he went. And when the celebrated doctor
of philosophy met the old nun, she reached forward, traced the
tips of her fingers across his forehead and down the cheeks. "Yes,"
she said, "this is my Willy. My Willy." She was blind.

Mrs. Durant reminded her husband that, when she arrived at
the wedding on roller skates, he had forgotten to buy a wedding
ring. They borrowed one from a clerk. Ariel held her left hand up
for my wife to see. It was bare. "He never bought one for me," she
said, "and I have never missed it."

The doctor covered her hand with his. This was the true bond.
My wife looked at me and laughed and wiped her eyes. "I'm so
silly," she said, "but isn't it a lovely world . . .? "

Arthur Carney

He stands on the edge of the waves, the face red and half frozen,
the fleece collar up, hands deep in pockets, and he stares out
across Long Island Sound toward the sea. The thunderous surf
brings peace. He watches the white terns walk the lacy hem of the
waves and he lifts his eyes at the lonely cry of the gull.

Few men are more serious than Art Carney. No one has less
glamour and greater inner sensitivity. He is much more than a
funny man. Mr. Carney is a fine actor, a man who can run the
range between a slapstick waiter and a maudlin alcoholic on a
telephone. He's a pro.

The big house up on the dunes is his. It's in Saybrook, Connecticut, and he and Jean bought it so that they could be close to
the sea. Jean is economical. They heat only a small part of the
house in winter. She has been saving Art's money for twenty
years. The lady is petite and pretty, and she knows her man better
than he knows himself.

Arthur met Jean in A. D. Davis High School in Mount Vernon.
At the dances, he was the kid standing against the wall. He was
too shy to join the dramatic society, but not too shy to come home

from a movie and do a deadly imitation of Ned Sparks, John
Barrymore, Jimmy Durante and Fred Allen. In school, when Art
was called upon for a recitation, he blushed and stammered, "Miss
Stimson, I'm unprepared."

Before television, Carney worked in radio and he could do it
without blushing because there was no audience. He was an unknown mimic on a world news broadcast. The announcer would
say: "At Ten Downing Street in London yesterday, Winston
Churchill got to his feet and said . . ." and Carney would imitate
Churchill's words and voice.

It was nothing at all for Carney to do Franklin D. Roosevelt,
Wendell Willkie, Cordell Hull, Mohandas Gandhi, Adolf Hitler
and Benito Mussolini on one broadcast. He was one of the few
mimics who made it pay. But he wasn't acting.

He did not know he was funny until Morey Amsterdam hired
Carney for the part of a wild waiter with plastered-down hair and
dizzy opinions. After that, he went with Jackie Gleason and "The
Honeymooners." Gleason built Art's salary up to $3,000 a week
and told the world that Carney was one of the greatest talents he
had ever seen.

Now, in his forties, Carney has come of age as an actor. He stars
in the "Art Carney Show." He works only in the big ones—sixty
minutes and ninety minutes—and he does eight of them a year.
He rehearses in an old bar mitzvah room on the Lower East Side
of New York.

He does not play the big star to the rest of the cast and, when
someone else utters a funny line, Carney's face breaks into a
hundred tiny chips of laughter. He listens to the director, takes
correction gracefully, runs through the same scene over and over
until it's right.

Carney can't be pushed. Once, when Gleason presented him
with a fat contract, Art declined it because there was a clause
which said that, if the show moved to California, he would have
to go. The actor said that his children were going to school in
Yonkers, and he would not consider moving them.

Since then, he has sold the old fifteen-thousand-dollar house
and has bought a big beautiful one near the Bronxville line. It has
an acre and a half of trees and lawn, a big white brick colonial
residence with black shutters, and, over the garage, two extra
bedrooms and a bath.

The children are, like their parents, normal. Eileen, seventeen,
is a senior at Roosevelt High; Bryan, thirteen, is in the eighth
grade at P. S. 8; Paul, seven, is in the second grade at P. S. 30.
They don't know yet what they will do with their lives. Eileen has

discovered rock 'n' roll and boys; Bryan rigs his own hi-fi sets; Paul is interested in finding out what he's going to get for Christmas.

On the weekends, Art and Jean go off by themselves to the big summer house in Saybrook. She putters in the kitchen. He stacks wood, or reads by the fire, or digs himself into a windbreaker and goes for a lonely walk along the beach.

The wind comes fresh and cold from the southeast and combs the long swale grass on the dunes. The waves curl bottle green on the sand. A gull wheels overhead and cries. The man on the sand looks up. He's the audience of one.

François de la Rochefoucauld

He was a man for devising aphorisms and making love. With two such talents, one could hardly live more delightfully—or more dangerously—in France three hundred years ago, but François de la Rochefoucauld was intoxicated with his own charm. He cultivated shoulder-length dark wavy hair, a mustache with a delicate droop, heavy-lidded eyes which could denote passion or sleepiness depending on the beholder, boots overhung with ochre lace, and a sword which clanked at his side.

In time, he became a more intimate friend to Queen Anne than the King. He joined the army when he was sixteen and married blonde Andrée de Vivonne at once. De la Rochefoucauld farmed a little, but he was not a man for watching vegetables grow. He tired of farming and Andrée at the same time, and directed his charm toward the celebrated Madame de Chevreuse, a court favorite of Louis XIV. From the madame to the Queen was but a step through a door for François.

Still, in spite of his boastfulness, he did not spend all his time tiptoeing into darkened perfumed boudoirs. De la Rochefoucauld found time to fight in battle for his king, was wounded three times, and fought Cardinal Richelieu too. If this man sacrificed anything, it must have been sleep because he also found time to write three books, and this may account for the drooping lids. The books are: *Letters, Memoirs* and *Maxims*.

His amatory excellence is now lost to history, but the maxims are alive. Thus François sustained his fourth wound after death, because if he had a choice, it would be the other way around. One cannot kiss a maxim, or entreat it for a special favor. No warm affectionate man wants to remain alive in a dusty book on a library shelf.

And yet, this is what happened to de la Rochefoucauld, and his maxims are as adroit today as they were in the seventeenth century:

"We often do good that we may do harm with impunity."

"We must confess to small faults to create the impression that we have no great ones."

"Self-love is the greatest of all flatterers."

"Passion turns the cleverest of men into idiots and makes the greatest blockheads look clever."

"We all have the strength to endure the misfortune of others."

Sometimes, when the mellow mood was on him, François de la Rochefoucauld invented flowery maxims with fewer thorns. "Grace is to the body what clear thinking is to the mind." And: "It is difficult to define love: in the soul it is a thirst for mastery; in the mind a harmony of thought; in the body a delicately hidden desire to possess, after many mysteries, whatsoever one loves."

Conversely, the grand seigneur often became the sharp cynic: "There are successful marriages, but no blissful ones." "We get so much in the habit of wearing a disguise before others that we finally appear disguised before ourselves." "Some people revolt us in spite of their virtues where others please us in spite of their faults."

"The man who thinks he can do without the world is indeed mistaken; the man who thinks the world cannot do without him is mistaken even worse." "Absence weakens lukewarm feelings but intensifies great ones as a wind snuffs out a little candle but feeds a great fire."

His world was sharply split by likes and dislikes. As a popinjay, he saw no neutrality anywhere. "We always like people who admire us, we do not always like the people we admire." "We can forgive those who bore us; we cannot forgive those whom we bore." "What keeps husbands and wives from tiring of being together is that they talk of nothing but themselves."

His words are borrowed with impunity, but his real cleverness consisted in not being caught. He would have preferred to die, I am sure, defending a woman's honor, or assailing it. De la Rochefoucauld made the mistake of living on until he was sixty-six. He found that he could no longer make love, so he wrote about it. His deeds were reduced to words.

At the end, no irate husband claimed his life; no jealous woman lifted a dagger from a warm bosom. Gout got him. . . .

Edward Leach

It was hot and sunny at the country club and the golfers waiting around the first tee leaned on their number one woods or stood in the shade. The caddy master called out "Mr. and Mrs. Leach" and a stout giant of a man in Texas boots stepped forward with a petite woman. "Okay, Polly," the big man said. His voice was three miles below sea level. The crowd watched the woman step up, tee up, and whack the white ball down the fairway.

A man standing in the shade watched Edward Curtis Leach, Jr., a fiftyish man who weighs 264 pounds, step up, flail at the ball, and send it bounding like a baby bunny forty yards into the rough. "There's your typical Texan," the watching man said. "He's fat as a hog, rich as Croesus, wears cowboy boots with spikes on a golf course, and can't hit a ball."

Maybe. Maybe not. If the man who stood in the shade reads this, he may revise his opinion. Ed Leach's mother was Marguerite O'Sullivan Leach. She was six feet two inches tall, weighed two hundred pounds, and sang in the Metropolitan Opera House as a mezzo-soprano. His father was six feet three inches tall, 160 pounds. The big man in the Texas boots was their only child.

He was born in Cleveland in 1913. His feet were on backward, with the heels to the front. At the age of eleven days, the infant was operated on by a doctor from Mt. Sinai Hospital. Other doctors had examined the infant and said nothing could be done. The one doctor said, "I promise you nothing. The baby will need many operations. Each time, I will turn the toes in, toward each other, a little at a time." Each time, the infant's feet and legs, all the way to the hips, were placed in casts.

The parents could not bear to listen to the screams of the infant. The doctor perspired as he worked. "Little babies," he said, "have bones like gristle. We will turn a little at a time." The operations continued for three and one half years. So did the hip casts. After that, he wore steel braces. No one expected anything from him in his life ahead. He was fat and his feet were almost straight, but he could hardly walk. He was jolly enough, but when he laughed, tears of pain shimmered in his eyes.

His father bought him a tricycle. It wasn't easy to pedal, wearing steel braces, but he was ordered to keep riding. "Edward!" his mother called from the window, "turn your feet out." Ed wore

braces until he was nine. He walked like a slow rocking horse. His
feet hurt. His hip joints ached. The boy wanted to quit. The
parents wanted no quitter in the family.

Ed Jr. was ten when he was taken to Tatanagra, in Bengal. His
father had a big contract to build the Tata Steel Works. The
Leaches had a lavish home, lots of servants, and a promise of lots
of money. The fat little boy would not have to amount to anything
in life. The money would soon be there. The father supervised
hundreds of workmen and the big plant took shape. Edward Sr.
was a health faddist. He believed in raw vegetables, exercise,
Bernarr MacFadden, and no doctors.

One morning, a year and a half after they arrived, the engineer
had a fever. In thirty hours, he was dead. Four hours later, in spite
of the tears of Mrs. Leach and the boy with the club feet, the
Hindus buried Ed Sr. The cause of death: black smallpox. The
widow and child were taken from their mansion and thrust into a
small room.

For the rest of his life, all the boy could remember was the
small room, draped mosquito netting, food slid to them through
an opening in a door, and his mother talking aloud to his dead
father. When the quarantine period passed, the Bengalese government gave Mrs. Leach some money and two tickets on an
ocean liner.

Mrs. Leach was a one-man woman. She fought the horrifying
dreams alone. When they got home, she waited awhile and sent
her son to the Tennessee Military Institute at Sweetwater. There,
he drilled every day on bad feet and soothed the blisters all night.
The other freshmen nicknamed him "Twinkletoes" and "Beef."
The kid had to pretend that these names were funny.

One of the freshmen was Mead Johnson. His father manu-
factured baby food. Mead was a good competitor. When he found
that there were medals and decorations to be won, he went out for
all of them. So did Ed Leach. Both boys went through the acad-
emy ranking first and second. In the senior years, Cadet Leach
won almost all the medals, and finished school with a four-year
average of 98.75 per cent.

This mark has never been surpassed. The boy with the chronic
pain told his mother he wanted to go to West Point . . .

It was never easy for Ed Leach. He had been in West Point
nine months when he sustained a spinal injury playing football
and was sent home. His mother was in Florida, dabbling in real
estate, and he found himself in Mineral Wells, Texas, working at
the Baker Hotel for fifteen cents an hour.

Guts was never a pretty word. But that's all Leach had. He was
a big kid, weighing 235 pounds and he had neither a room nor a
suit of clothes. He was staked to both by Henry Love, manager of
the Baker. Ironically, Love did not like the boy, and the boy did
not like Mr. Love. Still, no one could stop Ed Leach. He worked
harder and more intelligently than anyone else and he rose from
assistant gardener to manager of the coffee shop to assistant
maître d'hôtel.

Then Love took him out on the sidewalk and said: "See our
hotel? It's going to stay in business long after we're both gone. But
you're going first. You're fired. Know why? You're arrogant." After
that, Leach tried all the harder, as he had once tried and won
school honors over Mead Johnson. But nothing went right. And,
truthfully, he was arrogant.

Jobs? He sold cars. He tried selling ten-cent insurance to Negroes. He started a window-washing business. He opened the old
Period Hotel in Mineral Wells on borrowed money because a
Baptist convention was coming to town. He had no electricity, no
gas, no water. Leach begged and borrowed. He cooked, served
meals, made beds, ran luggage and, when the convention left, he
had $1,500.

He drove an oil truck, was food manager at the Holt Hotel in
Wichita Falls, hired a bankrupt band which was trying to hock
horns, and, in 1936 was assistant manager. To draw business, he
even baked three one-dollar bills in the lunch rolls, and made sure
that one was served to the local newscaster.

He did so well that the Raleigh Hotel in Waco offered Leach a
job as food manager at 10 per cent of the profits. When he arrived, big Ed found that there were no profits. Income was $1,500
a month; expenses $3,000. So he fired everybody, did his own
marketing at dawn, cooked, served and washed dishes. He made
so much money that the manager changed the deal to $350 a
month and 5 per cent of profits.

In 1939, he took his bent feet to Fort Worth and sold Campbell
soup. He was twenty-six years old. He hitched rides on long-dis-
tance trucks to see his mother in Florida. His weight was over 300
pounds and once hit 345. Ed quit Campbell and took a job as
maître d' in the Texas Hotel, a flashy place with six hundred
rooms. He got $190 a month and a room. In one year, Amon
Carter awarded Leach a pin as the best salesman in Fort Worth.

This led to an offer from W. L. Moody III to become manager
of the East End Motor Court in Galveston. Few had ever heard of
motels in 1940, and what the few had heard was bad. Leach
offered a hundred dollars for a better name for the place. A

thirteen-year-old girl suggested Jack Tar, because that's what the British call their sailors. It sounded good. Leach paid her.

He worked thirteen years for Moody, and they fought every inch of the way. The only thing Leach learned from Moody was to pause to appreciate beauty in a painting, a cactus bud, a green rock on the edge of the sea. One of the beauties was Leach's secretary, Polly Norwood, who had paused for a second look; he married her.

She taught him much. One was that if he wore Texas boots, they would hug his ankles and his feet would hurt less. He has worn them ever since. In 1953, a quiet man named Charles Sammons bought the Jack Tar. He owned insurance companies. Sammons and Leach became a team. Sammons was rich and quiet; Leach was poor and loud.

They bought the Fort Harrison Hotel in Clearwater, Florida, the Key Colony in Marathon, Florida, the Francis Marion in Charleston, South Carolina, the Grove Park in Asheville, the Grand Bahama in West End, the Jack Tar in San Francisco, and kept going. The body with the club feet and the spinal injury got a lifetime contract at a big sum, plus retirement benefits so that he will never have to worry about finances.

Leach runs hotels from Charleston to San Francisco, from Lansing, Michigan, to the Florida Keys. There are three children: Peggy Ann, nineteen; Betsy Kay, seventeen; and Edward, thirteen. When he stepped off the tee at the country club, a man in the shade looked at the cowboy boots and said, "There's a typical Texan . . ."

At lunch, Mrs. Leach ate heartily. Ed Leach drank a glass of fluid. "What do you call this reducing stuff?" he asked bitterly. "Metrecal," said Mrs. Leach. "Who makes it?" Leach said. The lady smiled. "The boy you beat in school, Mead Johnson. He's now taking you down a peg. . . ."

Joan Crawford

The long aluminum needles flew through the skein of yellow wool like nervous chopsticks. The woman whose skillful hands made the afghan heard the phone, set the needles and wool on her lap, reached one hand for the phone, the other to pet the gray poodle on her desk, and her voice said: "Yes? Yes. This is Joan Crawford. What's that? Oh. Thank you." She hung up and the fingers went back to the needles.

She sat in an office-library, high over Fifth Avenue, New York. The room is part of a rich duplex apartment, a plush hive for the queen bee. She has been a motion picture star for thirty-five years and, at a time of life when most glamour women have stepped back into the wings of oblivion, she is at stage center, more dynamic than ever.

She stars in one motion picture a year. She is on the board of directors of Pepsi-Cola. She has made a pilot film in color for television. She is the mother of four adopted children. She has had four husbands. Miss Crawford, physically, is a large head on a small body: black stenciled eyebrows, a pair of pain-racked blue eyes, and a slashy red mouth covering clenched teeth.

Joan Crawford is an assortment of twanging nerves exploding in productive work. She has starred in eighty-three motion pictures, has earned an Oscar, world adulation, and ten million dollars. She still has the Oscar and the adulation. Once she had a big mansion in Hollywood. Today it is owned by Donald O'Connor. Miss Crawford keeps a small apartment in the Loretta Young Building.

The star has dimmed, but it will not die. If Joan Crawford can no longer play the sexy flapper, she can play the maniac. She and Bette Davis slugged it out toe-to-toe for honors in *What Ever Happened to Baby Jane?* The newest Crawford picture is *Strait Jacket.* The title tells the story.

Joan Crawford picks her scripts, can earn $250,000 a year for one picture, and has it arranged that she gets a small amount each year over a long period of time. She also gets a good salary from Pepsi-Cola, and has traveled 870,000 miles as Pepsi's pepper-upper. She opens new bottling plants, shakes hands with salesmen, and makes four-word speeches in a suffusion of shyness: "Thank you. God bless."

Still, her personal life is full of luck, most of it hard. She loves knowledge, and never got beyond the sixth grade. Her clenched teeth, her innate stubbornness, taught her to read, to learn, to fight, to climb. She is still fighting, still climbing. Three marriages in a row—Douglas Fairbanks Jr., Franchot Tone and Phillip Terry —ended in divorce.

She found a mature love in Alfred N. Steel and married him in 1955. He has since died. Joan Crawford adopted five children. One was returned to her natural mother because the mother's demands were excessive. One, a boy, does not work and has a psychological problem. A daughter is in Hollywood, acting. Twin girls, Cynthia and Cathie, are sixteen, in high school.

The fingers fly, knitting. The work is compulsive. The dictation machine at her side is silent now, but she writes enough letters to keep three secretaries busy. Upstairs, one closet is full of wool yarn. One is full of hats, from top to bottom. All closet doors have full-length mirrors, all hold cellophane-covered gowns, dresses, skirts, suits, slips, and all insides of doors hold forty to fifty pairs of shoes in racks.

Now and then, the big blue eyes lift from the yarn to scan the room. She sees something, and drops the needles. It's an ash tray with two burned cigarettes. She empties it, runs a paper napkin inside, and sets it back in place. Everything in Joan Crawford's life has a place. As she enters a room, a book which sticks out an inch beyond the others will catch her eye.

She is impatient with herself, with life, with people. She walks fast, thinks fast, acts fast. A busy signal on a telephone will make her swear. A servant slow-of-foot brings Miss Crawford to her feet to do the work herself.

Absent-mindedly, she will fold and refold a napkin on a table until it looks like an air-mail stamp. She writes thank-you notes by the hundreds. A lot of her time is spent alone in this Fifth Avenue duplex. She is in bed by midnight, surrounded by portraits of Joan Crawford. She reads until two. She is up at six cooking breakfast.

One evening the needles were flying and a woman friend said, "Will you marry again?" Joan Crawford sighed. "I hope so," she murmured. "I hope so." She returned to her work, and the teeth clenched into a hard line. Once again, she was a little girl who looked at the hostile world and said, "You aren't big enough to hold me down."

Far below, in the dark of night, the high screech of brakes could be heard. Joan Crawford looked at the ceiling. "Ooh," she whispered. "Get between them, God . . ."

Family

Our family was plain. Often, we were rich in poverty. There were the Bishops on one side, and the Tier family on the other. They were friendly, in a polar sort of way. The Bishops all came from Innescorthy, Wexford, Ireland. They were farmers who lived in thatched huts, lived in the shadow of the Roman Catholic Church, and feared God more than loved Him.

The Tiers—my mother's side—were Irish and Dutch. My grandfather, Alonzo Tier, was a policeman who had a big blond mustache. His wife, Mary McSwiggen, was shrewd and thrifty. The Bishop side had more laughter, and more belligerence, than the Tiers. But the Tiers owned a house, when Grandma Bishop had a boardinghouse and, as a widow, worked scrubbing soap trays.

No childhood is fun. It is a time of growing, learning, loving and being disciplined, and only when it is far behind does it assume the character of loveliness and innocence which it never had. In the following pages, I have spared you my adolescence. The stories I have to tell concern the family, past and present.

They are presented, not to impress you with a unique clan, but to show that there is much in common between the Bishops and millions of other families. The mistakes we made, the attitudes of our children toward the world, the small triumphs and the needling, the jests, the ceremonial meetings, the raucous laughter and the tears are all here.

From these stories, I can tell you, you will learn nothing except a little bit about yourself and your family.

1943

The parlor was warm, and the stout, corseted women sat a little too erect on the camp chairs. Over near the front windows was the casket, and in it were the hundred-odd pounds of tissue, bone, and hair which, until three days ago, had been Mary Murphy. Two vigil lights flanked the big gold crucifix, and they wavered fitfully against the threat of the January gale which whistled outside the window. The women whispered sibilantly of children and measles and husbands and jobs and forgotten friends. In the dining room and in the bedrooms the younger groups laughed and giggled and preened. In the kitchen, the men sat around, smoking cigars and drinking whisky and talking, as the Irish always do, of better days.

Jimmy sat in the parlor. He was the son of the son of Mary Murphy and he leaned forward with his elbows on his knees, looking toward the casket and trying, in his mind, to measure the greatness of his grandmother. He placed her courage beside that of Joan of Arc, and he found St. Joan lacking. He measured her religious faith against that of the Little Flower and found that they were equal. He pitted her as wife, as mother, and as grandmother against every woman he knew—but none was worthy of her standards.

His judgment, of course, was clouded by affection. And there was true irony in that because, like Mary Murphy, he had never been able to show the deep love he felt.

He remembered so many and such varied things about her. The brogue was Corkonian and she said "certifiCAT" when she meant certificate. She never said "you"; it was always "ye." He was always Grandma's boy, but now, as he leaned forward on the camp chair, his hair was splashed with white and his eyes were puffy.

Through the years she had told him little bits about herself, and he learned other bits from his father and his Aunt Margaret. Now he was piecing them together in his mind and they were far from being a complete mosaic, but there was enough to see.

Mary Murphy was born on a ship going through the Straits of Gibraltar, The year was probably 1861. The vessel, a square-rigger, carried a regiment of English soldiers en route to the Middle East. Mary's father was a Color Sergeant and, in those days, men of good character were permitted to take their families with them. As the infant was born, her mother died.

Mary's first conscious memory was the cobbled streets of Cork and a proud young woman who came in on her father's arm and demanded to be called "Mother." Mary Murphy couldn't do it. She tried, but her tongue stuck to the roof of her mouth.

She left home for America when she was eighteen. This was a time of mass emigration to the New World, and the pale, slender young girl had read the letters sent to neighbors from expatriates in New York. They did not say that the streets were paved with gold, but they gave the impression of vastness and freedom of opportunity. She brought two things with her: complete independence and a sublime faith in her God and in her Church. These things were to stay with her, as strongly as her brogue, through the eighty-three years of her life.

The mosaic is scattered at this point. She did get a job as a "living-out girl" in Washington Heights, New York. There she was maid-of-all-work until, in early 1882, she married a boy from Wexford named Jim. He was short and stocky, and he had met some boys from Wexford in Jersey City and had got a job in the Eagle Oil Works there. Mary was no swooning romanticist. She got to know her man well before she consented to marriage. He had black burnside whiskers and big black mustaches. He had a healthy, roaring sense of humor and he was unafraid of hard work.

It was then that they were married, and they posed for a picture with Jim sitting gravely in a high-backed chair and Mary, frail and pale, standing behind and slightly to his left. Their first son, John, was born a year and a half later and, when the doctor said that he might not live, she insisted that he be christened the following morning—no matter the cold—and he was wrapped in a big blanket and taken to St. Patrick's Church in Jersey City on the morning of October 30, 1883, and given the name John Michael.

He lived. So did the next boy, Tom. Then, rapidly, came James and Margaret and Mary. At dawn, Jim left by the back door with his lunch pail and he wasn't seen until sundown. His earnings at the Oil Works were pathetic, but Mary Murphy dominated the household and she had no time for worry. She had time only for work and prayer. She taught Johnny to polish the black kitchen stove until it gleamed. She taught the little ones to stack firewood, to ask the butcher the price of meat, and to watch the scales when he weighed it. She taught them manners and devotion and respect.

Mary Murphy had known nothing but work, but more tests were to come. Her husband developed asthma. When the attacks came, and he convulsed on his bed gasping for the air that would not come, she knelt by the bed and said her rosary. There was no other medicine. The nearest to relaxation she ever achieved was when Jim felt good and invited some of his Wexford friends home. They would break out clay pipes and split a pint of whisky while they reminisced about the little people of Ireland. She would hear these stories upstairs as she tucked the children into bed and would chuckle as she listened and as the men bent the truth until fact and fantasy became one.

It was the week before Christmas when little Jimmy complained of a sore throat. Then Margaret had one. And Mary. The throats constricted until they screamed hoarsely for Momma, and the doctor looked and said "diphtheria." There was no cure. So Mary Murphy tended her brood and bowed her head and said "Thy will be done." Those words were hard to say. But there was no rancor in her heart when He took all three in Christmas week. It would have been easy for Mary Murphy to have bent her spine and wept. But she sat straight, and she asked no pity.

For some reason which no one can fathom, she promised God that if He blessed her with more children, she'd name them after those He took away. Two girls were born around the turn of the century, and these were christened Margaret and Mary. The latter was a baby when the final test was put to Mary Murphy. Her Jim died.

She was still young, but her friends knew better than to mention the possibility of another man. Jim had been her husband—he would remain her husband. John and Tommy were growing up, and they were put to work. They wanted more schooling, but there were mouths to feed. Tommy went to work in the oil yard, and Johnny tried a steel mill, and, later, a job as brakeman and fireman on the railroad. When family duties permitted, Mary Murphy did the neighbors' washing for small sums.

The boys handed over their pay envelopes intact. If they asked for money, they got nothing. If they kept their mouths shut, she gave them each a few coins. They were young men now, but they were still under the delicate thumb. They had to be in by ten, and they had to be out for early Mass.

Somehow, Mary Murphy managed to save a dollar now and then. This thrift went on year after year, and, when Johnny decided at twenty-four to marry Jenny Tier, Mary Murphy went downtown and bought herself a sizable house at 218 Fifth Street, Jersey City. Tommy went off and married Kitty O'Keefe and now, with Margaret and Mary growing up, Mary Murphy began to look old. The iron in the Bishop family was becoming malleable.

She took a job in Durkee's spice factory, and she worked long hours. The house she bought was an old brick one, with basement floor, parlor floor, and top floor. The back yard was adjoined by the Pennsylvania Railroad trestle, and the buckling of long lines of freight cars could be heard all night long. Tom became a foreman in the oil yard and John became a policeman, and both urged her to let them help. When the independence was upon her, Mary Murphy had a habit of clasping her wrists across her bosom. She did it then. She refused "to take a five-cent piece" from them.

When Margaret grew up, she got a job in Durkee's too. Then Mary got a job. It was then—around 1918—that Jimmy developed a love for Grandma. He was nine, the son of John, and, on Friday, if his schoolwork was good, he was given a nickel carfare to ride down to Grandma's house and to stay there until Sunday afternoon. He didn't know it at the time, but he bore a remarkable likeness to his dead grandfather. That may explain the favoritism. One of Grandma's prime dishes was pig's head, but her daughters made grimaces when she mentioned it. She taught little Jimmy to like it and used him as an excuse for buying it on Saturday for Sunday's dinner.

Here too she had a black stove shined to the highest. She used tall white mugs for tea and, when the downstairs bell rang, she always moved the old teapot from the back lid of the stove to the front before she answered the bell. It didn't matter who was at the door. It could be the mailman or the insurance man or a man selling brushes. Mary Murphy always asked him in for a cup of hot tea. In the downstairs parlor, she had a round black stove and curled under it in age was Dewey, her dog.

There was an old Victrola in the parlor too, and there was very little choice of records unless the music lover wanted to hear John McCormack. On some evenings, he sang "I Hear You Calling Me" for hours on end as Mary Murphy rocked in her chair.

In the upstairs parlor, reserved for occasions of state such as weddings and funerals, there was a big, gilt-framed picture of Mary Murphy and Jim on the day they were married. In the hall leading to the top floor, there were niches in the wall, and here little statues of saints stood in silent watchfulness. On the top floor was Mary Murphy's bedroom. It had a tremendous feather bed and, on many a cold weekend night, she tucked little Jimmy in, making sure first that he knelt beside the bed, shivering, to say his Our Father, Hail Mary, and an Act of Contrition.

The boarders were few, and they were always young men. Before they were acceptable, Mary Murphy Bishop questioned them about their faith, their devotion to what she called "juty," and their morals. One who got by was a U.S. Navy sailor named Tim

McManus. He liked Margaret, and for a time it looked serious, but Margaret noticed that, when he had shore leave, Tim liked to hit the bottle a little. Many a morning, Mary Murphy sat by his bedside and lectured him on the evils of drink, at a time when he was least able to assimilate a lecture, and she told him repeatedly that Confession and Communion, repeated often enough, would help him to lick the curse.

Then Margaret met Ed McCarthy, and this time it was serious and they were married in St. Mary's Church. The reception was held in the parlor floor, and Mary Murphy Bishop had the finest of food for the guests. However, none of the male guests could understand why they had to make trips to the corner tavern when thirst impelled. John and Tom had to explain that their mother had never tasted liquor and wouldn't permit it in the house.

It was after this that events began to move too swiftly for Mary Murphy. The impact of years was catching up with her, and she was now a little old lady with a bun of white hair. John was a lieutenant of police and had three children; Margaret started on the first of eight children; and young Mary was moving toward marriage with Johnny Foley, and the grandchildren were growing so fast that Mary Murphy sometimes called them by the wrong names.

She sold her downtown house and bought one in Greenville and moved in with Margaret. Despite her advanced years, she still refused help, no matter how the children tried to "browbeat" her into acceptance. She took a job scrubbing soap trays with the Colgate-Palmolive-Peet Company, and it was the hardest kind of manual labor. She kept it for almost twenty more years. Mary Murphy seemed to grow tinier with age. Now her head shook perpetually in a small "no." On Sundays, in good weather and bad, she trudged the two long uphill streets to Sacred Heart Church. She heard one Mass in the basement and one in the main church. At home, she wore a faded maroon bathrobe against the chill, and her habit was to walk up and down the rooms with her hands in the pockets. In the pockets were her rosaries, and she said them even when someone was talking to her.

At night, her pleasure was twofold: she delighted in checker games and penny card games, and, when the children cheated purposely to make sure she'd catch them, the board would go flying in air, or the cards and the pennies, and she'd go off into her room muttering and slamming doors. The other pleasure was reading Western magazines. She devoured them one after the other, being careful to place them under her bed when she was through, because within three months she had forgotten the stories, and when she read them again they were new.

Little Jimmy, who was now approaching forty, sat at the wake and thought of these things and many more. He thought how God had reserved one final sorrow, for her when she grew old: the death of her son Tom. He remembered how she had sat silent and stiff-spined at Tom's wake, and her eyes barely turned when she heard the weeping of other women.

Now, only three nights before, she had come to the final scene. It was after midnight and her tired heart convulsed a few times. She had called Margaret. Mary Murphy knew that this was the end; she had called Margaret for a last look of longing, but what she got was fright and hysterics. Margaret ran to the phone and, instead of calling a doctor, she called a priest. This was exactly the way Mary Murphy would have wished it, if she had felt the need of assistance. But the truth was she wanted no one but Margaret.

It was a bitterly cold night and, when the young priest arrived, Mary Murphy was perhaps fourteen minutes away from death. But even *in extremis* she was so surprised that she raised herself on one elbow, squinted at him quizzically, and said, "Sure and phwat would I be needing ye for?" The priest smiled as he unpacked the appurtenances of Extreme Unction. "It's a shame," said Mary Murphy. "A young man like ye needs yer sleep. Go back to the rectory." And she lay back on her pillow. He asked her to be quiet. "What would an old woman like me have to confess?" she demanded.

There was no answer to that. But, in the presence of the Host, she subsided. After it was over, she died easily, almost gratefully. The tests were all behind her and she had passed them all.

As Jimmy left the wake, he paused outside and looked up at the shaded windows. He whispered the two words she had whispered to him when he had been a little boy: "Pleasant dreams."

1928

In the spring, the little students brought tender shoots of pussy willows and curving branches of forsythia and gave them to the nun shyly. She thanked them, blinking her glasses, and sent them to their desks without a smile. She was writing a letter. The snowy fingers glided over the paper like ghostly skaters on a small pond. Now and then she paused to look at the subject of the letter.

He was the boy sitting in the fourth seat near the window. He was a husky boy, big and dark and quiet. The nun was certain that he had talent. He had always been at the head of his class. He had skipped a grade every year. He was mannerly, diffident, neat and ambitious.

She looked down at the letter:

"April 10, 1892

"Dear Mrs. Bishop:

"Your son John is a student in my class. I am moved to tell you that I am impressed. I predict that he will be a great success in life."

There was nothing more to write; no point in being flamboyant. He was clever, and she had said so. The white fingers spun the pen: "Sincerely," they wrote, "Sister M. Wenceslaus." She sealed it, and called to the boy.

"Take this to your mother," she said. He glanced apprehensively at the envelope. "Yes, Sister," he said. He went back to his desk and wondered what he had done to displease her.

He walked and ran his way home, up Old Bergen Road to McAdoo to Jackson and Warner, then through the woods to Fulton. He ran up the steps of the little house. He was hanging up his coat when he gave the letter to his mother.

She was a careworn woman and she wiped her hands on her apron and opened the envelope. When she read it, she looked at John with a smug little smile and roughed his ears and showed the note to him.

He was proud, but she was even prouder. The family never had much. The letter became a talisman. When company came on Sunday, the letter was taken from between the leaves of a big book and shown. It brought nods of surprise, and sometimes a visitor would give John a penny as a means of congratulation.

Sometimes, when the father was upstairs in an asthma attack, fighting for the next breath, someone would tire of the tireless prayer and go to the big book and read the letter again. It came from a nun. A nun had said that Johnny would be a great success in life.

That made it so. Then the father died, and Mrs. Bishop, in her pride, worked to support her children. Young John took a job on a farm, weeding from dawn until schooltime, and from three until dark.

They were all good children and when they grew up they went to work. In time, each went his way in life, getting married, having children, struggling for the rent.

John had a succession of jobs, and, finally, the Police Department. In this, he worked as hard as he had at school. He read all the books on police procedure, obeyed orders, tried to be fair, and raised a family of his own, in which I was the eldest.

Later, he became a lieutenant and wore a single gold bar on his uniform cuffs and on each side of the collar. The years went by and his hair became as white as Sister Wenceslaus' hands. One day he stopped on police business at St. Paul's Church.

"Many years ago," he said to Monsignor Monaghan, "I attended this school." The priest nodded politely. "There was a Sister Wenceslaus," the lieutenant said. The priest became interested.

"She's still here," he said. The policeman shook his head. "Not this one," he said. "She'd be ninety." The priest beckoned. "Follow me," he said. They went across the street to the convent. In the kitchen, an old nun sat in a wheel chair. Her head was permanently bowed. She was deaf. "I have an old student of yours," the priest shouted. "His name is John Bishop."

She was silent, staring at the floor. "His mother had a house on Fulton Avenue," she said. Another silence. "Once I wrote a note and predicted that John would be a great success in life. What did he do with himself?"

The proud policeman pushed the priest aside. His chest was out. "I'm a lieutenant of police, Sister," he said.

She shook her head. "What a pity," she murmured. "What a pity."

1952

The numbness was still on me when the doorbell rang. Three hours ago—returning from church—I was told that Virginia Lee, not quite fifteen, was going out that afternoon with a—well, a boy. It was all done over my dead body, as I should have known all the way back to the day when I brought Virginia Lee home from the hospital in an ordinary washbasket with ribbons on it. Somehow, it didn't occur to me that, when it comes to growing up, some children can be sneaky.

We were driving home from church when the news was fed to Father. I remember the words clearly. "We're having early dinner," Elinor said. "Virginia Lee has a date." Maybe I choked. Maybe I just hung onto the wheel. I don't know. But I do know I muttered, "You're kidding!" and the two words rattled around inside the car in silence. It was then that I realized that a conspiracy was on; that the women in my family knew all about this matter, and that dear old Dad, as usual, was the last to know.

In the back seat sat my mother-in-law, Maggy. When fuses are lit, she remains quiet and becomes inordinately interested in scenery she committed to memory years ago. Also in the back seat was Virginia Lee, an inch taller than her mother, looking eighteen when she hadn't reached fifteen. She has dark brown hair and blue eyes and is a bit too pretty to suit me. In the front seat was Gayle Peggy, eight years old and the nearest thing to an anarchist in town. No matter what the subject, G.P. will give you the best of her advice whether you want it or not and, for one so tiny, her belligerence always reminds me of a Peke growling at a great Dane. When the time comes for her first date, we'll all be worried about the boy. Elinor sat in the front seat too, on the outside, a petite person with black hair and a moonlike face, trying to pretend that she hadn't said anything startling.

"Are you going to let her go?" I said, closing down all the stops so that what came out was a sanctified whisper.

"Of course," she said. "She's a big girl now, and a little matinee date at the movies isn't going to hurt her." She sighed a long sigh. "Don't worry. We've had talks." More silence. I swung the car into the driveway, a thing that can be done without thinking. My mind was trying to trace the history of natural events up to this shocking event. Only a year ago we couldn't get the kid out of dungarees and into a dress. First she was going to be a nun when she grew up. Then she was going to buy a ranch with one H. Cassidy out West and chase the rustlers up and down Channel Five. Now it was boys.

"Come on, Pops," said Virginia Lee, and helped me out of the car. I don't need the help, yet. But it was offered, and accepted. Once we got inside the house, pots and pans clattered, dishes and condiments were tossed on the table, the oven temperature was set higher, mother and daughter were rushing upstairs and down on the double, the sibilant sound of whispering could be heard and Gayle Peggy said accusingly:

"Somebody's got a secret around here and they ain't telling me."

"Virginia Lee has a date," I said dully.

"What's that?" the little one said.

"She's going out with a boy."

"What's his name?"

"They forgot to tell me."

"Big boy or little boy?"

"Big."

"How do you know if you don't know who he is?"

"Frankly, I don't. Now will you keep quiet for a moment?"

"Why do I always have to shut up? She doesn't."

"Who doesn't?"

"Virginia Lee. She just talks and talks and talks."

"Believe me, kid. She'll listen today. It's part of the plot."

"What's that?"

"A scheme. The women plot to trap a man. They're all in on it right now: Nanny, your mother, and your sister. Today, the beautiful butterfly comes out of the cocoon."

She smiled. "You talk funny," she said.

It was shortly after early dinner that the bell rang. It is most astonishing what a front doorbell can do to our house. Virginia Lee was standing in the downstairs hall in a bathrobe, trying to apply the first delicate tracings of lipstick under her mother's tutelage. Upstairs, Maggy was ironing a slip. The bell gave a short brr-r-t and Virginia Lee moaned, "He's early!" and, without a word, mother and daughter tried to race each other up the stairs. On the second floor, Maggy, unnerved by the commotion, dropped the iron. The sound of women wailing went through the house. I sat transfixed. Gayle Peggy had sense. She opened the door and said, "Hello," the way a warden might say it to a lifer who has just jumped back over the wall. It was here that the boy made a mistake. He tried to tousle Gayle Peggy's hair in a patronizing way. She pulled away and turned on a glare that should have melted his glasses.

I stood and introduced myself. I was right—he wore glasses, big black frames which seemed to enlarge his eyes. He had hair the color of a general alarm fire and it hung in a way that suggested that a bulldozer had spent time in it. He was short and so thin that, for a split second, I almost forgot my animosity. I kept thinking "A good meal would . . ."

We chatted about baseball. This is the on-guard stage. Keep the conversation neutral. Remember, it's her old man. I said I favored the Giants and it was no surprise that he liked the Giants too. On the other hand, I thought that Roy Campanella was the best player on the Dodgers and that Jackie Robinson was a pop-off. He concurred. I asked him what his name was and he said, "Eddie." That wound up that conversation.

After a while, there was a noise on the stairway. We looked up together and it was Virginia Lee, coming down as regally, as slowly, as elegantly, as any girl who has just received the last-minute signals from her mother. She did well for the first four steps. Then there was a commotion and she almost fell headlong to the bottom. When she straightened up, on the landing, Eddie and I saw the cause. She was wearing a pair of her mother's high-heel shoes and she was now standing on them on the outsides of her ankles and trying to smile a hello at the same time.

Perhaps it was at that point that my numbness began to warm toward the sentimental. For a moment, I grinned and thought of the time I first brought her mother home from a dance and Maggy stood in the dark behind the screened window and bellowed, "What kind of a time is this to be bringing a decent girl home. . .?"

Then, when he helped her on with her coat and they said good-by, I felt bad again. Miserably bad. Until now, this child's present and future lay in my hands. Now it was in the hands of an anemic-looking kid whom I didn't know. All the murder stories I had worked on as a reporter came back to mind. Many of them started off more innocently than this.

He had a car out front. Well, I say a car. It was really four fenders sagging against some metal and glass. He untied a rope to help my daughter in the right-hand side. The car shuffled off slowly in a cloud of blue smoke.

"Where's he taking her?" Gayle Peggy demanded. She was still angry over not being dealt in on the secret.

"Movies," I said.

"I know that!" she shrieked. "Which one?"

"I don't know," I said. I was about to explore the possibilities of a cold beer when the phone rang. It was Virginia Lee's girl friend and classmate, Mary O'Brien. I said that Virginia Lee was out. "She's on a date with a guy," I said. Mary emitted a squeal of delight. "Please tell her to call me the minute she gets in," she said.

I went to the kitchen table. I ruminated, which means that I drank the beer slowly and did a lot of thinking. In my mind, I could still see the face on Eddie when Elinor came downstairs, wiping her hands on an apron and trying to look pleasantly motherly. And then Maggy came downstairs and, with Gayle Peggy, the cast was complete. At the time, I was moved to commiseration for this boy, and I mumbled to myself: "Oh, Eddie. If you could only see the same people at eight any morning. The bedlam, the bathrobes, the hair, the exasperation, the breakfast, the panic, the clock, the sagging faces, the line-up at the bathroom, the last-minute bus, and that pretty girl scowling at her Quaker Oats, pursing her lips as though to blow her hair out of her

eyes. Oh, Eddie. If you only knew how the whole world of
females is in league against you. None of us ever stood a chance,
kid."

"Nice boy," Elinor said, coming into the kitchen.

"Very nice boy," said Maggy, right behind her. "Mannerly."

"Yeah," I said. "Just peachy. What's his name?"

"Eddie," Elinor said airily.

"Eddie what?"

She stopped and stiffened. Her mother stopped behind her. The
scene took on the aspects of a Halt-or-I'll-shoot movie.

"I . . . don't . . . know," Elinor said slowly, almost horrified at
her own words.

I poured the second half of the beer. "That's peachy," I said.
"Our precious daughter goes out on her first date and we don't
even know the kid's name." Maggy rubbed a tired hand across her
forehead. "It's Eddie something or other," she said. I nodded happily.

"What time does the show get out?" I said.

Elinor looked at the yellow kitchen clock. "Quarter after five,"
she said. "The picture is just starting, quarter after two."

"Well," I mumbled helpfully, "in case they don't come back, we
can always explain to the police that you—not I—permitted our
child to go out with a fiend whose name is Eddie Something-or-
Other. By the way, where does he live?"

"He wears black glasses," Gayle Peggy said brightly, "and he
has a big tooth in front. I'll tell the cops."

"You shut up!" she was told from three directions.

"Frankly," Elinor said, "I don't know exactly where he lives. But
it's somewhere around here."

"Good," I nodded. "Very good. His name is Eddie and he lives
somewhere in this county. The county only has seventy-two towns
so it should be a cinch to run him down. Many a nice mannerly
boy has turned out to be a secret maniac, but then . . ."

"He is a fiend," Gayle Peggy said. "I saw him—"

She wasn't told to shut up. She was shoved into the little television room and the door was slammed. She started to cry and said
that everybody had secrets on her. Besides, Howdy Doody wasn't
on yet. I reassured Elinor and Maggy that, despite the excitement
and the subsequent fears, everything would turn out all right and
that this Eddie really seemed like a very nice boy. Did anyone, by
the way, know what faith Eddie practiced? Nobody knew. Nobody
knew anything except that he was a mannerly kid named Eddie
who had walked out to a strange car with our daughter on his arm
and both had disappeared. It was as simple as that.

Although I told them not to worry, I was scared into a state of frozen digestion. The kitchen clock moved imperceptibly. For the first time, I noticed that the faucet dripped. Susie, our English bulldog, lay silent on the cellar steps. This was unusual and I wondered if there was anything to that stuff about a dog's intuition. The car was either an old Chevy or an old Plymouth or an old Ford or something. Gayle Peggy asked would anyone like to look at television. The answers came back softly, gently: No.

People moved by the front of the house and they seemed happy. Boys and girls arm-in-arm on Sunday afternoon strolls. All walking. All friendly and compatible. Only ours stepped into a strange car. Only ours. The hands of the clock moved on with excruciating reluctance.

"Where did she meet him?" I asked suddenly. "Maybe . . ."

"The ice cream parlor," Elinor said. "He works there."

"Oh," I said sarcastically, "one of those soda-jerking sheiks, hah?"

"He's a good boy," Elinor said.

"Is he?" I said. "Then maybe you tell me why the heck we're sitting around frightened stiff. Of what does a nice boy consist, if I may ask."

"Not your type," came the answer. I had asked for that one. Someday I would learn not to ask questions which can be answered with disparaging comparisons. Still, it was a mark in Eddie's favor. The clock moved on and on and on, and outside, the sun masked itself behind the houses across the street and a brisk blueness came into the air. A few cars passed with lights on. The clock said five fifteen.

"Okay," I said. "You can start to worry right now."

I didn't know it, but Elinor was close to tears. "I won't," she said. "The show is due out right now. You've got to give them time to get home, or do you figure they ought to fly?" I detected the edge in the voice and the tiny break in the tone. I remained silent. The clock ticked on to five thirty. It seemed suddenly to have taken on speed. It went to five forty and then to five forty-five. Nobody spoke. Maggy sat rubbing her head, Elinor paced up and down, puffing on a cigarette.

"I can go out and look for them," Gayle Peggy said helpfully. Nobody admonished her to be quiet. One of us—I forget who— patted her on the shoulder. The clock moved to five fifty. I turned the palms of my hands upward on the table and beads glistened like tiny brilliants.

The front doorbell rang. Everybody jumped to answer it at once. Gayle Peggy had a slight lead and Maggy was a poor fourth.

Gayle Peggy arrived first and opened the door. There stood Virginia Lee, beaming and radiant, and Eddie. Suddenly, everyone seemed to start breathing at once. Elinor got so excited that she kissed her own daughter, hugged her, and laughed immoderately at nothing. Before anyone could stop her, she had invited Eddie in for something to eat. He said no, thanks, that he had to be getting home. They had stopped, he said, for a soda and he was now a little bit late for supper. At the mention of the word soda, Elinor gave me one of those glances. Without a word being spoken, I knew that the whole thing was my fault and that everything would have been fine if I had kept my mouth shut.

Everyone said good night. Virginia Lee got a nudge from her mother—it was gentle enough to move a Mack truck uphill—and Virginia Lee immediately thanked Eddie for such a nice afternoon. Eddie said it was he who should thank her, and, after all the lies were dispensed with, Eddie went home and the door closed and mother and daughter immediately went off somewhere for a private talk.

I hunted for another bottle of beer, but there was none. I sat and waited, not even looking at the clock because now I didn't care where it went, and soon they came downstairs. Elinor's arm was around Virginia Lee's waist, but Virginia Lee looked coldly angry.

"A very lovely boy," Elinor said right at me. "Mannerly and considerate and not a bit fresh."

I nodded vaguely and kept looking at Virginia Lee.

"What's the matter with you?" I said.

She made a face. "Mommy asked if Eddie tried to kiss me. Huh! Why the very idea!"

I haven't worried since.

1956

We were dreamers, my mother and I. We would sit on the beach, digging our toes into the heavy, wet sand, and watch the big, slow breakers come curling in, green and white, and we would dream. I was ten. She was thirty-four. I dreamed that I wanted to own a house by the sea. She dreamed that she wanted real diamond earrings.

She was a short, plump woman in those days. She had a calm,

exquisite face and a straight nose with a tiny tilt on the end. There
was bronze in her hair. I was short, shorter than my younger
brother John, and I had black hair and slit eyes. We used to sit
and dream, and watch John and little Adele race each other up
and down the beach. In my dream, I owned a big, beautiful house
behind the sea wall at Sea Bright, New Jersey. I could sit on my
imaginary front porch and see the big ocean liners—the *Levi-
athan*, the *Berengaria*, the *Olympic*—as they left New York harbor
loaded with rich people who were always laughing and gay. In
my imaginary house, servants went around with silver trays
loaded with chocolate bars and jelly beans and ice cream.

Jenny Tier Bishop didn't really know how to dream well. She
dreamed of small earrings, about half a carat apiece. Her ears had
been pierced long before by her mother and she knew that if she
ever got those earrings she would not lose them. So she told me.
Her dream came true first. On her next birthday my father gave
her the earrings. He was a lieutenant of police, a big man and a
bright one. I remember that he did not like other men to look at
my mother.

Mother wore the earrings only when she was dressed to go out.
When matters didn't go well for our family, she said that she did
not need a new dress as long as she had the earrings. In the
Depression, matters went bad. We always had food on the table,
but the city was paying my father partly in scrip. I didn't miss the
earrings for quite a while. But they were gone. And, when I grew
up, my mother showed me a pawn ticket and said that someday
she would get the earrings back. She worried that she would
forget to pay the interest on the ticket. And, one year, she forgot.
And she lost the earrings. She didn't complain. Mother wore dollar
earrings clipped on, and all of us forgot about her dream. Each of
the three of us got married and had children, and the years flipped
off the calendar like dry leaves from a lawn.

It is exactly thirty-eight years since we started to dream together. Jenny Tier Bishop is seventy-two. She is no longer plump.
She is tiny and thin, and she says that her cane is her best friend
and she will not go anywhere without it. Sometimes she gets
mixed up in the names of her grandchildren and the great-
grandchildren.

Four years ago I brought her and my father down to Sea
Bright. I showed her my house on the sand dunes. It wasn't a big
house. It was small. But it was behind the sea wall. There were no
servants, but there were some jelly beans in a coffee canister.
Mother said it was a nice place. A real nice place.

I gave my mother the tiny felt box, and her hands shook and

she laughed at her own nervousness. "John," she said, "help me with this. I'm so clumsy." Dad opened the box and told her that they were beautiful. "Real beautiful," he said. She kissed me and mussed my hair. She was always a crier anyway. She screwed the earrings in tight and said, "Now, how do I look?" And we told her fine. She couldn't see them herself. She was blind. . . .

1957

The yellow bus sighs to a stop. No cars pass it. They wait. A youngster gets aboard. She exchanges loud greetings with thirty other children. They sprawl, rather than sit. The conversation is boisterous, insulting and thoroughly friendly. School has started. The girl is mine. Her name is Gayle. She is thirteen, as willful as a filly under a halter for the first time. The hair is dark, the eyes hazel, the body slender and barely beginning to bud. She is still a half-head shorter than her mother. She prefers dungarees to dresses and regards her married sister, Ginny, as a sissy. The bus moves along the inner edge of the sea wall to the Borough of Sea Bright. It passes the shops, turns right at the pharmacy and stops at the red-brick school. It is a good school. From 8:30 A.M. until 3 P.M. Gayle will be under the discipline of Mrs. Helen Young Sawyer, the principal and also the teacher of the eighth grade. Like scores of millions of other young Americans, her ears will be assaulted with knowledge from now until the third week of June. A little of it will stick. A lot of it will be vague the day after it is absorbed. Some of it will never be understood.

Gayle doesn't like school. She looks toward graduation as a convict looks toward parole. She is fairly well behaved, is inclined to try to do as she is told, but, to her, homework is drudgery. To me, she is the most lovable thing in the world. To Ginny, she is a pain in the neck. To Rocky, our German shepherd, she is the only person who can run your ears off and who will tease you and wrestle with you and pretend to be angry at you. She is easily moved to pitty by anyone in distress. By the very same token she has the shortest fuse I know. No one bridles as quickly as she. At the hint of a detracting remark she will go off to her room and play records. If you want anything—a cup of tea, a sweater, nail polish or just the lights turned off—no one can beat her bouncing to her feet to get it. When her grandmother was ill, it was Gayle who tore herself away from the television set to get the glass of water with three ice cubes, or to run upstairs and help Nanny to the bathroom, or to run to the store for the second or third time, or to lie on the bed beside her grandmother and relate the latest gossip from school.

She is impossible, she is wonderful. She is not a little girl, not a big one. She is as innocent as an infant and as wise as an old shrew, as good as a saint and as mean as a tomcat. Her biggest pride is that, in emergencies, she does not panic. If Nanny slices her finger instead of the steak, it is Gayle who stops staring at it in horror and runs to the medicine chest, and she knows exactly how to clean the wound, fix a dressing and phone for a doctor. She laughs at her grandmother's fears, but she will not go to bed at night unless Nanny kneels beside her. They say their prayers together.

Maggy is seventy-seven. She's the last of the breed. She is short and stout and has a big round face and a shoe-button nose. She looks like Cork and Limerick and Galway and Wexford. She was really born in Hoboken on February 4, 1880, and her real name is Margaret Lanigan Dunning. She's my mother-in-law.

Maggy has been living with us for twenty years. Her husband died. My Elinor was her only child. What else? Where else? She was a good cook. Her meat sauce was so good that I never ate the spaghetti; just a bowl of the meat sauce and a half loaf of Italian bread. No soup. No dessert.

The kids called her "Nanny" as far back as I can remember. They loved her with a devotion that matched what they had for their parents. In some ways, they pandered to her, and this pleased the old lady and she did nothing to discourage it.

Maggy had a code of her own. If she liked you, she liked you all the way and she could never get herself to believe that you could do anything wrong. If she didn't like you, it was equally difficult for her to believe that you could do anything right.

She lived by this code, and it distressed her to have to place me in one category and then the other. Maggy could never quite make up her mind about me. When I did something nice for her—like bringing home a pair of dollar earrings—she would study them in silence and the tears would shimmer on her lids and she would present her cheek to be kissed.

If I did something wrong—like ask her how she could lecture a child on how to eat with a fork when she herself was shoveling the food with a spoon—then I paid for two or three days in a cold blue glitter.

Best of all was to see Maggy at a bar. She loved bars, and she was always first on the mahogany with the five-dollar bill. The children got dimes for potato chips and dimes for the jukebox. Only two songs made her cry: "When You and I Were Young, Maggie" and "Lover, Come Back to Me." She never wanted to go home.

She always weighed better than 180 and she was exactly five feet tall. As far back as I can remember, Maggy was going to start a diet in the morning. She hated a corset, and she would rather skip a good wedding than put one on. But, once she got into the harness, let no man be caught looking at a watch and saying, "Isn't it getting a little late?"

My mother-in-law had little knowledge of the world, and you could tell her that Europe was four miles south of El Paso, and she'd believe it. Her only outside interest was in rooting for the Brooklyn Dodgers. When they were a run behind, she said nothing. But, in her housecoat pocket she had a rosary, and she would tick off the beads in petition for two quick runs. I asked her softly what would happen if our Lord was on the side of the Giants and, that time, she didn't speak for a week.

A few years ago, I took the family on a Grace Line cruise to South America. We went on the *Santa Paula* and all of us agreed that it was the best time we ever had. The food, the service, the weather were so wonderful as to be unreal. The ceiling of the dining room peeled back at night and we ate under the Southern Cross.

When we got back, Maggy clutched my arm and said: "Take it easy. I'm short-winded. Listen. I want to tell you something. Before we got aboard, I was scared to death. Know why? I didn't know what a ship was like. So help me, Jim, I didn't know it had rooms in it."

Last week, I brought Maggy and my wife down to the Jersey Shore and there was a stillness in the family, an uneasy quiet of the kind which sometimes occurs before summer lightning. It was a hot July night and Maggy kept murmuring, "I'm disgusted with myself. Completely disgusted." My wife wrung her hands and beseeched her mother with her eyes. "Can I get you something, Momma?"

Maggy shook her head no. There was a fresh offshore breeze and the old lady's straight brown hair, parted in the middle, freed a few strands and they wrapped themselves around her face. She moved from the car to the front porch and said, "I don't know if I can make it." The weakness of the old lady was a sorrowful thing to watch for several reasons. She enjoyed life and laughter, and a good fight too. Her daughter Elinor had an abnormal attachment for her mother and this had pleased Maggy until now. Suddenly, she spurned the extra attention, the supine and automatic agreement.

She got to her room upstairs in slow stages, two steps and a rest, and I suggested a doctor. She waved me away. "Jim," she said wearily, "I have been afraid of doctors all my life, and I've lived a good long while. I'm not going to have one now." This was final. I knew something that she did not. Obesity had enlarged her heart until it stretched almost halfway across the rib cage.

The slow decline in Maggy's health in the past year was matched by increasing nervousness on Elinor's part. My wife lived in apprehension every waking moment. To keep from flying apart with nervousness, she would take more tranquilizers than the doctor ordered, and chase them down with a drink of straight Scotch. This made her heavy-lidded and did nothing for the nervousness. If she would drink enough to become intoxicated, it might smother the tension, but two Miltowns and one Scotch were too little too late.

So, I watched Maggy fade away slowly, and, helplessly, I watched Elinor drag herself down until she sat alone, bent over at forty-six, hair disordered, the big dark eyes forever frightened, studying the shaking hands in her lap. I played gay music and no one listened. I made jokes and nobody laughed. It was a time of stillness, a time of waiting.

Yesterday, I was at breakfast with Elinor, and Maggy called her daughter from upstairs. Elinor dropped the toast and ran up. It was not an emergency. The old lady was asking a little help to get to the bathroom. In a few minutes, she came down. "Momma wanted to go to the bathroom," she said softly. I nodded. "I know," I said. "I can help her back to bed." "No no," my wife said, "I'll do it." She bolted the breakfast, drank the coffee, and hurried back upstairs to stand outside the bathroom door.

She had to be of service. After ten minutes, she came down. "I called to Momma," she said cheerfully, "but there was no answer. Do you think she's all right?" I was worried by the lilting tone. It begged for reassurance. "She's all right," I said. "I'll go up and make sure." I went upstairs and tapped on the door. There was no answer. I tried the knob. The door was unlocked. I turned it and looked in.

The old lady was leaning across the basin. Her eyes were wide open. She was staring at the ceiling. I listened. I felt for a pulse. Then I went to the head of the stairs. "Honey," I said, "I think Mom has fainted. Call the doctor and call Father Sullivan." "Is she all right?" she said. What could I say? "Sure she's all right. She felt a little faint. It could be serious at her age, so please hurry with those phone calls."

Elinor did. She was still of service. It was, of course, too late. The old lady was modest and I did not want her to be pronounced dead in the bathroom. So I took her under the arms and dragged her backwards to the bedroom. She was a heavy woman. I got her on the bed, adjusted the nightgown and the hair, and closed the eyes. Then I pulled up the bedclothes, smoothed the cool cheeks, and left the room on tiptoe.

I wondered what the scene was going to be like when the doctor told Elinor that her mother had left. . . .

That was July second. August fourth was a Sunday. My mother and father came down to the shore house for the weekend. We had a colored cook and my mother told me to be good to her. "Don't ever be bossy," she said. Then, late in the morning, she began to have trouble breathing and she kept calling "John, John!" My father fanned her with a newspaper and told her that everything was going to be all right. I made the phone call, and the four men from the volunteer ambulance corps came in bathing trunks. They were big. Jenny Bishop was seventy-three. She was a pale wisp of a woman, who smiled at the big men she could not see.

She asked my daughter Ginny to fix her hair before she went to the hospital. Ginny trimmed the ends. The men placed her on the stretcher tenderly and looked at me and looked away. "We'll take good care of her," one said.

Jenny Bishop never understood much of what was going on in the world. She understood her man and her children. Sometimes, for no reason at all, she would take us in her arms and hold us close and rock us back and forth and kiss us behind the ear. She could also, on occasion, reach far back and send a hand crashing across a cheek and, at those times, her eyes sparkled with fury.

Now she was old and blind and finished and the nose was still cute and turned up a little at the tip. The eyes were still sky blue, but they could not see. The men of the Sea Bright First Aid did not know this and they put her in the ambulance, talking sweetly as rough men sometimes talk, and they slid her into the back.

In the driveway, Captain Dougherty of the Police Department sat in a squad car and turned his blinker on and led the way down the beach five miles to Monmouth Memorial Hospital. On the way, one of the volunteers turned the bed up and pointed out the old mansions on the dunes. My mother had to explain to him that she had recently lost her sight.

He said, "I didn't know," and he proceeded to describe the mansions, color by color, and how the sun hit the big green rollers as they crashed white on the sand. He told her that she had nothing to fear, that she was over the worst of it. Nothing bad could happen to her, he said, on such a sunny day.

My father and I got to the hospital five minutes behind the volunteers and they yelled not to worry, that she was doing fine. She was. We got to the top floor, and Jenny Bishop was in a corner room. John M. Bishop felt bad because, many times, he had promised Jenny that he would never put her in a hospital.

He was more worried than she was. He didn't understand that he had no choice in the matter. If he had kept her in my house, and she died, he would have said hospitalization might have saved her. If she died in the hospital, he would feel that he might as well have kept her home. In this situation, he was the only one who couldn't win.

However, he was always all man and he fussed around her, adjusting the sheet, feeling her forehead, asking in a growl if there was anything she needed. She said no. We left at nine o'clock. A priest came in. It was not discouraging for my mother to make her peace with God, because she had done it every day of her life.

At ten thirty I was watching television. My father was sitting in the kitchen, reading the newspapers. He came into the living room. "Did you hear anything?" he said. No, I said. He shook his head. "I must be hearing things," he said. "I distinctly heard your mother calling 'John! John!' " Sit down, I said, and watch TV and take your mind off it.

At ten fifty, the phone rang. It was the doctor. "Better get your father to the hospital," he said. "I don't think she's going to make it."

I hung up. "Get your hat," I said to my father. "We're going to the hospital." He didn't ask why. He knew. We rolled down the beach fast. I wanted to get there before she made the last graceful bow. I don't know why. We hardly talked all the way.

There was a doctor in the room and a nurse. My mother was sleeping as I had seen her sleep from childhood, the small hands clasped together on top of the coverlet. My father pushed the doctor aside and kissed my mother on the lips. Then he stood away and looked down at her.

The nurse was talking to the doctor. "There was no problem with this patient," she was saying, "until ten thirty. I was walking down the hall and I heard somebody calling 'John! John!' so I came in. I called the resident at once, but it was too late. . . ."

We are in a dimpled blue saucer. The ship moves swiftly, but it never leaves the center of the saucer. To see progress, you look backwards. The four big propellers leave a white crack in the saucer, all the way to the horizon. It will be like this for five days.

Down in the ship's library, a fourteen-year-old boy thumbs through a volume of Shakespeare. His little sister looks up at him and asks: "Who wrote it?" Without looking up at her, the boy says, "A square." My room steward, Señor Pedro Benitez, says that to gat de soots press, you have but to press de button. A congressman's wife nibbles at raisin cake while listening to the ship's orchestra play "Only Make Believe." A skinny girl links arms with her husband on the promenade, and, without looking back at her five little children, smiles up at him and says, "They're all here."

There is no rock, no roll. Just a small steady hum as though someone had left an air conditioner on. The ship will move eastward, hour after hour, day after day, at thirty-five miles per hour. It can do forty without strain. The *United States* weighs fifty-three thousand tons empty and is as long as three football fields. It is the fastest ship in the world.

This is the first day out. I have been lost twice. The corridors seem to be endless. I have seen so many beautiful reading rooms, writing rooms, smoking rooms, sitting rooms, ballrooms, observation lounges, dining rooms, and playrooms that I have trouble finding my own room—which is G on the Sports Deck.

Nine hours ago, as the *United States* backed away from her New York pier, I waved farewell to my clan. Why this should make the heart heavy, I do not know. All of us have been through it before. But, as soon as the first basso blast sounds, I'm dead.

Down on the dock, Elinor covers her eyes with a hanky and waves. I asked her to come along, and she said no. No, thanks. As the liner backs away from the dock, she weeps as though it is the end of the world. Ginny, tall and attractive, gives Daddy the rich smile. She knows that I must go to England for the publication of a book of mine. Gayle appears to be moody, then breaks into a grin when she catches me looking.

My father puts on a brave, permanent smile. What does he think of, down there on the dock? I don't know. Maybe he thinks of his mother, who made this trip from Ireland in 1879 in a sailing

vessel. The five-day trip required three weeks. Maybe he thinks of
my sister Adele, who stands beside him. She can become sentimental saying good night to the lady next door.

The ship turns down the Hudson River and stewards tap little
bells announcing lunch. I'm not hungry. Parting is not sweet sorrow. There is an atavistic fear in it. Each face on the dock is
studied and traced with the eyes. Is there one among them that is
being seen for the last time? If so, which one? Each of these faces
is important to me. There is a compulsive stupidity in thinking
primly portentous thoughts.

The work is done. The British and French ritualistic publication
of my book is concluded. I have been gone a month, and I miss
my domestic harem. It is good to be going home. It is always good
to be going home.

Coming out of the harbor, we see the brown hills of Spain, like
cookies on a blue plate. As I watch, the cookies grow smaller. At
the bottom of the plate, grains of sugar glisten in the sun. These
are the rooftops of Barcelona.

At three this afternoon, Gibraltar began to fade behind the
taffrail. A group of us stood on the sports deck watching. Eight
miles north was the coast of Europe. To the south, the gray Atlas
Mountains of Africa scarred the sky.

Now we will be at sea for seven days. This is the last leg of the
trip home. I am alone. Each time, I think that my wife will make
the trip. Each time she turns it down with thanks.

In twenty-seven years of married life, Elinor had made but one
trip with me—last summer to San Francisco. Why is this? I do not
know. She is an attractive and nervous woman whose fears are
multitudinous and petty.

There is much to tell my women when I get home. Nothing
tickles them more than laughing at something silly Daddy has
done. I must tell them about the brown suede shoes I bought in
London and found, inside, a sign saying "Handmade in Italy."

My French cost me $250. I can't speak it and all of France
knows it. I was playing roulette at Cannes and my number was
twenty-nine and I kept playing until my chips ran out. I asked for
twenty one-thousand-franc chips. The croupier no comprehend. I
tried again. The other croupier spun the wheel. My man did not
understand me. He asked me to say it again, but in English. This
hurt my pride. I said it again in French. The ball dropped into
number twenty-nine and I went home.

Then there was the time, at Cannes, when the young blonde
woman stepped into the waiting room weeping. Passengers would

board the *Giulio Caesare* in fifteen minutes. If she wanted to cry, it was her business. I had to ask why. She spoke Spanish, one of the many languages I do not speak. By sign language, I learned that her little redheaded son was lost. The tender was almost ready to leave with the passengers. I ran out in the street, looking for a little redhead. I came back puffing. No youngster. I ran for a gendarme. He spoke French. She spoke Spanish. I spoke English, I think.

In three minutes, we were running all over the Cannes waterfront. The gate was ready to close. I apologized to the woman for leaving her in a most distressing moment; she was going to miss the ship. A man standing nearby listened to her and said: "She says her little boy runs away all the time. She is not trying to make the boat. She is seeing someone off."

When I finished the previous paragraph, a steward said I was wanted on the phone. My heart was leaden because the only people who would phone me on the ship are those at home, and then only in an emergency.

It was Ginny. She said that Mommy (my wife Elinor) has been in a hospital for four days and was operated on this morning for peritonitis. My voice cracked. So did my nerve. This was ridiculous. Elinor was well when I left home. I had phoned home at each stop and she was feeling fine. Ginny's voice swelled and faded over the thirty-five hundred miles of ocean as though in a moaning gale. Why didn't you tell me this eight hours ago? I asked. I could have left the ship at Gibraltar and caught a plane at Lisbon. The voice faded. The connection was gone.

A cruise ship is a gay place, but not for me. It's a prison.

The monsignor moves slowly across the little ship's altar. There is a Force 6 wind outside. In the chapel, the worshipers cannot see the twists and plunges of the liner, but the feet feel them and the yellow tongues of flame on the candles wave slowly back and forth. Monsignor Luigi Floran is saying a Requiem Mass for my wife. She died yesterday.

There are things a man does not want to write about. This is one. At 3:35 P.M. yesterday Ginny called me from Sea Bright and her voice lifted and died with distance. "Daddy? Dad? Can you hear me? Mommy died this morning. Yes, this morning. Can you hear . . . then the doctor . . . peritonitis and pneumonia . . . I can't hear . . . Please don't worry. . . ."

The monsignor moves to the right side of the altar. I try to pay attention. The black chasuble seems strange on a cruise ship. To my left kneels Father Matthew Houlihan, of Floral Park. Behind me is Mrs. Estella Viviano, who asked the monsignor to say this first Mass.

But my mind will not stay here. It is with her, and with my two girls. The thoughts are confused and irrational. I see Elinor on the deck of the liner *United States*, posing for a picture with me. She looks dark and attractive, as she has in all the twenty-seven years we have been together.

I see her when we were keeping company. The fights. The tears. The mutual recriminations. I see her at the altar. I see her young and laughing. I see her with her mother; so often with her mother. I see the slow, interminable surrender to "nervousness." The first baby was born in July 1937. We called her Virginia Lee. The one born in the war years, Gayle Peggy. There were two other girls who died at birth. Ginny and Gayle were important. They steadied her. From them she could demand love and withhold approval. She loved them and admired them, but she kept it locked in her heart. Elinor was more a daughter than a mother, and more a mother than a wife. When her mother died in July, Elinor began to sit in a silent vacuum. Once, in exasperation, I had said, "What the hell *are* you afraid of?" and she shrugged and said, "Dying, I guess."

On June 30, 1957, there were three women in the house at Sea Bright. One was Maggy, seventy-seven years old, upstairs in bed; one was my mother, blind and leaning on a cane in the living room; one was Elinor, approaching her forty-seventh birthday.

In two days, Maggy was gone. In thirty-two more days, my mother was gone. Sixty-six more days and Elinor was gone. Morbid? Far from it. I am thankful that we were permitted to have each of them as long as we did. Always, the sun must set, the wind must stop, and stars must fade. They are all still present, as she is present.

When I left for Europe, I held her chin in my hand and said, "Remember, you're not in charge of your big girls this time. They're in charge of you."

On the pier, she waved a handkerchief and cried into it. And I thought: How typical! You'd think that it was the end of the world.

Home. . . .

It looks the same. The back gate is still unhinged. Hairpins are on the dresser. Elinor's watch has run down. Her dresses and shoes are in the closet. The pills stare silently from vials. My daughters look at me when they think that I am not looking.

Gayle is quiet. Too quiet for a youngster of thirteen. Ginny, a
married woman of twenty, is a distressed little girl. Her husband,
Charles Frechette, at twenty-one is a man. He took care of everything; made all the arrangements. He stands a little bit away, tall,
solid, redheaded, silent.

There is nothing to say. Suddenly, the girls fall into my arms in
tears. In a minute, it is over and the children move from tears to
inordinate laughter and back to tears again. Conversation becomes babble; everyone wants to do everything for Mommy. Or
as Mommy would want everything done.

The children remember a score of things that Mommy did, and
they echo all of her favorite expressions. They were always good
kids, and affection around this house was as common as crumbs.
Four months ago, this house was full of women. Even the echoes
have died.

In Gayle's case, I'm the only one she has left. It isn't much for a
child who stands on the edge of adolescence. What can I tell her?
What should I tell her? Ginny has her husband. Gayle has a father
almost fifty years of age, a short gray-haired man with a whim of
iron. Should I be strict? Lenient? She isn't even aware of her own
innocence. Besides, she suddenly forgot how to cry.

In the morning, she insists on getting up alone and making her
own breakfast. This is new. The children of her class sent flowers
to her and she nodded a brief "Thanks." She will crack soon and I
must be there when it happens.

Ginny is under control until there is no work to do. Then she
sits. The beautiful face stares at a piece of rug. The tears come in
silence and, as quickly, they are gone. She is the sentimentalist in
the family. Everybody watches everyone else without watching.
Each morning, on awakening, the world is all right. Then the news
comes crashing into the consciousness anew. It fades and then, at
odd times, it hits again. Nothing improves faith in God like death.

We are lucky. We have God, and faith in our Church. On the
ship coming home, I said a prayer to Our Lady of Guadalupe. She
is the patron of all Americans. Back in 1531, she appeared to an
Indian on a hill outside of Mexico City.

She told him to go to the bishop and to have a church built in
her name. Nobody believed the Indian. The priest thought that he
was insane or drunk. The bishop told the Indian to ask for "a sign"
as proof. The Indian told the lady, and she sent him with a load of
dewy roses in his robe. Roses do not grow in Mexico City in
December. When the flowers fell from the robe, the bishop saw
the image of Our Lady of Guadalupe on the garment. He fell to
his knees. He believed.

Almost 426 years later, I asked Our Lady of Guadalupe for "a sign" that Elinor was in good hands and not suffering. On Sunday, I attended Mass on the ship, and behind the altar was a banner with the image of Our Lady of Guadalupe. I asked the priest why an Italian ship would use a Mexican saint. "I don't know," he said, "someone gave it to me and I thought it would look nice this morning." It was a long, unusual coincidence.

I forgot about it. Today, Ginny said to me, "I meant to tell you something strange. That statue of Our Lady of Guadalupe you put upstairs in the hall. On Sunday, it fell off the shelf when nobody was up there."

Who knows? Who knows?

Ginny leans back in the rocker and says that, from now until after the baby is born, she thinks that Charlie ought to spoil her. He is a big and gentle redhead and he grins as he pretends to strangle her. Ginny, in mock warning, yells, "The baby!" and he stops. Gayle, watching the horseplay, says, "All the girls in my class use lipstick."

My family is growing up.

Ginny says that Gayle should be permitted "a little bit of lipstick." I say no. The child is not fourteen yet. From where I sit, Ginny is a child who will have a child in August. "Your mother didn't permit you to use—"

"I know." "So?" I said. Ginny shrugged. "Gayle is still tomboyish. She's in pants more than dresses. If you permit her a little lipstick, and get her a nice hairdo, she'll be more feminine."

"Someday, you're going to say something that makes sense to me."

"All right, Dad. When you were fourteen or fifteen, didn't Grandpa buy you long trousers? After that, didn't you pay more attention to the crease in your suit and didn't you comb your hair and shine your shoes?"

"Lipstick. Your mother would have a fit."

"No she wouldn't. I know what Mommy would want."

In the end, I said okay to the smidgen of lipstick (to be as transparent as chapstick), and a haircut with the ends curled up a little.

Ginny decided that she had better get this done before I changed my mind, so she and Charlie and Gayle drove off to the village. I was reading when the doorbell rang. It was a prominent lady from town. She wanted to know if the ladies could expect my support in a Friday night teen-age dance.

"We want to take our teen-agers off the street," she said. "The

Fire Department will permit the ladies to use the old firehouse to
stage dances for the kids."

"Will boys attend this thing?" I said casually.

"Of course," the lady said. "You don't want the girls to be dancing with each other, do you?"

"No," I said. "I don't. It's a good idea, this dance thing. I will
support it in every way I can. But if you're here to ask Gayle to
attend, the answer is no. She is too young."

"My own daughter is thirteen, Mr. Bishop."

"Fine. Different families have different standards. And please
don't tell me I'm too strict. My older daughter was allowed her
first matinee date at fifteen. The same applies to Gayle. I want the
children to have all the childhood they can get."

My children came back. I was reading. I looked up. Gayle stood
smiling behind a little bit of lipstick. I swallowed hard. "Great," I
said. "Gee, hon, you look wonderful."

She was pleased. And suddenly shy. When she walked, I
watched the ends of the dark hair bounce like springs. There was
an aching feeling that I was losing everything in this house. A few
more years, and there would be me and the dog. That is, if Rocky
didn't run off with some silken-haired female.

"There are going to be some teen-age dances at the firehouse," I
said casually. "Find out who's chaperoning those dizzy kids."

1958

The long wait begins. . . .

Ginny's time has come. Charlie came downstairs this morning
and nudged me. "Ginny woke up dreaming that she was swimming," he said softly. "We're leaving for the hospital." I didn't
know what he was talking about. In five minutes, my older daughter was downstairs, leaning backward as she walked, the shoes too
tight for swollen feet, the face wrapped in a big smile.

"D-Day," she said. "The D stands for delivery." I felt a pang of
worry, even though this is what we have been looking forward to
since last November. I must keep telling myself that she is not the
three-year-old blonde who ran around the back yard in sandals
and a pair of cotton panties with two guns hanging from the
hips.

She's a woman; a wife. As they left, I yelled to Charlie, "Take it nice and easy." The ride to Teaneck, New Jersey, is a long one. We are at Sea Bright. Distance: fifty-eight miles. There are fine hospitals much closer than that.

Holy Name is administered by the Sisters of St. Joseph of Newark. When we lived in Teaneck, Ginny became a volunteer worker at the hospital after school. Her first love was babies and she worked hard to be transferred from Medical 1 to Obstetrics. There, she was permitted to feed infants who were on formula and who were slow to eat. She fell hopelessly in love with every one she fed and, now and then, if a baby died, she came home and said to her mother, "I don't feel hungry tonight."

Ginny has no fear. Long ago, she read all the books one can read about babies. She wants no needles, no twilight sleep, nothing. She expects a little pain; not much. "It won't be beyond what I can stand," she said a week ago.

It's a new generation. New ideas. New thinking. When Ginny was born, if Dr. Arthur Trewhella stuck a needle in Elinor's arm, I fell down. I vowed that if Elinor came through that one all right, I would join a monastery. Ginny's attitude is: "If all pregnancies are like this, I want to have six in a row."

The time is noon and she and Charlie have been gone three hours. The phone is silent. The housekeeper looks out into the office and says, "Would you like another cup of coffee?" I would.

The clock ticks slowly. It ticks for thousands of young ladies in many lands. This is the moment of truth for all of them. And, when it is over, all of them will look like tired gray dolls. When the doctor comes in, the ladies will summon small smiles and all will say the same thing, "Doctor, may I see my baby for a minute?"

At the same time, the father's responsibility begins. No matter how young he is, he is now a family man. He has responsibilities and obligations. He cannot take chances with his career and he guards his wife and child the more jealously. The carefree days end right here.

It would have been nice to see Elinor's reaction to all this. She would have bossed Ginny and told her what to do as though the girl were an idiot. It would have been nice, but it wasn't meant to be.

Still, there is a consolation prize. He took Elinor away in October. The new baby was conceived a month later. He takes one; He gives one . . .

The seconds ticked by like wet grains of sand running through

an hourglass. To ease the silence, Gayle and I phoned our relatives. "Ginny is in Holy Name Hospital, in Teaneck. Yep. Any
minute, we hope." This is a mistake. My father, who already has
four great-grandchildren, called the clan. Soon, the hospital was
hit with inquiries. "Mrs. Charles Frechette? Sorry, we have no
patient by that name."

This confused everyone. They phoned me to ask if there was a
baby on the way or not. We said there was. The hospital said
there was no Ginny. The truth was that Dr. Albert Higdon told
Charlie to keep his wife out of the hospital until the contractions
were five minutes apart. So she sat in the medical office.

The least worried was the mother-elect. She had complete faith
in God, the Blessed Mother and her doctors. The women in the
family were shocked to find that Ginny looked forward to the
birth as one might to a new adventure. No fears, no pain, no
anxiety.

At 11:15 P.M. she felt contractions. She told her husband about
it later and he looked at her and looked at his watch. A little later,
she said, "There's another." Charlie nodded. "Okay. That's exactly
five minutes. Let's go."

They went. At midnight, she was in a silly nightshirt waiting.
Charlie was in another room, smoking. Dr. Fox took care of all the
preliminary work. Time ticked on slowly, on a hot night.

At 7:30 A.M. Dr. Fox called Dr. Higdon. He told Ginny what to
do. She did it. He asked her if she felt any bad pains. "No," she
said. He smiled behind the mask. "Any minute now," he said.

At 8:10 A.M. he gave her a needle. She tried to turn it down. "I
want this to be natural. I'm not in bad pain." He shook his head.
"We have a minor complication," he said. "Take the needle." She
did.

The time was 8:23 A.M. A baby girl was born. It was a feet-first
birth. She weighed six pounds eleven ounces, and she had straight
red hair and blue eyes, like Charlie. She hung upside down in the
doctor's hand, and a moment later, she grimaced and cried.

Dr. Higdon handed her to a nurse and Ginny sighed and smiled
a tired smile. She had her own baby. She knew it would be called
Robin. The masked doctor nodded to the nurse and began to
probe. His eyes opened wide above the mask. Then he grinned.

At 8:27 A.M. a second girl was born. She had dark hair in wet
ringlets. Ginny smiled and shook her head from side to side and
murmured, "Pamela." The baby weighed seven pounds eight
ounces.

Later, Sister M. Bartholomew, who is the hospital librarian,
found the new father in the corridor. He had a mechanical smile

and glazed eyes. "Twins," she said happily. She received no reply, no glance of recognition.

He walked to a phone booth and called me. "Twins," he said. "Twins. Both girls. Both doing fine. Ginny is fine. I'm fine too."

He hung up. I wanted to say something but nobody was listening. The operator cut in. "Number, please?" she said. "Two," I said . . .

The ladies were ready. They slept across the crib, heads down, diapers up, the knees tucked under their stomachs. Both left hands were clenched in tiny fists next to their mouths. This was the day of the christening. The twins were sleeping.

At the ceremony, in St. James Church in Red Bank, they wore dresses with lace along the hem. Father August Neumann almost christened Robin as Robert—which shows how much he knows about the birds and bees—and Pamela cried and wore her little white hat over one eye.

Aunt Gayle was godmother to Robin. David Frechette, the father's kid brother, was godfather. Ray and Lorraine Zewicki were godparents to Pam. The twins were taken back to the house, where each one knocked off about a fifth of the best formula, and then they were sleeping again.

The relatives arrived. The Frechettes came from as far away as Waltham and Miami. The Bishops came all the way from the corner tavern. Jim Sullivan, a neutral, refused to be quoted on the state of the weather, which was beautiful. By three thirty the men from Henry's Delicatessen were setting up the food.

Chief Dundas set up the bar in the kitchen, and guzzled six beers to offset his natural shyness. There were about fifty people, the very old, the old, the middle-aged, the young, and children. It was a gathering of the clan—which occurs only at solemn ceremonies—and the men from opposite sides felt each other out with careful remarks.

Max Lewis arrived looking for me. "I got my piano in the car," he said simply. "Can you help me carry it in the back yard?"

Piano in the car? Well, who was I to argue? I went out front and, in the trunk, he had a piano in a box that looked like a casket for a midget. It is called a Wurlitzer Electric Piano. The piano was opened up and the man sat down and rapped out "Come to Me, My Melancholy Baby."

Ray Stone started to sing and soon my brother John and Margie Waldron were singing "Let Me Call You Sweetheart" while Emil Herman shot candid pictures of the crowd. The Angerami and

DiSiena babies were crying in a playpen under the trees and Sid Goldberg saw them pulling at the bars and he said, "They're stir crazy."

Emil Steencken, my gigantic brother-in-law, peeked out a screen door and said, "I'm lining up at the table with a paper plate." Inside, Charlie was feeding one of his babies; Ginny was in another chair feeding the other.

Someone posed Great-grandma Frechette with one baby and Great-grandpa Bishop with the other. When the lights stopped winking, both seemed relieved to get rid of the little burdens. There was a face missing in the crowd and Ginny and Gayle and I thought about it and we looked at each other. "She'd have loved the twins," I said.

It went that way until dusk. Someone said, "Well, I've got quite a drive ahead of me," and soon everybody was kissing everybody else good-by. It was over. On the porch there were some plates with bits of potato salad and ham on them. The lights of many automobiles brightened the neighborhood for a few minutes. Then the directional signals winked and disappeared.

The stars slept through the whole thing. . . .

The babies are ten weeks old. They are twenty-three and one half inches long and weigh twelve pounds apiece. They are identical to everybody except their mother and Gayle. Faint wisps of reddish hair are beginning to show on the backs of their heads. The toothless smiles are the same. There isn't a mole or a wart to tell them apart and when one weighs 190 ounces and the other weighs 192, and the moon-shaped faces are the same, I am disturbed by the thought that it's a poor grandfather who does not know one child from the other.

When I pick one up, I say, "This is Pamela, no?" And Ginny grins and says, "No. That's Robin." How, I ask, do you know? She shrugs. "I just know." It is too early to tell whether they look like the Bishop side of the family or the Frechette. They have china-blue eyes, three chins, Buddha bellies, and fat little arms and legs with dimples.

The twins even cry identically. When they are hungry, they screw their faces into grimaces and thrust the pink lower lip out. Then the lip begins to tremble. The trembling increases until they work up sufficient self-pity. Then the hands curl into fists, the little legs work the pedal of an imaginary bicycle. They take a deep breath apiece—and blast off.

They eat baby cereals and vegetables and, if the little spoons aren't jammed into their mouths fast enough, they cry between mouthfuls. They knock off eight ounces of formula at a time.

Both are beginning to focus on faces. They stare at me gravely, especially if I am wearing glasses. Robin tries to speak, works her arms and legs into a frenzy, and ends with a big sigh.

Ginny has no help with them, and doesn't want any. She thought that she could do the diapers herself, but she gave that up. The girls use between eighteen and twenty-four a day. Ginny calls them sieves. Now she uses a diaper service, and she sings the familiar dirge that nobody told her it was going to be like this before she was married.

The first faint signs of personality are beginning to show in the babies. Pamela is quiet and observant. Her daddy can set her down anywhere and she studies the ceiling open-mouthed, and turns her head to look at a wall. Robin wants attention. She is the first to try to talk; the first to smile; the first to scream at the top of little lungs if anyone sets her down.

When the infants leave Lincroft, New Jersey, to come to my house, their bottles and impedimenta go with them. When they arrive, they are placed crosswise on my bed. After a few looks around, Robin takes a deep breath, puckers the lip, and emits a wail that would peel the paint off the wall.

Six inches away, Pam decides to ignore the noise and go to sleep. How this is done I don't know. They sleep on their stomachs and do not smother. This is another thing I do not understand. When Ginny was an infant, I was the one who tucked her in, and I had clasps with ribbons on them all around the crib. The hands, with long sleeves, were outside the blankets.

Oh, what am I saying? Who wants to listen to how it used to be done. . . ?

Night out. . . .

It starts at 3:40 P.M. Gayle comes in from school with the white trappings of the crossing guard. The nose is red. The hair, in bent twigs, peeps from under the knitted hat and muffler. The hazel eyes sparkle. Rocky labors upward on lazy legs. The tail wags three times and the dog collapses in ruins.

"We goin' out tonight, Daddy-o?"

"Where? And stop calling me daddy-o."

"Okay, Pops. The movies?"

"I guess so."

The ninth-grade homework is done at once, because she must be home and in bed by ten thirty. This means the first show or nothing. And, to get to the first show on time, we must have dinner at five thirty.

A night out, to us, is important. It is a ritual. This time, she asks if we can take Frances with us and I say yes. Frances is Mrs. Frances Platt, the housekeeper-of-the-week. She is tiny, and she lives with us in a room across the hall from Gayle. Mrs. Platt comes from Mullins, South Carolina. She is a good cook and she can talk girl talk with the fourteen-year-old.

Frances says she'll be glad to go with us. At five fifteen it is dark as we ease the car out of the drive. We turn south and, in Sea Bright, we stop at Tom Longo's restaurant. We always order the same thing: small pizza to start. Then a bowl of spaghetti with meat sauce and meat balls. Also a loaf of Italian bread, warmed in the oven. Plenty of butter. One large glass of milk; two coffees.

Back in the car, then south through Monmouth Beach, Long Branch, West End, Deal, Allenhurst, and into Asbury Park. Total distance: nine miles. In Asbury, we go to Reade's Mayfair Theater. Gayle looks at the stills outside. *"Don't Go Near the Water,"* she quotes. "That isn't one of those love pictures, is it, Daddy-o?"

"No it isn't, and stop calling me daddy-o."

"What's it about?"

"It's about the Navy."

"Shooting? That's good."

"No shooting. No rock and roll. No outer space."

"Oh, gee."

I bought three loge seats, and we stopped at the candy counter. This, too, is a ritual. We bought enough goodies for a tiger hunt. Then we were ready for the movie.

We climbed the stairs, irritated the loge usher by not being able to find the ticket stubs, sat, heard nice things from Gayle about her friends Petra Welch and Marie Johnson, and then the movie started. We looked and ate and laughed and ate and flapped our arms and wiped our eyes and sent Gayle down for more candy and howled.

At ten twenty we were out, en route home. The beach road was deserted, and snow began to build up around the metronomic wipers. We pulled into the driveway.

Inside Gayle arranged her books for the morning. Frances got the breakfast foods out. The child let Rocky out for his final airing, went upstairs, changed into her nightie, said her prayers, and came down, said good night to Frances, gave me the hurry-up kiss on the cheek, and she was off, sneaking her little transistor radio under her pillow.

I watched the late news, and hardly heard Frances say good night. Then a little of Jack Paar, and I went off, yawning and dousing the lights.

Night out. . . .

Next week, John M. Bishop will be seventy-five. He will leave for work, as he has been doing for sixty-six years. It will be another day in an endless belt of days. He will get out of his car many times and talk to the merchants with whom he does business. They will recognize the snowy hair, the gleaming shoes, the neat crease from a block away.

He is my father. He is also my best friend. We have disputed every public and private issue for the past thirty years. We were pinochle competitors; we went to ball games, the mountains, the shore; we have laughed together until tears dimmed the eyes; we have wept together when our women were taken away; when I was broke, he dug up the money; when he didn't have the money, he borrowed it.

We knew each other's faults better than the virtues. He was always a responsible person. He knew that he would have to get through school quickly, so that he could get a full-time job.

John found time to serve as an altar boy in the church. When he graduated from school, he went to work and, at night, attended sessions in P. S. 14. He had many jobs. No boss ever fired him; no boss ever wanted him to leave. He met Jenny Tier and, after a long courtship, they were married on January 15, 1907.

He looked bigger than he was. He was five feet eleven-and-a-half inches tall, and about five and a half feet broad. When he was a police lieutenant, he weighed 254 pounds. He was never a flat-foot and had an inborn contempt for a man who would not continue to study. When he retired, at the age of fifty, he said, "Now I'll begin my career."

He took a job in a chemistry laboratory because he wanted to know something about the mysteries of chemicals. When plastics first came on the market, John Bishop got a job in a big plant as a receptionist. In a year, he had been promoted to the job of personnel director in charge of 3,000 employees.

When he met Bennett Fishler and Ed McNamara of the Ridgewood, New Jersey, newspapers, he stopped looking for new fields to conquer. He wanted to be credit manager and he worked hard at it until he understood the problems of merchants who place advertisements in the newspapers. He has been at this job for ten years and wouldn't quit if he were offered full salary for life.

He is as eager to learn at the age of seventy-five as he was at nine. He loves life and people and he has an insatiable curiosity to know all about everything. He is religious and he fears the wrath of God. He says his prayers every night and the last phrase he utters is "Good night, Jenny."

He lives with my sister in a little house in North Bergen, New Jersey. When his day's work is finished, he eats lightly—sometimes only cereal for dinner—and he watches television. He sleeps in a Barcalounger chair with a sheet tucked under his chin.

Over the years, he made a lot of mistakes. He remembers all of them. The characteristic which I admire most is that he was always 100 per cent man.

1959

The twins were in their playpen. They looked up, blue-eyed blondes with tiny pony tails, mouths open. Mommy was saying good-by. Daddy was taking her to the hospital to have another baby, and the twins felt vaguely uneasy. Why did she hold them so tight this particular time? Why the long, wet kiss, the nuzzling behind the ear?

They watched. Mommy stood up, pulled the dress down over the awkward form, blew one more kiss and followed Charlie and the little valise of clothes out. Gayle told her sister not to worry. "Lil and I will take care of them. They'll be good."

This is the moment of trial for millions of young women. This is the hour when there is no future, just the present. Charlie drove her up to the hospital as he did at the same time last year. The Sisters of St. Joseph were waiting. So was Dr. Higdon.

He knows that some things start, and then stop. It's an aggravating truth. That is what happened. It was like this all day. Virginia Lee Frechette put her robe on and walked the corridor and met other young women. To some this was a new story. To some it was old.

"Mine has got to be a boy," Ginny said. Everybody laughed. "It's simply got to be. My father had girls. He never had a son, so he must have a grandson. You know what their vanity is like when they reach fifty."

The red ball of the sun hung above the deep green trees on the horizon. Nothing. Some of the girls were taken to the labor room. Not Ginny. She sat on the side of her bed and shrugged. The pretty face broke into smiles. "Nothing," she said to Dr. Higdon.

It was night and the antiseptic dinner came up on a tray. The nurse at the desk made notes on charts. The clock on the wall dragged lazily and silently. The gleaming corridor was quiet. Then something happened. It was no maybe-I-imagined-it thing. This was real. The doctor was called. It was all right.

There was no fright in Ginny. No panic. "This is fine," she said. "I wouldn't want to go home and start all over." She's a sensible girl who believes that most of the pain is emotional. So she asked for no medical crutches.

But, before the night was over, her eyes were wild with fright and a doctor was sitting behind her holding a cone to her nose, murmuring, "If you'd only breathe deep as I tell you, you won't feel the next one." Before dawn, she heard the doctor say, "Get her husband. I want to talk to him," and she thought sadly, This is what it's like to die. This is what it's like. She was wrong. The doctor wanted Charlie, sleeping on a hall bench, to be awakened because the time was near.

The sun came up over Leonia mean and hot. Only the snowy statue of the Sacred Heart in front of the hospital braved the rays in cool splendor. Breakfast trays rattled and doctors hopped out of parked cars to visit patients in many parts of the hospital

The nuns walked the corridors in silence, their rubber heels making kissing sounds on the linoleum. "All right," Dr. Higdon said softly. "Now. Now. There. There." There was the sound of a slap, and a loud, thin wail assailed the walls of the delivery room. A second doctor got the silver nitrate, and the blue eyes, which did not want to look at the world, were opened by force.

It was 10 A.M. The doctor was tired. He went into the hall. "Charlie," he said to the big redheaded father, "everything is fine. Ginny is all right. The baby is fine. Weighs about eight pounds."

Charlie grinned and sat down. "Boy or girl, Doc?" he said. The doctor smiled. "Boy," he said. "I asked Ginny what she's going to call him and she said Jim Bishop Frechette."

"That's good," Charlie said. "Fine." It didn't occur to anyone that he might like to have the first boy named after him.

Five years ago, Elinor bought a wedding ring for me. It was a plain yellow band. Inside, in tiny figures, it said "14k." I shook my head. "You think this is going to scare some woman off?" She smiled at the children. "Get him," she said, and everybody laughed.

It wasn't much of a symbol. Still, it reminded me that I had been too poor to buy her an engagement ring in the long ago. So I went to Nick Napoli's jewelry store and ordered a fancy wedding ring. Nothing plain, please. I wanted something that could be worn only with smoked glasses.

Nick got a good one. It was made of platinum, filigreed in curving orange blossoms, with a diamond in each blossom. It sat in its dark plush case like the constellation Orion over a moonless sea. One evening at dinner, I presented it by sliding the box across the table.

Elinor took a look and did the usual: she burst into tears. It was too beautiful, she said. Oh no, I said gallantly, it doesn't mean any more than the yellow band you gave me. That ended the dinner. Only Gayle and I ate.

My wife was a great saver. When she appreciated a tablecloth, or silverware, we never saw it again. It was put away. That's what happened to the wedding ring. This led to arguments. "Why did I buy it," I said, "if you're going to hide it?"

When she felt that I was being unreasonable, she had a habit of rolling her eyes toward heaven, as though appealing to God to witness all she had to put up with from me. "Do you think I'd put a ring like that in dishwater?" she moaned. "Why did I have to marry a man who is out of his mind?"

Okay. If her ring could be put away, so could mine. I have a tray in a bureau drawer, and there I keep cuff links, collar pins, tie clasps, and the police shield my father used when he was a lieutenant. The gold wedding ring went in there.

The next day, when I was dressing, I looked for it. The ring was gone. I turned the drawer upside down on the bed. No ring. I accused Elinor of hiding it for spite. She denied it. After that, she wore her ring on state occasions, holding the hand a little limp so that the sparkle would blind her friends, and this would remind me of my ring.

This was enough to start an argument. There was nothing secret about our battles. We disagreed, toe-to-toe. There was nothing subtle about our devotion to each other either. We did all right for twenty-seven years.

Then she died, and overnight the book had been slammed shut. I buried myself in work because it was the only way in which I could stop the carousel of maudlin thoughts. There were no tears, because I had lost the knack of weeping.

The first thing I noticed was that the ring was not on Elinor's finger. I whispered to Ginny. She shook her head. "We looked everywhere, Daddy. The ring is gone." It had been in the pale blue jewelry box on top of the dresser. It had been there with all

the cheap earrings, the ice-cube wrist watch, the beads. It was
gone. Both rings were gone.

Another ring was slipped on Elinor's finger. I felt awkward
about it. When we came home, the girls and I sat around in a
daze. We talked about Mommy because we couldn't think of anything else.

A week later, the beautiful wedding ring was found. It was
sitting on top of Elinor's jewelry, in the pale blue box where it
belonged. Ginny shook her head. "Believe me, Daddy," she said,
"we searched through this box a dozen times. It was not here."

I said nothing. What could I say? Silently, I kept thinking that
maybe she wanted Gayle to use the ring someday. There was no
other answer to the riddle.

Two years have slipped by on soft winds from the south. There
have been springs and autumns and Christmases and three grandchildren and she knew none of these. There have been good days
and bad ones, and she has been deaf to these too. She rests near
her mother.

A year ago, I took the diamond wedding ring and put it in an
envelope and marked it: "For Gayle." Next Saturday will mark the
second year since Elinor slept away. Last night, as I undressed, I
put the cuff links on the tray in the drawer. On top was a plain
gold wedding ring. I tried it on. It was mine. . . .

They were here all afternoon and evening and now it is nine
o'clock and they've gone home to Daddy. I speak for all grandparents, I think, when I say that we can see babies grow. That's
because we do not see them often.

The twin girls—Robin and Pamela—are fifteen months old, and
Jim Bishop Frechette is ten weeks old. The girls are identical ash
blondes and, in red leotards and plaid skirts, they look like miniature beer barrels. They weigh twenty-two pounds apiece, and they
can say a few words like dada, popop, brother, Gayle, and
mommy. At that, it is necessary to know how to tell them apart. If
I hand a rubber toy to one, and the other one tries to snatch it, the
snatcher is Pamela. If one bursts into tears and then slaps her
sister it must be Robin. It's a poor system of identification.

They love music. When the hi-fi set is on, and they are in the
playpen, they bob and weave like a pair of cobras in a basket.
This, I have been given to understand, is rhythm. They also love
to eat. When I see Ginny spoon-feeding them with that glop, I
turn away. So does our dog Rocky, and he was never particular.

Rocky is a big black police dog and he suffers the presence of the babies as the Christian martyrs did having tea with the lions. They rub his back, try to hide little objects in his ears, and make cooing humming sounds, as they pat his brown eyeballs. He permits this, but he keeps looking at me with that when-are-they-going-home look.

JB is different. He has auburn hair, a cleft in his chin like his father, a broad, almost Slavic face, a deep chest and big feet. He weighs fourteen pounds and he has no time for hysterics. Most of JB's time is spent sleeping, or staring at the ceiling making a big O of his mouth. He doesn't cry often, but when he does, JB is hungry. He imbibes a lot of milk and a lot of that warm-colored glue which is so good for the little man of the family.

When his sisters want to show him how much they love him, they press the sides of their heads against his face and murmur, "Ahhhh." The "Ahhhh" goes on until they run out of breath. He resides in a small old-fashioned wooden cradle and, when Virginia Lee isn't watching, the twins sometimes rock him until his little head spins.

It seems that the last time the twins were here—or perhaps it's the time before—they tried to stand in the playpen and they had to look at me through the bars. Now they stand in it, and lean their elbows on the top rail. Both of them, when paroled, walk through the room in a rocking-horse gait. Their feet remind me of Charlie Chaplin.

Now and then when Charlie Frechette works late, Ginny and the babies come to Sea Bright, and this was one of those days. Aunt Gayle, who will be sixteen this month, takes them to the village and buys presents for the girls.

She is clever at taking care of babies and knows by instinct which type of cry is make-believe and which is serious. She also understands the danger of complete silence when youngsters are playing. Gayle and I look forward to the visits because, at the twins' age, they are forever learning new things and they are fun to watch.

If Ginny says, "Go love your sister," each of the babies, no matter how busy, will struggle to her feet and go toward the other. They clinch, put one arm around the other's back, pat it lightly with fingers and rub cheeks and say, "Ahhh."

Although they are identical, the girls have different personalities and this shows already. Pamela is serious. She is forever investigating a toy piano, an ash tray, or pointing at something she recognizes and letting out little high-pitched yips.

Robin loves fun, loves to be swung high, laughs at anything you do three times in a row, and has a little mother instinct. If she hears JB cry, she stops her play and hurries to mother to tug at her skirt.

Some say it makes a man feel old to be a grandfather. This, I now know, is untrue. On the other hand, after wrestling with the babies all day, it doesn't make a man feel any younger. . . .

He drove up for his weekly appointment with the doctor and, within three hours, my father was in Holy Name Hospital. I have never seen him madder. He was muttering. This is not the spirit of Yuletide. "I was in the hospital last Christmas and the Christmas before," he growled. "Is everybody crazy?"

John M. Bishop felt well. He is seventy-six. Behind his back, we always called him "Big John," for he once weighed 254 pounds. Now he is a wisp of a man at 139, although he still has all the snowy hair, and the eyes still twinkle when there is something to twinkle about.

Now he ships water. Some is in the lungs; some is in the ankles. Dr. Bernard Krull pumps him out with diuretics but, around Christmastime, he wasn't bailing properly so he was slammed into the hospital.

Big John was always the boss in our family. Still is. What he says not only goes, it goes fast. My sister Adele still shivers when he says "Good morning." And yet, he was never a stern man. He was precise and articulate and he had no patience with stupidity.

He was a man who put every last collar button in its place and, if I borrowed a pencil from him in January, he'd ask me in June when I planned to return it. He could not stand laziness, lack of ambition, and lack of interest in world affairs. He was on the ball before anyone knew it was round.

They gave him a private room and he didn't like it. They said they had one in the old wing at nineteen dollars a day and one in the new wing at thirty. Big John said he'd take the thirty-dollar one and he hoped that the hospital had heard of an invention called the telephone. The admission clerk said he could have a phone.

Near the door was a recessed chest of drawers, and there he hid his cigarettes because he knew that if the nurses knew that he was smoking, they might keep him in until New Year's. "It's tough enough," he said, "that they won't allow a man to eat what he wants, and a highball is against the law, but they're not going to keep me from having a little smoke now and then."

They put him in an old sheet that ties up the back and he walked across the room looking like Mahatma Gandhi. "Things

have come to a pretty pass," he said. "Look at me." He reached for
the drawer of cigarettes just as a nun came in.

"Where are you going?" she said. He glared and then smiled.
"The bathroom, Sister," he said meekly. She nodded curtly. "It's
over there," she said jerking her head. As he disappeared, she said,
"I hope I never smell smoke in this room." I could hear the
commode lid slam all the way down the corridor.

He got into bed and the swollen ankles began to thin down. He
read all the papers and used the phone like a field marshal. He
phoned Adele and read off a list of items he wanted delivered at
once: his old slippers, three pairs of clean pajamas, a bathrobe
and, if the nuns would allow it, his portable television set.

In the morning, he was transferred to a semiprivate room where
he could talk with another man. The man's name was Kaplan and
he was too sick to talk and he may never be forgiven for that. Dad
read all the newspapers, called a barber to shave him, combed his
hair, permitted an orderly to bathe him from the stomach up and
from the knees down, read part of a book brought by Sister M.
Bartholomew, and asked his doctor if the man had no conscience
putting him in a hospital at Christmas.

My father is home now. For Christmas he bought himself a
hospital bed and he now feels that he's got everything they've got
in Holy Name except it's more comfortable and he can issue
orders louder. He can turn himself up into a sitting position and
watch the Late Show on television, while smoking a cigarette,
without anyone daring to tell him what to do.

For Christmas he gave me a beautiful piano. I gave him a fitted
leather liquor case. If he must listen to my music, he might as well
be in the proper mood. . . .

1960

The sultry, breezeless days of August will be here in six weeks. So
will another baby. This will be the fourth in two years, and Virginia Lee, tall, stately, with deep chestnut hair and the self-assur-
ance that goes with being twenty-three years of age, is as happy as
I've seen her. She says she wants a big family. My feeling is that
she will kill herself doing all the work alone, but she wants no
help.

At the moment, she looks more like a bungalow than a beauty. She has twin daughters, twenty-three months of age, and a boy eleven months old. If she could only have managed to have them a little closer together, they'd all be in the same class in school.

As my younger daughter Gayle is the wit and the sparkle and the fun in my life, so Ginny is the heart and the soul of it. I can see you nodding wisely, thinking of your children, and murmuring, "I know what you mean." That is the reason why I write about mine—so that, in them, you will see yours a little more clearly.

Virginia Lee was born in Leesburg, Virginia, while her mother and I were on vacation. She wasn't expected for at least a month. Everything happened so fast that we merely switched the name of town and state to get a name for her. She came home in a basket on the back seat of an old car. The only time she cried was when I stopped for a red light.

I was her favorite, I guess, from the beginning. And she was mine. I had a workbench in the cellar and she would sit on it by the hour on Saturdays and Sundays while I tried to repair whatever was broken around the house. At the age of three, she knew every tool in the chest and could get them for me almost as fast as I could call the words.

When she was four, she told me in confidence that, when she grew up, she was going to marry Gene Autry and live on a horse ranch out West. It was a solemn secret and I kept it for a long time. Another time, when I was shaving, she was standing on the lavatory seat watching, and she asked me to sing a cowboy song.

I can't sing a cracked note, but I tried one chorus of "The Last Roundup." When I finished shaving, she was in tears. I didn't realize that one so young would understand that the cowboy in the song had died.

We loved dogs and horses and music and, until she got too big for me, we went everywhere together. When the first date arrived, in thick lenses and a twenty-dollar car, to take her to a matinee movie, I knew that I was through. My time was over. Hers had begun.

Virginia Lee was born a pale blonde, but her hair darkened as she grew. Her life ambition was to win the approval of her mother, who loved both girls to distraction but dreaded to show it. Elinor thought that any show of affection was a sign of weakness. I did the loving. And the spanking, too.

In Teaneck High School, Ginny studied journalism and put it to practical use. At the age of seventeen, she wrote her first and only book—a biography of Father Duffy of the Fighting 69th. She did the drudgery. I looked over her shoulder and suggested small refinements.

A big redheaded kid with a rich smile began to show up in the evenings. His name was Charles Frechette and somehow Elinor and I knew from the start that this was to be the man in Virginia Lee's life. He was studying truck management—a course I never heard of—and, the more I sat and talked to Charlie, the happier I became that he was to be the second and last man in Ginny's life.

It required no courage on my part to stand in church and place her hand in his. They belonged to each other. After a few years, they bought a house in Lincroft, New Jersey. Both of them love children, so they now have a flying start on a personal day camp.

It's a ranch house, and Charlie has fixed up a room in the cellar for fun when the children are in bed. There is a big back yard, some shady oaks, and a lawn that burns brown once a week. They also have a female German shepherd named Tammy. She's big and she runs for cover when the babies teethe on her ear.

There is also a hysterical parakeet who talks in sign language, and, until recently, a cat with a bent tail who climbed draperies. The Frechettes are as happy as any couple has a right to be.

We were whispering low over a table at Le Bistro in Atlantic City. Kokey and I were watching a kid named Duke Hazlett sing in the manner of Frank Sinatra and Kokey was saying, "The kid is even losing his hair like Sinatra. Next week I'll buy him a little piece of carpet." I looked at my watch. It was nine.

"Excuse me," I said. "I have to call a hospital. My daughter is having a baby." Irving Kolker nodded. "I know," he said. "This makes four—right?" I left the good steak for a moment and went into the booth and called Teaneck. It always takes a long time when the heart trembles. When I got the number, the operator was reluctant to connect me with maternity. "Let me speak to the nurse," I said.

The nurse came in faint and far away. "You have a patient named Mrs. Charles Frechette," I said. "I want to know—"

"Yes, Mr. Bishop," she said. "She had her baby." I swallowed. "What was it?" I said. "Just a minute," she said. "I'll check." I said, "Wait a minute. How is my daughter?" but she had gone. When she came back she said, "Mother and child are doing fine. The baby was born at seven forty-five. It's a boy. He weighs nine pounds eleven ounces."

"Ginny thought that this was going to be a small baby," I said weakly. She giggled. "Shall I tell her you called?" she said. I nodded dumbly at the phone. "Tell her that I love her dearly," I said, "and I will be up to see her as soon as possible."

I went back to the table. I told Kokey that I must leave, that I wanted to get aboard *Away We Go II* at dawn and head for home. Back at the Flamingo Motel, I packed and left an early call. Then I went to bed, but couldn't sleep. Four grandchildren in two years—holy mackerel.

Bill Armstrong and I got the Richardson gassed up early and we cleared Absecon Light and headed north-northeast in a southerly breeze. Five hours and fifteen minutes later, we rounded Sandy Hook and headed up the Shrewsbury. We docked the cabin cruiser behind the house.

I phoned again. Everything was fine. I sent two dozen long-stem American Beauties. This would at least let her know that Gayle and I were thinking of her. In the morning, I answered the mail and got in the car and headed for the hospital.

Grandfathers aren't allowed to visit. Fathers only. So I sneaked in, got past the receptionist, and took the elevator. Ginny was lying on a sheet, dozing. I sneaked into Room 212 to tickle her bare toes. She awakened, gave me the big-surprise smile, and we fell into each other's arms.

They have new systems today. The baby had been born only forty hours before, but the mother was allowed to get up and walk down the hall to show the baby. He was in a basinette behind glass. His name, she said firmly, will be Kevin Gerard Frechette.

I looked in at my new grandson. He has a big round face, eyes squinted shut, coal black hair, a ruddy complexion, and his big hands were tied to his sides to stop him from scratching his face.

"Dr. Higdon calls him Moon," she said, laughing. I shook my head in wonderment. "He looks like a moon," I said. "A full one." He's a big buster and so is his one-year-old brother Jim.

The nurse wheeled Kevin away and we walked back to Ginny's room. Time spins so swiftly and so many momentous things happen so quickly.

"Where are the flowers?" I said. Ginny shook her head. "Sister Canise brought them in for me to see, then took them away. She says the nurses don't like to take care of big bouquets. Small ones are all right."

There was time for a brief chat, and then farewell. This is rapidly becoming the essence of existence: hello, good-by. I am in several places, it seems to me, simultaneously. When a friend asks the names of the four grandchildren, I must stop and think and then tick them off slowly.

When I left Virginia Lee, I said—tactfully, I thought—"Now that you have four infants, are you going to skip a year?" Her eyes flashed dangerously, and she said, "Daddy, Charlie and I want a big family and we're going to have them just as fast as God sends them."

Any more questions, Grandpa?

Gayle eloped. I didn't expect it, and I think she did it without much thought. There is something about a secret marriage which worries me. It may work. It may endure. Certainly, the event itself has robbed me of the right to criticize. It happened in Maryland when Gayle was supposed to be spending a weekend at a girl friend's house.

Somewhere along the line, I made a mistake. I was the aloof father when the child needed a warm mother. Since Elinor's adieu, Gayle has fallen into long, moody silences followed by the old sparkle and wit which made my tomboy a happy hoyden. Gayle never complained, even when I was absent on story assignments for days. She was left in a house which was empty except for a colored cook and a German shepherd.

Or maybe this was the way it was intended to be. Frank Gerace is twenty-one. He is short and slender and polite. He aspires to be a jockey. He is an exercise boy at a racing stable. He earns about three hundred dollars a month. When I ask why an elopement was necessary, Frank says, "If we had asked you, you would have said no."

I told him, somewhat grimly, that there is going to be a church wedding, whether he is ready for it or not. The two stand listening in silence. She is sixteen, eager to escape the old sorrows in this house. But she doesn't see it as an escape. She sees it as the one, everlasting love. Her idea of marriage is a guy, a convertible, some rock and roll music and pizza.

His idea of marriage is simple. He wants to provide for a wife, and all the wife has to be is to be obedient and not question him. It is, with some exaggeration, like handing a Stradivarius to an orang-outang. On the other hand, when I married Elinor, I was a cub reporter with no future and earned twenty-five dollars a week. Also, I was a smart-aleck who did not want to listen to advice.

Next week, for the last time, I will give a bride away. Also, I expect to give them enough for a start in life. The leaves of autumn lie russet and dead in the driveways, and I wonder how my little one could have kept the secret since last spring.

Soon, she will be leaving with him. Maybe that's the reason why

I am confused. Perhaps I am thinking only of myself, of being truly alone. Gayle and I were always close, and we traveled alone to many parts of the world. We just weren't close enough for her to confide her heart's desire.

In some ways, I failed successively. I tried to explain to the young couple that marriage is not perpetual ecstasy. In time, one strives solely for contentment. Some are satisfied with a truce. Marriage is bills and babies and bargains and belligerence and bitterness and, once in a while, bliss.

I knew by the silence that my message did not get to them. They listened, and nodded, and held hands. I had the same sense of betrayal that Gayle had when Ginny walked in from the hospital and said, "Mommy died this morning." The Little One has not recovered from it yet. I am going to try to face the new truth with a phony smile . . .

He is bent over the sink, washing the breakfast dishes. This gives me time to write. My father has been here a week. For a proper appreciation of what has happened, one must recognize that he is seventy-seven, has an auricular fibrillation, edema of lungs and ankles, his feet shuffle slowly, his head is inclined, hair white, teeth new, eyes blue and twinkling, manner courtly and diplomatic.

When my mother died, over three years ago, John M. Bishop, Sr., retired to his room in my sister's house. He seldom came out. The man who sits alone is in poor company. He built up nervousness, fears and, in effect, marked time.

He was terrified of planes, afraid of trains, nervous in automobiles. I goaded him into leaving the room. My brother John shoved him on a train at Newark, and I met him the next day at Flagler Street in Miami and yanked him off. I had no intention of babying him. I said, "If it is God's will that you may have to go, let Him take you in bright sunshine rather than in that stuffy room."

Dad agreed. His leg muscles were so flabby that it hurt to walk more than a hundred yards. The first night, I took him to the Jai-Alai games. When we got back to the Key Biscayne Hotel, he said he couldn't sleep without his pill. He was snoring before he could reach for it. The next day, I asked him to play nine holes on a pitch-and-putt course.

"Oh, no," he said. I gave him an eight iron and a putter and dragged him out. He shot a forty-four. The next morning, he was out by himself and shot thirty-four. His snowy skin became red, then brown. We went everywhere together.

Sunday we went deep sea fishing on the *Elkam II*. My father is afraid of the sea. He relaxed, held his face to the warm sun and ate as though food had been outlawed. Monday, he played eighteen holes of golf and drove to Hialeah to visit Frank and Gayle Gerace.

Tuesday we went to Hialeah. He knew nothing about horses, but would bet the whole wad—two dollars—on anything Bill Hartack was riding. He won seven dollars, and got back to the hotel in time for a corned beef and cabbage dinner. He was now averaging two miles a day on his feet.

Wednesday, he visited the Seaquarium, saw a three hundred-year-old turtle, and murmured, "My friend, you've got me by a few years."

Later he visited Dr. J. V. Hankwerker, accompanied by a note from his Northern doctor. Hankwerker examined the tricky heart, searched for fluid in lungs and ankles. The doctor said, "He's in good shape. Heart is all right and no fluid. He's dry as a bone."

Now he is washing the morning dishes. I'm trying to write and he wants to know "What's next?" Last night, we stood along the edge of the sea, looking at the little pinholes in the sky.

"This," he said solemnly, "is the closest I expect to get to heaven."

1961

The phone rang. I snapped the light on. It was 3:20 A.M. I got out of bed. My father was sleeping, as he has for years, on a chair. His legs were on an end table. A sheet covered him to the chin. The white hair, the face in repose, made him look like a dead cardinal. I fumbled for the phone. "Hello." A young man's voice said, "Dad? Gayle had her baby ahead of time. It's a girl."

"Yes," I said sleepily. "Her baby." Then I came to. "Her baby! Gayle had her baby?" Frank Gerace told it again. I was wide awake. The questions flew like missiles: How is she? How is the baby? A little girl? Why didn't you tell me Gayle was in labor? When did it happen? What do you mean you didn't want to bother me? Where is she now? What does the doctor say? Is there anything I can do?

It was incredible that my little onion had become a mother. This child could drive a car, pilot a speedboat, swim in a heavy sea, shoot a basket, climb a fence, handle a crisis without losing her head—but motherhood?

Now she was an old married woman of seventeen. I went back to bed thinking. Virginia Lee has four. Now there is a fifth one, a little girl born to be a girl. I got out of bed and nudged my father.

He opened one eye. "Hah?" he said. I said, "Gayle has had a little girl." He closed one eye. "Is that so?" he said dreamily. There was a silence. Without opening the eyes, he said, "That makes my tenth great-grandchild." More silence. "My family sure comes up with the goods."

In the morning, I phoned Ginny. She wanted to fly right down to Miami. "Daddy," she said, "Gayle is only a baby herself. She needs me to explain things to her." Virginia Lee is an old crone of twenty-three. I said, "Your own babies need you more than Gayle needs you."

I went to the hospital. The nurses had all the bassinets lined up behind glass. Relatives were saying "Ooh" and "Ahhh" and the infants looked red and wrinkled and their tiny arms and legs jerked spasmodically and the little mouths contorted with tears. This is the way life begins. This is the way it ends.

Some women were saying, "Who is that one in the back? Over there on the left." It was an infant whose skin was pale pink, a baby with cheeks so fat that they hung like eggdrops. Its eyes squinted open and the tiny fingers kept moving, one by one, in slow motion. "What a pretty baby!"

The masked nurse looked at the card at the foot of the bassinet. She held it up for the women to see. "Gerace" it said. Two buttons went off the front of my jacket and bounced on the marble floor. Gayle's baby. Frank's baby. Of course. Who else?

Gayle looked good. She was in a robe and Frank was helping her to walk around the room. A flood of memories came back on a windy tide. It was yesterday—maybe the day before—that Gayle used to come bouncing in from school yelling, "Hey, Daddy-o! What's new among the squares?"

I put my arms around Gayle and kissed her. "How do you feel, Ox?" She grinned. "I'm fine, now. Did you see the baby?" I told her that the baby was beautiful, and that I wasn't saying it to please her. "Now you have your own live doll," I said. "Have you and Frank decided on a name yet?"

"Yes," she said, and the grin died and a frown came to life. "We're going to christen her Elinor. . . ."

* * *

It cannot happen twice in a lifetime. Love comes but once. I renounced marriage four years ago because the one I had was the best—and at times, the worst—and it endured a long time. Also, some of my spirit was under sod. The great and profound things happen but once.

Now I have remarried. She is a tall attractive woman with long, honey-colored hair caught in a bun at the back of the neck, and her name is Kelly. She is thirty-two years old—a disadvantage because I am fifty-three. She has two beautiful blonde daughters —Karen, eight, and Kathleen, six. This is another disadvantage because I have brought my children up, and feel happy to have survived it. I am not in the age category to begin the old admonitions, the old lessons painfully taught, the supervision of schoolwork, and facing the female penchant for putting questions to father.

There is one more disadvantage to this marriage. My faith is Roman Catholic. I believe in it. Kelly recently divorced an old friend of mine, Raymond T. Stone. My church excommunicates those who marry divorcees. Then, too, I am not in the habit of marrying old friends' ex-wives.

All the portents are against this marriage. And yet, when I met Kelly at her place of business—the Diplomat Hotel in Hollywood, Florida—there was a slipping, sliding, skidding feeling in me when I invited her to bring the little girls to the swimming pool at the Key Biscayne Hotel. My father and I were staying there in a small bungalow alongside the pitch-and-putt course.

A few visits led to a few movie dates. The few dates led to a few serious talks. As a species, men are ridiculous figures in love, but no one was sillier than I. Most of our time was spent with me giving her reasons why she should not, under any circumstances, marry me. One was the age difference. Two, the children. Three, the Church. Four, she had looks and charm to spare, and could easily find a much younger man.

She listened, and smiled. If I did not want to marry her, she said, it would be better to stop discussing it. She said that I spent most of our time together giving excellent reasons why the marriage could never occur. So, last week, when the first weak sprigs of green adorned the old poplars in front of New York State Supreme Court, we walked inside and were married.

It was the most difficult decision of my life. I am not one who can fall into or out of love easily. It is accompanied by a resounding crash, like the fall of timber. But, even when I knew that it was pointless to fight permanent feelings, I was fretful about marriage because it involved two children already hurt by a divorce.

What about them? Could I, in the fifties, be an adequate father? I understood the problem, and would rather forego the conjugal happiness than add another scar to their lives. I knew them, and had known them from birth, and liked them. But like isn't love. Children need love. Besides, they loved their father—a good man—and would regard me as an interloper.

Kelly had no doubt that everything would resolve itself for the betterment of the youngsters. The more I worried about it, the more certain she became that I would "make the grade." So, I have taken the plunge and I have even decided what kind of a father I am going to be. I am going to treat the girls exactly the same as I did my own. I will not try to purchase their affection by being overly indulgent, nor will I be overly strict. In time, love will become a reality between us.

Time . . .

Another birthday is coming up. In a few days, I will be fifty-four. What have I to show for all this time? Very little, I'm afraid. A house, a boat, a car, some money in the bank. My real riches are in my family. They are the lovingest, kissingest, battlingest group of Irish revolutionaries in town.

I've been in the midst of this group since 1907 and I still find it difficult to keep up with their activities. My father celebrated his seventy-eighth birthday a few weeks ago and we had a gathering of the clan. It's like a wake, with jokes. Everybody sits in the living room while my sister Adele fusses and perspires in the kitchen.

After the second or third round of drinks, the relatives stop glaring at each other and begin to grin. My father opened the loot—a few ties, two pairs of slippers, a bottle of Scotch to keep the ticker in tune, six pairs of bobby sox, and he told a few stories. At every paragraph, his sister, Mrs. Margaret McCarthy, corrected him on the date or event. His younger sister, Mrs. Mary Foley, laughed at all the old stories and told everybody to keep quiet while the recital was on.

My brother John, portly and dignified in a new topcoat, left early with his wife for a Polish wedding reception. A photo of my mother, as a young handsome woman, stood on the television set. In the cellar, some of the men shot pool between the clotheslines and the furnace.

The riches are right there. Adele had two functions: make the salads and keep her husband Emil out of the kitchen. He will eat anything that won't eat him first. She waved a big wooden spoon at him and he snarled like a tiger at bay.

The next night we went over to Ginny's house. Her twin daughters are three and they were dressed as Irish fairies, with green stockings and ragged tunics with wings on the back. Ginny said she made the outfits because she didn't have anything else to do. Little Jim was trying to run a model truck through an electric socket. Kevin, the fat laughing boy of the outfit, sat in his high chair showing how he says his prayers. He can't say a word. He just presses the palms of his hands together.

My younger daughter Gayle came up to visit us with Frank. Her little Elinor is now ten months old and, somehow, more beautiful each day. Gayle has short dark hair and wants to get it cut shorter. Frank says that if she does, he won't drive her to church.

Me? I'm back in the homework department. Our two little girls come in from school laden with brief cases and lunch kits as though they were trying to make it across the Sahara without refueling. I check the homework and once, when the conscientious Karen subtracted when she should have added, Mrs. Heliker marked the paper with a big zero.

Have you ever tried to stem tears at 3:20 P.M.? Kathleen has to write numbers from one to sixty. She also draws pumpkins and clowns and Santas. Through all this, Kelly is the epitome of the patient wife, always understanding and never impatient.

Five grandchildren, two children, two stepchildren, a wife, a father, a sister, a brother, numerous in-laws and nieces and nephews—this, my friend, is living. Almost all of them are forever in some form of emergency. The quo is never status; something is always going on—like the twins off to the hospital for tonsillectomies, Dad off to Dr. Krull to check the rising tide of fluid in the ankles, a report card which could be better, all the women on the phone at once to tell each other which niece is pregnant, or which in-law who is pleading poverty has just blown twenty dollars for a new hat.

At fifty-four I have my share of worldly goods. I'm not knocking it. I've been lucky with a few books, and, now and then, a column scores a hit with a few readers. I'm as happy now as I ever was. There are swings in the yard again, and a doll with a fractured skull stares at the ceiling. Rocky finds a corner and curls up to nap with one eye open.

It's not an exciting life, but it's not dull either. When I can't think of an idea for a column, all I have to do is rap out the truth about my family. Of course, no one speaks to me after it's published, but, at the age of fifty-four, there's a blessing in that too. . . .

1962

Kelly and I are in our room now, so it's safe to kick the shoes off and relax. The little ones are in the room next door, and my father is in the room beyond that. There is nothing in the world as fascinating as traveling with little ones, and a man of seventy-eight. It is anything but dull.

At Idlewild, my wife was checking the baggage when she picked up a small valise which almost tore her arm from the socket. "What," Kelly said to my father, "is in that one?" He looked slightly irritated. "My medicine," he said. "Why?" "Nothing," she said. "What have they got you on now—iron?"

Big John is becoming slower of foot and faster of mind. He misses nothing, is interested in everything, and has opinions. I can recall the days when it was possible to start an Irish Rebellion by merely observing that it was a nice day. His brows are snowy, and his head is down and he walks a few feet and says, "I'm winded again."

We took him on the jet anyway. He's game. He wanted a window seat, and he got it. He also wanted a highball—"Double, if you don't mind." Karen and Kathleen wanted window seats too. So did Kelly. So, although the trip from New York to Miami is only two hours and a few minutes, we played musical chairs.

The stewardess was serving the double hooker to Kathleen and the Coke to my father, and everybody on the plane was confused except us. We knew where we were all the time. When we got to Miami I rented a car and was halfway out of the airport before I realized both the children were standing in the back seat tossing little goodies at cars following us.

We arrived at the Diplomat Hotel worn. At least, Kelly and I were tired. The others looked great. The Diplomat has a big classy lobby and we walked in as though we belonged. I signed the register with what I thought was a flourish and Karen said, "Mommy, didn't you used to work here in the cellar?" Some of the eyebrows behind the desk went up.

Kelly worked here once. She was a stenographer in the publicity department. "Not the cellar," Kathleen said, "it's much nicer to say the basement." One must know children well before the desire to slug them becomes irresistible.

The bellboy showed us to our rooms. Big John said he could not sleep on the bed, even though he had two of them in his room. "I need something that will keep me sitting up," he said. I telephoned the housekeeper. She sent a porch glider. Now my father has two beds, with a glider between them.

His medicines are all over the room, and you would have to be a Chinese pharmacist to decipher what they're for. The girls have their room littered with dolls, and beachballs.

My father calls for a newspaper to be delivered in his room—252—but, by the time the bellman arrives, Dad is in our room. The bellman tries our room as Dad goes through the connecting door into the girls' room. The bellman never quite makes it, but he tries.

The family has barely arrived, but already the hired hands are asking the kids, "How long you staying, honey?" with the sweet sad smile. There is a bottle of vodka which has bounced between the two rooms so many times that no one is sure where it is. My guess is that it went out with the clothes to be dry-cleaned.

My father took a sip, and said, "Is this a Russian drink?" I said that the Russians could stake a claim to it. "What do you call it?" he said. Vodka. "That's right," he said. "I keep forgetting." I told him that he didn't have to remember, because his doctor will allow him but two drinks a day, no matter how they are pronounced.

He shuffled back to his room. That evening, after dinner, I asked my father to join us for television in our room. He declined, with thanks. He said he wanted to get to bed early because, in the morning, we would be flying to Grand Bahama Island. I never knew my father to go to bed early.

At 11 P.M. a bellman delivered the morning newspapers. I tipped him and he said, "How did your dad like the vodka?" I said, "What vodka?" The man said, "The fifth I delivered after dinner. Your father ordered it."

In bed, he must have looked like a Christmas tree.

On the fourth day, he sat in a chair next to a tall lamp. The lamp was lit and, even with the drapes drawn, the light etched the loose individual strands of white hair, the lean cheeks hugging the old bones, the wool pajamas open at the top, the blanket covering the legs, the facing chair which held the feet.

The eyes opened briefly as Karen and Kathleen bounded into the room. The little bathing suits dripped, the blonde hair hung in wet strings. My father smiled briefly. The eyes flickered closed. The hands were clasped across his stomach. The lower lip stuck out in sleep.

Kelly crouched beside him. "You all right, Dad?" she said. The eyes opened. The smile came back. "Fine," he said. I came in from an adjoining room. "You can't be all right," I said. "You can't sleep through a vacation." He thought about it, looking up at me as though afraid to start an argument. "I'll be all right," he said. "I'm tired."

He's seventy-eight. He'll be seventy-nine in October.

"I know you inside out," I said. "You started sleeping at The Diplomat." "The Diplomat?" he said vaguely. I nodded. "The hotel in Hollywood, Florida. You started sleeping there and you haven't stopped. Now you're sleeping through the Bahamas."

"I'm all right," he said. "Honest."

"Any pain?" I said. He shook his head no.

"Are you taking your heart medicine?" He nodded yes, but the eyes were closing again.

I phoned Dr. Adolf Richter. He's the only doctor in West End. "I'll be over," he said.

What could I tell him? The medical facts were simple enough: auriculuar fibrillation; edema in ankles and lungs—both under control. The fibrillation is an uneven beat of the heart due, in this case, to childhood diphtheria which killed a node called the pacemaker. The edema—or fluid—came from weakness in the heart muscle. Nothing unusual at seventy-eight.

The doctor arrived, listened to the story, and began his examination. When he finished, he said "This man needs a hospital." There is no hospital on the island.

"The small arteries of the brain could be rupturing. Little strokes. How far is home?" "New York," I said. The doctor shook his head. "He is weak and getting weaker. Can you get him to Florida? He should have some oxygen."

I said I did not know. I would try. The doctor was sympathetic. He would be back. The patient was in no pain, just fading away. I couldn't take it. I looked at my father. He slept with his chin on his chest. He looked tired. We had been through a lot together. He must die. I am aware of it. I have been lucky to have him this long. But there is something sad and helpless about fading away. In an acute illness, like a heart attack, there is something to fight. Who can battle a four-day nap?

A mile away there was an airstrip. Who? What? How? Ken Calendar of Miami Goodwill Industries had a plane. He was going to pick us up and fly the family to Miami. Did it have oxygen? I didn't know. Could we afford to wait? A good question. I went back in the room and awakened him.

"Did you take your medicine?" I said. It appeared to be difficult for him to concentrate. Yes, he said. "What day is this?" I said. He wasn't sure. "Where are we?" I asked. He smiled a little. You know, he said, those little islands—hydrangeas.

I got his medicine. "Which one is for the heart?" I asked. He studied the bottles a long time. "They're green," he said. I became exasperated and frightened. "There are no green pills," I said.

The phone rang. I answered. As I spoke, my father fell back into a deep soft sleep. It was the nurse at the Jack Tar Hotel. "I'm coming right down with some oxygen," she said. I thanked her. The sight of the tank would make my father feel that the end was near, I knew.

I was boxed. Trapped. After all this man had done for me, what could I do for him? Nothing. Why had I insisted that he join us on this vacation? He had been comfortable in his little room with his newspapers and books and the baseball games on TV.

The flight to Miami is about forty-five minutes. I needed a plane with oxygen, some strong hands to lift my father, and a prayer that he would live through the journey. I told him everything was going all right. He didn't hear me. . . .

It was morning again. The door was ajar and the sun traced a hot ingot across the rug. The palm trees on the lawn whispered to the birds to be quiet. John Bishop was comatose. The head was on the chest and it could be turned in any direction and he would not resist. The white whiskers were long on his cheeks.

The doctor had been there, and had left. Pulse: fifty-five; Heart: weak and erratic. Respiration: thirty. Temperature: 100.2. Feet: swollen and blue. Lips: cyanotic. "He needs a hospital bad," the doctor said, "but he is very weak for travel." That was the little crisis. The hiss of the oxygen was steady. In the yellow mask, my father looked like a retired spaceman.

Bob Brumby phoned. "There's a DC-3 ready to leave for Miami," he said. "The pilot says he has oxygen and he'll take your family." I thought about it. I understood my own fear very well. If I left him here, he'd die. If I bounced him in a plane, he'd die. "Let me talk to the pilot, please," I said.

He said he was Roger Byrne of Jacksonville. He worked for Owens-Illinois Glass Company. It was a company plane, but he was sure his superiors would not mind if he helped a sick man. I thanked him, and decided to ask my father. This is the cowardly move. He was in no condition to make a decision. I slapped his cheeks and, at last his eyes opened and he looked up at me. The mouth hung open. He smiled briefly and fell asleep.

"Okay," I said to the pilot. "We'll go. Thanks for thinking of us."

Kelly finished dressing the children and combing the hair. The little ones had dozens of questions. Why is he so sleepy? What does die mean? We could take him swimming. Would he like that? Does he always sleep on a chair? Yes. And yes. Yes. Yes.

None of it was easy. It required two strong Jack Tar bellboys to change the pajamas. The oxygen mask fell off three times. Kelly packed his clothes and his medicines. We no longer knew which ones he had taken and which ones he had skipped. A Cadillac was backed up on the lawn.

John Bishop was lifted onto a wheel chair. When the sun hit his face he squinted his eyes tight. It was the only sign of life. Lifting him onto the back seat of the car was an engineering problem. The children were taken to the airport in another automobile and put on the plane.

The pilot met us beside the Owens-Illinois DC-3. He had passengers. I felt that our case would depress them. "Think nothing of it," Mr. Byrne said. "They understand. On our way into Miami, I'll call for an ambulance and a doctor. They'll be waiting." He grinned. "Stop worrying. He's going to be all right."

My father looked like a lump of blankets as he was hauled backward onto the plane. Getting him into a seat was another problem. Kelly stood behind him and held the yellow mask to his face. I had a sheaf of five-dollar bills for the bellhops. They spurned the money. They left perspiring and heaving for breath. Brumby waved good-by. "He's Irish," he yelled over the noise of the engines. "He'll make it."

The pilot brought the ship to the head of the runway, turned, and let her go. As we cleared the jungle, Kelly drew the curtain next to John's face, so that the sun would not bother him. In forty minutes, we were coming down at Miami International. It was as Pilot Byrne said: below was the revolving red light of the ambulance.

A short pleasant man introduced himself as Dr. J. C. Frell. In ten minutes, I was riding the front seat of the ambulance. The back was air-conditioned, and Dr. Frell worked over the patient as the ambulance raced to Jackson Memorial Hospital. There was a cluster of cream-colored buildings. Inside, everything was starched and cool and orderly. Swiftly and silently, my father was moved out of my jurisdiction. He was wheeled to Room 788-S. Someone put in a call for Dr. Martin S. Belle, a cardiovascular doctor. Around-the-clock nurses were ordered. A young man in a white uniform rolled the bed down. I asked him to put it up. "My father has slept in chairs for years," I said. "He can't breathe if he's down flat." It was rolled up again.

Nurses moved in and out of the room like swans. I kissed my father and went into the hall. "He's not going to make it," I said to Kelly. "He's too far gone."

"Let's go downstairs for a cup of coffee," Kelly said. "These hospitals always have a coffee shop." "Where are the kids?" I said. They were in the admitting room prattling about their dolls. "Did you ever see anything like that pilot?" Kelly said as the elevator started down.

"There's a story about that man in the Bible," I said. "It's called The Good Samaritan. . . ."

The word spreads. It was on local radio stations and television within an hour. John M. Bishop, retired police lieutenant, had suffered a heart attack at West End, Grand Bahama, and was now in Jackson Memorial Hospital. Mr. Bishop is seventy-eight.

The sympathy of strangers is very sweet. Phone calls offering help came from everywhere. A woman sent a poem and a prayer. Some offered financial help; a man named Schwartz offered a suite of rooms free at the New Everglades. "You'll be closer to the hospital." Women offered to watch the children. Miami Beach police sent flowers.

Friends called. George Beebe, managing editor of *The Miami Herald,* said, "Name it. We'll do it." Hank Meyer said, "Whatever you need, we'll take care of it."

The action in Room 788-S is impossible to describe. Dr. Pedro Greer and Dr. Maurice Rich supervised tests. The chart began to show pages of notes. Night orders. Day orders. E.K.G.'s. X rays. Oxygen at nine. Medication. Liquids. Sip through a straw. Breathe through a green tube. A little blood out of the arm; a shot into the buttocks. A chemical balance test.

Patient on the critical list. He's nauseous. Call the doctor. Stop the medication. Try something new. Pulse stronger at sixty-three. Arms cold.

Let's not try anything radical with this patient. Too old. Take one thing at a time. Congestive heart failure first. One thing at a time. Nice and slow. He has an old ulcer. We'll pass the ulcer. Okay, now. Easy does it.

It was like that for days. Inch by inch, John Bishop began to climb back up. The eyes flickered open. They looked at Kelly. One of them winked. The man was making his own fight. He heard the nurse say he needed fluids. "Beer," he said, forming the word slowly, "Get . . . me . . . a . . . barrel."

He received Extreme Unction, the heavenly passport, and he felt better. The patient never mentioned anything about his chances of living, but I saw the lingering, longing look in his eyes and I knew that he didn't think he would make it.

His will had been handwritten a long time ago. He disposed of his cherished possessions among his three children and, at the bottom, it said: "No tears. No grief. In my time I have lived a life and a half—maybe two—and there is nothing to feel bad about. Please take sufficient cash to buy dinner and a drink for all who come to pay their last respects."

The days dragged. There were phone calls home and visits to the sickroom. The monotonous plea of prayer was offered again and again.

The television set on the dresser remained blank. For the first time in forty years, he did not care about the New York Yankees.

The doctors and nurses came and went, riffling through the chart, frowning, whispering, writing. On the fifth night, he had Scotch and water through a bent straw. The doctor said it might do a little good.

In the hall, I talked to the doctor. "He's still in heart failure," he said. I said nothing. "Everything depends," he said, "on how much heart muscle he has left." I was learning something grim. He would not recover fully. Much of the heart muscle was dead. The chances were that he would, with luck, live out his remaining time in a wheel chair.

John Bishop is not the type for that life. He had once been a flashy second baseman, a rugby player, a lieutenant of police with big strides, a man who held up one end of a piano while my mother swept the rug under it. Now, he was just another old man dying, paying an account overdue. For a moment, I wondered if he and I would be praying for the same thing.

The following day, we arrived at the hospital to hear laughter in the room. We looked in the doorway. A stout nurse was halfway across the bed. "There," my father said, kissing her. "You want to know if I feel stronger?" The nurse got up, ruffled, and straightened out her skirt. She patted her hair and looked at my wife.

"He's a terror," she said, shaking her head. "He'll make it."

He did.

Last spring, I bought a gold watch for my father in Hong Kong. It had a Swiss movement. It was priced so reasonably that my wife and I walked in and out of the shop on Cameroon Road three times before we put up the money. We brought it home in a plush case. When my father saw it, he shook his head in wonderment.

"Beautiful," he said. "It's the most beautiful watch I've ever seen." It was something to look at. There were thirty jewels, and the watch not only told the time of day, it also told the day of the week and the date of the month. It looked like a gold alarm clock on his wrist.

"You can't use two watches," my brother John said. "Can I have the old one?" My father shook his head. "It didn't take you long to figure that out, did it?" he said. Johnny got the old watch. That turnip only told time. The new one did everything but cook the breakfast.

"Now," my father said, "let me get one thing straight. This thing not only tells time, it also gives me the day of the week and the date. Suppose I forget to wind it?" "Well," I said, "there must be some way of adjusting it." "Okay," he said. "How?"

I took the watch, pulled the stem out a little, and turned it. Nothing happened. "Here," he said. "Give it to me before you break it." He took it and gave the winder a few turns and, in a moment, it was giving us the wrong date, the wrong day, and the wrong time.

My father began to study Johnny as though he was going to ask for his old watch back. We fiddled with the new watch for an hour, and finally got it to tell the right time, but we couldn't get it to say Wednesday the twelfth no matter how hard we tried. When we got it to show Wednesday, it gave the date as the four-teenth. When we got the date right, the day was Monday.

The watch lacks imagination. Also a calendar. My father fooled with the thing a few days, and finally got the right date, the right day, and the right time, except for one thing. The watch was busted. So he took it to Nick Napoli's jewelry store and said, "Nick. Fix this thing, will you? I'll wait."

Napoli took a look and said, "If you're going to wait, you're going to be here a long time. I don't think I ever saw this make of watch before." My father said his son picked it up in Hong Kong. Napoli nodded. "We may have to send it back there to fix it," he said.

The jeweler sent it to New York. New York sent it to Switzer-land for a new part. The new part took time. Weeks went by. My father was watchless. Every time he passed my brother he said, "How's the old turnip doing?" Fine, Johnny said. Just dandy.

The watch came back and it told the correct time, the day of the week, and the date. "This thing is okay," my father said, "if nobody touches it. One touch and it's out of business." So all he did was wind it. He said it was the only watch in the world which required eighty winds each morning and still felt loose.

One night he found the watch fast, so he moved it ahead eleven

hours and some minutes, and managed to pass midnight. At once
the day and the date changed, and now he had the right time, but
the watch was on tomorrow. He began to glare at me and mutter
under his breath. We tried to get it back on the rails, but when we
got the correct day and the date, the hour was wrong. So it went
back to Napoli. He tried. The stem-winder was bent. The watch
was sent to New York, and then to Switzerland and, weeks later, it
was back on my father's wrist.

Everything is fine right now. My father shows it to his friends
with a little scorn. "Wanna see my Chinee watch?" he says. "It
tells Chinee time."

I don't mind. But I think I'll avoid him for the next week or so. I
just looked at the calendar and February has only twenty-eight
days. On the first of March, his watch is going to read: "Friday,
Feb. 29."

The family moves onward. The oldest member, John M., attended the christening of the youngest a few days ago. My father
will be seventy-nine this month; the new little boy, of course, is
age zero. There is not only a broad reach of the time between
them, but of wisdom and future and outlook. The things they
have in common are strong maleness, anticipation of the next
meal, and a desire for service.

This is the fifth baby for Ginny and Charles Frechette in four
years. Pamela and Robin are four; Jim Bishop Frechette is three;
Kevin is two; and now Chip. He made his bow weighing nine
pounds one-half ounce. He looked like a small bull. There was a
round head, no neck, a fat body with a deep chest, short legs and
arms in layers of fat, and hunger.

The Frechettes, with an ancestry of French Canada, have big
families. Great-grandma Frechette, a handsome and poised
woman with a radiant smile, told me she has forty-three grandchildren. Strangely, her maiden name was Frechette and she
thinks that sometime, far back, two wings of the family had separate farms in Quebec.

It is a truism that the more babies one has, the more casual the
mother becomes. Ginny almost missed the hospital. She barely
arrived. Dr. Albert Higdon thought he had time for a cup of
coffee. He got off the elevator and saw his number flashing silently
in the corridor, and hurried back up again.

The other four youngsters were with the Frechettes in Waltham, Massachusetts. They seldom believe what they cannot see.
Five days after Chip was born, they were still asking God to "send
a new baby to our house."

The day after the birth, there was some speculation about a name for the new boy. After a little waiting, the word came. He would be called Jonathan David Frechette. There were a lot of funny-looking expressions around the family. "Jonathan?" Who's that? All hands understood that the David would be a compliment to Ginny's father-in-law, Dave Frechette of Miami. But Jonathan? So Kelly and I sneaked into the hospital to ask. Ginny looked tired. Bone-weary. She said she chose the name Jonathan because she likes it. "I think we'll call him Jody," she said. Charlie just smiled. Anything that makes Ginny happy makes him happy.

Kelly asked me what I thought of the name Jonathan. I made a face. "It's better than Sean," I said. "I sometimes think that Ginny is more Irish than her forebears. She wanted to call this one Sean Frechette."

My wife said, "Sean Frechette?" I said "Yup. With a name like that, the child would have to learn to fight." We went back home. The following day, Dr. Albert Higdon arrived at the hospital to make out the final form of the birth certificate. Charlie stood with him beside the bed.

Higdon put on his best smile. "What name?" he said. Ginny said "Jonathan David." The doctor stood, with pen poised, and the smile died in a long, slow fadeout. "Jonathan David?" he said. She nodded.

The doctor shook his head. "Nobody," he said, "ever names a baby after me. I deliver one after the other, day and night, and each time I see a big healthy male, I say, 'This one is mine.' But it isn't. It always ends up with a name like Jonathan. Or Leslie. Or maybe Rollo."

"What's in a name, Doc?" said Charlie. He was grinning through the kidding. "Plenty," the doctor said. "A name is important. Take you for example. Five babies—three of them boys— and none named after you. After all, Charlie, you and I have to stick together. You start all these babies. I finish them. She puts any name on them but ours."

In a moment, the father and the doctor had the mother in a corner. "Yeah," Charlie said. "How about that?"

"All right," Ginny said. "All right, fellas. You win. I don't know how I get talked into these things. We'll call him Charles Albert Frechette. It's a nice name and we can call him Chip, because that's what I want him to be—a chip off his father."

Dr. Higdon winked at Charlie, and left before any change of mind could occur. An hour later, a nurse came into the room with a pill and a glass. "What happened to Dr. Higdon?" she said. Ginny shrugged.

"I was down in the nursery," she said, "and the doctor came in beaming at all hands. He went through all the bassinets until he came to yours and he picked it up and held it and said, 'Careful with this one, girls. He's mine.' "

And so there was another christening. It was a clear, cool day, and the two families gathered under the big oaks and maples in the back yard, eating ham and turkey and roast beef, and drinking Scotch. Afterwards, my father asked for some milk. At the same time, there was a cry from the nursery. Someone else wanted some, too. . . .

1963

The sunbeams bounce off the sea hot and silent. On the beach, the breakers barely make it, collapsing in thunder on the sand. The umbrellas look like hundreds of wild petunias. Women sit under them, streaking unguents on their shoulders; their men doze and bake their bellies in the sand. Solemn children build sand castles; some skip along the edge of the waves; some sit around mother.

Four are sitting around one mother. She has a round, pretty face. She wears a black bathing suit, a floppy straw hat with blue ribbons for tying and she laughs at what Kevin is saying in her ear. Kevin is two, a wrinkle-nosed laugher with a figure like a barrel of beer. What he is saying is "Happy do do . . . Happy do do . . ."

Mother translates for the others. "He is trying to sing happy birthday to me." The four-year-old twins think Kevin is funny because he can't say "Happy birthday." Ginny is twenty-six today. She is rich because, in Charlie, she has the right man and in the number of her cherubs—five—and another to be born in five months, she has an assortment of miniature mirrors.

This is an off day for Ginny. Instead of fretting and worrying about the children at home, she is doing it at the Ship Ahoy Club. Like most mothers, she automatically watches other little ones frolicking around the swimming pool. Behind the sun glasses, her eyes miss very little.

A lifeguard comes over in a flaming red shirt to ask her if he can watch the four while she takes a swim. She says no, thanks. The most work she plans for today is to walk around the pool to the soda stand. I live across the street from Ship Ahoy, so I finish some work and hurry over to sit beside my onetime girl friend.

The babies crowd around. They call me "Pop-Pop" and their love for me is built around my boat. They fall over each other trying to ask if we are going on the *Away We Go*. Yes, I say. Yes. Yes. Kevin points at me, falls over my legs, and says: "Bo . . . Bo . . ."

Our new little girls, Karen, nine, and Kathleen, seven, help get the babies across the street and all hands, including Mrs. Katherine Rook, our housekeeper, get aboard the boat. There is a big white life raft on the foredeck and all the children sit in it. The boat turns her bows downstream on the Shrewsbury and sails sedately toward Sandy Hook.

I'm on the flying bridge and it is easy to watch all the children in the raft. Also, by turning around, I can see Ginny and Katie and Kelly in the animated chatter of women. Rocky sits forlornly on the dock, watching the boat and crying through his nose. He wants to go, but it is impossible. The dog has been on the boat three times, and each time he gets seasick before the craft leaves the dock.

The children begin to sing "I'm Popeye the Sailor Man." When they reach the boop-boop, I make the mistake of hitting the twin horns. The kids almost jump out of their skins. Now, they sing chorus after chorus and, at the proper time, I'm expected to tap the horns.

As I go under Highlands Bridge, the bridge tender comes out and glares down at me.

He thinks I'm nuts. I am. Once or twice, one of the little ones almost falls out of the raft and the heart, for the moment, beats in fright. By the time we get back to the dock, Charlie is waiting to kiss his wife a happy birthday. "What's new?" he says. She shakes her head. "Nothing," she says. "Just a quiet day at the beach."

Nothing beats a lazy Sunday at home. . . .

We had one a few days ago. It was a dream. The air conditioners were in a hushed roar. I read the papers, with part of my mind on the news, another small part on the ball game on television, and a large part debating whether to fall asleep on the couch or fight it sitting up.

Kathleen, eight, who is learning to sew, had made a blue doll's pocket, but was having a problem. Somehow, she had sewed it to her slip. Karen, who is ten and tall, had a little difficulty lifting her feet over the dog. She managed to flatten herself twice. Kelly was in the kitchen with a roast, asking herself out loud whether it is better to put the thermometer in the meat when the inside is still frozen, or whether to wait until it's partly cooked.

The doorbell rang. It was Mr. and Mrs. Charles Frechette. Also their tribe of Comanches. The children—all blond—always come in timidly, smiling shyly. Nothing in the world is guaranteed to bring brighter smiles to Kelly's face or mine than the appearance of the Frechettes.

The twins—Pamela and Robin—are now five. They have Buster Brown bobs. Pamela is the little serious mother of the tribe, and Robin is the hell-raiser. Next comes Jim, who is four, a tinker and thinker. He is a crew-cut who will sit for hours over knots in a piece of string.

Then Kevin Gerard who is almost three, a moon-faced con man who can smile you out of the fillings in your teeth, and who is built like a runaway pickup truck. Then there is Chipper, who is really Charles Albert, and he will be one next month. Last, there is a sixth child, who will be born around Christmastime. What am I saying—last?

They arrived in a station wagon, and should have a bus. We decided to play African gin before dinner. Rocky, the worrisome police dog, sits under the dining room table and I rub his fur with my bare foot. I was rubbing some time before I peeked under the table cloth and found that I had my toes in Chipper's hair.

Pamela skidded down the steps into the living room and mother managed to assuage her tears while keeping one eye on the cards in her hand and one on Jim, who was trying to smother Kevin with pillows. Charlie didn't know the game we were playing, so he asked questions and won. Kelly kept excusing herself to go out into the kitchen and look at the roast and the vegetables.

Gayle, who will be twenty in November, works nights at Riverview Hospital, so she was sleeping in her room. Or, so we thought. The kitchen door swung open, and Gayle emerged, saying a hurry-up hello and banking the turns on her way out to get something from the car. She washes it more frequently than she bathes her patients.

Kelly said that the children would have to eat on the porch and the adults inside. Someone switched the ball game off because the children wanted to watch a relaxing horror movie featuring people with no heads. Gayle busted back in the house in time to jam the door against Rocky's nose and Kevin tilted a chair so that Kathleen almost flew out of it.

The phone rang. It was my father, who said that if I was missing the ball game I was missing half my life. He said that something must be wrong with his ears because he could hear all kinds of funny noises on the phone. We had dinner, and the kids on the porch kept coming in with minute-by-minute reports on who was eating his dinner and who was not.

Karen took Chipper out on the front lawn and managed to fall into the petunias. I decided to go out into the office and write a column. My twin granddaughters watched gravely and said, in unison: "Why you do dat, Pop-Pop?" I couldn't think of a reason.

Kelly took the leftovers and put the meat in a tin plate for Rocky, and she and Ginny washed the dishes and talked woman talk. It was several minutes before they looked down and saw that Rocky and Chipper were eating from the same dish. Rocky is generous. He was not offended.

It's an exciting and wonderful thing to have the whole family together. Exciting and wonderful and terrifying. In the evening, when they departed, and Gayle had gone to work and Kathleen and Karen had said their prayers and were in bed, I grinned at Kelly. She was sprawled on a chair, blowing the hair out of her eyes.

Nothing beats a lazy Sunday at home . . .

The visits to the cemetery are not for me. Nor would I want to be visited if I were a tenant. The tilted headstones, the mangy grass, the events beyond recapture are good for those who feel penitential, or guilty, or morbidly triumphant at still being alive. For me, prayer is everything. The walk in the cemetery is a pointless sacrifice.

My mother and my first wife, Elinor Dunning Bishop, are a row apart in the granite ranks. Six rows away is Helen Scanlon, the dark sprite with the laughing eyes. Little Frankie Westphal is nearby. So are my grandparents, my mother-in-law, cousins, friends beyond number.

Is a prayer said there of more value than one said in a church? Or at home? The setting of a wreath—does it please the clay beneath? A bouquet of roses—who sees it? Who smells the fragrant goodness? The giver? Or the recipient?

Still, I must admit that I was touched recently by such a visit. To tell it properly, I must explain that when Elinor died, our daughter Gayle was sick in bed. She was thirteen, an age of delicate emotional balance in young ladies. She was verging on pneumonia. I was on a ship. Virginia Lee, our older daughter, was at the hospital with her mother.

Gayle was too young, too sick to be told that her mother was not doing well. Ginny walked into the bedroom one day, tears standing on her lids, and said, "Mommy died this morning." As simple as that. Gayle pulled the bedclothes up under her chin, stared at the ceiling, and wept.

After the funeral, the children and I tried to recall happy things about their mother; fun things. Sometimes, in the midst of the laughter, there was a mist of memory, too. But always, Gayle set her lips grimly and left the room. Ginny and I felt that she was callous.

The opposite was true. Gayle was the one hardest hit. We did not know it. We forgot that, in the final two years of her life, Elinor had used Gayle as her exclusive slave. We failed to recall that it had been Gayle who doled out pills at all hours, went to the stores innumerable times, got the glass of water, held the hand, patted the cheek, and became a wise old lady when she was still a child.

All of which led to a nervous breakdown. It required two years of grief to crush Gayle. Two years of inner sorrow coupled with a feeling that it was unjust of her mother to die suddenly. Two years when a girl is transmuted into a young lady. A delicate time to be left with a father and a police dog.

The breakdown led to a sudden elopement, a poor marriage and a beautiful baby. The marriage broke when a young energetic husband could not understand his wife's depression. Gayle came home. It wasn't easy because now her father had a new wife, and two new little girls were in the house.

But Gayle was determined to bury all the sorrows. It required a lot of work and a monumental will to succeed. Day by day, she won a little ground. Inch by inch, she pulled herself upright. She decided to study to become a practical nurse. By day and by night, she immersed herself in nursing books. She took jobs in nursing homes where the old and the chronically sick were not sure what they wanted. Or why.

All last summer, Kelly and I watched the laughter come back into Gayle's heart. She became the breezy, witty tomboy she had once been. Life became fun again. She reached the ripe old age of nineteen, a dark woman with mischief in her eyes. Her career became increasingly important.

Immersion in work is strong therapy. Little by little, she found herself able to talk about her mother without feeling hurt. Little by little, she found herself seeking Kelly's advice. Little by little she began to confide in Kelly. Then one day she called out, "Hey, Mom!" and the new mother, who knew she could not replace the real one, realized that she had an additional daughter.

Christmas Eve came. The weather was clear and cold. Chunks of ice floated like giant cakes of soap down the Shrewsbury River. Gayle said, "Are you going to visit Mommy's grave?" I said no. Her soul was not there, and her soul was what lived. "I think I'll go," she said.

"Well," Kelly said, "it's quite a drive." Gayle smiled. "Stop worrying about me. I'm going. I want to decorate the grave." She went. I worried a little because it was going to be a severe test. The young lady was going to face this one alone.

She went. At five o'clock, I heard the front door slam. I waited in the office at the back of the house. No use appearing anxious. She came out, and kissed me on the cheek. "Like you said," she murmured, "there's nothing there. But I'm glad I went."

John said that the name of the car was Teapack. My father said he had never heard of it. He wasn't aware that the Japanese make their own automobiles. "What is it?" my father said querulously. "A kind of a Chinee car, would you say?" No, my brother said, Japanese. It was a little secondhand job, and John said he might have to learn to speak Japanese to run it.

My father shook his head. Everything that happens in our family is either hilarious or tragic. The car is a Toyapet. John is sort of Art Carney born to be fleeced. He does everything with the best of intentions, and the shrewdest of suspicions, but he talks his way into fraud. Once, he went for $400 for a beautiful cabinet radio and, after he got it home, he found that the music was coming out of a secondhand automobile radio.

Now it's a Japanese car. My father asked if it was a good one. "Oh yes," John said gravely, "you turn the key and geisha girls hop out the back." Dad kept shaking his head. He wanted to know how much it had cost. "Nine hundred," John said, "and it's a steal." "For whom?" Dad said.

My brother is the only man I know who moonlights in the daylight. He works as a night watchman and, in the early hours of the day, he's a bartender at Louie's Tavern on Broadway in North Bergen, New Jersey. He needs a car. The one he had was dragging its tailpipe. Sometimes it took off in a proud plume of blue smoke; at others, it just sat and ground its gears.

"How is it," my father said, "that you don't know the correct name of the car you just bought?" My father is eighty years old, and has everything in correct order. John has a glib reply. "Because," he said grimly, "everything on the dashboard is written in Japanese, that's why."

"Ha," my father said, "it must be like that Chinee watch Jim gave me." Now his blue eyes glittered with suspicion as he asked questions about the Toyapet. John said that it is basically a good car except that the battery runs down. He is pleased with it, in fact, and hopes to teach it to run without a battery.

"Why doesn't the battery run?" Dad asked. Well, John said, the brake light remains on permanently. "You mean you can't shut off the light?" John nodded. "So what are you going to do?" Dad said, wondering how my mother managed to raise such an assortment of numskulls. "Unscrew the bulb," John said.

"I see. Tell me something, John. When this heap falls apart, where do you go for repairs—a chop suey joint?" My brother pays no attention to such jokes. He has better ones. "It's not the bulb that bothers me," he said. "It's the heater." Dad held his hand over his heart to make sure that he wasn't verging on an attack. "What," he whispered, "is the matter with the heater?"

"It won't shut off, winter or summer," John said. Dad nodded agreeably. "That must be nice," he said. "You bought a car you can't pronounce—secondhand—and it has a brake light that won't go off, and a heater that keeps percolating all the time, plus a battery that is out of order, and you can't read the dashboard. Anything else?"

"Yes," John said. "I get thirty-three miles to the gallon." "Gallon of what?" my father said sarcastically. John smiled. *"Sake,"* he said. "What else? Does it have an automatic shift?" "Oh, no. This is a stick shift." "I suppose it was driven by some retired school-teacher up and down her garage?"

"No. It was a young nurse. Most of the time, she couldn't get it to move." "That's nice." "Well, it kept the mileage down, didn't it?" "What happens if you need a part?" "I don't write to Tokyo, if that's what you mean." "How does it run—sort of sidewards?" "Come on. I'll take you for a ride."

My father declined, with thanks. The Toyapet stood out at the curb, sapping its own strength. My brother's wife Anna thought that, if the car had to be fixed, maybe John should drive it to the United Nations. Everybody thought that this was very funny. The car was referred to as John's Hiroshima Bomb.

That was a week ago. Now they have all revised their thinking. After the first ride, my father took John aside. "Listen," he said confidentially, "I wouldn't make this offer to anybody else, but would you like to buy a Chinee watch . . . ?"

John M. Bishop, Sr., is beginning his eighty-first year. The difference between this man and the one of long ago is consider-

able. When he was a police lieutenant, he weighed 254. Today he
is 150. He used to swing his arms and take long steps with his chin
high. Today, the head is bowed, the hair is snowy, and the step is
a hesitant shuffle.

He spends his time in a small room at my sister's house. In it are
pictures of my mother, a few holy pictures, a gold clock, a hospital
bed which he never uses, a big chair, a portable TV set, a hassock,
a bridge table, hosts of newspapers, a small library and bottles of
pills.

The mind is quick and sure. He reads everything, loves conversation, and appears to slip only on names. He shoots an excellent
game of pool, loves to go to sea on the boat, complains of his
"wind," adds up his great-grandchildren and comes up one short.
Sometimes he winks at proper ladies and when I asked him why,
he said, "That's what I've got left."

He lives in North Bergen, New Jersey, but the geographical
love of his life is Florida. He insists that there is no place in the
world like it, although he has never been west of Chicago, nor east
of New Hampshire. He comes alive in Miami, even though he
almost died there of a sleepy heart a year ago. On occasion, when
I mention the name of Dr. Martin Belle, my father lifts his hat
and bows his head. He was saved by the Belle.

He cannot bear to see a child punished for any infraction, although he was a pretty tough parent in my time. He believes in
ghosts, spirits and the Little People of Ireland, although he smiles
derisively at anything which is not "scientifically logical."

He has opinions on everything and everyone. If you do not
agree with him, he will explain patiently and in some detail. If
you still do not understand, you are beyond hope. In his world,
there are two seasons: one in which baseball is played, and the
dull season. Christmas is a milestone because it is 110 days until
the opening at Yankee Stadium.

He cannot understand a policeman who will not do a minor
favor for another policeman. Nor can he abide politics in a Police
Department. He still feels—with good reason—that he should
have been chief in Jersey City, but that he was kept down to
assist chiefs who had little talent.

He likes two highballs in the evening because we won't give
him three. John enjoys food, and likes to flatter the cook. Years
ago, he used to love salt herring for breakfast or yesterday's beef
stew. He is meticulous about his person and his morning ablutions
require considerable time. He comes to the table sparkling—even
the shoes.

Long ago, he was afraid of age and didn't like to face it. Now
he tries to pretend he's an ancient who has outlived everybody.

He enjoys an automobile ride for its own sake. At night, he waits until everybody is in bed, then he starts to read books. He will read until 3 A.M. Sometimes he writes reminder notes to himself. Before he retires, he lays out tomorrow's pills in a special bottle, as precisely as he lays out fresh underwear and shirts, and goes to bed in a chair thinking about all the wonders he gleans from books.

John Bishop is a romantic, a sentimentalist, a logician—terms which are not always compatible. Neither is he.

1964

The New Year's Eve party was at my house. We sat in the dining room around the table. My brother John looked up from the score pad and said, "Whose deal?" His wife Anna said, "You look tired." My wife said, "Why not? He worked last night and hasn't slept today." I pointed to the bottles on the table. "Make yourself a highball," I said. "It will keep you awake."

My father was dozing in his chair. "Who's having a highball?" he said, lifting the lid of one eye, in case it wasn't worth it to open both. "I am," Johnny said. My father opened the second lid. "Am I in?" Anna nodded. "You're in," so he sat up, and John made two modest highballs.

"Nobody asked me," my wife said, "but I'll take a beer." She went out into the kitchen and got a can. She pulled the tab top off it, and then went into the bathroom for a Band-Aid. "My deal," I said, picking up the cards. I riffled the deck and four cards fell on the floor. It required determination to stoop to get them.

My father turned the television set on. It was very exciting. There was a picture of Guy Lombardo waving his hands in front of a band, and some people dancing in Grand Central Terminal. We could hardly contain our enthusiasm. At one minute to twelve, the set showed a picture of a lighted ball on top of the Times Building. We were told that, at the moment the old year died, the ball would come down to the bottom of a flagpole.

Well, you can't see this kind of living history every day, so we quit the card game for a moment, adjusted our bifocals and dental plates, and sat watching. I ran into the kitchen and dialed my son-in-law, Charlie Frechette, to wish that branch of the family a Happy New Year. There was no answer. Charlie and Ginny were in bed. So were the six—count 'em—babies. The new one, born just before Christmas, is Christopher John. The twin girls, oldest in the group, are now five years of age.

I phoned Gayle in Red Bank. "Happy New Year," I said. "Thank you," she said, "and a Happy New Year to you, Pops." That covered the topic. I hung up and the phone rang. It was my sister, Mrs. Adele Steencken. "Happy New Year," she said. "And many more to you," I said.

The thrills were too much to bear. My father downed his high-ball before the lighted ball came down, and he refused a second. "Well," John said sadly, "this is the day. This is the day." My father paid no attention to him. He was back on his chair, tilted back, dreaming of New Year's Eves of long ago.

I wanted to go upstairs and wish the little girls a Happy New Year, but Kelly reminded me that Karen and Kathleen were sleeping. I don't drink, so I poured another cup of flaccid tea from a lukewarm pot, and dealt the cards. John murmured "Mixed deal" and shoved them back at me.

It was so breath-taking that I went out on the porch. There wasn't a person in sight. The only sound was the basso profundo of the breakers pounding the sea wall. I came back in and my father opened his other eye and said, "Snowing?" I said no. He said, "The radio says it's going to snow." John poured himself another highball and studied us through the bottom of his glass. He was surprised to find that we appeared to be more interesting.

The ball came down the staff, and on television there was a loud cry of "Happy New Year!" Now that it was official, we kissed each other, shook hands, and wished each other many, many more. The ladies became emotional about it and, for a moment, it was a tossup whether Anna or Kelly would burst into tears.

Kelly decided to toss caution to the winds, and drank her beer out of the can. I went to the bathroom and got a Band-Aid for her lip. My father got out of his chair, tottered over to a box of Christmas cookies, and tossed one to our police dog. "Rocky is entitled to a New Year celebration," my father said. Well, you can't start a fight over that, so we all sat and watched the dog eat the cookie.

Then the dog sat and watched us. It was almost twenty minutes past twelve when he went to sleep. My father was working up a small snore. John pushed all the cards together in a neat pile. "Whose deal?" he said. I was no longer certain. At once, it became the most fascinating topic of the whole evening.

We were still at it when twelve thirty rolled around and we all went to bed. It was, as they say, just too much.

The best man can do is to appreciate his women. The worst is to try to understand them. Take Kathleen. She is nine now. Nine going on ninety. Until a few weeks ago, she was like a blonde kitten. She has long hair, parted in the middle, round china-blue eyes, a nose the size of a shoe button, and a figure which comes through a filmy pink nightie like Miss America.

Overnight, she has changed. She is at least two persons, perhaps three. Sometimes she is grave, sensible, old-fashioned and overly modest. The Sisters at St. Matthew's School teach Spanish in the third grade and Kathleen is still struggling with English. She is beset by holiness and villainy. One moment she is praying for all the afflicted people of the world, and the next she collapses in my arms and murmurs: "Growl at me, Tiger!"

She is reading a teen-age biography of Clara Barton, but she does not neglect the comic strips. She and her older sister Karen are the kissingest kids of all time. It is not unusual in this house for the girls to blow farewell kisses to all hands en route to the bathroom. And more on the way back. They call all male visitors "uncle" because it gives them a license to kiss them.

They think boys are "icky"—which is an aboriginal term of denunciation. Their bedroom is pink and white; the bedspreads are laden with dolls, and aliens like me gain admission only by knocking, and waiting until a flurry of feet and excited whispers dies down. They watched a movie star on TV one night and Karen said, "I don't like her. She's too sexy." Kathleen looked at her sister. "What's sexy?" she said. Karen shrugged. "Sort of show-offy," she said.

Kathleen has been under the shadow of her sister for a long time. Suddenly, the little one has become boss. Karen is beautiful and lazy, a dreamer. Kathleen is now her advisor and counselor. Karen listens gravely and says, "Oh yes. You're so right."

Karen can play imaginary games alone and does all the character parts out loud. Kathleen cannot. At breakfast, they try to speak in fractured Spanish. It comes out: "Se habla usted?" The other one, afraid to acknowledge that she doesn't know what it means, nods and says: "Sí."

A few weeks ago, they got into their parents' room and found a garter belt. Kathleen held it out, grimaced, and said, "What's this?" Karen smiled with superior wisdom. "It's a bra, you dope." Kathleen shook her head negatively. "Can't be," she said gravely. "Look, there are four of them."

Sometimes, when they go off to school in a good mood, they hold hands and skip, with the book bags bouncing at their sides. They look like Mutt and Jeff and sound like a runaway junk wagon. Karen likes to pretend that she doesn't understand her homework so that I will do it for her. Kathleen likes to pretend she understands everything, and requires no help.

Both girls are feminine and vain, and would rather be in pretty frocks than in shorts. My older girls, Virginia Lee and Gayle, in their early years, would rather climb fences in dungarees than be caught dead in a dress.

When Kathleen does not like something I say, she grins and shows a little gap between the front teeth and says, "Funn-eeee." In a similar situation, Karen pouts, or weeps. Kathleen is now at the stage where love has become the most important thing in the world.

"Everybody should love everybody else—right? Well, I'm trying. You know what? It isn't easy to love everybody because I don't know everybody. But I don't hate anybody, even that boy who sent the funny valentine. I think of him as a sort of an ox, you know?"

She edges up onto one of my knees and continues her speech. "Where would we be if there wasn't love? Nowhere, that's where. People have to love each other pretty good. Sometimes when they first say hello, they don't like each other. This is wrong. Tell me, are big people stupid? Or maybe they're afraid.

"Did you see the six o'clock movie last night? Well, this man comes home and his girl is there and he grabs her and crushes her with kisses—you should have seen him. Why aren't you like that, Tiger?"

I thought about it a moment. "Okay," I said, "I'll be your tiger. Wait until I put my teeth back in."

A house is important. It is more than a roof and walls; more than an abode. It insulates the contentment of the heart against the world. It can be exalting or depressing, exciting or dull, loving or cold. Within its walls occur the ecstasy of birth, the grief of death. Without love, it is wood and cement. With it, a house is a castle, a fortress, a refuge. It is a place of infant cries, adolescent shrieks and, in time, the silence of two old people alone.

We bought a house in Golden Isles, Hallandale, Florida. It is a red-roofed pagoda, with beams curving upward at the ends. There are Chinese characters on the garage doors, and palm trees with hidden green lights in the base to light the fronds against the dark velvet of the night. A man named Don Tucker did an excellent job of building a knotty-pine office in the garage. He also built a replica of the Chinese house as a mailbox.

The house is fifty-nine feet across the front and about twenty-five feet deep. There is a master bedroom with deep closets behind white-latticed doors. Each closet has its own interior light. The bathroom has two basins—His and Hers—a shower, and is decorated in black and white tile. It also has a back door leading to a thirty-five-foot oval swimming pool. The pool holds twenty-five thousand gallons of water. It is in the center of a screened Florida patio measuring fifty-nine feet by forty feet, with formal Chinese gardens around the pool. Kenneth Hoobler, who used to landscape for Arthur Vining Davis, designed the gardens and the Chinese lighting.

Rocky shows a shocking contempt for these gardens. Behind the patio is a white concrete dock with orange lights. There, a thirty-five-foot cabin cruiser, *Away We Go IV*, sits at ease in a canal only one thousand feet from the Intra-Coastal Waterway. In the canal, big snook chase the small fish, which leap clear and silvery in the fight for life.

There is a front bedroom for Karen and Kathleen. They have a white desk, a vanity, twin white beds, pink accessories, and shelves for their dolls. Next to it is another bedroom, this one reserved for Gayle when our twenty-one-year-old has time to visit. The bathroom across the hall is a dream in pink and gold marble, with twin basins and a sunken marble tub.

The living room is about twenty-four by twenty, and has a gold couch which runs ten feet along one wall, and nine down the other. The room is decorated in Chinese black and gold. The center hall is in red and white flecks of terrazzo with a guest closet on one side and a huge mirror on the other.

Everything is covered with broadloom, except the kitchen. This is in Chinese red with tiny tracings of gold Chinese temples on the walls. There are two sinks, and two electric ovens recessed. A pull on a stainless steel handle brings out a tray with four electric burners. Even the blender is concealed in a drawer. The drainboard is red formica and runs around two sides of the room.

There is a disposal unit, a dishwasher, and two white filigreed gates which open on the dining area. The dining room table is white, with high-backed gold chairs. Looking toward the patio, the entire wall of the house is of sliding glass doors with Chinese characters chased on them. There is a breakfront with dishes which we are not allowed to use.

The walkways to the front and side of the house are made of huge stone discs, like coins. On the side, there is a room for our housekeeper, Mrs. Pradseda Miskiel, who was a successful businesswoman before she agreed to join us. She runs the place.

The entire house has air conditioning concealed in the ceilings and, whether it is blazing hot outside or chilly, the temperature stands at seventy degrees. Mike Susik built the place, and it couldn't be more perfect.

This morning, I was looking around it and the thought occurred to me that it ought to have a name. I do all of my writing in it and all of my living. It represents a happiness I thought had died seven years ago. It is far from being a mansion, but it isn't a log cabin either.

So I called a Chinese friend. He asked me what the house means to me. I told him exactly what I'm telling you. He said, "Call it Sum Shen Shang Fai." What, I said, does it mean? He said, "It means The Heart is Content. . . ."

Human Interest

These are my favorites. Early in life, I became addicted to the terse portrait, the surprise last line. It is a difficult type of writing because the character and the action, leading to the important last line should be done in about eight hundred words. The masters of this craft—De Maupassant, O. Henry—required more space, but they lived in a verbose age when long sentences and interjectory clauses were the hallmark of the literary man.

In a more modern era, the tradition was carried on by Collier's Magazine *and a Broadway columnist named Mark Hellinger. Fortunately for me, I studied under both—first, as an assistant to Hellinger, and secondly, as an editor of the magazine. Now and then the columnist penned some memorable "Short-Shorts," but, as he was paid to write one a day, the quality dropped and many of the last lines were forced. The magazine, on the other hand, produced but one a week and had a reservoir of authors from whom to choose. Still, now and then the editors bought one which had been stolen. Once, five hundred dollars was paid to a writer who lifted the characters, the plot and the last line from Mark Hellinger.*

Hellinger wrote to an editor, and produced evidence that he had published the same story years before. Collier's *wrote to the columnist and asked how much he wanted in damages. A week later he replied: "First," he wrote, "I must find out who I stole it from."*

Most of the following human interest stories have a basis in fact. I would like to claim that they are my inventions, but this is not true. Almost all of them are true, except that names and characterizations have been altered to fit the story.

In all, I have written fifteen hundred of these. Here are the few survivors.

The hills looked like vanilla cupcakes in the late snow. The cars cut black scars around them and, where the road dropped steeply to the river, the bridge looked like a child's Erector set. On the far side were the town, a few church spires and some old-fashioned houses and two or three traffic lights, which were brighter in the gloom of a snowy day.

Bob ordered one more fast one. He was careful about his drinking because Ymelda worried. It wasn't that he was alcoholic. She claimed that it affected his judgment. Not much. A little. Liquor made him happier and more ebullient and more confident and less cautious.

This made Bob smile. Women, he felt, never really understand their men. They are always afraid of something that never happens. Nervous Mel, he called her. He snapped the shot glass up, tilted his head, and nodded farewell to the bartender.

The car outside was his. It was old, but it was all his. He patted it and pulled his gloves on and sat behind the wheel and ran the engine a little. A sweet-sounding baby, that engine. It had a quiet roar of authority. Bob chewed on a mint as he swung the car around, watching in both directions for traffic, and on across the bridge and up into the hills.

He thought of his happiness. He had so much of it. Not much money, but a fortune in contentment. He had come home from the war safely and Ymelda had been waiting for him as though she had not stirred since he kissed her good-by.

Both had jobs. His paid $118.50 wtih time and a half. He cannibalized old cars in a junk yard and he had a boss who trusted him all the way. Bob and Mel had bought a four-and-a-half-room house—he called it a bungalow—for $7,250 and little Mickey had been born in it suddenly and unexpectedly eight months ago.

Now there was another baby coming. A girl, he hoped. A real girl with a yellow pony tail and a saucy mouth and laugh-squinted eyes and big wet kisses for Daddy. Bob drove through the hills, swelling with pride. He was richer than Rockefeller and he knew it.

He looked at his watch. Mel should be almost through at the doctor's office. He started back, around the bases of the hills. He was happy. Extraordinarily happy. He moved the car up a notch or two and spun it a little on the snowy turns. There was no traffic up here. Nothing to worry about. He had promised Mel that he would not take a drink. Bob removed the glove on his right hand, dug into his pocket, and popped two more mints into his mouth.

What a woman doesn't know cannot hurt her. He came to the brow of the hill leading down to town and he knew, the instant he passed the edge of it, that he was going too fast. It is a knowledge that a good driver feels, without looking at a speedometer.

Bob knew, the moment he tapped the brakes lightly, that he would never make the bottom turn onto the steel bridge. A man full of liquor would be unintelligent and in a situation like this he would panic. But not Bob. He had thirty seconds left in which to think. So he figured all the angles.

He was glad that Mel wasn't with him. She'd scream. She'd complicate everything. The best thing to do, he knew, was not to turn the wheel. The car was going faster and faster, down the icy road. He would stay in his lane—luckily, there was nothing ahead —and, when he reached the river, he would permit the car to go through the wooden handrail. Before it left the road, he would open the door on his left and jam his foot in it so that it would not close.

The moment it hit water, he would push the door all the way, and strike out. How far would it be to the muddy bank? Thirty feet? Forty? Bob thanked God that he was a man who used his head.

The old car went down, down, faster and faster. People coming up saw it and knew what was going to happen. They held their breaths. Bob opened the door, jammed his foot in it, and swung the wheel slightly so that the vehicle, instead of crashing into the steel girders, splintered the wooden handrail and arched gracefully over the river and splashed in.

He struck out and headed for shore, shivering in the icy current. He could hear the cheers as he staggered up the bank. Then he remembered that he had left little Mickey in a basket on the rear seat . . .

The Old Man was dying. He was doing it the right way— slowly, painlessly and consciously. The I.V. jars hung over his bed, dripping into tubes which, somehow, had found a few veins not collapsed. The Old Man had asked the nurse—the starchy one with the blue BB eyes and the automatic smile—to take them out, that they were useless. He knew he was going.

"No," she said, singing the words as though injecting cheer into dreadfulness, "we must try hard to get well, mustn't we?" The Old Man watched her from the wrinkled sheet. Middle-aged and single, he thought. Can't stand a man because she can't stand herself.

"Please get me two more pillows," he said, and the cheeks flapped like loose sneakers because they had taken his teeth away. The nurse thought about it. She tried to think of a medical reason why he couldn't have the pillows, but she couldn't. At last she got two and fluffed them up, and lifted the old head and placed them behind him.

He tried to reach a bony hand to rub his chin, but his wrists had been strapped to the bed so that he wouldn't break the I.V. needles. "I need a shave," he said. "What day is it?" "Tuesday evening," she said. "Well," he said, shaking his head with resignation, "I must look like Santa Claus."

She sat on the edge of the bed to listen for a moment. He was a bright old codger. Sometimes, in the past two weeks, he had come up with some cute ideas. He told her that he had been born in this old house. She nodded, and said she knew. He had told her before.

"Well," he said, "I'm eighty-seven and I never would have dreamed that the place would outlast me." He looked around at the faded wallpaper, the walnut washstand, and the Morris chair which had burst its seams. "We never know, do we?" she said. He nodded emphatically.

"I came here an innocent babe," he said softly. "I leave laden with crimes." The nurse said she wouldn't say that. The Old Man smiled. "You wouldn't know," he said. "In my time, I think I broke all the commandments. Now I make a journey to the great perhaps." He grinned, and his face seemed to fall apart. "Either there is a God, or there is no God. There are no other alternatives, young lady. And I will be punished, or I will float off into silent darkness. One or the other."

Personally, she said, she believed in God. "So do I," he said brightly, and the old head came up off the pillow. "So do I." The head went back. "But that doesn't make it so." He thought a moment. "Looking doesn't make it so." He thought a moment. "Looking back, I would say that I had a successful life and an unhappy one." He saw the frown. "You don't think they go together?" The nurse shrugged.

"I made a lot of money," the Old Man said, "and I had a lot of women and wine in my time." He shook his head from side to side. "None of it was worth a tinker's dam." The nurse regarded him closely. He appeared to be rambling a little, and this might precede a comatose state.

"Add it up," he said shyly. "When I got rich, I emptied other men's pockets; when I made love to the ladies, I was yanking them off their little pedestals; when I emptied bottles, I was filling my head with crazy dreams." She smoothed the skirt, and decided to get up and go back to work.

"The doctor will be here soon," she said. The Old Man smiled. "He isn't going to do me any good and you know it. I'm going, and I'm glad. I never told this to anybody before, but my life practically started off on the wrong foot. I was ten years old, miss. Ten. I was washing in that basin over there one morning and there was a knock on my bedroom door. I opened it and a policeman was standing outside. He said my mother and father had been killed in the family carriage, at a railroad crossing."

The nurse shook her head in sympathy. "Do you know what that does to a ten-year-old?" the Old Man said. "Do you realize that the guts turn to jelly and the mind freezes? I never got over it. It was the God-awful moment of my life. When I grew up, I used to leave doors open, so that people wouldn't knock. I couldn't stand it."

"Well," she said cheerfully, "you had your fun." He nodded slowly. "I suppose," he said. "But most of it was at the expense of others. I tell you, miss, I'm sagging with sin. That is exactly why I would like to know for certain if there is a hereafter. If there is, I'm going to be punished. The worst would be to have to live it all over again."

It was morning when he awakened. He knew he had been dreaming. It took time to reassemble his mind. Then he jumped up, and went to the washstand, shivering. The house was cold. He looked at his rumpled black hair, the boyish face, and he thought how good it was to be ten years old.

Then he thought about the dream, and the childish face was troubled. How could he have dreamt he was a dying old man? How could it have been so real? The room was cold and he hurried to the washstand, and broke the film of ice in the water. He was trying to forget the bad dream. Then he heard a knock on the door . . .

In the room, the nurse packed her things. The doctor was writing on a pad. "When?" he said. She thought a moment. "About an hour ago, Doctor. He just sighed, and I hurried over, but the Old Man was gone. . . ."

. . .

There had been toys around the house before. Many of them. But little Dennis loved the twenty-five-cent turtle more than the Erector sets, the book of games, the orange scooter, or the baseball mitt. The turtle was about as big as a coin. On his brown shell was his name: Oscar

Dennis loved him and Dennis was eight years old. He saved for a ninety-eight-cent goldfish bowl and he packed small brightly colored stones in it, so that, when water was added, Oscar had his own private beach. Then he placed Oscar and the bowl on a window ledge in his room so that the afternoon sun warmed the cold wrinkles in the turtle's legs and moved him, now and then, to slip and slide down the stones into the cool clear water.

When Dennis came in from school, he hurried to his room to see what Oscar was doing. Oscar was the first live thing that Dennis had ever owned.

One afternoon, Dennis hurried up the stairs and found Oscar on his back floating. As young as he was, Dennis understood the finality of death. His shoulders shook and his breath caught and a wail came from his lips.

His mother hurried upstairs. She saw her little boy standing, arms hanging straight down, chin on chest, and she heard the sobs. She knew the genuine sound and she stood in front of him and held him to her breast. It took her a moment to find out what the trouble was.

He was promised a new turtle if he would stop crying. It didn't help. The crying continued and no promise on her part could slow the sobs.

She phoned her husband at his office. He was irritable. He had a business to conduct. He got into his car and came home. He hurried straight up to Dennis's room and put his arm around his boy.

"You can cry as long as you like," he said softly, "but it will not bring Oscar back. When God calls us it means that He loves us so much that He cannot bear to be apart from us any longer. God must have loved Oscar a great deal."

The sobbing continued. The father kept talking quietly, insistently and inexorably. "Coming home, I kept saying to myself, 'Well, now that Oscar is dead we should be asking ourselves what we can do to show him how much we love him.' Crying isn't the answer. It won't bring him back, son. What I think we ought to do is to have a funeral service for Oscar."

The sobbing began to slow. The boy was listening. He brushed his shirt sleeve against his eyes and he tried his first few words.

"What can we do for him, Dad?"

"Personally," the father said in a tentative tone, "I think we ought to bury Oscar in the back yard. We will invite Mommy and all the children of the neighborhood and I will attend too." Dennis stopped crying. His father took a solid silver cigarette case from his pocket. "See this? This is Oscar's casket. He will be the only turtle in the world buried in solid silver."

The eyes of Dennis glistened. "Will we have a solemn procession?"

"Certainly," the father said. "And I will get a big rock and chisel Oscar's name on it so that centuries from now, everybody will know that Oscar is buried there."

Dennis was smiling. He looked at the goldfish bowl in time to see Oscar flip on his stomach and swim toward shore. Dennis looked up at his father.

"Let's kill him," he said.

The Atheist slept soundly. He was a good man, a just man. His balding head was flat on the white pillow, the lips blowing out rhythmically, the pudgy hands clasped over the sheet. His wife slept beside him, her back toward him, her hands flat under her cheek.

God appeared in the bedroom. He was a vague luminescent figure, something which appeared to be a tall bearded figure with the sorrows of the ages in His eyes, but the light caused the figure to fade and reappear. God called to the Atheist, and the man stirred in his sleep. But he did not awaken.

A hand appeared out of the ring of light. There was a hole in it and an old crust of blood on the palm. The hand touched the Atheist and he awakened at once. He blinked tight against the light and opened his eyes in a suspicious squint. He looked quickly to make certain his wife was beside him. Then he lifted himself and leaned on one elbow and said, "Who are you?"

"I am God," the voice said. It was surprisingly soft, touched a little with pity. The Atheist thought about it a moment, half in sleep, half awake. "Is that so?" he said sarcastically. "Well, as there is no God, then I must be dreaming. If I'm dreaming, permit me to do it in comfort," and he dropped his head to the pillow.

"Why do you not believe in me?" said God. "I believe in you." The Atheist chuckled. He studied the light again, and the vague bearded figure within it. "Of course you do," he said. "I'm real. You're not. You're the dream of billions of people who are afraid to return to the dark nothing."

"Can you not believe," God said, "when you can see me?" The

Atheist reached down to the floor and picked up an ash tray and
some cigarettes and put them on his belly. He lit the cigarette and
puffed deeply. "Mind if I smoke?" he said. There was no answer.
"Tell me," the Atheist said, "which God are you? Are you the
Christ of the New Testament; Jehovah of the Old Testament; the
God of Islam; Buddha—which one?"

"There is but one God," said God, "though His name may make
many sounds in many tongues." "Very clever," said the Atheist
"Why do you disturb my dreams?" "I have come," said God, "to
ask you not to tell your children that there is no God." The Atheist
began to bridle. "My children?" he said. "By what right—"

"I gave them to you." The Atheist came back up on his elbows.
He tried to speak softly to keep from awakening his wife. "You
did nothing of the sort," he said. "There were some cells which
split, an ovum, some chromosomes or whatever they call them—"
"I give all," said God. "I can take all."

"Is that a threat?" said the Atheist. God bowed his head. "I ask
you not to teach the little ones that there is no God," he said. The
Atheist smiled wryly. "You want me to lie to them? You want me
to tell them that you're real?" "All I ask," God said, "is that you
give their souls a chance to flourish. Permit them to mature, and
decide for themselves."

"If you are not a dream," said the Atheist, "why don't you show
yourself to all men?"

God lifted His head and fixed His sad eyes on the Atheist. "I put
men here," He said, "to have faith in me. If they see me, and
acknowledge my works, they do not need faith. From man I ask
faith."

"Why then," said the Atheist cunningly, "do you appear before
me?" God held out His bloodstained hands. "You are an atheist.
You will not believe, even though you see."

"Right," said the Atheist. "I have been trying to awaken from
this dream, but I cannot. You are just a figment of my indigestion
last night."

"You will give the children a chance?" said God. "What you do
to them is worse than murder, because you are strangling their
souls, as yours has been strangled."

"It is a logical argument," conceded the Atheist, "even for a
dream. I will permit them to decide for themselves. If they suffer
the poison of the preachers and the Bible now, they will become
firm atheists when they mature."

The vision of light began to fade. "You have one good work to
your credit," the voice of God said, "and I will not forget it.
Blessed are they who do not see, and who still believe."

In a moment, the Presence was gone. The Atheist yawned and returned to sleep.

In the morning, his wife called him to breakfast. He arose slowly, scratching his bald head and thrusting his feet into his slippers. He tightened the cord on his pajamas and shuffled out to breakfast.

His wife kissed him and stepped back. "There's a spot of blood on your shoulder."

The Atheist looked. "Hmmmm," he said. "I must have scratched myself in my sleep."

This city sits in the bottom of a serrated pie crust. It's a rich filling. It is as green as a $10,000 bill and it comes alive out of a beige desert rimmed by mountains. I told Mr. Tracy that it is misnamed; it should have been called Jericho. Mr. Tracy is a short, slick-haired person who talks by pulling his mouth to the left side. He is long on hospitality; short on humor. He lives here.

"You writers never stop writing, do you?" he said.

"Oh, please," I said.

"No," he said. "I'm not impolite. Writers always see things that other people don't see."

"Have you ever seen Jericho?" I said.

He shook his head. Together, we looked out the window of Room 822 at the Adams Hotel. Ahead were a dozen streets full of business buildings, then a residential valley, and then the big mountains, purple in the late sun.

"Jericho," I said, "is so much like Phoenix that they appear like brothers. You know about Jericho?"

"The Bible," he said.

"The Bible. That's right. Where those mountains are dead ahead is called the Wilderness in Judea. The ones behind us are called the Mountains of Moab."

"Who was Moab?"

"I never found out. The Bible says that Jesus spent forty days fasting and praying in the Wilderness. When He was at His weakest, the devil appeared and offered the whole world below to Him if He would bend His knee to Satan.

"Jesus refused. Your city is a ringer for Jericho."

"This your first time in Phoenix?"

"You have a Salt River. Jericho has a Jordan. Each one runs along the edge of town in the same way. The Jordan is smaller than a creek."

"You're not going to write about Phoenix," said Mr. Tracy. "Maybe. Maybe I'll write about how similar—" "People will laugh." "This is not new, my friend."

I studied Mr. Tracy when he wasn't looking. He is very bright and very informal. He introduced himself to me in the club car of the train. He was on his way home to Phoenix from the East. He said, "My name's Tracy," as though no one else in the world had that name and therefore I didn't need to know the name that went with it.

Now, as he had promised, he stopped at the Adams the following afternoon to bid me welcome again, in that peculiar left-handed way. Most of the time, I wasn't sure whether he was being brazenly candid with me, or just brazen.

"I have to go," he said. He stood and his gun creaked in the leather cartridge belt.

"Come again," I said.

"No thanks," he said. "I may get downtown next week and see you at the ball park. Have you seen the players yet?"

"I'm still unpacking," I said.

He shook hands. "Will you have a drink before you go?" I said. He declined. Mr. Tracy walked out. I was about to walk him to the elevator, and then I thought that it might make him angry. At eleven years of age, boys have a lot of pride.

Mack trusted nobody, not even himself. He was a little man with a big ego and a one-sided smile. Nobody, he was fond of saying, ever did nothing for nobody. He worked hard as a maintenance man in a big oil refinery and he brought sandwiches and saved his money. When he had enough, he married a girl who looked good and stupid and who had a little money of her own.

Mack had it made. Her money and his money made a nice down payment on his house. After the honeymoon, he had a little heart-to-heart chat with Mazie and told her that, from now on, he would do the thinking for both of them. All household bills would be called to his attention. For herself, she would receive four dollars a week and he would not expect her to buy clothes with it, but he didn't want it squandered, either.

She voted his way. She thought about the things he wanted her to think about. She adored Mack because he did too. When he said, "No children. We can't afford them," Mazie gulped and said, "Yes, Mack."

Mack was a happy man. He manicured his lawn; he did his own carpentry, he did his own plumbing. He almost electrocuted himself changing a 110-volt line over to 220, but he saved a few dollars. The fellows at the oil refinery wanted him to join their bowling club, but Mack was too smart for them.

He knew that it was just a beer-drinking racket at a quarter a game. What for? To throw a sixteen-pound ball down an alley? Nothing doing.

One day a watchman told him that Mazie had a boy friend on the side. Mack laughed so hard that his stomach hurt. He began to think about it. There was a boy in the neighborhood who used to do odd jobs for Mack at a dime a job. Mack asked the boy if any stranger ever stopped to see Mazie during the day.

The kid thought about it. "Well," he said, "my mother said she'd kill me if I opened my mouth, but the milkman takes about an hour every morning to drop the homogenized at your place. Everybody knows about it—except you.

Mack seethed. He had spent every waking moment trying to keep the world from outwitting him, and now he had been foxed by a woman who meant no more to him than a down payment on a house.

He didn't love Mazie, but she was a good buy. She worked hard in the house; she did his laundry; she saved money for him; she gave him the adulation he needed; she was obedient to the point of terror.

The watchman had said she had a boy friend. The kid had said it was the milkman. Mack didn't need any more evidence. One morning, he watched Mazie making his sandwiches. When she was finished, he said, "I'm not going to work today." She seemed surprised.

"Stop looking goggle-eyed," Mack said. "I know all about everything. Do you love the guy who's been seeing you?" Mazie looked as though she would collapse. Her head nodded dumbly. "Yes," she whispered.

Mack cackled. "Does he love you?" She nodded. Mack went into the broom closet and got a mop handle and unscrewed it. "I'm dying to meet your boy friend," he said casually.

Mack waited inside the back door. When the milkman arrived, Mack beat him insensible, broke his nose, and kicked his ribs. It was a good job all right. But the milkman sued. And Mack no longer owns a house or a wife.

The man he almost killed was the substitute milkman . . .

The scene was sickening. He knew it was coming. He braced himself against it. When it came, Joe Walsh's skin paled, the pegs on his violin nerves tightened, and he shook. He kept pleading with her that it wasn't lack of love; it was only that he didn't have the nerve to get married Saturday. That was all.

Later. Six months maybe. Alice stood in the plain living room, shaking her head. "Six months? Why not six years, Joe? It will give you more time to get your nerve up."

"Please," he said softly. "Please, hon. I love you. I want to marry you. I don't care for anybody else. Is six months going to kill us?"

"If you say that once more," she said through locked teeth, "I'll scream. My father is not a rich man, Joe. You know this. You know he took every dime he has to put it into this wedding. Fourteen hundred dollars, Joe. The invitations are out. Holy Trinity Church is ready. It's Saturday, Joe. This is Wednesday."

He shook his head and sat. There was no use talking. She wouldn't understand. She didn't understand. It was lucky, in a way, that her mother and father were out. Her old man had never thought much of Joe.

Good they were out. The old lady would be hysterical by now. She wouldn't even go to a movie unless she got a good cry out of it. Still, Joe Walsh was sincere in the things he was saying. He did love Alice. He did want to marry her. He had gone through a couple of rehearsals at Holy Trinity and he felt his nerve slipping like a tired garter.

He knew that if he could get Alice to postpone this thing, that he could win her back later. She'd be mad. She'd stay mad for weeks. But she loved him as he loved her. She was talking. He picked up the monologue in mid-flight.

" . . . but after six years, what can I tell people? I'm thirty, Joe. Who wants me now? It's you or nobody. What girl gets jilted after six years? Not this one," she said, tapping her chest. "Not me."

"I'll tell you what," he said. "Let me take the rap for this. It's not so hard on a man if a girl jilts him. I show up at Holy Trinity Saturday with my best man. We wait. You don't show. You send some girl friend with a note. You have examined your conscience and you just don't love me. You feel mixed up. You're sorry for me and sorry for all the guests and all that stuff."

She listened. And nodded. "Okay," she said softly. "Okay. You're the boss. How about the gifts upstairs?"

"Send 'em back, hon. They can mail them to us again at Easter."

Alice shook her head. "There will be no Easter wedding," she said. "No wedding, period." She said that she would send a messenger to Holy Trinity on Saturday with a note for Joe.

On Saturday, Joe and the best man waited in Holy Trinity

sacristy. Through the partly closed door, they could see relatives and friends coming down the aisle, the women in big hats and bouffant dresses, the men exchanging little jokes with the ushers. "Stop fidgeting," the best man said. "I got the ring. You got the girl." Joe waited. He felt sorry for all these people; sorry most of all for Alice. He waited and waited. Where the heck was that messenger? Then he heard the organ break into the solemn notes of the wedding march from *Lohengrin*. He looked up the aisle like a trapped animal. Here came the attendants and, behind them, the radiant, triumphant Alice . . .

Assistant Chief Inspector Edward Feely is in charge of Manhattan Homicide East. To him, police work is mathematics. There are over a million people in his district and they range from the abject poverty of the Lower East Side to the swells of Park Avenue and Sutton Place and on up to Harlem. When a murder is committed all Feely has to do is to eliminate 999,999 people and he has his man.

Mathematics. Sometimes it keeps him awake at night. Last week for instance. He was lying in bed thinking of a little Negro girl. The name: Robin Joyner. She was four, product of a broken home at Seventh Avenue and 146th Street. She was sweet and believing, and her mother tried to instill goodness into Robin's heart.

She went out to play at 4:15 P.M. She wanted to play in the PAL shelter around the corner. She walked down Seventh Avenue, turned the corner at 146th, grabbed the hand of a cousin, and edged between two parked cars to cross the street.

Her cousin saw the taxi coming. It was coming fast, knifing along the edge of the parked cars. He dropped Robin's hand and stood still. Robin went out. The cab hit her and she didn't cry. She skidded on her face across the cold asphalt.

Some people stopped. The cabdriver got out. He was a big Negro. "Don't worry," he said. "She ain't hurt bad. I'll take her to a hospital."

He picked up the thirty-five-pound doll. He placed Robin on the front seat. Then he got in and drove off. The cousin ran back to tell Mrs. Joyner that Robin had been hurt, but the big man was taking her to the hospital.

She ran down the staircase into the street. Tears made shiny satin furrows in her skin. She took a taxi to the nearest hospital. The nurses checked the records. No little colored girl; no taxi driver.

She tried another. And another. No Robin. No record of an accident. Mrs. Joyner went home. Two hours later, her Robin was found a half mile away, by a man who thought he saw a doll under a parked car. Her body had been placed in front of one of the rear wheels so that, when the parked car was moved, she would be run over.

The medical examiner said she would have died within a half hour of internal injuries, even if the cabdriver had taken her to a hospital. It wouldn't have been his fault; she had run out from between parked cars. Now it was homicide. Hit-and-run. It came to Assistant Chief Inspector Feely's desk, and the game of mathematics began.

He had seven witnesses to the accident. They told their stories separately. Each was certain of his story. The taxi was a 1960 Chevrolet; it was a 1958 Fairlane; it was a 1959 Plymouth; the license plate had an 029 in it; it had a 211.

The driver was six feet and very dark. He was six foot four and light-skinned. He was nervous. He was self-contained. He wore a sweater. He had on a coat.

Feely and his boys tried another tack. They eliminated the 975,000 people who were not cabdrivers. This left 25,000 suspects. Then they eliminated the 17,000 white drivers. This brought them down to 8,000. From this number, they checked off those who were not working between four and five that afternoon, and they further discarded those with old taxis and those in the far reaches of New York.

They now had 140 suspects. They questioned these and narrowed them down to twenty-six Negro cabbies who were in the Harlem area at the time. Of these, only one, a big man, claimed that he had remained in the cab company garage washing his cab between four and five. No one there remembered seeing him.

"I'll pick the man with the alibi," said Feely. He did.

The ambulance stood double-parked. The blinker winked on and off, on and off. Some little girls stopped skipping rope to watch. It was a cheap neighborhood. On the lawn a sign read: Furnished Rooms. Upstairs, a stout landlady stood in the doorway wringing her hands.

The old man was on the floor. A young intern in white peeled the eyelids back, unbuttoned the old sweater and shirt, and crouched to listen to the fading footsteps of the heart. He refolded the stethoscope while studying the waxen skin, the half-opened eyes, the thin blue lips pulling air against toothless gums.

"Cardiac," he said to the policeman. "Could be malnutrition, too."

The intern tapped a little vial with a syringe and held it up and watched the stuff bubble out of the top before he cleaned the old man's arm with alcohol and made the puncture. The policeman opened his notebook and asked questions. The landlady answered them nervously and once she cried.

As she talked, the intern and the ambulance attendant wrapped the old man in blankets, and lifted him easily onto the stretcher and carried him in the breeze created by the motion of the stretcher. Downstairs, the little girls watched and one said, "That's the old guy who gave me a nickel for getting the newspaper."

The cop upstairs dismissed the landlady and examined the room. He didn't like this assignment because there was no crime involved and nothing worthy of his talent. Still, his eyes missed nothing and he ransacked the room carefully, like a considerate burglar.

There was a bowl, half-filled with breakfast cereal. It was old and dry and the milk in the bottom looked watery. An iron cot in the corner had an army blanket spread neatly on top. There was a dresser and two photographs. One was a picture of a smiling buxom woman in a hat with flowers. An Easter picture, perhaps. On the back of it was a yellowed clipping. It was dated September, 1938, and it announced briefly the death of Mrs. Kenneth T———. The other photo showed the old man and two little girls and a boy. The old man looked young and vigorous.

The policeman checked his notebook against the photos. Mr. Kenneth T. had been a widower since 1938. He had worked as a compositor on an Ohio newspaper and had not remarried. Apparently, he had brought the children up himself. The record showed the next of kin to be John T., engineering consultant; Mrs. R. K., housewife and former registered nurse; Mrs. Peter Mc., schoolteacher.

The old man must have given the children good educations. The policeman opened the bureau drawers. There were three shirts with frayed collars; two ties; a half-dozen worsted sox, some shorts and undershirts; an Elk pin; three pairs of bronzed baby shoes and a bundle of letters tied with string.

He riffled through the letters. A half-dozen snapshots fell out. These showed young family groups. On the back, in a shaky hand, the old man had written the names of his grandchildren and their ages and the dates of the pictures. From this, the cop deduced that each of the children must be six or seven years older than the photos.

The letters were signed "Your loving son, Jack" and "Love, Miriam" and "Best, Jane." They were postmarked from nearby and all started off saying that matters had not gone too well lately. One child had measles; a husband needed an operation; the mortgage payments were heavy. Reading them, the policeman gathered that the old man's children didn't want him to come live with them. One of the daughters kept repeating: "Your place is with Jack, Dad. You would feel more at home with a son than a daughter. Besides . . ."

Two of the notes signed Jack said, "May has enough on her hands with three children. You wouldn't want me to ask her to take care of you, too. You're not young any more, and it would be like having a fourth child . . ." The daughter Miriam wrote: "I wish I could help with a few dollars a month, Dad, but times are difficult for us, too, and George says your Social Security should be plenty for your needs. . . ."

In the hospital, the intern wheeled the man into the emergency room and ordered oxygen. Then he looked at the old man again and canceled it. The old guy had no more fight in him. The nurse searched through the old man's pockets for effects. She found a tiny piece of wood with a miniature loving cup on it.

It was old and the metal legend had been pitted by time. She could decipher the words. It said: "To the World's Greatest Dad."

The wonderful thing about Sam was that he knew everything about everything. Love, for instance. He knew that loving anyone else was futile, so he loved only himself. It was a loyal affection, almost touching. Next to himself, he had a high regard for money. Sam ran a New York night club and he took the customers as well as the employees for every dollar he could get.

He ran three shows a night, and had a good-looking chorus line. "Give the people what they want," he used to growl, "and they'll flock to see it." Sam always had a fading headliner to draw the customers, also a good young male singer, and a dizzy comedian or a dance act. Sam gave the people what they wanted, and they lined up nightly, hungry to be fleeced.

Sam despised everybody and did not try to hide it. He stood inside the front door, ordering the customers around, herding them into queues, a bald little man with a big roaring voice. If they complained, he merely pointed to the door. "Go," he would say. "Who needs ya?"

There was a stout woman attendant in the rest room. Sam fired her when he caught her keeping some of her tips. When a chorus girl began to show a few lines in her face, Sam put a friendly arm around her shoulder and had a talk with her. "You can't make it any more, honey," he would say. "You're beginning to show up in them bright lights. You been with me seven seasons, so I'll give you a good recommendation."

The headwaiter was a worried Frenchman named Henri. He had little white wings in his dark hair, and people liked him. He was a horse player and he was always in debt, so it was difficult for him when he was let go to give Sam's brother-in-law a job. Sam did it only because he was tired of supporting his married sister.

Once in a while, Sam gave an unknown a chance. When this happened, he signed himself as manager, and took 50 per cent, then signed the kid into his White Way Club at $200 a week. If he liked the youngster, Sam would advance a little money at six for five per week.

Still, he had his softer side. It is a matter of record that, year in and year out, Sam gave ten dollars to the Red Cross, ten dollars to the Catholic Charities, ten dollars to the National Foundation. He opened his heart equally to all.

Sam never married because, as he said, "Dames is for suckers." He lived alone in a little flat over the club. He had a few close friends and played gin at a tenth of a cent a point. Those who beat him didn't remain close. Those who lost were surprised to find that Sam had invested in a high fidelity set and liked good music.

One night Sam was in the office of the White Way after closing hours. He hated to waste time, but he was wasting it this time, because he was going over his books and he had only about ten minutes to live. His desk light was on, and he ran down the columns of figures swiftly, the point of the pencil aimed at each digit in turn.

The figures were fat, but they brought no smile to Sam's scowl. He was working up a trial balance sheet when all the lights went out. Sam's head fell on the blotter, and he sighed like a tired baby. The hand still held the pencil. He remained in this position until the cleaning women arrived in the morning.

The newspapers gave Sam quite a play because he was a well-known club owner. Two of them published one-column cuts of Sam's hateful features. A few old-time stars were quoted as saying that Sam was the last of the old Prohibition barons and would be missed. Like Prohibition, perhaps.

The funeral was announced for the following afternoon at Campbell's up on Madison Avenue. There were no flowers, except the palm fronds that usually ornament such festivities. Sam looked younger in repose. And he no longer scowled.

The big surprise was that so many people were present. The place was crowded for the short service. To some it seemed a waste to have the cleric pray for Sam, because he wouldn't want Heaven unless he could butt into it and throw a five-dollar cover charge on the place.

Outside, the mobs made room for the funeral cortege. Everyone was there, including the stout woman who had been fired, and Henri, the headwaiter, and some of the unknowns who remained unknown. The stout woman looked at the crowd and shook her head. "How come," she said to Henri, "that so many people are here?"

Henri smiled. "Sam had the answer to that," he said. "Give the people what they want, and they'll flock to see it."

The football turns end over end high in the sun and it comes down between the palm trees in the big back yard. Kathy, twelve, sets herself for it. She takes it as one would cradle a baby and she yells to Kelly, ten, to block for her. She runs it fifteen yards before she is touched. Kelly says he took his little sister Trudy, eight, out of the play, but he couldn't get by Jean, thirteen.

They line up. The yard is full of shouting and the play swirls around little Willie, who is six. He is not in the game. He has a white ball and he throws it up and then misses it.

The father of the five sits on the back porch, watching. His name is Rube Faloon. He is thirty-eight, and lives at 6832 S. W. 68th Street, in South Miami, Florida. He was a good sports writer when he had a paper. His job is executive secretary of the Rotary Club of Miami. He is also part-time press agent for the Jack Tar Hotels. He could use a little good luck.

Mrs. Faloon comes on the porch with a cup of black coffee. Rube calls her Peter. She is jet-haired, slender, a swimming teacher.

Six years ago, Mrs. Faloon was in Doctors Hospital having little Willie. They told her it was a boy. Rube hurried to the hospital. Dr. James Lancaster stopped him in the hall. "Rube," he said, "there is something I want to talk to you about."

They went to a room. The doctor fidgeted. "Do you know what a retarded child is like?" Rube nodded. "Sure I do. What's that got to do with it?" Dr. Lancaster sighed. "You have a mongoloid son, Rube. No, wait a minute. Before you go off the deep end, let me call another doctor to have a look."

The second doctor studied the baby boy. He saw the stubby fingers; two toes on each foot were fused. The lines on the infant's palms ran the wrong way. The eyes were slanted. The tongue was a little thick for the mouth.

It was Rube's job to tell Peter. He wanted to start by saying that there are a million babies in the United States. It didn't sound right. Instead, he said, "Honey, we have a problem." "What problem?" He fumbled a little. The voice fought a tight throat. "Our baby is going to be a little boy—always."

Rube tried hard to be the man. He didn't make it. He barely got his arms around her and half lifted her off the bed and buried his face in her hair. After the tears came the buoyant bounce of optimism. "We can keep him, can't we?" "Oh, sure." "It will work out."

No one knows what causes a mongoloid. Some say that they have forty-seven chromosomes per cell, whereas normal people have forty-six. Some say that a subacute virus in the mother causes it. Most doctors admit they don't know. The Faloons took Willie home. He needed more attention than the others. They sent him to Sunland Training Center at Gainesville when he was four.

The others—Jean, who is going to be a pretty woman; Kathy, the tomboy; Kelly, who wins trophies swimming; and Trudy, who couldn't get a good schoolmark if she wrote the report cards herself—moped around the house. Everybody missed Willie.

Rube and Peter went back to Sunland and got him. He beamed and gurgled at his family and they hugged him breathless.

A month ago, Trudy's teacher told the class to write something about the happiest day in their lives. Some wrote about vacations; some wrote about sports events; some wrote about a flight in a plane. When the teacher came to Trudy's report, he glanced at it, swallowed, and looked away.

All it said was: "The day Willie came home."

It was cold and dry and the hard winds of winter roared up Cedar Lane and snapped the Christmas decorations hanging across the shopping center. The wreaths danced a rigadoon and the cars inched over rusty snow, laden with trees and gifts. The stars were brighter, and they winked plainly.

The reporter wore no hat. His blue overcoat collar was up and his gloved hands were deep in the pockets. He walked up the steps of Holy Name Hospital. It was the last stop. Inside, he turned to the left and saw Sister M. Evelyn, a tall dark nun, genuflecting outside the chapel.

"Anything new?" he said. She looked around the corrugation of her habit and smiled. "What would be new here?" she said. She pointed to the chapel. "In two days, a child will be born." They talked—the reporter and the nun. They were old friends, but they sniped at each other like relatives.

"I'm glad to see that you were in there praying," he said. "You wouldn't dare say one for me." She showed some white teeth. "The would-be saints never need it," she said. "I was praying for a little girl who has leukemia." The reporter shrugged. "A waste of prayer," he said.

Sister Evelyn talked about the little girl. She was eight, and she believed in Santa, but Santa didn't believe in her. The doctors said that she had a good chance of lasting through Christmas Day, maybe a day or two beyond, but she had no folks, no visitors, no gifts.

"Little Miss Nobody," the reporter said, and made a few notes. He said good-by, and Merry Christmas. In a tavern he phoned four little stories to the city desk. Little Miss Nobody became a one-column box on page seven. She wasn't worth any more.

Christmas Eve was a day of military gray skies and icy puddles. Many people read the story about Little Miss Nobody. Three men did something about it. The first was Charlie Pearl, owner of a candy store and in debt to his brows. The second was David Musicant, a florist with no patience. The third was a furrier on Queen Anne Road.

They were Jews. They did not believe in Christmas. The nuns were surprised when they arrived, at almost the same time, in the late afternoon. They had packages. They were for Little Miss Nobody. The receptionist said they had no one by that name. Musicant showed the clipping. "Oh," she said. "She's on two."

They went upstairs. Little Miss Nobody had a private room, not because she could afford it, but because her exit would disturb the other children. The three went into the room with their hats off. Charlie said "Hello" with a bright smile. The others swallowed.

They saw yellow hair on a white pillow. There were two big blue eyes with no pain in them. Two snowy hands were clasped on the bedspread. She had no one to talk to, no one to hold close, no one to give her a good-by kiss. Her mouth was grave. "We come from Santa," the furrier said. "He told us to deliver some stuff."

Rapidly, they crouched and untied the parcels. There was a

black honey bear with eyes that lit up. There was a small brunette doll in an expensive gown. There were crayon books and crayons and a big blonde doll half her size who could go to sleep and wake up. There was candy and there were nuts and a stocking which, with a thumbtack, hung off the edge of the dresser.

There were so many things that Sister Filomena, who was on the floor, permitted only a few things on the bed. The rest was set up on chairs and the dresser. "Merry Christmas," said Charlie Pearl. Musicant nodded. "From Santa Claus," he said. "It's special for you." The furrier turned away. "I hope you make it," he mumbled.

The little girl said nothing. As they turned to leave, she said, "Thank you. I mean, thank Santa." They turned to look at her. They didn't see the reporter in the corridor, watching them. The furrier clapped his hand to his forehead. "I almost forgot the most important thing," he said. He ran back down the stairs to his car and came back puffing, holding a little silver Christmas tree.

The three men put it on the dresser and set the colored ornaments on the branches. The reporter turned and left. He had a lot of shopping to do and his wife was griping. Downstairs, he dialed the city desk.

"Nothing," he said. "It's very quiet. I'm going home." There was a silence. "I have a little feature but it's not worth anything, to be frank. I just saw the magi. You know, the three wise men bearing gifts . . ."

There was a small breeze in the evening. The mists came up the Avon slowly, like transparent fingers imparting a blessing. In a half hour, fog had engulfed the Cotswold Hills and smothered Bristol. The hilly streets were obliterated in patches. The roofless church, opened to heaven in an old air raid, the neat shops, the university, all died one by one.

Paddy Smythe sat to supper in the kitchen. He was a young, lean man with small, alert blue eyes. He drank his soup slowly and noisily, the right arm and the spoon forming a metronome for dull music, the left elbow on the table, with the fist against his cheek. His wife stood on the far side of the table, buttering slices of bread for him.

"It's a bad night," she said. "Will you be staying home?" He did not answer. Paddy shook his head. He looked up at the window and watched the night fog coat the pane with thin milk. He was going out. "Another card game?" she said.

"Another card game," he said in a deep growl. He looked up as though to divine the intention of the question. Bridget Smythe stared impassively. She was difficult to read. She was a short brunette with a big-eyed face and an exaggerated figure. She finished buttering the bread and sat to her soup. "Nothing," she said. "I don't like to be alone nights."

"Ah now," Paddy said. "That's sad. Indeed it is. Me heart is bleeding. All I ever see of you when I'm in the flat is you talking on the phone to your domn girl friends or ye're off to night services. I hope ye're saving my soul as well as yer own."

"Sometimes," she said softly, "I go to the cinema." He slammed the big spoon into the bowl so that it made a splash of soup. "Not unless they're playing *King of Kings*," he said loudly, "or some holy picture." Bridget looked frightened. She did not like loud voices. Paddy saw this and modified his tone. "It will do you no good," he said, "to make a smell about it. I have me cards. You have the church." She nodded. "And the rugby pool," she said.

"All right," he said resignedly, "I won a few quid on a game. And I may win some more at cards. I'll be home in the morning." He went inside and washed and dressed, while she did the dishes. Bridget was still cleaning up as Paddy pecked her on the cheek and left, reeking of cheap cologne.

He got into his small car and drove to the main part of town. Paddy drove slowly, not so much because of the fog, although that was a factor, but because it gave him a better chance to look for unescorted girls. Mr. Smythe had no intention of playing cards. The extra money he displayed at times came from small burglaries.

These were random jobs. He had learned a lot about places to rob, while delivering merchandise for companies like Shipwards and Framptons. Women were his hobby. The small robberies and the smaller conquests made the little man feel big. Paddy was smart, but he had to keep telling himself how smart he was.

He toured the fronts of the cinemas, tooting his horn and making gay remarks to lady pedestrians. It was a dismal evening. No one was interested in Paddy, or his car. The cheater felt cheated. Was it possible that he was losing his charm? His hair, perhaps, but not his charm.

After two hours he gave up and went to a hotel. He would not go home under any circumstances. What man wants to study a silent rebuke? He got into his room and rubbernecked out the window, but there was nothing but fog. Nothing to see. Nothing to do.

He went down to the bar and drank a couple of gins. There was only one other customer, an old lady with a can who sat at the end of the bar sipping half-and-half. Paddy swapped pleasantries with the bartender and, in a confidential tone, they reached the subject of women. The bartender was a man after Paddy's own heart. He knew them all. In fact, he could lie better and faster than Paddy Smythe.

He told Paddy about a woman who could make life interesting. The more Paddy listened, the more he wanted to hear. "This one," said the bartender, "is not available all the time. She'll cost a few bob but she's worth the best dinner in Bristol." Paddy said to please call her for him. He despised commercial women, but it was a foggy lonely night.

Paddy went back to his room. He waited. He reset his tie, slicked his hair, and waited. Nothing happened. Maybe, he thought, the bartender couldn't reach the lady. His impatience was bordering on despair when he heard a timid knock on the door.

He ran and threw it open. There, smiling blankly, stood Bridget. . . .

Now we could hear it plainly. The cold hail came slanting out of the night, tapping against the front windows. The little boy pressed his forehead against the glass, but he could not see out. His mother had finished stacking the dinner dishes and she came into the living room, a stout, busy person, to straighten the antimacassars on the sofa and put the piano rolls back up on top, where they belonged.

She asked the little boy what he was doing. "Looking," he said. "Dreaming," she said. That was a better word. The little boy said nothing. He kept listening to the salty tap of the hail. His heart was exultant. Tomorrow was bound to be a snowy Christmas. Bound to be. . . .

When she had sent him to the store for a box of thyme, he had seen the thick slow flakes spinning downward. He had stuck his tongue out, trying to catch one. At the store, the street was already white and he had seen naked turkeys hanging by their feet in the window, and rosy apples gleaming in barrels, and busy clerks in white aprons weighing mixed nuts and sugary, colored Christmas candies.

He was a dark, unlikable boy with a slab of black hair slanting over his eye. He was past eight now, and they told him that God would grant anything within reason. So he had spent the week saying, "Please, God. Make it snow." And see?—it was snowing.

The boy had run all the way to the store because his heart was glad. Now, with the box of thyme in his mackinaw, he ran all the way back. The fat flakes kissed his face coldly and the kid tensed all the muscles in his body and had to restrain himself to keep from screaming with joy.

Christmas. Christmas. Oh, beautiful joyous Christmas. Oh, beautiful tree in the living room tomorrow. Oh, beautiful smell of the boughs and the look of the colored ornaments on the tree. Oh, beautiful lumpy stockings on the mantel, full of fruit and striped candy canes. Oh, beautiful white sheet winding under the tree, laden with fire engines and games and maybe a Flexible Flyer. Oh, beautiful Jesus in the manger, too young to understand the wonder of Christmas.

The boy had promised the Infant a gift this Christmas if He brought snow. He had told himself that, even if snow didn't come, he would present the gift anyway. Maybe. The kid had bought the gift with his own money. Funny, it was Jesus' birthday, and everybody got presents except the Baby. Well, what could you give one so young?

The kid was still holding his cold forehead against the cold window when his father told him to go to bed. The little boy said it was early. His father said it was time. A younger brother and sister were already in bed. His father was a big man. He put his arm around the little boy and told him it wasn't good to be awake when Santa arrived.

The small one remembered he had heard that last year. He went into the kitchen and his mother leaned down sidewards and he kissed her on the cheek and said good night. Then he kissed his father and went into the dark bedroom and undressed in the chill. He said his prayers swiftly, got off his knees, and hopped under the blankets and pulled everything over his head.

"Dear Jesus," he murmured in his mind, "please make it snow. Make some men come out tomorrow in big sleighs so I can see the steam from the horses' noses. Make Santa give me lots of presents because you're his boss and he has to do what you tell him. Make me good. You can forget the Flexible Flyer if you make it snow hard."

He was still thinking when sleep came. In the morning, he was up before anyone and his mother peevishly ordered him back to bed. When the proper time came, the parents got up and dressed the children for church. The little boy was not allowed to go into the living room. He was not allowed to see.

When the family left, the front steps were thick with vanilla icing and the whole world was white with silence. Voices sounded funny across the snow, and big people yelled Merry Christmas! A black horse turned into the street, pulling a sleigh with bells jingling on the harness and big plumes of white smoke were coming from his nose.

At Mass, the high altar was laden with red flowers and all the lights were on. The little boy broke away from his parents and hurried up front and knelt before the manger. His dark eyes were dancing with radiance as he looked at the cows and the sheep and Mary and Joseph and the little plaster image of the Infant.

The boy sneaked his gift beside the Baby, and went back to his parents. They looked at him, and said nothing. The snow had stopped. There was a great joy in the world. Later in the day, a priest stopped by the manger and lifted the gift out, and put it back.

"I don't know that the Christ Child needs a rattle," he said to himself, "but it's the only gift He got."

The cab bounded downtown, fighting the lights, stopping and starting, the rear end sounding like a child making up its mind to cry. Frank drove the taxi, using 5 per cent of his mind. He could think of dozens of things while driving through the city traffic, without making any mistakes in his work.

What Frank usually thought about was money. He loved cash. He loved it a little more than he loved his wife. Once he asked himself if anyone gave him a choice between fortune and his spouse, what would he do. He decided he would take the money. One can always locate a new woman, but a fortune is not easy.

Now he had an old lady in back. This was his last trip before lunch. The old lady had some bundles beside her, and she said she was late in exchanging some Christmas gifts. She had snowy hair, nicely coifed, and a perky little velvet hat sitting on top. She wore a beige coat with dark brown fur collar and cuffs.

Probably had money, Frank decided. When he had an old lady like this, Frank was in the habit of centering his conversation on his children and his poverty. The fact that he had no children did not bear on the matter. He could rattle off names and ages and school status with authenticity.

So, while she talked about gift exchanges, Frank talked about how he had to repair a four-dollar used bicycle for his oldest boy because he could not afford a new one for Christmas. A little glue patched up an old doll for his daughter Melinda. "She's nine," he said, "and stops in church every day after school to pray to God to keep her daddy safe."

The old lady got out in the department store area. The fare was seventy cents. She gave him a five-dollar bill and told him to take out eighty cents. Frank had wasted the whole pitiful story. So he doled out her change—$4.20—and hoped she would fall on the sidewalk with all her bundles and perhaps break a leg. He watched, but she disappeared in the crowd of shoppers with no trouble.

Frank went on to lunch in a West Side beanery. He had two frankfurters, a cup of coffee, and a doughnut. It came to sixty-five cents. He paid with the five-dollar bill and the girl cashier turned it over and over. "This is a phony," she said. "Somebody stuck you."

The cabdriver was shocked. Who could believe that a sweet old lady—oh well. He'd stick somebody else with it. He paid the check and went back to the taxi, picking his teeth with a free toothpick. One thing was certain, Frank was not going to take a five-dollar loss from any old lady.

So he got back into his cab, and drove up and down Fifth Avenue and Park and Madison. He was looking for someone who appeared to be in a hurry and who might pay with a ten-dollar bill. Frank had several disappointments. He picked up a few fares who paid with dollar bills, or fives.

He would be going off duty around four o'clock, and he wasn't going to report in with this phony five. So, as quitting time approached, Frank was reduced to worry about a five-dollar dent in his day's pay. Then, when he was about to despair, the cabdriver was rescued. A young woman with an infant in her arms hailed his taxi.

She asked him to take her crosstown to Polyclinic Hospital. The woman seemed nervous. Her baby had been ill with measles and she was too poor to afford a doctor, so she had been taking the infant to the hospital clinic. Today would be the final visit.

He looked at the woman in his mirror. She wore a red sweater. No coat. "Why didn't you take a crosstown bus?" he asked. She shrugged. "It's a walk," she said, "from Forty-Ninth Street and I don't want her to catch cold." Well, no use telling her about his hard luck, and his children. She could match him, line for line.

He stopped at the hospital. This would be a very small tip, he knew. She would probably pay the seventy-five cents with a dollar bill. But, surprise of all surprises, she paid with a twenty-dollar bill. Frank beamed. He no longer cared about the size of the tip. He made a great show of carefully counting out the change, being careful to put the phony five-dollar bill on the bottom.

The young lady counted it quickly, and said "Thank you. I'd give you something, mister, but this is all the money I have."

Frank felt generous. He said it was okay. He understood what it was like to be in hard luck. The woman left and Frank took off for the company garage.

His heart was singing and he backed the old crate into its proper slot. He reported to the cashier with his call sheet and his cash. Once more, he could afford to think of the beauty of money. The cashier tallied the money and flipped a twenty-dollar bill back to Frank.

"You'll have to keep this one," he said. "It's counterfeit. . . ."

There is an old sorrow in the hill. It stands bare, like a clenched fist, on the left of the Turnpike nearing New York. Laurel Hill. The name is an irony because it was a poorhouse. There are no laurels in poverty; no infirm legs ever negotiated the front steps of that old red brick building with honor, or with hope.

The building is coming down. It never accorded pity to the old, and now that it too is old, it gets none. Once, there were three main buildings: the poorhouse, the prison and the hospital for communicable diseases. The felon, the infected and the ancient wept in separate structures.

They put Grandma Flynn in the poorhouse years ago. You do not know her, but I want to introduce her because she was a giver, never a taker. She was so completely Christian that she was comical. She gave and gave until she had nothing left. She ran a boardinghouse, an old place with a high stoop and a furnished basement, and she took in loafers and bums and drunks, and sometimes she mended their minds.

She made thick hot soups for them, washed their shirts and underwear on an old washboard in a galvanized tub, baked bread in an old stove, pressed their suits, made their beds, scraped up pennies for the next meal, and never asked a favor.

Grandma Flynn was not my grandma. Her grandson was my friend, and he was a handsome kid with deep wavy hair. He lived with Grandma because his father had died of tuberculosis and his mother found another man. The kid was a taker. So Grandma gave him spending money, and bought his suits and ties, and took whatever was left and gave it to the Summit Avenue Church.

He drank a lot, and, when he had a job, he gave Grandma nothing.

Once, long before I was born, Grandma had had a husband but he had died early too. When I asked her about it, she said she had had her love and she had no time for it.

She was a shuffling old lady with nothing to distinguish her from millions of other old ladies. She shopped. She worked. She prayed. She forgave everybody who ever cheated her.

Then I moved away, and forgot her. I forgot her grandson too. Fifteen years went by. Then a detective from the Elizabeth Street precinct phoned and said they had a tubercular bum on the Bowery. His name was Flynn and he named me as next of kin.

I went to see him. He lasted long enough to get to Sea View Hospital. I could carry him on one arm. He told me that Grandma Flynn was at Laurel Hill and I didn't believe him. She must have been older than the hill. Still, I stopped there one day—in the grim red brick building—and they asked me to wait and they brought her out.

She wore a cotton thing with no belt, no ornamentation. On her feet were brown wool stockings. She sat, shyly, looking and trying to remember, and rubbing those old knees with parchment hands. I wanted to tell her that the boy was dead, but I couldn't.

"You see," she said slowly, the lips slapping against the gums, "he's been sick. Very sick. But he wrote to me and he told me he's going to take me out of here." I said nothing. "You understand?" she said. "He's going to take me out because—well, nobody wants to die in a place like this, Jim." Even her church had forgotten her.

I had two dollars folded postage-stamp size. I owed money and I had nothing. She didn't want to take it. I pushed. She held it in the shaky hands. "Nobody wants to die here," she mumbled. "It's not money. Nobody wants to die here. He's going to take me out all right."

It was a mistake to have made the visit. I sat fidgeting. Then I said, "That's what he wanted me to tell you," and I gave her the Judas kiss and left.

She died then. Now the big hill is becoming bare again. They're tearing the building down. They can't tear Potter's Field down. There's a radiance in it. . . .

The old car bounded down 601 like a lame rabbit. The sun was high, and it filtered through the tall cool pines in a cascade of small gold coins. Grandpa and the Little Girl had been on their way for a long time. They rocked with the rhythm of the road, he with arthritic hands tight on the wheel, she with pale ones listless on her lap.

It didn't seem right to see a small one so quiet. He wished that she would squirm more. Or talk a little. The last time she had spoken was away back between Pageland and Kershaw, South

Carolina. She asked why her daddy had been killed. The old man said, "Because he was running. Somebody stole something and a policeman saw your daddy running."

She had never seen her father run. He had been a fat whining man with stubby legs and he had complained to her mother about things the Little Girl did not understand. Then her mother had died. Her daddy had held her up to see her mother's face. Now the Little Girl could never smell flowers without being sick. She hated flowers. She hated big people, too, but she didn't know why. All except Grandpa. Grandpa loved her. Really, truly.

"Why did you bring the printing press?" she said. The old man looked at her sharply. "It was your daddy's and it fit in the trunk of the car," he said. She thought about it. "Is that why the luggage is up here with us?" He nodded, and the old squinted eyes were on the road ahead. "Me and you," he said softly, "have to get a fresh start. We ain't got nobody 'cept each other."

She said nothing. He had made the speech before. They were going to Florida and Grandpa would get a pension and he had a nice little place in mind. He had told her that dead means a long, long sleep and her mommy and daddy were dead. The Old Man and the Little One had each other. What they had for each other was respect.

Out of Pageland, she saw a police car in the tall trees. She told Grandpa. He nodded, and stepped on the gas. The child looked surprised, then relapsed into prissy apathy. The Old Man looked in the rear-view mirror and the car rocked with the violence of speed, but the policeman did not follow.

Grandpa slowed to seventy, and pushed the car up the long hills and down the far slopes. "That printing press," the Old Man said, as though he had not thought of it since she asked, "will give us a little start in Florida. Then we dump it in the river." The Little One lifted her chin because, even with the pillow underneath, she could barely see over the dashboard. "Why?" she said. He said that when they got to Florida, they wouldn't need it.

She was going to ask why once more, but she saw a police car up ahead and watched the policeman swing it out parallel to Grandpa with the red blinker turning on. "You're going to catch it," she said. The Old Man smiled. "I know," he said. "I know." He pulled off the road and stopped the car.

The policeman had a beige uniform and a big floppy hat and a gun at his belt and a big belly. He talked to Grandpa, and the Little One heard him say, "You ought to know better, mister." They talked some more, and Grandpa got out of the car and walked ahead, bent forward the way he always walked. She saw

Grandpa give his license and she could hear the policeman because he was loud and mad. She wondered if he was the one who shot her daddy.

"I don't care where you're going, mister," the policeman said. "Either you come back here to court Friday morning or you forfeit your bond. Bond is ten dollars." Grandpa reached fumbling into his wallet and gave the policeman money. Then the policeman reached into his pocket, and gave Grandpa some money back. They had to wait until the policeman did a lot of writing. He gave the writing to Grandpa on a blue piece of paper.

Grandpa got back into the car. He thanked the policeman. The cop said nothing. He pulled his hat down over his forehead and swung his car around. "They have a speed trap here," Grandpa said. The Little One was going to ask him how it worked, but it was too much trouble. She felt that Grandpa was about to talk, so she concentrated on her blonde hair, and wondered who could wash it now that her daddy was gone, and she thought about her Barbie Doll on the back seat. The doll had been naughty of late, and the Little One put it to bed every sundown as punishment.

"There ain't a crooked bone in my body," Grandpa said, as the car picked up speed. "But I have to do something to get us a start. We been stopped by four policemen in Tennessee, North Carolina and South Carolina. If we can get seven more to stop us, they're gonna keep taking your daddy's twenty-dollar bills and giving me ten dollars' change. When we get to Florida, we can dump the flat-bed press and start all over again.

"Them cops ought to be glad to help the little girl they made an orphan. . . ."

Does evil triumph? Sometimes . . .

Take Al Deg. He was a short bald man of many roundnesses. He had a tall skinny wife who looked like a frightened apostrophe. He had all the brains. She had none. Al was a wholesale salesman in the Midwest. He was so shrewd that he weighed the possibilities of every word before uttering it. By the time he got around to murmuring hello to a friend on the street, he was a block away.

Deg bought his wife a new car. She was allowed to do anything, like washing and waxing it, except drive it. She was forbidden to do this, so, on the very first day, she waited until Al went out to peddle magazines, and she drove it to her girl friend's.

That evening, she barely made it home before he did. She flew out of the car and into the kitchen, donned an apron, and turned up all the gas burners. She was just filling a cooking pot when he walked in. He didn't kiss her. "I told you not to drive the car," he said. Muriel stared at him with her mouth open.

"Come here," he said. He took her outside to the driveway. "Look," he said. The right side of the car had been shoved in. The wife began to weep. "Stop it," he said sternly. "You disobeyed me. This is the penalty. You were probably in your girl friend's house when some lunatic sideswiped the car. You came out and got in on the driver's side and never noticed it."

Muriel begged forgiveness. Al decided to make her pay a little more for trying to outwit a genius. Then he phoned the showroom where he had bought the car. "Your man delivered our new car two days ago," he shouted. "I've been too busy to look it over. Now I find that someone has creased the right side. What are you going to do about it?"

The dealer said that if it was his fault, he'd make good. He couldn't prove that it wasn't. So the car was refinished like new. A few days later, Al Deg received a phone call. "Does you car have a license plate number 27936528?" said a man's voice. Al was cautious. "I think so," he said. "Why?" The man said that he was Edward Lewis, owner of one of the biggest department stores in the city.

"My wife," he said, "had a slight accident. She was out driving last week with our dog and the dog was leaning too far out the right-hand window and my wife reached for him and the car swerved into a parked car. It made her hysterical, so she took the license number and hurried home. Now she has told the story to me. If it is your car, Mr. Deg, I'd like to make good . . ."

"No, no," said Al magnanimously. "We have already taken care of the matter. I wish you would reassure your wife that no great harm has been done, and the car is already repaired." Mr. Lewis insisted. "It is my responsibility," he said. But Deg wouldn't hear of it.

"You are a rare person," said Lewis. "I wish you would stop by my office some day so that we can say hello." Al got off the phone in ecstasy. He danced his wife around the living room. "I couldn't get in to see Lewis in a million years," he said, "but now I'm invited."

Two months later, Deg received a notice of a contest. A national magazine was offering a free trip for two to Hollywood to the salesman who sold the most copies of the June issue. Deg wanted that trip. He wanted it badly. So he went to the big department store and asked to see Edward Lewis.

Mr. Lewis received Deg effusively. They talked, in the plush office, like old cronies. Deg was modest. "I want to win that contest," he said, "and I think you can help me. My idea is to place copies of the magazine beside every cash register on the main floor. That is, instead of merely in the magazine section. This will increase sales . . ."

"Wait a minute," said Lewis. "I have a better idea. Why not place them beside every cash register on every floor?" Deg said that this would be beyond his wildest dreams. It was done. And Deg won a trip to Hollywood for two.

He took the plane tickets and cashed them in. Then he and Muriel drove West, living like royalty all the way. "A man has to think ahead," he told Muriel. "A buck here. A buck there. It mounts up."

They saw Hollywood and movie stars and they went south to Tia Juana and came back up to La Jolla and drove up into the tawny hills and got out of the car to look down at the sea. Al was breathing in beauty when, out of the corner of his eye, he saw something move. It was his car. It started slowly and, before he could run to it, it rolled off the hill, out into space.

Muriel began to cry. It was the thing she did best. Al threw his hat down and jumped on it. "After you had that parking accident," he roared, "I canceled the insurance. Nobody gets a second accident with the same car. We're going to lose two thousand dollars on this mess."

There is a word for Clement: cheap. He was a tall, bald man with a mustache big enough for polishing shoes. He liked to refer to himself as thrifty. The six other tellers in the branch bank said that Clement was so cheap that his fingers squeaked when he paid bus fare. He said they were jealous.

They weren't. Nor were they envious. Clement never married because he said that he could prove, arithmetically, that two could not live as cheaply as one. Two, he said, couldn't even live as cheaply as two because, even if the wife had a job, her salary would probably be less than her husband's. That, according to Clement, would constitute a loss.

He was in his forties, and no one knew him to go out with a girl. Clement said that it would be pointless to solicit the attention of any female for an evening because she would be thinking romantically and he could not afford to think along those lines unless she had lots of money.

No woman with lots of money ever looked at Clement twice. So romance was dead, even though it had never been born. He was the only teller in the branch bank to bring his own lunch. He made the sandwiches in a neat little apartment on the East Side, and he ate them. Sometimes he brought a container of milk; sometimes he washed the sandwiches down with water.

At work in the cage, he wore a linen duster because he wanted to save the jacket of his good suit. He called it an "all weather suit" because it was light enough to wear on hot summer days, and warm enough—at least, so he said—to keep him comfortable in winter. Some of the other tellers, especially Johnny Axelsen, who worked the next cage, tried to socialize with Clement; "loosen him up," they said.

But he resisted this, too. And he was blunt in his reasoning. Axelsen was a fairly young family man who lived not far from Clement, and he invited the thrifty one to dinner. "No," said Clement after thinking about it. "No, thanks. If I go to your house, then it is only proper to invite you to mine. I'm a bachelor who likes solitude, so I'll have to decline with thanks."

Others tried. But no one ever saw Clement after office hours. They knew he saw a movie now and then because one of the depositors managed a movie house and he left passes with Clement. They also knew that he saved money, and bought sound stocks. They also knew that he had no television set. "Instead," he said, "I have a card at the public library."

The bank examiners arrived regularly, but everyone knew that it was a waste of time going over Clement's accounts. They hadn't been off balance by two cents in fifteen years. However, they went over the books one day recently and they finished with the tellers by lunchtime.

Clement had his sandwich, as always, in a back office, and, when he returned to his cage, he thanked Johnny Axelsen for watching his cage. Then, before he removed the "Next window, please" sign, he riffled through the cash drawer and emitted a long moan. "Somebody," he said loudly, "has been in this cash drawer. Quick," he yelled to the policeman at the door, "don't let anybody in or out."

The bank officers came running; so did the bank examiners. They had checked all the cages, and all the cash was in order. Now, as they studied Clement's cash balance, it was obvious that a matter of four thousand dollars in big bills was gone. Well, it couldn't have been Clement, because the thrifty one had never left the premises. After much searching, and discussion, suspicion turned on Johnny Axelsen. Clement said, "I must tell the truth. I must. The cash was all right when I left to have my lunch.

Johnny always watches the cage for me. He is the only one who had access to it today."

The police were called. Detectives questioned one and all. Johnny Axelsen finally broke into tears. "I never took a dime in my life," he said, "and I haven't taken anything now. But Clement is right about one thing. I was the only one near that cage while he ate. If anyone else had walked in, I'd have seen it."

A detective lieutenant booked Johnny on suspicion of grand larceny. Afterwards, he said, "I believe that Axelsen kid. I don't know why. I just believe him. He practically handed himself up to me."

Two days later, the detective walked into Clement's cage with a fat envelope. "The case is solved," he said. "I thought you'd like to know." Clement said he felt sorry for Johnny.

"Oh, no," the cop said. "Save your pity for yourself. You took the money before lunch, shoved it in a bank envelope, and mailed it to your apartment. You were so cheap you put a four-cent stamp on it. The letter has just come back, marked '8 cents in postage due.' . . ."

Religion

If it is true than man has three parts—a soul, a mind and a body—then religion is to the soul what knowledge is to the mind and food is to the body. Like knowledge and food, too much religion is almost as bad as none at all. And too little causes malnutrition, with its concomitant of sicknesses.

Religion was always a part of our family life because our parents made it so. All of us were aware of the presence of God, just as we knew that we belonged to the Roman Catholic Church, as our Irish forebears had for centuries before us. The narrow parochial view was never thrust upon us. My father's cronies were Jews and Methodists and Baptists and Lutherans and some had no faith at all. We were taught that these, too, if they lived by principles and delicate conscience, would someday be in heaven.

The family, with the exception of one, accepted God and the Church as naturally as they accepted coffee with breakfast. The one was I. My question was why, rather than what. I read deeply about my own church, and studied as much as possible of the others. I visited the Holy Land three times, always with the journalist's jaundiced eye on truth as it might be revealed to me.

Most of what follows concerns priests and popes. It is not favoritism on my part. I happen to know them best.

The Death of a Pope

The time of triumph for a Pope, as for many millions of people, comes when he saves his immortal soul. This is certain only at the moment of death. His work is finished. He dies in a state of grace. He who called himself the "servant of the servants of God" is now summoned to the Almighty's presence to render an accounting. Thus the act of dying—as it was to Jesus—is the supreme moment in the life of a Pope. It is the moment of victory; the beginning of true peace; the time of reward.

When God called Pius XII, the first sad words come from Professor Antonio Gasbarrini, one of the Pope's doctors. The two men who listen to the words are the Cardinal Grand Penitentiary, who administered the Sacrament of Extreme Unction to His Holiness, and the Cardinal Camerlengo, who will administer the financial affairs of the Vatican until a new Pope is chosen. The gray-robed Friars of the Franciscans, the priests who hear confessions in all languages in St. Peter's Basilica, are summoned to the private apartment of the Pope. They kneel. The Cardinal Camerlengo prays for the soul of Pius XII. Then he peels back the square of white linen which covers the face of the Pope and, three times, he calls, "Eugenio Pacelli!" The Camerlengo turns to the Friars and announces, "The Pope is truly dead!" Doctor Galeazzi-Lisi and the Papal Master of Ceremonies sign a certificate of death. The Gray Friars, in solemn concert, pray for the repose of the soul of Pius XII. The Vatican Radio announces to the world in twenty languages that the glorious reign of Pius XII is at an end. Old printers in the composing room of the *Osservatore Romano* reverse the rules of their newspaper, so that they will print broad and black for three days.

Within the Pope's apartment, a monsignor hands to the Cardinal Camerlengo the huge Fisherman's Ring. In the stone of the ring is an engraving of St. Peter with a fisherman's net. Around the perimeter is the name of Pius XII. The Camerlengo holds the ring and the young monsignor hurries into another room and returns with the Papal Seal of Pius XII. The Cardinal removes the circle from the ring and makes it unserviceable as a seal. He scores the other so that it can no longer be used to authenticate documents in the name of the dead Pope. The Gray Friars strip the body and bathe it. Afterward they clothe it in Papal vestments. In the morning the first of the nine Masses will be sung for the Pope. These are said, not at the main altar in St. Peter's, but in the apse behind the main altar. Each Mass is celebrated by a Cardinal.

The Camerlengo leaves the private apartment and, holding the broken ring and the scored seal in his hands, enters his office, and there, waiting for him, a Cardinal-Vicar asks for permission for the bells of Rome to be solemnly tolled. When permission is given, the large bell on Capitoline Hill crashes out the first basso note, followed by hundreds of bells large and small.

On the second day the priests and monsignori attached to St. Peter's appear at the door of the Sistine Chapel and ask the Gray Friars to deliver the body to them. The penitentiaries permit the priests—about forty in number—to take the body, but the Gray Friars, by custom, remain close behind the procession. The time is dusk. By the light of tall candles, surrounded by the priests of his own household, the Pope is carried on his bier through the dark halls. In the cathedral sacristy, the priests, in a final act of devotion, attire the body in full Pontifical robes with the triple mitre on the head. When this is done, they carry the body into the cathedral, followed closely by the watchful Frairs, and they set it before the altar in the Chapel of the Most Holy Sacrament. Here, for the next twenty-four hours, the people of Rome are permitted to file by the catafalque. The reason this privilege is accorded them is that, besides being Pope, Pius XII was their Bishop. They will queue in thousands, the rich and the powerful of Rome standing in line with cabdrivers and porters, nurses and housewives.

Now the Holy Roman Catholic Church will go into mourning. The red of the Cardinals will not be seen. They will wear purple mozzettas, rochets and birettas. Members of the Papal Court will be attired in long purple cloaks and black stockings. Nuns, priests and lay brothers will, in thousands, be on the roads to Rome. Masses for the repose of the soul of His Holiness will be celebrated in churches all over the world.

On the third day after death, the body of His Holiness will be moved from the Chapel of the Most Holy Sacrament to the altar in the apse. Those who have received their red hats from the dead Pope will carry the body. Now the last rites will begin. St. Peter's will be filled with dignitaries and statesmen and nobles and members of the Pacelli family. All will wear severe black. The ceremony will be long and a prelate will announce each stage of it. Absolution will be given by a Cardinal-Bishop, probably Micara of Italy. During the nine daily Masses, nine more absolutions will be given.

When the Requiem Mass is over, three Cardinals will carry the body to a cypress wood box and lower it. When the body is inside, the vestments and triple crown will be set aright, and medals of gold and silver and copper will be thrown into the box. The number is determined by the number of years the Pope has reigned. Now the first Cardinal to be created by the Pope will cover the face of Pius with a purple veil. Afterward he will lay a red ermine blanket on the body. The box will be locked. It is then placed inside a lead coffin. The caskets are blessed. The Pope is carried down a short marble stairway to the vault beneath the big main altar. There the caskets are placed in an oblong space and masons seal it with concrete. In front, a marble square will be screwed into place. On it is the name of the Pope. The Cardinal-Bishop will lead the College of Cardinals in a recitation of the Lord's Prayer.

The burial ceremonies are finished.

A Day in the Life of a Priest*

Father McWilliams arises at six thirty. He used to get up an hour earlier, but now he has two assistants to take care of the early Masses. He washes and shaves and dresses in twenty-five minutes. At seven he strolls through the corridor between the rectory and the church and reports to the sacristy to prepare for Mass. Almost on the stroke of seven thirty, he is before the main altar of his church with one altar boy and fulfills his sacred duty. At eight o'clock, Mass is over, and he spends fifteen minutes in a prayer of thanksgiving. After that Father McWilliams has breakfast alone in the rectory. This consists of fruit juice, one soft-boiled egg, whole wheat toast, and coffee. At his other meals he drinks water. At eight thirty-five, Father starts on his sick calls. On some rare days there are none. On others there are four or five. On first Fridays the calls swell into the dozens.

St. Michael's Roman Catholic Church in Jersey City, New Jersey, is one of the biggest little parishes in the United States. Geographically, it measures six blocks in one direction and about seven in the other. But it is stacked with flats and tenements, and

* The first of "The Day" stories. It was written in 1949.

it is not uncommon for ten families at one address to be parishioners. In other days, when the Horseshoe section was laden with the laughter and the tears of immigrants from Wexford, Mayo, Tipperary, and Cork, St. Michael's was bigger numerically than any other parish in the city. But now the Irish have prospered and the third generation has moved up "onto the hill" into the parishes of St. Patrick's, St. Aloysius, St. Aedan's, and Sacred Heart.

Father McWilliams is back in the rectory by nine twenty-five on the average day and begins to read his mail. This is a formidable correspondence, because Father McWilliams supplements his spiritual work with civic duties. He is Moderator of the Mount Carmel Guild and each year raises about $30,000 for their charity work. He is also vice-chairman of the Community Chest and a member of the Board of Governors. He is Chaplain of the Catholic War Veterans and is one of the top officials of the Red Cross. He is also chairman of St. Francis Hospital Nurses Training School, an official of the American Cancer Society, vice-chairman of the Citizens Planning Board, and during the war was chairman of the Food Panel of the War Price Rationing Board.

So his mail is heavy. Most businessmen would consider it a day's work in itself. By ten thirty it is answered, and Father is off to make hospital calls. St. Francis Hospital lies diagonally across the street and the Jersey City Medical Center is two miles away. If, by odd chance, all of his people are reasonably healthy, Father McWilliams uses this hour to visit his grammar school and his high school. Slightly more than a thousand children are enrolled in both. They are taught by twenty-four Sisters, nine secular teachers, and three athletic instructors, all under the supervision of Sister Superior Grace Antonia, who may someday surrender her Brahmin Boston accent for the brand of base Brooklynese spoken on Erie Street.

Father McWilliams is the boss. He is so short that, when he stands on a sidewalk with his great Dane Michael and the dog's ears are up, the priest is the shorter of the two. He bristles at public injustice, issues statements to the press, browbeats merchants into employing boys fresh out of prison, referees chronic fights between married couples, is a Fire Department chaplain with a red light and a siren on his car, and a white fire helmet and raincoat in the trunk. He enjoys fighting for the helpless, and in these Father McWilliams is rich.

At eleven thirty he pauses for prayer in the church. As a supplicant he kneels in a pew. The church is big and Romanesque in design. It was built seventy-five years ago and is one of the few equipped with a round tabernacle. A priceless sarouk rug cascades down the main altar steps, and the Italian chandeliers are equipped with fluorescent lighting. In the basement is a huge auditorium, once damp and dismal. It is now warm and bright and has a stainless steel soda-and-snack bar, a fully complemented kitchen, and is used by all parish groups from the Holy Name Society to the Catholic Youth and Sodality down to youngsters who want to put on a play. Father McWilliams ripped out half of the old basement windows and walled the auditorium with marlite. During the Depression, scores of thousands of the poor were fed free in this room.

At the stroke of noon Father McWilliams has dinner in the rectory. This is the big meal of the day and consists of meat, vegetables, dessert, and a glass of water. The writer had dinner with Father on a Saturday and, when fish cakes were served, the priest made a grimace and growled, "They don't feed you here." He is finished at twelve thirty and, at that time, goes into a conference with his two assistants. They confer on the business of the parish. There is a free exchange of ideas and a fair sharing of duties. Each curate has his own sitting room, bedroom, and bath. The rectory, a big brick building, was built by the late Monsignor John A. Sheppard in 1916. Everything is spacious, including the kitchen. There are thirteen rooms in all.

At one o'clock Father McWilliams goes into the front office. This is equipped with a desk and chairs and the customary gilt-framed portraits of archbishops, monsignori, and pastors of the past. One, between the two front windows, is of Monsignor Januarius de Concilio, a pastor whose name is barely recalled by the few. He was laboring at St. Michael's in the early days when his superiors asked him to draw up a catechism. He worked hard and when it was finished said: "That's the last I'll hear of that. It will go in somebody's wastebasket." He was wrong. What he wrote is what we call the Baltimore Catechism, an instrument used to teach the fundamental precepts of our Church to scores of millions. It was in use for fifty years without the change of a comma.

In this hour after lunch, parishioners come in with all sorts of problems. Poverty, hardship, and heartache come in to sit close to the sheen of the black cassock and plead for help. Some, of course, are amusing. This is one of the few parishes, in this enlightened age, where an irate wife and a tooth-grinding husband will arrive together to submit their dispute to the arbitration of the priest. Now and then a young wife will come in unexpectedly to report that Paddy came home with more than a drop in him, and should she leave him now or wait until morning.

At two o'clock Father McWilliams goes out to keep whatever

appointments have been made for him. Many of these are public meetings of charitable organizations. Father believes that the priest's prime and never-ending duty is spiritual work. But he also believes that a priest can do incalculable good by identifying himself with good works. "The priest," he says, "is the window through which the non-Catholic sees our Church. The presence of a priest often tends to break down prejudice and disposes people kindly toward our Church." Recently a well-known Protestant publisher, after serving with McWilliams on a charity board, grabbed the priest's hand. "You've opened my eyes," he said. "I didn't know that a priest could be helpful and so human."

At four Father is back in the rectory. After making sure that all parish business is under control, he takes a walk. As a one-time athlete, he places a high value on physical trimness. When he goes for his walk, he is ostensibly out to get the afternoon newspapers but usually walks through a good part of his parish, nodding and swapping pleasantries. When he returns, he stops in the church for prayer. After that, when eye fatigue permits, he scans the papers and tries to keep abreast of the world.

At six o'clock supper is served. This one is long on conversation and short on food. His curates tell him what they have been doing. In the old days Monsignor Sheppard used to have a blackboard in the rectory hall and priests had to write on it the exact time of leaving, the destination, and the time of arrival back in the rectory. Anyone who was overlong on a trip was given time at the next meal to give a detailed explanation.

At seven o'clock the rectory doorbell begins to ring. These are the evening callers. Like the afternoon callers, they have problems. They want to arrange for Requiem Masses, Nuptial Masses, christenings, or maybe Paddy came home stone sober and beat his wife up. This goes on for two hours, unless there are evening devotions.

Around nine Father McWilliams retires to his room. He has been at his work fourteen hours, a situation no good union man would tolerate, and yet he has done no more than thousands of other parish priests. He sits in a deep leather chair and reaches for the magazines and books he has promised himself to read when he "gets the chance." There is no sound at the door, but Father suddenly stands and says, "It's Himself wants to come in." Himself is Michael, one of the biggest great Danes in captivity.

Years ago a parishioner phoned the priest and asked if he'd like to have a dog. "Yes," Father McWilliams said, "I always liked dogs. How big is he?" The parishioner sighed windily. "Roughly, Father," he said, "about half your size." It was a Dane. When he died, Father got "Himself." And no feet tread the precincts of a rectory with more quiet dignity.

The dog settles himself halfway across the room with head on paws, watching the priest read. Father McWilliams turns on his radio if there is a good "Whodunit" mystery. If not, he leafs through *The Catholic Messenger, The Sign,* and *Baxter's Economic Service.* If his eyes tire he dwells, like most of us, on boyhood days when his father was commissioner of the Police and Fire Departments of Paterson, New Jersey. Two of Jim McWilliams' sons became priests. The third graduated from Annapolis and became a Navy officer.

Today, Father McWilliams thinks that his long talks with Father Paul Guterl, first assistant at St. Joseph's in Paterson, had a big bearing on his decision to study for the priesthood. LeRoy McWilliams went to Paterson High School and then to Seton Hall. He spent four years in the college and three and a half in the seminary. There was a war on and priests were needed, so LeRoy McWilliams was ordained on December 21, 1918. Two days later he was sent to St. Michael's Parish in Jersey City. After thirty-one years, he is still there. He has been pastor for the past eleven years.

Toward eleven o'clock, his head begins to nod in the chair. Himself watches unblinking. Father gets up, yawns, and goes into his bedroom. Michael gets up, turns his huge frame around twice, and drops to the floor. His eyes squint closed. The bedroom door shuts and, barring accidents, gunplay, or emergency calls, Father McWilliams' day is done.

The Practicalities of Christ

When did Christ die?

The answer is in perpetual dispute. No one knows. However, in the nineteen hundred years since His death, the great scholars of each century have added bits to our knowledge of the Messiah. These are clues—nothing more. However, they point in one direction and it is possible by equating them, to arrive at certain conclusions about the date of His birth and death.

For example, there are certain provable historical facts in the Bible. We can fix the reign of King Herod, who administered the affairs of a large part of Palestine when Jesus was born. We can also fix the reign of Tiberius Caesar, who ruled the known world, including Judea, in the time of Christ.

Tiberius appointed Pontius Pilate as Procurator of Palestine. Historians can almost fix the exact date.

Pope Gregory, centuries later, assigned a monk, Dionysius, to devise a calendar and ordered him to fix the date of Christ's birth as the year one, *anno Domini*. Our troubles in fixing the birth of Christ come from a mathematical error committed by Dionysius. The year which he set as A.D. 1 is now thought to be the sixth year in the life of Jesus. How the monk made the mistake, no one knows, but it has upset Biblical calculation ever since.

When the Magi came to Judea to worship the infant Messiah, they said that they had seen a bright star in the East and had followed it. They told this to Herod, an insane king. Astronomers of today calculate that, in the year 748 A.U.C. of the Roman calendar, or the year 6 B.C. in our calendar, there was a remarkable conjunction of the planets Jupiter, Saturn and Mars, which appeared to be fused together into one gigantic star in the constellation Pisces. This occurs every eight hundred years.

It is a provable fact that Herod, hoping to destroy the Messiah, ordered a slaughter of all male Jewish babies up to the age of two. This occurred in the year 4 B.C. and leads us to believe that Jesus was born when the giant star appeared in 6 B.C. This would account for why Herod wanted all male babies "up to the age of two" killed.

Also, Jesus was about two years old when His mother and Joseph took Him to Egypt. This explains why Jesus was not among the infants killed.

Another clue is contained in the Gospel according to Luke, where he mentions the fifteenth year of the reign of Tiberius (which is easily computed) and the fact that Jesus was "about thirty years old."

The death of the Messiah carries its own historical clues. The date to be sought must be the eve of the Passover (the fourteenth day of the month of Nisan, according to the Jewish calendar) and this feast must fall on a Friday. If Jesus was a man "in His thirties," then the probable date of His death is April 6, A.D. 30, because that particular Passover began on a Sabbath (Friday).

These things are deducible. If they are correct (and the majority of Roman Catholic and Protestant archaeologists in Jerusalem subscribe to them) then Jesus was born in the winter solstice of 6 B.C. (the week of December 21) and died on April 6, A.D. 30. He was thirty-four years and three months of age.

Prayer

Prayer is a secret thing. I've been to church thousands of times with my family and I have watched their lips move silently, but I never knew what they said. They never knew what I said. Prayer is a personal call to God; it isn't a party line.

Some prayers are answered. Some are not. The thing I prayed hardest for was a two-wheel bicycle. I was twelve and it seemed that every boy on the street but me had one. It didn't occur to me that God's ears might be busy listening to the pleas of the dying, the petitions of the poor, the supplications of the sick at heart.

Still, the prayer was answered. I was about to give up when the school announced that, as part of a bazaar, there would be a popularity contest for boys. The winner would get a bicycle. Votes would cost a penny apiece. If there was anything that I was not, it was popular. Among my fellows, I was a cipher.

However, God works in mysterious ways. This time He used my father, who was lieutenant of police. Dad got a bunch of popularity books and gave one to each of his merchant friends—some of whom, as I recall, were saloonkeepers. I won. No bicycle ever got the meticulous care accorded to that one. I used to dream about it.

I thanked my father for all that he had done. I think I neglected to thank God.

I've been short-changing Him ever since. Under analysis, my prayers are always asking him for something. I pray for the infant twins, for the children, for my father and brother and sister and their families, and for me. I ask for health, happiness, prosperity, long life, and grace of a happy death—the works.

All I want is everything. All He asks is adoration. I don't ever remember dropping to my knees and murmuring, "You are all. I am nothing."

Not long ago, I wrote a book about a prayer. It is called *Go With God* and, if it is interesting, it is because the prayers are not mine; they are the thoughts of hundreds of faithful minds. This represented my first glimpse into the hearts of others.

Admiral Arthur Radford, for example, prayed "that I and all the military leaders of the free people of this world may perform our tasks so well that, with Thy blessing, ours may be vanishing positions . . ."

Franklin Clark Fry, president of the United Lutheran Church, prayed for "peace that the world cannot give, that our hearts may be set to obey Thy Commandments . . ." Harry Truman's favorite prayer contains the phrase: "Help me to be, to think to a T what is right."

Francis Cardinal Spellman, writing a prayer poem while the nation was at war, penned these lines: "Dear Christ, some of the altars we have built, With all the skill that science could command, With all the speed our genius could beget, Have graven golden images enshrined." Bishop G. Bromley Oxnam of the Methodist Episcopal Church, wrote, "When we say Our Father we know that the Eternal, who keeps the stars in their courses, notes the sparrow's fall and knows each one of us by name . . ."

Mary Pickford's favorite prayer contains the line, "It is I who have wandered from your love." Clare Boothe Luce's is: "I may forget Thee. Do not Thou forget me." General Douglas A. MacArthur's prayer opens: "Build me a son, O Lord, who will be strong enough to know when he is weak, and brave enough to face himself when he is afraid. . . ."

Henry Knox Sherrill, presiding bishop of the Episcopal Church, asks: "Grant unto Thy people that they may love the thing which Thou commandest . . ." Rabbi David de Sola Pool closes his prayer with the words: ". . . as I open my mind, my heart, and my soul to Thee, I shall know peace within my own being, and shall further peace on earth among Thy children." John D. Rockefeller, Jr., hits close to the mark when he says: ". . . may we face the unknown, calm and unafraid, because of an abiding faith in Thee!"

The most touching, I think, is Elizabeth Barrett Browning's prayer for a dying baby:

> I am not used to bear
> Hard thoughts of death; the earth doth cover
> No face from me of friend or lover:
> And must the first who teaches me
> The form of shrouds and funerals, be
> Mine own first-born beloved? he
> Who taught me first this mother-love

Now I know why my prayers must have sounded so weak to Him. . . .

Good Friday

The Romans always kept the body on the cross until the birds and the dogs finished with it. This one was an exception. At sundown this day, Passover and the Sabbath would come. It would not look good to the pilgrims crowding the Gennath Gate to see this one in death with a mocking sign over His head hailing Him King of the Jews.

He came down in midafternoon. There had been a wind and a momentary night sky and the rocks of Golgotha had cracked, but that too had passed. Now He was taken down by a Sadducee, a Pharisee and a pagan. John wanted to help, but the others said no, that he should console the Dead One's mother.

John was ashamed. Only last night he and his brethren had beaten their breasts at supper to argue their love for God and the Son of God. Where were the others? They were hiding. The death of Jesus, they were sure, was the ultimate defeat.

Nicodemus sent a servant for a hundred pounds of spices, some myrrh and aloes. Joseph of Arimathea, who owned the little garden tomb next to the execution place, bought the wide linen bands. He also sent for the unguents and a downy feather.

John left the women and helped to rock the cross arm loose from the crucifix. He helped to lay the body on a flat rock. It wasn't much to look at. The body was that of a fairly tall man, brown haired, brown bearded, the dark eyes half closed, the mouth partly open, as it had been when He had willed Himself to die and had said: "It is finished!"

The Arimathean knelt behind the head and wiped the face soothingly. It had to be patted because the bits of bones at the tips of the scourger's lash had whipped little pie wedges of flesh out of the cheeks. When the face and shoulders were fairly clean, a strip of linen was wound from chin to top of head, to hold the mouth closed.

The men worked against the sun. Furtively, they watched His mother approach the rock and sit beside Him. They could not bear to look at her, and they wished that she would go. Two held the body on the side as John washed it. The two Marys held the hands of the mother and wailed with her.

Nicodemus unrolled the sheeting. The three lifted the Dead

One and placed His body on it. They anointed the body with spices. A feather was placed under the nose. The men watched it. Under law, if it moved while shielded from a breeze, the burial could not proceed.

The feather did not move. Joseph could not bear the weeping of the women. He suggested that the remainder of the obsequies take place in the vestibule of the tomb. The women were too spent to object. The men carried the body 120 feet north-north-west to Joseph's tomb.

John carried the rolls of linen back to the women and asked them to impress the spices into the cloth. They were pleased. They had been asked to assist. The tomb was not ornate. It was set in the side of a twelve-foot hill facing east. From front to back, it measured fifteen feet. From floor to ceiling, it was seven feet, from wall to wall, five.

The entrance was five feet tall, and a rolling millstone was set in a rock groove so that, if it wasn't held back by a chock, it would roll closed. The rolling stone was sixty inches in diameter and nine inches thick.

The sun was heavy lidded on the mountains when Jesus was buried. More than one hundred fifty thousand pilgrims came down the marble steps of the great Temple of Solomon, after the final sacrifice of the day. Some of the seven thousand priests of the temple began to light the lamps of the evening. Along the east wall, a cluster of gold grapes, four stories high, caught the reflection of sunset and the grapes turned lavender.

Joseph and Nicodemus and John finished the burial and, together, they rolled the stone in place. Soon, the tomb was quiet. Somewhere, a bird trilled a final phrase and tucked its head under its wing. The Marys sat before the tomb and wept.

They had missed the point. This was the moment of victory. . . .

A Man Named Roncalli

The future is an opaque mirror. Anyone who tries to look into it sees nothing but the dim outlines of an old and worried face. . . .

In 1905, four Italian priests were friends. One was Radini-Tedeschi. Another was Della Chiesa. The third was Achille Ratti. The fourth was Joseph Barto, who was Pius X. These men had respect for one another, and affection too. Of them, only Radini-Tedeschi would not, in time, become a Pope.

Della Chiesa became Benedict XV. Achille Ratti became Pius XI. Barto was already in his pontificate and would someday be canonized.

Radini-Tedeschi was content to remain in Bergamo. There, in the small hills outside of Milan, he tended his flock. His greatest help came from his young and vigorous secretary, Father Angelo Roncalli. The young priest was born in the area and he knew the people. Like his boss, he had sympathetic understanding.

When young Father Roncalli heard that Radini-Tedeschi was to be consecrated a bishop, his pride was enormous. The ceremony occurred in Rome on January 29, 1905. It was a thing of splendor because it was the first consecration by Pius X.

At the conclusion, the Pope embraced the new bishop and whispered to him. This little thing intrigued the diplomats and church dignitaries. They wanted to know what the Pope had said. Neither the Pope nor Bishop Radini-Tedeschi offered to satisfy their curiosity.

Back at Bergamo, young Father Roncalli, with some trepidation, asked what the Pope had whispered. The bishop regarded his secretary and said that the Pope had told him that, after his death, he would come back to take Radini-Tedeschi with him, and they would be together for eternity.

The young priest did not mention it. He went about his duties quietly. He was not one to try to look too far into the future. The bishop never mentioned the matter again. Neither did the priest.

Had any of them been able to look into God's mirror, the future would have been a depressing sight of age and unfinished work and death. Pius X had nine and a half years ahead of him, and he used it to work hard for the poor and the workers.

This kind of work is never completed and men who put compassionate hearts into it are always asking for a little more time.

In July, 1914, the crowned heads of Europe lit a giant bonfire. It burned across many countries and killed millions of people, but this too was not to be seen in advance. It had barely started, in July of that year, and many soldiers went off to war with high hearts, the salutes of their women still burning their cheeks.

A month later, Bishop Radini-Tedeschi became ill. It was a wasting, debilitating illness. He too had much work to do, but now he felt that the book of time was being slowly closed. In the hospital, he thought of many projects he had promised himself to accomplish to help his people. Now, someone else would have to carry the yoke.

At his side, young Father Angelo Roncalli held his bishop's hand and dreaded to see him go, not only because the strong young secretary had learned so much from his superior, but because he believed in his heart that a great man was dying.

Doctors came into the room, made examinations, gave orders to nurses who made notes on charts, and left. At times such as this, these are pathetic gestures. Man's science is pompous, even when it fails. Death, for a man of God, is the time of victory; the moment of reward.

On August 20, 1914, the doctors advised that the bishop's family be permitted to come into the room and say farewell. The young secretary stood aside in the face of grief. He too was saddened, but only because he was losing a saintly shepherd.

On the morning of the twenty-first of August, news came from Rome that Pius X had died the previous night. On the next day, the bishop died. The Pope had kept his word. The book of time had closed for both men; the book of eternity had opened.

It is good that none of us can see in that mirror the grave responsibilities and the suffering of tomorrow. Forty-four years after all this happened, Father Angelo Roncalli became Pope John XXIII. . . .

Jerusalem 2,000 Years Ago

The night watch at the Shushan Gate was the first to see the moon come up. It sat like an orange on the deep blue Mountains of Moab. Inside the temple, the high priest had been reading the twelfth chapter of Exodus. As he uttered the concluding words: "And the whole assembly of the congregation of Israel shall kill it," three Levite priests, standing over three lambs, lifted the jaws of the little animals and, with a single stroke, drew sharp knives across their throats.

It was 6 P.M. of the fourteenth Nisan in the year 3200. The Passover had begun. Within the walls of Jerusalem, three hundred thousand Jews were in solemn joy. Outside the walls, two hundred thousand others were in tiny shelters on the hills of the Mount of Olives and the Mount of Offense. Once more, their hearts were touched at the story of Moses and the deliverance of the tribes from the bondage of Egypt. Once more, they had come to the great Temple of Solomon to worship Yahweh in His one, His only, home on earth.

The blood from the lambs was caught in a golden basin and handed along a line of priests until the last one, standing at the sacrificial rock, dashed the blood against the stone. It ran down brightly over the ridges toward the drains underneath. The high priest watched the others pour warm water over the lambs and hang them on racks. The wool was peeled carefully from the animals because the skin had to be intact and free from wens or moles.

On examination, they were found acceptable and, on a signal, the Levitical priests cut the bellies of the lambs with a single downward stroke. The viscera fat, the kidneys, and the caul above the liver were removed. These were placed on a fire altar to steam until the logs were consumed.

The priests rubbed salt into the lambs. The right foreleg and part of the head were removed as an offering to the priests of the temple. In the tallest tower of the temple, a priest shouted down that he could see three stars in the east. There was a blast of silver trumpets from below, and the new day had begun.

There were seven thousand priests in the temple. There were twenty-four gates and ten priests manned each gate. They estimated that two hundred thousand lambs had been sacrificed this day. Every one of the three million Jews in Palestine, from the age of five onward, was bound to know that the Pasch signified that, when their forefathers had left Egypt hurriedly, the women had baked unleavened bread and the men had slain lambs, sprinkling the blood on the doorposts and lintels to identify the house to the Angel of Death.

Now the Jews were home, but God had tested their subservience to Him many times. He had visited them with plagues and pestilence and famine. He had tried them by exchanging the Pharaohs, as masters, for conquerors from the West. He had given them the Commandments and the tablets had been placed in the sacred Ark of the Covenant. They would lose it in a war with the Babylonians.

It wasn't a big country. From Caesarea Philippi in the north to Bir es Saba in the south was 150 miles. From the port of Joppa to Jerusalem on the east was fifty miles. There were so few trees in the land that it was an epithet to call a man "a cutter and the son of a cutter." The people worked hard and prayed hard.

They still had the temple. It was 1,600 feet long and 970 feet wide. It was made of marble and alabaster and, on the east side, a cluster of gold grapes stood four stories high to catch the first morning sun. It had courts for the Gentiles and courts for women and courts for the faithful.

The Jews could build synagogues anywhere, but these were places of teaching. There was only one place where God dwelt.

That is why so many people came to Jerusalem on the Passover. A Jew could live in Egypt and Syria or even Rome, but it was against the law for him to live more than ninety days' journey from the Holy City. At least once a year, at Passover, he was bound to come to the temple. It was not only his duty, but his joy.

At this time, he drew close, very close to God. He brought his family and he brought his unblemished lamb and made the sacrifice. Then, even his little ones began to understand the Jewish oneness: one God, one temple, one nation, one people, one tribe, one family.

His heart swelled with pride.

The Renegade

He was shrewd, and brilliant and had no character. His name was Flavius Josephus and he was born in A.D. 37, seven years after the death of Jesus. Josephus, a scholar in Hebrew, Aramaic and Latin, was the only person—except the apostles—to write about Christ in the century in which He lived.

He was a devout Pharisee, and he made ritualistic sacrifices in the temple of Jerusalem and once, in the zeal of religion, he spent three years in the desert with an Essene hermit named Banu. In the year 64, he went to Rome to intercede with Caius Nero in behalf of three rabbis who had committed a trivial offense.

Josephus could not get an audience with Nero, but he managed to see the Empress Poppaea. He charmed her, and she caused her husband to free the rabbis and send them back to Jerusalem. When Josephus got home, he found that the Jews were ready to revolt in Rome. He told them that what he had seen in Rome convinced him of the enormous power of Nero, and that resistance would only exterminate the Jewish race.

In the year 66, he went to Galilee to persuade the Jewish fighters to lay down their arms. When they refused, he joined them and became their general. He led them in battle, but a Jewish leader named John of Giscala saw Josephus as a traitor and tried to get him assassinated.

The next spring, Vespasian and Titus led the Romans against Josephus. He was beaten and sent word to Jerusalem, asking for reinforcements. None came. So he sat in the Galilean hill and cast lots with the remnants of his army. He said he was opposed to suicide, and arranged that the soldier who drew lot number two would kill number one, the man who had lot three would kill number two, and so on.

Josephus managed to draw the final lot. Everyone was dead except Josephus and the man he was supposed to kill. They surrendered and, when brought before Vespasian, Josephus boldly predicted that the Roman would some day become Caesar. This flattered Vespasian. When the prophecy came true, Vespasian liberated the shrewd man.

The new emperor took Josephus to Rome with him, made him a citizen under the name Flavius Josephus, gave him a lifetime pension, and bequeathed an estate in Judea.

Josephus was now a renegade Jew. However, he had great power in Rome, and the Jews made no move against him. He lived in a time when almost all teaching and all records were oral; the written word was rare. Still, being rich and secure, Josephus tried to regain favor with his people by writing Jewish history. One of his works, *The Jewish Antiquities,* consists of twenty volumes and professes to trace the history of the Jews from Adam and Eve down to A.D. 70, when Jerusalem was sacked and destroyed.

He also wrote an autobiography, called *Life,* in which he defended himself against the charge that he had started the Jewish rebellion against the Romans and, in the face of defeat and death, had renounced the faith of his forefathers and embraced the pagan worship of Rome. It amounted to a massive apology and was discredited almost at once.

However, his twenty-volume work has been translated into many languages, and lives to this day. The books are compelling because they represent the thinking of the Jewish sages of two thousand years ago. However, I do not trust his opinions. Some of them are shaded toward whatever was politically popular at that time. He was, of course, opposed to Jesus.

In volume three, page sixty-two of the Woodward edition, published in 1825, Flavius wrote:

"Now there was about this time Jesus, a wise man, if it be lawful to call Him a man; for He was a doer of wonderful works, a teacher of such men as receive the truth with pleasure. He drew over to Him both many of the Jews, and many of the Gentiles. He was the Christ.

"And when Pilate, at the suggestion of the principal men among us, had condemned Him to the cross, those who loved Him at the first did not forsake Him; for He appeared to them alive again the third day; as the divine prophets had foretold these and ten thousand other wonderful things concerning Him. And the tribe of Christians, so named from Him, are not extinct to this day."

Josephus wrote this between the years A.D. 75 and A.D. 80, about fifty years after the death of Jesus. He is amazed to note that the Christians, as a sect, have not died off. Also he notes something that Christians today try to forget—that Jesus had many more followers among the Jews than enemies. The men who carried the word, and wrote it, were Jews, too.

It gives me something to think about, at the start of Lent. . . .

Judas

The treasurer of the Twelve was Judas. He was the only one of the group who was not a Galilean. He was short and broad and dark and wore his hair in ringlets. His name was not Judas Iscariot, but Judas ish Kerioth (Judas from Kerioth, a town in Judea). He was vain, snobbish and wise. Judas regarded the other apostles as country boys.

Not much is known about this man, except the fragments which appear in the writings of Matthew, Mark, Luke and John. However, from the chips of truth, one can deduce other things. He wore a garment of white, as the others did, but, as treasurer, he also wore a leather apron under the garment. It had two big pockets. In these he stuffed alms.

On at least one occasion, Judas was accused of stealing. Some Jewish women who had given up their worldly possessions to follow Jesus demanded an accounting. The Messiah dismissed the complaint although some of the other apostles added testimony of their own about earlier thefts. So it is certain that Judas had inordinate pride, and no character.

It is reasonable to assume that he did not believe that Jesus of Nazareth was God and the Son of God. If he believed, no power could have forced him to betray the Master because, to do so, would be to forfeit his soul in addition to all the rewards promised to the apostles in Heaven. It is possible that he believed that Jesus had delusions.

His father, Simon ish Kerioth, did not subscribe to Jewish law. Judas was irreligious. Why then was he selected as an apostle? Because the ancient prophecies had to be fulfilled: the innocent lamb would be betrayed. Someone had to do it. Who better than a vain atheist whose prime interest in life was the acquisition of money? Who better than a thief who would steal from his Master? Who better than one who believed in no one except himself? Who better than a man who believed he was on the paying end of a good racket?

He pitied the thousands of Jews who believed in Jesus and who gave up their worldly possessions to follow Him. At the home of Martha and Mary, Judas protested when the feet of Jesus were anointed with an expensive unguent. He said it could be sold for three hundred denarii and the money given to the poor. To the poor? Poor Judas.

While Jesus was curing lepers, or raising the dead to life, Judas had no time to watch, and see for himself. He was busy threading in the throngs of people, asking for contributions. He demanded the strictest accounting from the other apostles, but rendered none himself. The man's hunger for money was insatiable.

Two things primed him for betrayal. One was the increasing references of Jesus to His imminent death. The other was the desire of the high priest Caiaphas, and his father-in-law Annas, to put Christ on trial for blasphemy, for claiming to be the Son of Yahweh. Judas calculated that, if Jesus was about to die, the racket was bound to die with Him.

Also, the few highly placed Jews who plotted against Jesus had more power than the thousands of poor Jews who believed in Him. The few might punish the many, and it is not good to be caught on the losing side of the struggle. So he went up to Caiaphas and promised to deliver Jesus for a price. The price was thirty pieces of silver, which was the price of a slave killed by an ox.

Judas refused to testify at the trial. He agreed to identify Jesus with a kiss. Then he expected to take his thirty shekels and disappear. He got the money. It jingled in his leather apron, but he could not leave. He hurried from Gethsemane down the Cedron to the Fountain Gate and on up to the courtyard of Caiaphas.

There, remorse smashed his mind. He saw the gentlest of men kicked, flogged and slapped, not because Caiaphas asked it, but because the guards wanted to show zealousness to their boss. Judas sickened. Instead of leaving, he whimpered behind the party all the way to the temple and the trial.

The rising sun deepened the hollows in his leathery cheeks as he waited on Solomon's portico for the verdict. When he heard it, Judas lost his mind. He raced north and into the sanctuary of the priests and shouted: "I have betrayed innocent blood!" He counted out the thirty shekels and watched them tinkle and dance and roll on the temple floor.

He ran toward the Valley of the Hinnom and hanged himself. The last human words Judas heard were from the priest: "That is your worry." As he swung from the tree near the wall, the bough broke. His body was dashed on the rocks below, and the money in the leather apron rolled down the hill, toward Potter's Field.

The First Christmas

The road out of Bethany threw a tawny girdle around the hill they called the Mount of Olives, and the little parties came up slowly out of the east leading asses with dainty, dark feet toward the splendor of Jerusalem. They came up all year long from Jericho and the Salt Sea and the Mountains of Moab and the north country of Samaria and Galilee in a never-ending procession to the great temple of Herod. It was a spawning, a coming home, a communion with God at His appointed house.

Joseph had never seen the city. The elders in Nazareth had told him that it was a rare, white jewel set in the green valley between Cedron and Golgotha and he had asked questions about it, but the elders—and his father too—seemed to lose themselves in arm-waving and superlatives. Now he would see it. He reached the rise of the road, his feet strong and dirty from ninety miles of walking, and he unconsciously pulled the jackass a little faster.

"Are you quiet?" he said. His bride, called Miriam in the Aramean tongue, and Mary in others, jogged sideward on the little animal and said that she was quiet. She felt no pain. This was the fifth day from Nazareth and, from hour to hour, she had progressed from tiredness to fatigue to weariness to the deep anesthesia of exhaustion. She felt nothing. She no longer noticed the chafe of the goatskin against her, nor the sway of the food bag on the other side of the animal. Her veiled head hung and she saw millions of pebbles on the road moving by her brown eyes in a blur, pausing, and moving by again with each step of the animal.

Sometimes she felt ill, but she swallowed this feeling and concentrated on what a beautiful baby she was about to have and kept thinking about it—the bathing, the oils, the feeding, the tender pressing of the tiny body against her breast—and the sickness went away. Sometimes she murmured the ancient prayers and, for a moment, there was no road and no pebbles and she dwelt on the wonder of God and saw Him in a fleecy cloud, a windowless wall at an inn, a hummock of trees, walking backward in front of her husband, beckoning him on. God was everywhere. It gave Mary confidence to know that. He was everywhere. She needed confidence. Mary was fifteen.

Mary had married a carpenter. He had been apprenticed by his father. Now he was nineteen and had his business. It wasn't much business, even for the Galilean country. He was young and, even though he was earnest, he was untried and was prone to mistakes in his calculations. In all of Judea there was little lumber. Some stately cedars grew in the powdery, alkaline soil, but, other than date palms and fig trees and some fruit orchards, it was a bald, hilly country.

A rich priest might afford a house of wood, but most of the people used the substance only to decorate the interior. The houses were of stone, cut from big deposits eighteen inches under the topsoil. It was soft when first exposed to air, and could be cut with a wooden saw into cubes. These were staggered in courses to make a wall. Windows were small and placed high on each wall, so that, daily, squares of sunlight walked slowly across each earthen floor. Mary's house, like the average, was small and set against a hill in Nazareth. At the front, there was a stone doorsill. Over it hung a cloth curtain. To enter, the curtain was pushed aside.

The interior consisted of two rooms. The front one was Joseph's shop. In it were the workbench, the saws, the auger, the awl, and hammers. There were clean-smelling boards and blond curls of shavings on the floor. In the back room was an earthen oven to the left, three feet wide, six feet long, and two feet high. The cooking was done in the stone-lined interior. The family slept on the earthen top of the oven. On chilly nights, the heat seeped through to warm the sleepers. To the right of the room was a table. There were no chairs because only rich Jews sat to eat, and they had learned this from traveling Greeks. Next to the table was a wooden tether for the ass. He was a member of the family, a most important member because he did the carrying of the raw lumber and the finished products, and he was also the sole means of transportation.

This was the winter solstice of the year 3700. The gaiety of the Feast of Hanukkah had ended as Joseph and his wife left Nazareth. They had come down from Nazareth through Naim and on down into the valley of the Jordan. It was hot along the valley floor, but the Jews of the upland country seldom risked travel by the direct route through Samaria and Sychar, where the people at the village wells were unfriendly and argumentative.

Each night, when the sun was gone and the road obscure, Joseph led the ass a little way off from the river, away from the road and into a clearing where there was very little brush and few insects, and then he tied the ass, tilted the goatskin until an earthen jar was full of water, and sat. There was not much to talk about. Their minds were troubled with momentous events far beyond their scope of thought; far beyond the rationalization of two single peasants of the family of David. On the few occasions when they discussed it, both Mary and Joseph became overwhelmed and shy. They lapsed into silences and Joseph would mend the conversational rip with a question about Mary's family.

Mary was big with the baby, and awkward, but she managed to fetch the food and the bread from the pouch on the near side of the donkey and to set it down as neatly and as appetizingly as possible. There was no meat. Even at home, they never had meat more than once a week. Mostly, it was lamb, chopped into cubes and roasted and then set on a plate beside charoseth and other herbs and fruits.

They slept in the open, saving what little money they had for the day of the baby. Sometimes, when there was no moon, Joseph set the lamp on the ground and Mary removed her veil and brushed her long, dark hair which hung to her waist.

In the morning, with the sun still behind the Mountains of Moab, Joseph arose, adjusted his tunic, and fed the animal. He worked quietly, whispering to the jackass, setting the folded blanket behind the withers, adjusting and balancing the goatskin and the food bag, before awakening his wife.

On the evening of the fourth day, they were at Jericho, a few miles above the Salt Sea and within glance of Mt. Nebo to the east. Joseph wanted to stay at an inn, where they could pay for space on the floor, but Mary begged him not to do it. "This is not an important day," she said. He knew what she meant.

"One does not see a great place like Jericho often," he said softly. "It will be just as well if we eat at an inn and, as you say, sleep in the fields." He looked away. "I was thinking of you."

In the morning, Joseph led Mary and the ass into the wilderness, and it was twenty miles to Bethany and, from there, three to the heart of Jerusalem. A man with a clubfoot could walk it, leading an animal and a woman, before sundown. The wilderness is a barren place in the mountains, where nothing of consequence grows and the tiny peaks look alike, ocher and white and chalky, a place where bandits await ornate conveyances and the sun smites the walker until the sweat inches down his legs and softens the straps of his sandals.

Joseph stopped at the top of the rise. "Jerusalem," he said, pointing. Mary looked. The wonderment of what she saw caused her nausea to fade. The eyes lost the glazed look. She had heard her father describe this place when she was a little girl. A glance told her that the poor man did not know how to make anyone see Jerusalem. Joseph opened his mouth to speak, but what his eyes saw made his mind drunk and paralyzed his tongue.

It was a thing to see. The late sun was ahead, across the hill behind Jerusalem. The city was a white jewel pronged by the great stone wall around it. Joseph pulled the ass to the side of the road because the pilgrims behind him were shouting. Without turning from the scene, he moved back along the flank of the ass until he touched Mary's hand. "Jerusalem," he said again. He said it as though it was an earthly anteroom to paradise, as indeed it was.

The sun would be gone in ten minutes and there was much to see, because he could not stay in Jerusalem. His destination, Bethlehem, was still five miles to the south, but he did not mind the night walk if he could stop a moment and drink in all of this and remember it when he was old as sharply as though he were still standing on the side of the Mount of Olives, directly above a little olive press called Gethsemane.

His eyes, and Mary's too, moved in little, darting glances, and they longed to exclaim to each other, but there were no words. This was where God lived.

Below was the Valley of Cedron, with the full, little river running cold below the east wall of the temple. Gray-blue smoke hung still in the sky over the temple proper. These were the last sacrifices of the day, the final baby lambs on the altar.

The Porch of Solomon faced them, the marble walk and Corinthian columns gleaming like teeth in a seven-hundred-foot mouth. Down the side of the great temple was the snowy, stone wall, hung with a cluster of gold grapes four stories high. In the valley, the Golden Gate and the Fountain Gate slowly regurgitated the last of the temple pilgrims for the day. From their height, Mary and Joseph could look across the enclosed city and see Herod's palace on the far side, a little south of the place called Golgotha.

"Darkness is upon us," said Mary. She had a feeling of foreboding. She wanted to proceed to Bethlehem for no reason other than that she was trembling and the baby was unusually quiet. Joseph led the ass westward into the valley and across the little wooden bridge over the Cedron and beneath the great wall of the city and then by the Valley of Hinnom and on up into the hills between Jerusalem and Bethlehem.

It was soon night and moonless. Joseph trod slowly, stumbling on stones underfoot and wondering how much of a man he would be if brigands sprang out of the dark. There was little traffic on the road; a few transients who lived near Jerusalem hurried by, trying to reach home without spending an extra night under the stars.

Something happened suddenly to Mary and she knew in a moment that this would be the night of the baby. She asked Joseph to stop and he became alarmed and asked if she was unquiet. "No," she said. "I feel no pain, but we must find an inn. The baby—with God's help—will be born tonight."

Joseph was frightened. He knew nothing of these things.

The thinking Mary did about the events leading to this night were a kaleidoscope of happy and mysterious and supernatural things calculated to unnerve the most serene young lady in the world. To have a first baby is, in itself, a towering, wordless joy, a living proof of the most common miracle, a sad tenderness to constrict the heart and mist the eyes. To give birth to a first-born who is God and the Son of God and the Second Person of the Holy Trinity is, at age fifteen or any greater age, a greater responsibility than any woman ever bore, an enormity of weight which could be maintained only by one too young to appreciate it to its fullest.

Mary was born and raised in Nazareth, the child of an average family. She played on the streets, as the other children did, and she was subject to the average parental discipline. Joseph knew her, even though he was four years older. All houses in Nazareth were in the same neighborhood because it was a small town. The people were knit closely in their daily lives, and the women met in the morning at the village well.

When Mary reached her thirteenth birthday, it was permissible to ask for her in marriage. The proper form was followed. Joseph asked his parents first if he could marry Mary. He was seventeen, an apprentice carpenter in the neighborhood and more than a year away from having his own shop. It was assumed that a serious-minded, young Jew of seventeen was a responsible adult.

Joseph's parents discussed the matter of marriage and, in time, paid a formal call on Mary's parents. They engaged in formal discussion. It was necessary, as part of the little ceremonial, to talk of a dowry, but Mary's people had none. Their economic status was no better, no worse, than Joseph's. As long as the man of the house remained in good health, they would not starve.

When the two mothers and two fathers were agreed, the formal betrothal took place. It had the finality of marriage. Once the marriage contract was negotiated, even though the marriage ceremony had not occurred, the bridegroom-to-be could not be rid of his betrothed except through divorce. The formal betrothal, in Judea, also entitled the couple to lawful sexual relations, even though each of the parties was still living at home with the parents. However, in the country of Galilee and south, the people had renounced the privilege, and purity was maintained through the final marriage vows.

Still, if Joseph died between betrothal and marriage, Mary would have been his legal widow. If, in the same period, another man had knowledge of her, Mary would have been punished as an adulteress. The waiting time was spent, according to custom, in shopping for a small home and furniture. The wedding ceremony was almost anticlimactic. A big part of the ceremony was the solemn welcome of the bridegroom to his bride at the door of his new home.

Throughout the engagement, Mary, of course, lived with her parents and accepted the daily chores set out for her. At a time midway between engagement and formal marriage, Mary was alone one day and was visited by the angel Gabriel. She was alarmed, to be sure, but not as frightened as she would have been had she not heard stories of such visits by the elders.

Gabriel stood before her and saw a dark, modest child of fourteen. "Greetings, child of grace," he said. "The Lord is your helper. You are blessed beyond all women." Mary did not like the sound of the last sentence. Her hands began to shake. Why should she, a little country girl, be blessed beyond all women? Did it mean that she was about to die? Was she being taken, perhaps, to a far-off place, never again to see her mother and father and—and —Joseph?

Gabriel's voice softened. "Do not tremble, Mary," he said. "You have found favor in the eyes of God. Behold: you are to be a mother and to bear a son, and to call Him Jesus. He will be great: 'Son of the Most High' will be His title, and the Lord God will give Him the throne of his father, David. He will be king over the house of Jacob forever, and to His Kingship there will be no end."

The words did not mollify Mary. Vaguely, she understood that she was to be the mother of a King of kings, but who might this be and how could it occur when she was not even married?

"How will this be," she said shyly, "since I am a virgin?"

It was Gabriel's turn to become specific. He stood in soft radiance in the room and explained. "The Holy Spirit will come upon you, and the power of the Most High will overshadow you. For this reason the child to be born will be acclaimed 'Holy' and 'Son of God.'" She now understood the words, but they added to her bewilderment. What the angel was saying, she reasoned, was something for which the Jews had been waiting for centuries: A messiah, a savior, God come to earth as He had promised long ago. Mary shook her head. Not to her. Not to her.

Gabriel sensed that the child needed more proof. "Note, moreover," he said, "your relative Elisabeth, in her old age, has also conceived a son and is now in her sixth month—she who was called 'the barren.' Nothing indeed is impossible with God."

Her eyes lowered to the earthen floor, and her head inclined too. She comprehended. She also understood that the angel had told her about her cousin Elisabeth, whom she had not seen in some time, so that the fruitfulness of her kinswoman would be the earthly seal of proof to the heavenly words. She, a young virgin, was to be blessed by the Holy Spirit and she would bear a male child who would be God. It was an enormous honor, but she had been taught to accept and obey the will of God from the first moments of early understanding.

"Regard me as the humble servant of the Lord," she murmured. "May all that you have said be fulfilled in me."

The angel stood before her in silence, fading slowly from her vision bit by bit until all that was visible was the wall. Exultation came and it was transmuted to anguish. It was not a dream. Or was it? Could one dream, standing wide awake in one's house?

No, it was not a dream. She knew that it could not be, because she could not have devised the words that Gabriel used. Now, for a moment, she had trouble remembering them. She wrung her hands and prayed for recollection. Full recollection. She had to know every word and, more important, to understand every word. She prayed and thought and prayed and, little by little, the words and phrases returned until, like a familiar litany, she could recite them without hesitation.

Surely, she thought, Joseph would know. He was her intended

husband. The angel would have to tell Joseph. If he didn't, then what would Joseph think when she became great with child and he knew that the baby was not his? Oh yes, the angel would surely tell Joseph.

Within a few days, Mary asked, as casually as possible, for permission to visit her cousin Elisabeth. Her mother thought of it as a touching sign of devotion and sent her off with a family traveling south to Judea. The young virgin said nothing to anyone about her secret; some of the time she seemed to her friends to be lost in a reverie.

Elisabeth was gray and wrinkled and had spent many years in the balcony of the synagogue asking God for a child. Her husband, Zachary, was a priest, a small-town teacher who had once been selected by the great priests of Jerusalem to be the one to enter the Holy of Holies. He felt sorrier for his Elisabeth and, unknown to her, he had prayed again and again for a child.

Sometime before the visit of Mary, the angel Gabriel had appeared before the old man and told him that God had answered his prayers. Elisabeth would give birth to a son in June, and she must call him John. Someday in the distant future, he would be called the Baptist, and he would go ahead of the Messiah, preaching and baptizing as he went. The angel told Zachary more. Much more.

Elisabeth was standing in the doorway as Mary came up the walk. It was as though she had expected the visit. Elisabeth felt her baby move within her and, in raising her hand in greeting, suddenly burst into tears: "Blessed are you," she said, "beyond all women. And blessed is the fruit of your womb."

Mary stopped, partway to the door. Her mouth hung open. She could not speak. Elisabeth knew! Elisabeth knew the secret! Elisabeth wiped her eyes and tried to smile. "How privileged am I," she said, "to have the mother of my Lord come to visit me. Hear me now: as the sound of your greeting fell upon my ears, the babe in my womb leaped for joy! Happy is she who believed that what was told her on behalf of the Lord would be fulfilled."

The last sentence was a quasi-warning for the young girl to erase all doubt from her mind and become reconciled to the greatest duty of all ages. Mary had not doubted. She had believed the words, but she could not convince herself that she was the one, of all the women on earth, selected to bear the Baby. Now she was convinced. She no longer tried to divorce her person from the prophecy. She had told no one of the secret, and her cousin Elisabeth not only knew about it, but was pregnant exactly as the angel had said she would be.

When Mary returned home, she saw her husband-to-be. She decided, from his attitude, that he knew nothing of the great secret. She would not marry him without telling something of it.

"I'm going to have a baby," she said. The shock to Joseph was beyond measure. Throughout the courtship, his intended bride had worn an aura of innocence; he was painfully conscious of her lack of knowledge. She had gone away three months ago, and now she returned to say that she was pregnant.

It is impossible to read the depths of sorrow in both hearts. He looked at her tenderly and she offered no word of explanation. She looked away from him and wished that she might tell everything. The baby was going to need a foster father—who better than the man she loved, the gentle and pious and patient Joseph?

On the tip of her tongue, Mary had the greatest secret of all history. She could not unlock her tongue. Joseph went away from her to think. Of the two, he was the more pitiable. He loved this girl with all his heart, and he had visions of a long and fruitful life with her. Now, he felt, she had betrayed him and he could not understand the betrayal, nor even force himself to believe that it was true.

Joseph kept his awful secret. He could divorce her publicly. If he did this, he would be impelled to tell the elders the reason. In that case, they would ask Mary if she was with child. If she said yes, Joseph would have to swear that he was "without knowledge of her." The priests would adjudge her to be an adulteress. There was only one penalty for this crime: stoning.

Joseph was being put to a test. He did not want Mary to die. He loved her. He could, under the law, pay money to put her away, to have her sent to some remote place. There, she could have her baby and remain. A third possibility would be for Joseph to swallow his pride, proceed with the wedding, and hope that there would not be too much comment in the town over a six months' baby.

He was dwelling upon the possibilities one night in bed. Suddenly, the carpenter made up his mind. He would put Mary away privately. It would break his heart and he knew that he could not love anyone else, but it would be just and, at the same time, merciful.

Within a few moments after the decision was reached, relaxation came to Joseph, and he slept. In sleep, he was visited by an angel. The spirit said to him: "Joseph, son of David, do not scruple to take Mary, your wife, into your home. Her conception was wrought by the Holy Spirit. She will bear a Son and you are to name Him Jesus; for He will save His people from their sins."

When Joseph awakened, he remembered the dream. He felt refreshed. He felt happy. The more he dwelt upon the dream, the more clearly he saw the hand of God revealing a great truth to him. It required restraint to go to work, making stalls and tables and wooden hangers for utensils and closets for garments. His impulse was to hurry to Mary's house, crying: "I know!" His patience manifested itself, and he waited until the proper time, after supper, and when she saw his first glance, Mary knew that he knew.

In Rome, Caesar Augustus learned that not all men are honest. He ruled the known world, but the amount of taxes was not commensurate with the number of subjects. He held a council in Rome, and his advisers told Caesar that he could not levy an equitable tax until he had an accurate idea of the populations of the several provinces. Caesar issued an imperial rescript ordering all subjects, in the winter solstice, to return to the cities of their fathers and there be counted. This, of course, would work hardship on millions of people, and, in a two-week period of migration, would upset the economic balance as men left their work to travel to distant cities—but it had to be done. Many of the subject peoples chafed when the law was proclaimed. They said that Caesar was not a just king to do this to them. Even in a small town like Nazareth, which Caesar Augustus would not know by name, the Jews said that it was not fair. Joseph sought the local tax merchant and asked if women in advanced pregnancy could be excused and he was told that no one could be excused.

Joseph and Mary started on the trip south, two young and solemn people with a short and slender jackass who bore the most exalted burden ever to honor an animal. Joseph consoled Mary by reminding her that, if he paced the trip correctly, and they were not halted by heavy rains or sandstorms, she would see Jerusalem at sundown. The final few miles were fatiguing. Joseph stumbled many times in the dark, and, over his shoulder, he asked his wife if she was quiet. When they were two miles from Bethlehem, she said no. She felt discomfort, she said, but it was bearable and she had no complaint. She hoped that they would reach the inn in time. The stretch of road into Bethlehem curved broadly and climbed steadily. To the left the valley was precipitous. Four hundred feet below, the whistle of shepherds could be heard and sometimes, in the deep silences, they could be heard exchanging greetings.

Joseph leaned forward to pull the ass a little faster. He reached the City of David and found, to his dismay, that there were multi-

tudes of people, some sleeping beside the road. He had not realized that there were so many who belonged to the House of
David. His heart sank as he found that Bethlehem consisted of
one main road running north and south and two cross streets. The
inn was to the left, built on a cliff of rocky soil overlooking the
valley. Joseph went directly to the inn, knowing that he would
find room here or he would find it nowhere. He left Mary and the
animal outside and assured his wife that he would make arrangements. She too could see the crowds. Some families were sleeping
outside the inn, against the wall.

Joseph went inside. The floor of the main room was full of
people sleeping in their clothing, with bundles propped under
their heads. The odors of the unwashed and of spiced foods filled
the place. The young man sought the proprietor. With supplica-
tion on his face, he begged for a small, private place for his wife,
who was with child. The owner listened and threw up both hands.
Where? he asked. Where would you go for privacy? His own
family had no room in which to sleep. Every cubit of space had
been rented three days ago, and some of the transients were taking turns sleeping in one space. My wife, said Joseph in a tone this
side of begging, is outside. She will have her first-born in an hour
or two. Can you not please find room? The owner became irritable. Every house, every field in Bethlehem, was filled with people
from all over Judea. Some of the regular caravans between Egypt
and the upland country chose to continue their journeys at night
rather than remain in this overcrowded place. Where then could a
woman have a baby? Nowhere.

The owner's wife heard part of the plea. She called her husband
aside and asked questions. The night was chill, she said. Look at
the men outside the inn, sleeping with their cloaks over their
noses. Why could not the young man take his wife to the cave
below: the cave where the animals were kept? The owner
shrugged. If Joseph wanted privacy, he said, the only place left
was down the side path to the cave where the asses and small
animals were kept. He was welcome to it, if one wanted to bring a
baby into the world in a place like that. Joseph inclined his head.
"I am grateful," he said, "I thank you."

He dragged his feet returning to Mary. He told her the news.
She was not vexed; in fact, she seemed to be relieved. "Take me,"
she said. "The time grows short."

There were paths leading from both sides of the inn down the
side of the cliff. In front, as on the bows of a big ship, there was
an entrance to the cave, which had been carved out a long time
ago. Joseph paused to light his small lamp, then led the donkey

inside. He turned to look at Mary, and in the yellow rays, he saw
that she was in deep fatigue. Joseph apologized. He said that he
was sorry that the Hospice of Chamaan had no room for her, but
she could see the crowds of people. He was ashamed that he had
failed her in this hour. He must confess that he had not been
much of a husband. For a moment, Mary conquered her discomfort. She brought a tender smile to her face. She told her husband
that he had not failed her; he had been good and tender. He hung
his head and listened. Mary looked around at the haltered cattle,
the few lambs, some asses, and a camel. If it is the will of God
that His Son should be born in a place like this, Mary would not
question the wisdom of it.

At the age of fifteen, she would undergo this trial alone, just as,
thirty-four years later, her Son would undergo His trial alone. She
asked Joseph to build a small fire on the path outside and to fetch
some water from the goatskin. Joseph did as she directed. He
found an extra lamp hanging on a stable peg, and he lit this one
and the stable brightened, and the animals watched in glistening-
eyed silence, their breaths making small, gray plumes in the
gloom.

Joseph collected clean straw from the feed boxes, cleaned out a
stall, and arranged the straw as a bed and placed his cloak over it.
Then he looked for wood outside, and found none. He went back
up to the hospice and bought some charcoal from the owner.
When the water was hot, he filled a jar and brought it to Mary
with some cloths. She was standing, hanging onto the wall of the
stall with both hands. Her head was down, and he could not see
her face. In fear, he asked her to name what he could do. She said
to go outside and tend the fire and heat more water and to remain
there until she called him. The animals watched him go, and they
watched impassively as Mary sank on the straw.

The fire outside burned brightly in the southerly breeze and
little trains of ruddy sparks flew off into the dark night. Joseph sat
beside it, heating the water and praying. He begged God for
mercy for his wife.

No one came down from the inn to ask how the young woman
felt. If there was any sound, no one heard except the animals,
some of whom stopped chewing for a moment to watch, others of
whom opened sleepy eyes to see. Time was slow; there was an
infinity of silence; a timeless time when the future of mankind
hung in empty space; when a woman stands in the doorway to
death to bring forth life.

Joseph had run out of prayers and promises. His face was sick,
his eyes listless. He looked up toward the east, and his dark eyes

mirrored a strange thing: three stars, coming over the Mountains of Moab, were fused into one tremendously bright one. His eyes caught the glint of bright, blue light, almost like a tiny moon, and he wondered about it and was still vaguely troubled by it when he heard a tiny, thin wail, a sound so slender that one had to listen again for it to make sure. He wanted to rush inside at once. He got to his feet, but he moved no farther. She would call him. He would wait. Joseph paced up and down, not realizing that men had done this thing for centuries before he was born and would continue it for many centuries after he had gone.

"Joseph." It was a soft call, but he heard it. At once, he picked up the second jar of water and hurried inside. The two lamps still shed a soft glow over the stable, even though it seemed years since they had been lighted. The first thing he noticed was his wife. Mary was sitting tailor-fashion with her back against a manger wall. Her face was clean; her hair had been brushed. There were blue hollows under her eyes. She smiled at her husband and nodded. Then she stood. She beckoned him to come closer. Joseph, mouth agape, followed her to a little manger. It had been cleaned and, where the animals had nipped the edges of the wood, the boards were worn and splintered. In the manger were the broad bolts of white swaddling she had brought on the trip. They were doubled underneath and over the top of the Baby.

Mary smiled at her husband as he bent far over to look. There, beneath the cloth, he saw the tiny, red face of an Infant. This, said Joseph to himself, is the One of whom the angel spoke. He dropped to his knees beside the manger. This was the Messiah.

A Day in the
Life of a Cardinal, 1953

Madison Avenue is a pleasant, subdued street at 10:00 P.M. At this tranquil hour one evening fifteen years ago, Archbishop Francis J. Spellman and Monsignor John J. Casey, then his secretary, were walking together along the avenue when they saw coming toward them a weary fellow priest, struggling under the weight of his luggage. They exchanged greetings. "Where," the stranger asked, "do I find the bus to Kingston?" "It is too late for the bus," the Archbishop said. "Where are you bound?" "I come from the Belgian Congo. Thirty years in that place. I got in New York half an hour ago. I am anxious to get to Kingston. In Kingston, I have relatives." "It is too late for a bus," the Archbishop said. "We will put you up for the night and tomorrow see you on your way."

They helped him with his bags. The priest was pleased. He felt that he was in friendly hands. So he said, "Who is the Archbishop of New York now?" "His name is Spellman," said the Archbishop. "Never heard of him," replied the missionary. The Cardinal glanced at Monsignor Casey and smiled.

His Eminence Francis Cardinal Spellman is now fifteen years older than he was that night, but he still strolls the streets of New York at night, and he administers his residence as though he was running an ecclesiastical motel. He knew better than to say "I am the Archbishop." It would have frightened the stranger. He is not one to "pull rank." For many decades, he has been conscious of his mother's repeated admonition: "Be a good priest. All else is vanity."

His life as a priest was never simple. He was the son of a Whitman, Massachusetts, grocer and, after ordination, came under the despotic thumb of William Cardinal O'Connell of Boston. The old cardinal despised ambitious priests, and, by august fiat, tried to replace their aspirations with his brand of humility. Young Father Spellman was, above all, a patriotic American. He volunteered to serve as a chaplain in World War I, and, as a matter of discipline, the old cardinal ordered him to remain in Boston and work in the dusty archives of the Archdiocese. Spellman, always obedient, did as he was told.

At sixty-four the Cardinal maintains a daily schedule which would fatigue a young athlete. In the Archiepiscopal Residence on Madison Avenue in midtown Manhattan, His Eminence begins his day at seven, and usually ends it at two the following morning. He sleeps only five or six hours daily. It is conceivable that at five past eight a vesting priest might be standing in the sacristy and, looking up, find His Eminence glancing at his watch, almost as if to say to the priest, "The people came for eight o'clock Mass, Father,"—for it is a rigid rule that no one is to be kept waiting—no one's time is to be wasted—whether it be at devotional services or during routine daily appointments or even on telephone calls— and the Cardinal is himself the strictest adherent to this rule.

The Cardinal's Residence is a gray stone building behind St. Patrick's Cathedral at Fiftieth Street and Madison Avenue. It was begun almost a century ago by Archbishop Hughes and finished by Cardinal McCloskey. It once looked spacious among the Madison Avenue mansions, but now it seems squeezed among the skyscrapers and towers around it. The ground-floor windows are ten feet high, draped with antique Irish lace curtains. The marble steps leading up to the two grilled-iron front doors are worn concave in the center by the feet of thousands of visitors.

When Andrew, the doorman, is off duty, a pleasant Irish maid, in blue uniform and white apron, admits visitors. The interior of the house is quiet, cool, and agreeable. The staircase and wall paneling are mahogany. Oil portraits adorn all the walls of the rooms on the ground floor. In the reception hall hangs a large picture of His Holiness Pius XII, who, as Eugenio Cardinal Pacelli, gave his robes to young Spellman when the American was consecrated a bishop. In the two sitting rooms on either side of the main foyer are portraits of Patrick Cardinal Hayes, John Cardinal Farley, Archbishop Hughes, Archbishop Corrigan, Cardinal Mc-Closkey, and Cardinal Spellman; marble busts, pedestaled statuary of the Saints and of the Sacred Heart, comfortable chairs, sofas, marble-topped tables, and other sedate, handsome yet simple furnishings, many of which were there in the days before Archbishop Spellman came to this home.

The dining room is spacious and simply furnished in mahogany. At its large oval table, His Eminence, almost daily, is host to at least eight, and more often fourteen to twenty-eight, guests—Governors, Ambassadors, visitors to and from nearly every country of the globe; Cabinet members; Presidents of countries near and far; Congressmen; military "brass" and simple G.I. Joes; friends from Australia, Italy, China, Spain, Africa, or from the Cardinal's home town of Whitman.

Here, too, no one is kept waiting. Midday dinner at one sharp; supper at six thirty, not six thirty-five! To those who serve him, His Eminence is as courteous and considerate as to his guests, and seldom does he leave the dining table without thanking those who have served him. He has the bubbling, cosmopolitan interests of a cub reporter, and this includes people as well as events.

Separated from the dining room by draperies is a parlor where, in deference to His Holiness, a gilt and red-velvet chair stands turned to the wall on which hangs on oil portrait of Pope Pius XII. On appointment days, the old but beautiful chairs in this parlor, as well as in the other two sitting rooms, are occupied by visitors awaiting a few minutes with the Cardinal. His Eminence sees as many as twenty people—Sisters, brothers and priests, military men and diplomats—some seeking assistance or counsel, others merely wishing to pay their respects to His Eminence while in New York City. And this is but one more phase of the varied spiritual and administrative work done by the Cardinal each day.

Two priests live with His Eminence—His Excellency Walter P.

Kellenberg, recently appointed Auxiliary Bishop, and Monsignor Gustav J. Schultheiss, a secretary to the Cardinal. Their quarters are on upper floors, where too is the suite which Archbishop John F. O'Hara of Philadelphia occupied when he was in charge of the Military Ordinariate. The Cardinal's private chapel is on the third floor. On one side of the small, simple, oaken altar is a statue of the Blessed Mother; on the other, St. Joseph and the Christ Child. Here there are six wide, oak benches and *prie-dieux,* and between them in the middle aisle of the chapel is a red velvet chair with its matching *prie-dieu* used by the Cardinal. The lighting effects and natural oak paneling carry out a pattern of rich simplicity. Here, each evening after supper, members of the Cardinal's household, and any guests who may be present, recite the rosary.

On the walls, mantels, desks, and bookshelves of the Cardinal's private office, his sitting room, and his workroom are many pictures and mementos, a few of which are of his mother. Bookcases line one whole side of his office, tables are covered with work in progress. Between the sitting room and his office is the Consultors' Room, although the Archdiocesan consultors now meet across the street in the Administration Building. Here a board-of-directors table, once used at the meetings of consultors discussing Archdiocesan affairs, is now used by the Cardinal for his writing activities. Books of reference, large and small, pads of paper, dozens of pencils and fountain pens, articles to be read and correspondence are spread upon it. It also serves another important purpose. All letters ready for signature are placed on one end so that, no matter how late the hour, His Eminence must pass and see them on his way to his sitting room.

The desk in the Cardinal's office is the same large, flat-topped walnut one used by Cardinal Hayes. On it is the latest-model dictating machine into which he personally dictates answers to his vast correspondence. Also on his desk is a Mercator's globe—since coming to Madison Avenue as New York's Archbishop, the Cardinal has circled the globe several times—and there too is a small silk American flag.

Two telephones control four trunk lines. To the left is a basket with five trays marked: Vicar-General, Chancellors, Secretaries, Catholic Charities, Military Ordinariate; when the Cardinal refers letters to them, he clips a little sheet of yellow memo paper on which he checks a square opposite any of the following departments: Building Commission, Catholic Charities, Chancery Office, Military Ordinariate, Propagation of the Faith, Secretaries, Secretary for Education, Superintendent of Schools, Tribunal. Under that, he can check any of these squares: "For your information,"

"For whatever action you consider appropriate," "Please return to me with your comments or recommendations," "Please note and return." If His Eminence should find correspondence on the chair to the right of his desk, he knows that this is either finished business or is being taken care of by someone else.

Across the hall is the large office assigned to the Cardinal's two secretaries, Monsignor Gustav Schultheiss and Monsignor John Fleming. These are the Cardinal's "Minute Men." The telephone calls which they take run a wide and varied course from clergy of the world, as well as from his own priests in New York, to boyhood friends, statesmen, manufacturers who want to put His Eminence on television, men and women in trouble, wives who think that if the Cardinal had a heart-to-heart talk with their husbands they would behave, the poor, the homeless, the hungry, the sick, the despairing, the complainers, and the bigots. But, if the secretaries know the answer to the question or the solution of the problem, they save the callers' time and the Cardinal's.

Handling telephone calls is only part of the secretaries' work, but a great part. They also arrange the Cardinal's appointments, carry out his requests, meet people in the sitting rooms downstairs to see if they can help when His Eminence is not available, alternate as his traveling companion, and act as his liturgical assistant on ceremonies. The Cardinal has given them only one suggestion: "Help everyone you can and never become impatient!" Besides being secretaries, they must, of course, attend to their own daily devotional exercises.

Though he is sturdy and vital, one of the worries of those constantly working with His Eminence is that he finds no time for recreation. Baseball is still his favorite sport, but he has attended just one baseball game since he became Archbishop of New York. It was a benefit game for a charitable cause. The Cardinal was seated in the front row of a box when the Dodger catcher, Roy Campanella, chased a high foul back toward the stands. Campanella missed. The ball caromed off the Cardinal's knee and bruised it painfully. The players felt bad, but His Eminence said, "Don't worry. The knees of a priest should be the toughest part of him!" Time would deal harder blows to Roy Campanella.

Under his immediate jurisdiction there are 391 parishes; fourteen Catholic residences housing 10,210 business women; a center which, during one year, helped 15,209 homeless men; two centers for the blind; the Society of St. Vincent de Paul, which last year cared for 4,236 families; an organization of "homemakers" who prepare meals and keep homes going while mothers are ill and unable to care for their families; a home for neurotic children;

three agencies for the care of unmarried mothers and their families; fifteen nurseries; fifteen general hospitals, including the well-known St. Vincent's and St. Clare's; five specialized hospitals; three convalescent homes; five orders of nursing Sisters; the Catholic Youth Organization; an employment office; swim schools for children recovering from poliomyelitis; twenty-three camps for children; 2,197 priests; 7,978 nuns; 981 brothers; and thousands of full-time lay workers.

All the invisible strings from all of these agencies lead to one man—Cardinal Spellman. Father John J. Donovan of Family Service said: "You might figure that your little corner of the world is too small for the notice of His Eminence, and then he walks in and hits you with questions that go right to the heart of the matter."

One might think that His Eminence would divide the complexities of his domain into distinct parts and assign them to his Vicars-General and Auxiliary Bishops. He doesn't. He has the services of Their Excellencies Joseph F. Flannelly, Administrator of St. Patrick's Cathedral; Fulton J. Sheen, National Director of the Society for the Propagation of the Faith; the two newly appointed Auxiliary Bishops, Edward V. Dargin and Walter P. Kellenberg; and William R. Arnold and James H. Griffiths, Directors of the Military Ordinariate, which has the responsibility of spiritual jurisdiction over the priests and Catholic personnel in the Armed Forces of the United States. The Cardinal is himself Vicar of these Armed Forces. His Bishops are able and talented churchmen. They help His Eminence with confirmations and they sit with him and the other priests and monsignori who compose the Board of Consultors. They advise, supervise, and administer—but it is Cardinal Spellman alone who must take complete and ultimate responsibility for every department.

Directly across the street from the Cardinal's Residence are the old Whitelaw Reid home and other buildings which the Cardinal purchased and named in honor of his predecessors Archbishop Hughes, Cardinal McCloskey, and Cardinal Farley. Contiguous to these buildings, with its entrance on Fifty-first Street, is another office building, bearing the name of Cardinal Hayes, in which the Military Ordinariate is located. In these buildings facing the courtyard on Madison Avenue are located the Chancery Offices, Institutional Commodity Services, the insurance and other departments where forty priests and two hundred secretaries and stenographers carry on a full, busy business day. If it were not for their Roman collars and black suits or cassocks, these priests would look like bright young executives of any advertising agency in the neighborhood. They average forty years of age—young to be department heads—and they appear to be forever in a hurry. They talk with precision and act with efficiency and their teamwork is so remarkable that, in vacation time, one priest moves into the office of another and carries on the business of the department without the slightest interruption of the office routine.

All the offices in these buildings are under the supervision of Vicars-General Bishop Joseph P. Donahue and Bishop Edward V. Dargin; Bishop Walter P. Kellenberg and Monsignor John J. Maguire, co-Chancellors of the Archdiocese. While their duties are correlative, Bishop Kellenberg is the supervisor of the building program, construction and maintenance of buildings, and Monsignor Maguire's responsibilities concern general administrative matters and the finances of the Archdiocese. The annual reports of the pastors of the 391 parishes come to Monsignor Maguire's office. These reports cover the spiritual welfare of these parishes and their economic status, as well as detailed statistics regarding all parochial activities.

Every building in the Archdiocese, including 106 high schools, 271 elementary schools, and twenty hospitals, is covered by insurance. Head of the insurance department is Monsignor Daniel Donovan. Priests and nuns are also covered by insurance. Everyone and everything in the Archdiocese is properly protected. Every time the Board of Consultors approve a new building, the insurance department is advised. The centering of all insurance business in one department simplifies supervision and reduces costs; and, in this Archdiocese, cutting costs applies not only to insurance premiums but even to the purchase of a loaf of bread, a ton of coal, and every other commodity no matter what its size.

The Institutional Commodity Services is located on the fourth floor of the Chancery Building. This is the department through which procurators buy food, fuel, medicines, and other supplies for use in hospitals and other institutions; because they buy in such huge quantities, some commodities in carload lots, great savings are effected. Shortly after coming to New York, Archbishop Spellman organized this department, which through the years has saved millions of dollars for the Archdiocese. In charge are Reverend John F. McCarthy and Mr. Edward M. Kinney.

Other departments, equally well administered, in the Chancery Office are the Confraternity of Christian Doctrine; the Diocesan Propagation of the Faith (which is in the charge of Bishop Fulton J. Sheen); the Secretary of Education; the Legion of Decency; the Cemetery Office; and the Superintendent of Schools.

In two large buildings at 122-130 East 22nd Street are the headquarters of Catholic Charities, another major activity of the Archdiocese. An idea of the extent of its work can be gained by its successful campaign this year for $2,477,000, which it will spend helping the homeless, the needy, and the sick. In a fifteenth-floor office one finds Monsignor James J. Lynch, P.A., Director of Catholic Charities, and, in offices of both buildings, priests and lay specialists work diligently and sympathetically with all those who seek assistance. Catholic Charities is the gigantic beating heart, the strong helping hand of the parish priest. There is no type of human suffering and misery which does not find its way to these offices.

Until 1950, when His Eminence decided to complete the streamlining of all Archdiocesan activities, Catholic Charities was many institutions located in many different parts of the city. Substantial savings were effected, since the new arrangement is more efficient and eliminates duplication of effort.

Father John J. Donovan, Director of Family Service, spent two hours merely sketching the story of Catholic Charities and its multitudinous operations. Here, a G. I. can get expert counsel on his rights. A family without funds gets quick assistance. A Guardian Service watches over children after they leave orphanages. An emotionally disturbed child can be treated here by psychiatrists. Hardship cases are investigated by teams of men from the St. Vincent de Paul Society, and, if the family has a long history of hardship, a counselor will be appointed to investigate and stay there. If illness strikes a mother, trained housekeepers go out to take care of and feed the family until she recovers. The biggest goal of Catholic Charities is to keep families together. A full-time, paid worker is assigned to the Court of Domestic Relations to work out reconciliations whenever possible.

At Catholic Charities, they also care for expectant, unwed mothers. They also care for the babies and, if adoption is desired, they handle that too. In more than two thirds of the cases where husband and wife are sure that they cannot spend another day with each other and ask Catholic Charities to put the children in a home, the conciliators of Family Service have found a basis upon which the entire family will begin living together again. There is an employment office and a vocational guidance clinic where aptitude tests may be taken under the best psychologists. Unhappily, more than 70 per cent of all job applicants are persons who have tried everywhere else first and now find that few jobs are open for boys under eighteen and widows over fifty-five. One of the best clerical interviewers is a blind man with a Seeing Eye dog.

Non-Catholics as well as Catholics seek aid from Catholic Charities and get it. Some of the biggest private donors to the annual appeal are persons of the Jewish faith who have seen, at first hand, what great dividends in service their contributions to charity receive under the wonder-work of Cardinal Spellman.

Infants in the care of this department get a complete physical checkup once a month. They are weighed, examined, watched, and tested. Father Gallagher, a young enthusiast who works in Child Guidance, never tires of watching babies take the psychological test, when a red ball is placed in the crib. They stare, they wonder, and then they reach. If a big mirror is put at the foot of the crib, the baby reaching for the red ball looks up, in surprise, to see another baby reaching for a red ball. The look of intelligent surprise on the infant's face tickles Father Gallagher. He works with young bullies too, and his knowledge of the psychological side of these boys is so intuitive that, after learning one or two facts about a youngster, he can come pretty close to telling the boy all about himself.

In one of the larger offices there is a remedial reading clinic where, for six weeks in the summer, nuns take a course in how to teach reading to backward children. There are nine psychiatrists on the staff, five psychologists and twenty-five trained social workers.

"You start off here," says Father John Donovan, "with a Master of Arts degree, and then you work yourself up!"

Headquarters of the Catholic Youth Organization are also located here and, making use of the Institutional Commodity Services, they furnish basketball teams with equipment and uniforms cheaper than they can be purchased elsewhere. The moderators plan all CYO activities, dances, games, rallies throughout the Archdiocese, and, now and then, when they meet a child with an emotional problem, they refer him to Child Guidance. If the youth needs a job, he is referred to the Employment Agency.

Reports of these activities and visitations of various organizations occupy the attention of His Eminence from day to day. None is neglected. The Cardinal is acutely aware that Bishop Flannelly, who administers St. Patrick's Cathedral, has learned that, no matter how expenses are pared, it still costs $5,600 per week to keep the Cathedral immaculately clean, hospitable and helpful, providing services and service for the thousands of people who come to visit this famed American shrine, which the Cardinal himself visits every day when he is in the city. His Eminence also presides at ten o'clock Mass in the Cathedral almost every Sunday, usually greeting visitors from other cities or countries after Mass.

Some of the Cardinal's work is seasonal, as, for example, attendance at college commencements. He will not delegate his Bishops to appear for him at these June exercises. During this month, almost daily he distributes diplomas to the graduates and then, even in hot sun or hard rain, he remains quietly listening to the speeches until the exercises are over, when he steps down from the platform and personally greets the parents of the graduates. At the end of June, the Cardinal goes on retreat for a week of prayer and meditation at St. Joseph's Seminary, in Dunwoodie.

On the warm day that I visited the Cardinal, he had not got to sleep until 4:00 A.M. He was up that morning at seven o'clock, with that perennial brightness with which he is blessed. He said Mass at eight in his private chapel, assisted by Monsignor Schultheiss. That morning Germany's Chancellor Adenauer, his daughter, Dr. Lottie Adenauer, and fourteen members of his group occupied the *prie-dieux.*

Chancellor Adenauer and his party remained for breakfast. By nine thirty on this particular morning, the Cardinal had seen his guests to the door and begun at once the series of interviews scheduled for that day. Most of them last fifteen minutes or less. Sometimes, as in the case of an old friend, it may be longer, but that is exceptional. A pastor in the Archdiocese was the first visitor. The next conference was with a businessman from Bogotá Colombia. This conversation was in Spanish. After that, a priest leaving for overseas duty as a chaplain came in to say good-by. The Cardinal, as Vicar of all Catholic Chaplains, likes to talk personally to as many of these priests as possible. Wherever they are going, the chances are that he has already been there and already knows the situation.

A visitor arrived to tell His Eminence about current conditions in Europe. He was followed by an old friend from Rome who remembered the Cardinal when he was working in the Secretariate of State at the Vatican. A pastor from the Bronx came in with a request for permission to plan a new school. After that, the President of the Society of St. Vincent de Paul arrived. A friend from Lima, Peru, followed. A mayor dropped in to say hello. Several visitors came with pleas to help some charitable or philanthropic cause.

Lunch was served at one o'clock. There were a dozen guests. The centerpiece on the table was decorated with bright flowers and flags of the United States, Papal flags, and flags of the countries of the Cardinal's visitors. After luncheon, as is his custom, the Cardinal gave the little vases with the flowers and flags to the guests as souvenirs.

Later, a series of business conferences took place with the Board of Catholic Charities, the Foundling Hospital, and the Trustees of St. Vincent's Hospital. He was back at six o'clock in time for supper.

On this particular evening, no public dinner was scheduled and His Eminence supped with Monsignori Kellenberg and Schultheiss. Even this could not be relaxing, because the Cardinal used the time to discuss matters concerning Archdiocesan affairs. At seven thirty, the three retired, as they do every evening, to the private chapel for recitation of the rosary. The Cardinal then attended a public civic function.

He was back shortly after ten. The streets were quiet. He went out for a walk. Sometimes he invites a priest to go with him. Sometimes he walks alone and meditates. His is a familiar figure and, in these nightly walks, he is stopped by many people of all faiths who merely want to shake his hand and wish him well, and, no matter how hard his day has been, he never acts hurried, never impatient to those who greet him.

When the Cardinal returns from his walk, he finishes his breviary, goes to the old consultors' table and finds there the usual stack of letters that have been typed that day. These he knows must be signed at once. At midnight, although his official day is done, there is still work awaiting him. It is then that he writes his addresses, invocations, articles—and always in longhand.

It is customary to be "kind" to ranking churchmen and statesmen concerning their writings, but it is not necessary in this case. Cardinal Spellman writes well. His works are inspirational and factual. One of his first books, *Action This Day*, was serialized by *Collier's Magazine*, not because the author was an Archbishop, but perhaps in spite of it. He made one stipulation regarding the sale—that all moneys were to be used for the welfare of soldiers and sailors visiting New York City. This is the usual practice—that the rights be given to a charitable institution. Thus far, some of the institutions which have been the beneficiaries of nearly one-half million dollars through the Cardinal's writings are the New York Foundling Home, Rose Hawthorne Home for Incurable Cancer, Little Sisters of the Poor, St. Joseph's Seminary at Dunwoodie, U.S.O. Canteen, the Lighthouse for the Blind, and many others.

The Cardinal's works have appeared serially, in single articles or verse, in *Good Housekeeping Magazine, Life, Look, American Magazine, Collier's, Cosmopolitan, McCall's Magazine* and *Reader's Digest*. His novel, *The Foundling*, has sold nearly four hundred thousand copies. One short book of prose, *The Risen Soldier*, first appeared in a national magazine and was purchased by one of the major Hollywood studios; while his book *What America Means to Me*, now in its second edition, included a poem he wrote to his mother who died in 1935:

To My Mother on My Birthday

Mother, how shall I thank you for my life,
Now that you are safe beyond the veil with God
While I, achieving, yet have unachieved
That final victory: to be at home—
Even as you—with God? Take then this gift,
The heart you gave me, give it back today
Into that other Mother's timeless care
Who loves and keeps us both, you at her Heart,
Me, Servant of her Son and prisoner
Here upon earth, yet Heaven is today
Quite near to me—in memory of you!

It is incredible that, having this talent, the Cardinal finds time to use it. The nature of his average day would make a man trained to heavy labor feel bone-weary and mentally exhaust a high-pressure, dyed-in-the-wool, top business executive; still, long after midnight a passing policeman can see a glimmer of light from an upstairs room, and sometimes the light may still be on at four!

When His Eminence travels, he literally flies. Last year when, for the third time, he went to Korea and spent the Christmas season with America's fighting soldiers in combat, on ships and in hospitals, he actually flew around the world, covering twenty-eight thousand miles in thirty-two days, arriving in Rome on the morning of the Consistory in which His Holiness honored Archbishop McIntyre, of Los Angeles, and twenty-two other prelates with membership in the College of Cardinals.

To give an idea of how His Eminence spends his time when traveling, a recent trip is detailed here. On a Sunday morning, Cardinal Spellman pontificated at the ten o'clock Mass in St. Patrick's Cathedral to open the annual Catholic Charities Drive and shortly afterward left for La Guardia Airport with Monsignor Schultheiss. At six thirty that evening His Eminence was in the Hotel Muehlebach in Kansas City, Missouri. He was guest of honor at a dinner for businessmen who were planning Rockhurst College Day. After dinner and an informal talk, he drove to the home of Bishop Edwin V. O'Hara, where he remained as an overnight guest.

On Monday morning the Cardinal offered Mass in the Chapel

of a community of cloistered nuns. After Mass he said part of his Office, greeted each nun, spoke briefly to them, and drove to the Church of St. Francis Xavier, where he presided at Pontifical Mass. At luncheon, he addressed the clergy on the topic, "The Challenge of the Priesthood Today." He laid the cornerstone of a new faculty building at Rockhurst College, addressed the gathering on "The Meaning of Catholic Education," added a gift of five thousand dollars for the college to his spiritual blessing, and, accompanied by Bishop O'Hara, drove through the diocese, visiting Catholic institutions.

At one hospital, he shook hands with all the Sisters and nurses and visited the patients. At six thirty the Cardinal was back at the Muehlebach as guest of honor at a dinner for six hundred persons. To Monsignor Schultheiss he seemed as fresh and as happy as though he had not been occupied every minute of the whole day. This is no proof that the Cardinal was not tired, but neither those who work with His Eminence nor his friends since American College days have ever heard Cardinal Spellman complain of being weary, overtaxed or overworked!

The Cardinal then delivered another address, this time under the hot glare of television lights. After dinner, he left the dais to go down on the floor and greet the guests.

Early Tuesday morning the Cardinal drove to St. Teresa's College for Women, where he offered Mass for the students and the Sisters. After breakfast, he drove back to Bishop O'Hara's house to meet Archbishop Hunkeler of Kansas City, Kansas. The Cardinal was concerned with news of the floods which had swept the Kansas valleys and deeply interested in the relief program that had been organized, to which he contributed ten thousand dollars. Within an hour, the Cardinal, the Archbishop, and the Bishop had arrived in the stricken area, where they saw the devastation at first hand. His Eminence then drove to St. Mary's College, at Xavier, Kansas, where he addressed the faculty, student body, and the novices.

At noon the Cardinal drove to the Kansas City airport and took off at twelve twenty for New Orleans. He arrived at five o'clock and was immediately taken to a studio for a television program. Later he was interviewed on radio and made a tape recording for a future broadcast. He discussed the consecration of Bishop Bowers at which he was to officiate the following morning. Bishop Bowers is the first Negro to be consecrated a bishop in the United States. His See is now at Accra, Africa.

At dinner, the Cardinal was the guest of Archbishop Rummel of New Orleans. Late in the evening, they drove seventy-five miles to

Bay St. Louis, where the ceremony of consecration was to take place. They stayed overnight at the Seminary of St. Augustine, where the Bishop-elect had studied and had been ordained to the priesthood. The next morning His Eminence led a motorcade to Our Lady of the Gulf Church, where the three-hour ceremony took place.

At the end of the ceremony, the Cardinal was guest speaker at a luncheon for the clergy; his topic was the great work that Bishop Bowers could and would do in Africa. He then presented the new Bishop with a check for five thousand dollars for his mission work. At four thirty, accompanied by Bishop Gerow and Monsignor Schultheiss, the Cardinal drove to Gulfport, where the people lined the streets to greet him. From there he drove to Biloxi, where he had been invited to visit the new school of Notre Dame. At the exercises, His Eminence was introduced to Mrs. David Powell and her six children. He had met her husband, a member of the Air Force, in Korea at Christmas. Since then, David Powell had been killed.

The Cardinal, wishing to perpetuate the memory of this airman, gave a check for two thousand dollars to Monsignor McConnell, Administrator of Notre Dame School, asking that the interest be used in perpetuity as a prize for an annual David Powell essay, the subject to be "What America Means to Me."

At six o'clock the Cardinal was at Keesler Air Base in Mississippi, where he was guest of honor at a dinner tendered by all the officers at the base. After dinner, he attended a mission service for the airmen in the post auditorium. The Cardinal addressed the congregation, celebrated Benediction of the Most Blessed Sacrament, shook hands with a thousand soldiers and near midnight was back in the Seminary of St. Augustine.

Next morning at five forty-five the Cardinal offered Mass for the seminarians and at seven was on his way to the airport in New Orleans. At nine o'clock with Monsignor Schultheiss, he was homeward bound. At two fifty he was in New York. On arrival at his residence he was met by the home secretary, Monsignor Fleming, who presented the Cardinal with matters of urgent importance concerning which His Eminence took immediate action! And that evening he attended a public function. That was an average trip, just as the single day of activity which the writer selected was an average day.

The writer, in personal conversation with His Eminence, looked for signs of wear but found none. The Cardinal is buoyant, almost boyish in his enthusiasms and his energy. He seems to have time for everyone and everything.

Cities

A city is a thing which can be seen and heard and touched. If it is far enough away, travel writers will depict it as quaint or awe-inspiring, or perhaps hot and full of flies and misery. If it is close, the political writers stake a claim to it, and write about its crimes and motivations and ruling clique. There is a middle ground, a ground in which one can draw a dispassionate portrait of a community, one which neither panders nor indicts.

This is a collection of such impressions.

And yet, the opinion of the writer creeps into his work. For example, if you were to ask for quick impressions of cities, I might say: Berlin: A cancerous patient who hasn't been told; Tokyo: Philadelphia on Monday morning; Miami:Mecca in neon; Washington: Termites in marble; Hong Kong: Fuse on a firecracker; Jerusalem: Tense schizophrenic; San Francisco: "Mirror, mirror on the wall . . ."; Toledo: The nice boy next door ten years later; New York: Broken two-man saw; Paris: Prostitute writing her memoirs; Copenhagen: Bicycles and fish; Rome: A cross on a bare bosom; Vienna: Flirtation over whipped cream; Chicago: Revolving door; Dublin: Intelligent poverty.

Some of these cities, spelled out in detail, follow. I have traveled much, but I am always more impressed with cities than with nations. Someday, I hope to return to all of them—the good and the bad.

Island in the Red Sea

Berlin, Germany. The sun came out. Nobody believed it. There had been no summer. The streets glistened with rain. Saplings grew awkwardly from the bombed-out walls of the Eden Hotel. It was Sunday and the deep chimes in church spires tolled as the city rang God's front doorbell. The people hoped someone would answer.

They are in the eye of the hurricane of World War III. They do not see it or hear it. They look confident and serene in the morning sun. War will not come, they say. "You'll see." Their fathers said this in July 1939, and their gradfathers said it in July 1914. It will not come. Each time, it came and each time Germany was beaten to her knees.

The city is flooded with warm sunlight. It is a big city—east and west—and stretches from Lichtenrade to Schoenerlinde, from Staaken to Mahlsdorf, twenty miles in each direction. The District of Columbia could be dropped inside it; so could Paris. Like its women, Berlin is big hipped and deep chested, and, like women everywhere, a complex of mysterious contradictions. It is yesterday and tomorrow, fatalistic and prayerful, courageous and fearful, ancient and modernistic, intelligent and also dull.

The city is flat on the Prussian plain. The only sizable hill is Trummerberg. It is composed of all the unuseable debris from the bombing of Berlin. The hill stands 250 feet high and 1000 feet wide. In it are billions of bits of brick encrusted with the blood of those who died. The people are making two ski slides down its sides. It is impossible to be sentimental about a people so sardonic. They will slide down their own dried blood. Still, they think of themselves as sentimentalists. About three and a half million of them live in an amalgamation of twelve towns along the Spree and the Havel. They worship strength. Today, they look helplessly to the West to save them, but, if it doesn't, they will genuflect to a Russian tank.

He who shouts the loudest, demands the most, and gives the least wins the neurotic heart of Germany. The morning sun cast identical shadows from two Russian soldiers guarding the Russian War Memorial on the Tiergarten. A third shadow approached. It was a blonde German girl. One Russian soldier spoke limping

German: "You will put out the cigarette," he said. "This is a place of worship." She did not turn away. She ground the cigarette under her heel, just as they had ground her under theirs.

The city lies 110 miles inside the Russian lines. It is alone, a roundish island far inside Soviet-occupied territory. Berlin is in East Germany and its 3,250,000 people are trapped. Their isolation is palatable, temporarily, only because there is a four-power administration of its affairs: American, British, French and Russian. In 1948, the Russians walked out of the quadripartite group and never returned. They stick to the East Zone, and permit the others to rebuild Berlin West. In the field of power politics, the city is a small thing, but it is now a big thorn to both sides.

The Western Alliance wants reunification of all of Germany. It has been divided long enough, they feel, and no peace treaty can be negotiated with part of Germany. The forces of the East—Russia and the satellites—want all of Berlin because all of it is in their territory. It is as though one world power had all of the United States from the Mississippi westward; another had the eastern United States, but the western group held a part of Pittsburgh.

The situation is insufferable. Berlin is a rip in the Iron Curtain. It is a peephole through which the United States speaks to oppressed peoples through RIAS—Radio in the American Sector. In sixteen years, the United States and Britain and France have permitted the West Berliners to grow rich and opulent; the Russians have permitted the East Berliners to starve slowly in their bombed buildings.

West Berlin is a glittering showcase. The Soviet Union is tired of having *their* Germans look at it, visit it, and envy it. Both sides of the city are laced with spies. The Russians have fifteen thousand agents working in West Berlin and the Federal Republic of Germany on a part-time or full-time basis. The U.S. Army has about seventy-five hundred agents working East Berlin and East Germany. A local injustice, or a change in the weather, in any part of East Germany is aired on Radio RIAS in the evening. The West Berlin government has several hundred spies of its own; the East German government of goateed Walter Ulbricht has thirty-five thousand Communists in West Berlin. Each month, the U.S. Army captures two hundred spies. None of it reaches the newspapers. One pleasant man in West Berlin runs a private spy agency. He works both sides of the street. Now he is afraid. He moves frequently and changes his name. He cannot make up his mind which side wants to kill him.

In the hotels and offices, all political conversation pauses when a maid walks in. No one talks politics in public except to tell jokes. The people of Berlin can make jokes about anything, even their own deaths. Up the street from the Berlin Hilton is the Kaiser Wilhelm Memorial Church. The top half of the steeple is blasted off. Berlin West has decided to let it remain this way, and build a new church around the steeple. Berliners refer to it as the Unfilled Molar.

About fourteen years ago, the Russians sealed Berlin off, permitting only air traffic. The air lift is history. It kept Berlin West alive. So, in front of Tempelhof Airport, Berlin built a three-pronged memorial of concrete to the British, French and American pilots who flew in two million tons of food and coal. The Berliners call it The Huner Rake.

Russia will find it difficult to blockade Berlin West now. Governing Mayor Willy Brandt and his people have built big warehouses all over the city, and have remodeled some of Adolf Hitler's bomb bunkers into warehouses. In them are scores of millions of pounds of butter and eggs and beef and pork, all frozen, and all moved out and sold for replacements every four months. They have mountains of coal and deep tanks of gasoline and bins of flour and powdered milk in many places.

The Havel River is pumped, and sweet water is stored in lakes around the city. Berlin West can remain alive and well fed for nine months without rationing. With another air lift, it can go on indefinitely. It is a big thing, keeping 2,100,000 persons alive and healthy. The East German government is having trouble keeping 1,150,000 people in that condition with no restrictions.

West Berlin is as complacent as a kept woman with two beaus. It cannot fight for itself because it has been disarmed, so it sits and watches the last two first-class powers fight for it. In a free vote, Berlin East and Berlin West would ask to be reunited with The German Federal Republic, but there will be no free vote. Russian fingers are at Berlin's throat.

It was a warm day with the sun out, and the sailboats at Wannsee moved proudly and slowly across the lake. At the zoo on Budapest Strasse, a band played old tunes. When the war started in 1939, there were two thousand animals there. Only ninety-one survived.

The young people stroll the Kurfürstendamm, hand in hand, as they always have, looking in the shopwindows and whispering. The windows are laden with every type of merchandise from toothbrushes to television sets, from tacks to trucks. Want to buy a car? A Paris gown? A pair of custom-made shoes from Rome? A piano? Luggage? Radios? Name it. It is on the Kudamm in a window. If a TV set is priced at 560 marks, divide the figure by four and you have it in dollars.

Down near the Brandenburg Gate, where the world ends, engaged couples shop for apartments in the Hansa District. These are the most modern apartments in the world and they sit where older buildings were demolished in the thousand-plane raids of 1944 and 1945. Sixty percent of Berlin was totally destroyed and almost all of the debris is cleared from the western sector, although, here and there, a big building thrusts four walls and no roof to the sky.

In Hansa, some of the apartments are eight stories high and stand on concrete V's. On the Altonauer Strasse, a two-room apartment with kitchen and bath, and a recessed porch with a big plaque in peach or pink or yellow costs 160 West marks a month ($40.00). It is an ironic city indeed. Eighty churches are without pastors. There are sixty-two hundred Jews in Berlin, but no rabbi. At night, the St. Pauli club is jammed with young couples who stare at the amateurish strip-teasers and laugh at the dirty jokes of the mistress of ceremonies. They drink wine and eat pastries smothered in whipped cream.

No one stands at the Bahnhof Zoologischer Garten to lift a hat to a refugee. When the border was wide open, most of them got off at that station, bewildered, frightened, hopeful. They carried babies and blankets and, tucked somewhere in mother's clothing, the jewelry and cash of the family. No one from West Berlin stands on the elevated railroad station to say "Bitte schön" and show them to the refugee center.

Altogether, over two million East Germans have made it to freedom. Last year, the figure was one hundred fifty thousand. On one weekend in August, the figure was thirty-two hundred. A man from Amerika Haus, across the street from the S-Bahn station, counted one refugee every thirty-five seconds. Most of these people boarded the train at the Friederichstrasse station in East Berlin, paid sixty pfennigs, and held their breath for two miles and three stops before reaching the Zoo station.

There is Neo-Nazism here. It isn't big. The government of Konrad Adenauer dismisses it as the product of young hooligans who should be spanked. Some of the young hooligans have gray hair. It is a resurgence of the Nazism of Munich in 1924. The Berlin West government stomps hard on Nazis. Recently the police arrested fifty of them who were in a park practicing a pagan ritual of sun worship. On another occasion, they caught a boy painting a swastika on an apartment wall. He was arrested, tried, found guilty and sentenced to eighteen months in prison, all within twenty-four hours.

Anti-Semitism is a soft whisper these days. No one embraces it openly. There used to be five hundred eighty thousand Jews in Germany. Now there are thirty thousand—mostly new families. They make a very small target for a political cannon. Still, when a Berliner trusts you, he will admit that he doesn't like Jews and he wishes that Hitler had found an easier way than extermination camps to dispossess them. Hate is a soft whisper these days. But then, so is war.

There is the smell of old dust in Berlin East.* It is like opening a door to an unused attic. All the accoutrements of civilization are here: buildings, people, streets, lights, but there is an intuitive sensation that everyone has left except the old and those too young to run. The people prefer to remain indoors. As far as the eye could see on Unter den Linden, there were four automobiles and two buses. Two old ladies in kerchiefs hobbled across the Alexanderplatz as fast as their stiff knees would take them. The blasted, burned-out, bombed buildings stand exactly as they did the morning Adolf Hitler sat on a sofa in his bunker with Eva Braun and stuck a revolver in his mouth and pulled the trigger.

At night, a few lights go on. Not many. The streets are ghostly, even in moonlight. There are no stray dogs or cats because there is nothing to give them. Berlin East is part of a socialist state. The state is East Germany. The Communists have had sixteen years in which to sweep the dust out of Berlin East and fashion it into the happy glittering showcase that is Berlin West. However, the failure of socialism is that it strengthens the state and weakens the people. Berlin East is a gray miserere. From the sky, this part of the city looks like a ragged half-moon with its blunt nose against the Brandenburg Gate. It stretches from Eichwalde in the south to Schoenerlinde in the north; from Mitte to Mahlsdorf. In there are 1,150,000 persons, trusties in the world's biggest prison. They can move about freely, so long as they remain in Berlin East or East Germany. They can use their wages to buy something, if they can find something to buy. They can talk about anything they choose, so long as they do not criticize the government. They can even quit a job and take another, so long as they have a good excuse.

The socialist state has channeled the energies of East Germany into heavy industry. There is nothing left—or rather, little left—

---

* Written in East Berlin three days before the building of the wall.

for building homes, furniture, making clothes or toys. There are some big new apartments on Stalinallee. They are fat dumplings, eight and ten stories high, and they house thousands of families. They are not pretty, but they are solid, except for the veneer on the façade, which is falling off in chunks.

The Café Warsaw is in this block. It caters to middle-class families and party functionaries. It is on the ground floor, and has an outdoor cafe, which was not in use the afternoon I went behind the Iron Curtain. There are some faded rugs on a terrazzo floor, some round tables from which white table cloths hang, small lumps of sugar which are served only with coffee, and some heavy drapes to keep the afternoon sun off the front tables. The vodka is Russian and mild and served in small stem glasses. The bread is white and cut thickly. The jam is heavy and oversweet. The coffee has chicory in it. A few families sat at dinner—the midday meal is the big one—and the men wore heavy suits with broad trouser legs. The young women, as in West Berlin, are inordinately pretty, but are addicted to Woody Woodpecker coiffures and cotton prints. All females wear "sensible" shoes with Cuban heels. They use good rayon stockings rather than nylon.

The newsstands sell a lot of German beatnik magazines. These feature rock and roll, stories about jazz musicians, and teen-agers. It is barely possible that these magazines represent the cohesive force which holds the Halb Starke together as a group, East and West. The Halb Starke—the phrase means Half Strong—are Berlin's beatniks. They affect black leather jackets, blue jeans, seek girls in long loose sweaters and skin-tight pants, and mock their parents as failures.

There were no East German soldiers on the streets. There are one hundred ninety thousand of them and one hundred twenty thousand reservists, all trained by the Russians for a single function: to take West Berlin. The Soviet Union has given them fifteen hundred tanks and two thousand pieces of artillery. The Russians expect to use this force to maintain internal order. In free translation, this means to quell riots, crush rebellions, and besiege Berlin West.

Today, they dam the flood of border runners. In July and early August, those who were dissatisfied with socialism to the point of leaving furniture, bank deposits, automobiles and, in many cases, businesses, amounted to fifteen hundred each day. They were not all native to Berlin East. Most of them came from East Germany in general, that is, the five provinces and parts of two others now administered by the Russians. Since the war, 2,280,000 Germans have left Mitteldeutschland. In 1945, there were 18,500,000 Germans living there. Today, even with new babies, the population is no greater than 17,000,000.

Although the People's Army did not appear in Berlin East in the last days before the gate was shut, there were plenty of Russian soldiers on leave. They averaged about five feet seven inches in height, dressed in brown field uniforms with a red star on the cap and wore wrinkled black boots. They moved around the city on the backs of army trucks, gawking and talking and pointing and, when the truck stopped, getting off to take pictures with miniature cameras. They seemed good humored. Some of them saw me making a movie of them, so they swung quickly and made a picture of me. This seemed to be a joke. They laughed, and pointed.

The only Germans in authority around Berlin East are the Volkes Polizei, called Vopo. They wear green uniforms, and they incur nothing but unappreciative muttering from the Germans because the Vopo work for the Russians. Their orders are obeyed sullenly and, whenever their green uniform is seen on a street, groups of Germans stop talking, and begin to stare.

They are not seen at all in the Russian Memorial Cemetery. They stay away, because Russian soldiers are emotional about their dead, and they recall, at a glance, that the Vopo are Germans. Over eight thousand Russians are buried in this cemetery, all of them lost in the fight for Berlin. It seems especially pitiful, to the Soviets, that men who fought the fascists across the broad face of Russia had to die here in the final days of victory. The cemetery is, by any standard, beautiful. The green grassy plots are neatly edged and stretch over hill and down dale.

Near the entrance is a huge granite statue of Mother Russia on one knee. The hair has one braid around the head. The eyes are wide open in deepest sorrow, staring at the grass before her feet. The left hand is against the breast. On the far side of the hill, a thirty-foot statue of a Russian soldier stands in black marble, holding a baby in his arms. This is the peaceful touch. Beneath his feet is a big granite rotunda, and under that, twenty-four dead Russian soldiers were buried standing at attention. The Vopo keep out of this cemetery. It is full of Russian soldiers every day and they walk among the graves, whispering.

Over on the Wilhelmstrasse is all that is left of Adolf Hitler's Third Reich. It was devised to last a thousand years, and it died at the age of twelve. Off the edge of the street is Hermann Goering's Air Ministry. Today, it is the seat of the East German government. From this point up to the Brandenburg Tor, almost everything is gone except slices of wall. Hitler's Reichschancellery was bombed to ruins. Then the Russians came in and finished it with artillery. Afterward, they tore it down, column by column and stone by stone. Then they buried the whole thing, including the back bunker where Hitler died, under fresh earth. When I was there, it was a field of lavender clover.

Across the street was Herr Goebbel's Reichsministry for Propaganda. It was a big square-front building, recessed from the Wilhelmstrasse. It was damaged, but not destroyed. Today it houses the offices of the National Front of Democratic Germany— the coalition of socialist parties under communism.

Where there is an intact building, one sometimes sees wheel chairs. In them are Germans who lost both legs in the war. Their women put them in the chairs and push them out into the sun. They say nothing. They do nothing. There are many of them.

Berlin East is harsh to the eyes and deadening to the heart, but, as part of the German People's Republic, it is prosperous. Last year, this satellite produced almost twenty billion dollars in heavy machinery, tools, optical works and textiles. There are more jobs than workers, and the manpower shortage has hurt the Ulbricht government. That is one reason why the gate to Berlin West had to be slammed shut. A West German mark is worth twenty-five cents. On the open market, a man can get four East German marks for one West German. Thus, an Ostmark is worth only six and a quarter cents, although the East German authorities insist that the rate of exchange is one mark for one.

East Germany was the Soviet Union's first big attempt to satellize a "Western" nation. They have been trying for sixteen years and, unless all the East Germans I spoke to are lying, the Russians have failed. The lack of success is not in economics, nor in welfare. It is in politics, which is the foundation stone of socialism.

The seventeen million Germans in the East still want to be reunited with the fifty-three million Germans in the West. The Germans of Berlin East want to be as one with their brothers across the border. Dr. Adenauer's Federal Republic warms and fosters this aspiration in all Germans, while Walter Ulbricht, in the East, tries to kill it with the novacaine of party discipline.

Ulbricht is sixty-eight. He wears a pale goatee and he has rheumy eyes. He is First Secretary of the Communist Party in East Germany and is Chairman of the Council of State. As a younger man, he studied in Moscow and, before the war, became more of a Muscovite than a German. He, and a small band of German Communists, followed the victorious Soviet Army across Poland and into Germany. They were ready to take over the country before the dust of war had settled. This man has made several errors. One is that he proclaimed himself to be an ardent Stalinist. When Stalin died, ranking German Communists turned away from him and some demanded his head. He has promised Nikita Khrushchev that he can make a socialist state out of East Germany, and in this he has lost. He inherited all the good elements of the pre-Hitler Communist Party in Germany, and he has been unable to work with them.

Ulbricht selected Gerhardt Eisler, who fled the United States on the Polish liner *Batory* years ago, as his propaganda chief, and the publicity has been weak and divisive. The Soviet Presidium gave Ulbricht as much latitude in running East Germany as they gave Gomulka in administering Poland—which is to say, considerable —and they couple his failure with his decisions, some of which led to the uprising of 1953, when East Germans fought Russian tanks with rocks. In that case, he signed a decree ordering higher work quotas. If he had not been remote from the people—aloof and brooding in the Pankow section of East Berlin—he would have known their temper in advance. Ulbricht didn't know. The Russians had to come in and suppress the rebellion. On December 11, 1957, he signed a decree forbidding East Germans from moving about in East German territory. This weakened the socialist party because many farmers and factory workers who were ready to embrace communism as "not so bad" could not tolerate going to the local Rathaus and getting written permission to go to another town on a visit.

There is a shortage of food. No one knows why. The farms produce as much as ever, if not more, Distribution of food is amateurish. One area will be inundated with carloads of onions one week, and will not see an onion again all season. This also applies to flour, rice and meat.

The government puts huge signs on building walls advertising "Big Sales in the Shops," but they do not tell what is on sale, nor which shops. Prices are low, to conform to the low earnings of workers, but savings are high in East Germany because the people find so little on which to spend money. They cannot buy heavy industry. They want lipstick and radios and gowns and nylon hose.

One more blunder is attributable to Herr Ulbricht. In 1954, he persuaded Moscow to let him put up Communist candidates in a West Berlin election. West Berlin, he maintained, was ripe for communism. Ulbricht had thirty-five thousand card-carrying Communists in Berlin, and still has them. This was his cadre of propagandists. Moscow watched. That year, 1,535,893 West Germans voted after an exciting campaign. The SED, which is

Ulbricht's party, polled 41,375 votes, or 2.7 per cent. The defeat was so resounding that the SED has not participated in any West Berlin campaign since. This makes the men in the Kremlin wonder if, in Ulbricht, they have backed the wrong German steed.

These failures make the West Berliners overconfident. They tell me that there will be no war, that the East Germans will not dare to cross the border. Perhaps they are right. They assert that if the East Germans were permitted to vote secretly, for or against the Ulbricht government, that the Communists wouldn't get 10 per cent of the ballots.

I don't believe it. If, after sixteen years of labor, the Communist Party polled less than thirty-five per cent, then Ulbricht and his government are doomed.

The room looks bare and chilly. There are some chairs, a sofa, a coffee table with schnapps and beer, and the Brestrich family. This is the last time they will be together for a while because the border is closed. There is no way for Grandma and Grandpa to come here from Berlin East.

The Brestriches are Germany. Germany is the Brestrich family. Whatever it is that is wrong with this nation, and right with it, is in this room. It is in a five-story walk-up off the Sassneitstrasse in the West Zone. At each landing there is a naked yellow bulb. At the top is Rudi's flat. It is four rooms, a kitchen and bath. Two of the rooms are unfurnished.

Rudi pours. He is tall, partly bald, and speaks German with a lisp. He is thirty-eight and works at the Berlin Hilton. He has been married two years to Ingrid. She is twenty-six and is a registered nurse. Her hair is dark red and she has fast eyes and a slow tongue. Their son, Hans, sleeps in his crib. He is one. His hair is pale yellow and his cheeks are fat and pink.

Grandpa is fifty-nine. He is short and fat. He has no neck and his head glistens in the weak light. His speech is rapid and guttural and he sits partly off the sofa to make room for Grandma. She is Minna. She is older than Grandpa and her face has been squeezed into a long, narrow shape. In her time, she had one baby: Rudi.

The lives of these people spread from Kaiser Wilhelm, across the Weimar Republic to Adolf Hitler, through two world wars, to communism. It is impossible to understand Germany today without understanding the people. The Brestriches are average Germans—economically, emotionally, politically. Here is their testimony about themselves:

Grandpa: "I was a cadet in 1917. Potsdam. One day I saw the

Kaiser himself on a horse. It was a birthday, you know? There was
a parade. Ach, that was a real Germany. We had horses and good
food and parades and music. They used to sing a song: 'The Kaiser
is a Nice Man.'

"Then came bad times. I was studying to be a butcher here in
the city. The war was over. There was nothing to eat and we had
inflation. The people papered their walls with millions of
Deutsche marks." He looks down at the red rug and shakes his
head and grips his fingers together. "Terrible. By 1928, maybe
1929, we had good times again." He looks toward Grandma for
support. "People dressed well. They enjoyed themselves. Everybody had a good time. It was the time of the Weimar Republic.
As a butcher, I earned twenty-five marks with free lodging and
food."

He looks sheepishly at Grandma. She laughs before he speaks.
"When we let one loose in those days, we let one loose, I tell you.
A big glass of beer was twenty pfennigs, cognac thirty pfennigs.
Who can pay it in these crazy days? A beer, cheapest, is forty-five
pfennigs; cognac eighty pfennigs. For ten marks, you could live
like a knight."

Grandma smiles with smug pride. "Black stockings we wore
then. Black shoes and big hats. Always, dark clothes with white
trim. My husband and I had a horse and carriage."

"Then Hitler," says Grandpa. "In all the years here in Berlin, I
never saw him. But I liked him. I voted for him. Ach, the politics.
In January 1933, the government asked me to be an officer in the
Brown Shirts. I was in sympathy with them, but Herr Goebbels
had too big a snout. He talked and he exaggerated. I liked Hitler,
but not Goebbels. Hitler created order. He ended unemployment.
I thought over the Brown Shirts. Then I didn't take the job. I
preferred the Stahlhelm. You remember the steel helmets? I liked
them. Anyway, came the big German Army and the music and
marching. You know what brings misery to Germany? Marching
and music. Every time it comes, we Germans go. The uniforms
look so nice and the music makes the blood to rise. When Hitler
threw the French out, and took Czechoslovakia and the Polish
corridor, he should have quit. There he should stop."

Grandpa brings the little glass of cognac to his lips, and takes a
tiny sip. "I saved money. Momma and me, we bought a beerstube.
We sold beer, schnapps, wurst and cold buffet. We still have it.
Same place. Across the border. Wrong side. It cost nine thousand
marks. I had some. The rest I pumped from God and the bank.
Money came easy. It is a workers' district near a big open market.
The women used to come in ugly dresses to sell vegetables and

before they would go home to the old man, they would stop in my place for a few. In July 1941, I was called up for service, and Momma had to run the beerstube. No longer did I believe in Adolf Hitler, but he didn't care. He didn't need my vote. Suddenly, when they decide to fight Russia, they need me. They made me—me!—a top sergeant in the Luftwaffe. Night fighters."

Grandma chuckles. Her beads shake on her throat. "I used to send him schnapps and wurst. He gave them to the officers and they transferred him to the kitchen." She too shakes her head. "I believed in Hitler. One man, one government, one God. One could be arrested for saying anything against him. Just like now with the Russians."

Grandpa: "Did I kill in that war? I killed and killed. All over the verdammt kitchen, cockroaches. And Momma, we also knew that Jews were being killed. Gassed. People who say now they did not know are lying. On every street, someone was missing."

Grandma closes her eyes. "A good seamstress I had. They made her put on a yellow star. Then my husband became afraid to let her come in the store. The customers might talk. So she came to see me in the back. My dear Selma, I gave her eggs and flour at Christmas 1943. 'Selma, you make for your dear mother a good cake.' Selma told me, 'You will lose the war. People who persecute Jews lose the war.' I told her to come back. I never saw her again. We all cried. Selma was good. I saw S.S. men on our street chase old ladies up ladders on trucks. They had whips."

Grandpa, patting his wife's hand to keep her quiet: "In the whole war, I sat in the kitchen. The Kaiser's army was much better. Even today, on the Kaiser's birthday, I raise a drink. When the war was near over, I was taken prisoner by the British. I rode into camp fashionably, in a car. Now I have lived to live under the Communists. Lousy and every day lousier."

Grandma, having her final say: "He was away. I was here. In the last three months, we in Berlin did not get to bed. In the morning, alarms. In the afternoon, alarms. All night, alarms. I used to push all the pots off the fire, turn the lights out, and run into the cellar. Always we said, 'This time we will be killed.' By this time I had slave labor in the beerstube. Estonians, they were. No more Germans. On the radio, there was a gong forty-five minutes before the air raids. Bong bong. When the bombs landed, we were afraid to lean against the cellar wall. It was shaking in."

Ingrid has said nothing. She plays the demure daughter-in-law. Now she points to Rudi, sitting beside her. "At ten," she says, "he

was a Hitler Youth." Rudi feigns great surprise with his hands and
eyes. "A man comes one day and says you are a Hitler Youth. I
didn't ask for anything. They sent a uniform—twenty-five marks.
This was 1933. I carried the banner. Later, they sent me to East
Germany. It was a good life. We had a music band, you know?
Also we had political classes. We were taught the Führer principle. Later, I came home and studied cooking at the Adlon Hotel.
This was a great place, this was. Very first-class. I was learning
fast because I wanted to have my own hotel someday."

Rudi is swift and nervous. He uses the eyes, the hands and the
lips extravagantly. "In 1940, I was in the Arbeitdienst, the work
battalions. This is nothing for me. I admired Hitler. I admit it. But
with the shovel in Danzig, no. I gave the leader some cigarettes
and he took me out of the hole and told me to hold a plumb line.
This was better. In April 1941, three months before my father,
Hitler called me up to the army. I was in the Wehrmacht as an
antitank man. You know what this is? They put you in a foxhole
and give you a small mine. When the enemy tank comes, you
jump out, stick the mine against the tank, and run. This is also
nothing for me. I was in the Central Ukraine in May 1943. Fighting Russians. We were falling back. I ran up to a Russian tank. I
stuck the mine. A grenade went off behind my hip. You know
what is the basin?" He stands, points to hips and pelvis. "The
whole basin falls down. I am eighty per cent injured. Eight
months in the hospital then you know what? They send me back
to the front."

Ingrid smoothes her skirt. "I must go to the clinic. Before I go, I
will tell you that I met Rudi at a dance. My people live near
Stettin in the Russian sector. I was alone here. Rudi showed me
pictures of the hotel where he worked. I said to my girl friend, in
the ladies' room: 'With this one, one could do something.' I am
happy now. We got married so fast we did not know each other.
It is strange. We live in the West Zone. My parents live under the
Russians. So do his. My father made a visit and when he got
home, a friend said, 'How is Berlin?' My father said, 'In Berlin, the
dogs eat better than the rich do here.' His friend told the police.
My father is in prison now, for nine months. This is a world only
for realists. I have a baby inside, and one more at Christmas. The
children will get much love so they can face tomorrow.

"It will probably be a Communist world. Democracy has lived
out its existence. If it is not a Communist world, there will be a
nuclear war. No other way can communism be stopped. If you do
not like communism, I say to you: At the clinic, we nurses cannot

get a window fixed to keep out the cold. But the doctors, they can go to Switzerland three times a year. You'll see. It will be a world of communism."

It is 11 P.M. Ingrid kisses her mother-in-law good night, and shakes hands with Grandpa. Suddenly, the third generation of Germans speaks his mind. He sits up in his crib and cries, "Momma." Someday, he may die uttering the same word.

The master race has its own ghetto. It is a clump of apartment buildings at Marienfelde. They are gray and clean and the grass between the buildings is patchy from the play of so many children. The walls are bleak and the halls are of chill stone. The refugees from East Germany have been coming through here for fourteen years. This is Freedom Allee. The traffic has been stopped. Or, almost so. The East German People's Army guards the approaches around Brandenburg Gate. Farther away, the Vopo (Polizei) walk the border twenty-four hours a day. On the western side of Berlin West, the Russian soldiers do it themselves. They roam the woods in pairs along the bank of the Griebnitz-See, which is really a broad canal leading into the Havel River.

I sat under the trees on the right side of the canal. There is a little picnic place with bright tables on the bank. The waitresses are stout and fast and they can swing six steins of foaming beer without spilling it. Small brown ducks swam in the canal. The Russians, with their slung rifles, patrolled the other bank. When they see a swimmer, they use the one word in German they know: "Halt!" If the swimmer doesn't, they unsling the rifles and fire at will.

The ducks swam across, against the tide. The water was shallow and they looked for small fish. In turn, they turned their beaks down, then their necks, then their bodies, until only the final feathers were showing. The Russian soldiers looked at them. They didn't say "Halt!" The ducks came up and looked, and swam back to the beer garden.

It is like this all around Berlin. The ring is tight and it chafes both sides. The East Berliners are, if possible, angrier than their brethren across the border. It is like splitting on orange and telling each half that it is a different fruit. No one believes it, even the Communists in the East. Germans are Germans and they are united in spirit everywhere in Deutschland. Their politics differ. They argue about Adenauer and Ulbricht and pinochle, but they are brothers.

When East Germany closed the border, it had lost 2,665,114 persons to Berlin West. The West had lost three hundred thousand who, in the same twelve-year span, decided to try communism. Many of these were disappointed because the government of East Germany does not practice communism, nor does it pretend to. It has the same type of government as the Soviet Union— despotic socialism.

It was a cloudy cheerless afternoon when I got to Marienfelde. It is in the southern part of Berlin West, below Tempelhof Airport. The streets and curved walks were jammed with people. They were jumping the border at the rate of fifteen hundred a day because the word was out that Walter Ulbricht, head of the East German government, had returned from Warsaw with a mandate to be harsh with unhappy citizens.

A stocky little blond boy, about two, stood in one place drawing in a long breath and shouting "Fath-errrr!" at the crowd. He did not cry. After a moment, he would draw in another long breath and the call went out again. His father was probably in one of the buildings filling out an application sheet for admission to the German Federal Republic.

Most of the couples were young. They had babies in arms, in carriages, deposited on blankets on the grass, even under trees. None looked happy. The move to this place is always made under pressure. They tired of socialism long ago, but kept postponing the jump. No one likes to make big sacrifices and all of these have left their furniture behind, their family ties, their cars, jobs, even the money they had in the bank, because to withdraw it is to create suspicion.

There were many ways of getting across the border. The favorite, however, was the S-Bahn. The little family, if it came from the deeper parts of East Germany, had to make its way to Berlin East first. There was no other way to squeeze through. This was the tiny top of the tube of toothpaste. Even families who lived to the west of Berlin had to travel circuitously to the east, then into Berlin East, and then await an opportunity to get across.

S-Bahn is an elevated railroad. A block and a half from Brandenburg Gate is a station called Friederichstrasse. Here, the family usually split. The mother and the babies and a folding pram loaded with blankets and small treasures went up to the ticket agent first. Usually, a Vopo stood by. Sometimes he asked questions. Sometimes he made arrests. Sometimes he said nothing. The mother always had a ready story. She was taking the children to see their grandmother. She was going to see a doctor. She was visiting friends and had to be back in the evening to make her husband's supper. The husband stood by, watching. If she was permitted to get on the train, he bought a ticket and got aboard the next car. Sometimes, guards held the train while soldiers went through it, asking for papers and destinations. Many were yanked back onto the platform, weeping. When the doors shut, those still on the train held their breaths. No one spoke.

The train moved out slowly, swung around the burned-out Reichstag Building, and stopped at Lehrter. This is on the West side, but not far enough. The refugees remained aboard through a stop at Bellevue, then a swing around the Tiergarten to the Zoo station at Kurfürstendamm. There they got off. No one had to tell them about Marienfelde. They knew. Sometimes, they stopped at Amerika Haus across the street for information and assistance. Most of them wanted to see something of the new flashy Berlin West before reporting to the refugee center. Even an alien such as I could spot them pointing to food and merchandise in shopwindows and talking excitedly.

When they arrived at Marienfelde, the sorting began. Bachelors went to one building. Single women went to another. Married couples went to a third. Children were placed in a nursery. Everyone had to be examined by a physician before taking the next step.

The first screening of the refugees is done by the occupying authorities: American, British, French. There are two reasons for this: one is to apprehend spies sent across as refugees. The other is to gather intelligence. The second screening is German. This is conducted by three commissioners, representing the Berlin West government and the Federal Republic.

In a ground-floor apartment, I was taken to a room to watch this. Three battered desks were jammed together. Some light came through two closed windows. A gray-haired man sat with his back toward me. To his left and right, two men sat—one stout, with thick spectacles; one a thin gray face with a huge pompadour of dark red hair.

All refugees, if admitted, are flown out of Berlin West by commercial airliner to Hamburg, Hannover or Frankfurt. They are met by officials, given shelter and food, and a job according to their skills.

The next case had not yet been summoned. The applicant was different. He already had a job in Berlin West if the commissioners would permit him and his family to stay. The old commissioner read the application aloud. Then he read the report of the refugee intelligence agent in the town where the applicant lived; he followed this by reading the newest intelligence about the applicant's town, so that the commissioners would be able to ask questions.

This was happening in several other rooms in Marienfelde. The screening goes on, even now that the border is closed. The old commissioner went out into the hall and called the applicant. He was twenty-four, blond, with longish hair, an open sport shirt, had two gold teeth; he was invited to sit at the foot of the three desks, facing the old one. He murmured "Danke schön" and sat. He looked nervous. His smiles met no echoes. The gray one read the application to the others. The other commissioners listened, rolling ball-point pens back and forth under their fingers. The tone was whispering, almost confessional in character.

When it was done, the old commissioner did the questioning. It was fast and incisive. Most of the time, he waited only for part of a reply, then went on to the next question. And the next. You are a truck driver? We note you also drove an ambulance. For whom? When? What were you paid? Who is the party leader in your town? What does he look like? You have a wife? Four children? How old? Why did you select now to come here? Are you in trouble in your town? Have you ever done anything to show that you are anticommunist? What, for example? What radio station do you listen to? Can you tell us something broadcast on that station within the past few days?

When the questioning stopped, the old commissioner asked the applicant to speak. He fidgeted. He shrugged. He smiled. The East German government, he said, is always saying that there is a labor shortage. Still they will not give a man a decent job. He came to Berlin East and crossed the border every day. He managed to get a job in Berlin West. It paid enough to keep his wife and children. Last week, he was ordered to report to the burgomeister at Brieseleng. His wife worried. She wept. The truck driver went to the rathaus and there was more than the mayor waiting. Two men from the secret police sat with him. "When will you give up your job in Berlin West?" one of them said. "When you give me another job," he had replied. This was the wrong answer. The wrong tone. One policeman made notes. One talked. "You have a job," he said. "A nice new one. It is in a factory and you get three hundred twenty marks per month, plus eighty for overtime."

Four hundred marks would come to twenty-six dollars a month. He told the mayor he would like to talk about it to his wife. He went home and told her that it was time to leave. She was afraid. She would be leaving her mother and all her family. The authorities might do something to them. The young husband said that each family had to seek its own salvation.

The wife cried. She said that she was going to leave the little one—aged two—with her mother. Then, if anything happened to the rest of the family at the border, at least one would be left alive. He reminded her that the East government had put through an order to force school children to work one day a week at the factory. Soon, their oldest would be eligible. The children walked an hour and a half to the factory, worked all day, and walked an hour and a half home. It was too much. She stopped crying.

They went to the Friederichstrasse S-Bahn station. The young man waited until he saw the Vopo. Then he made an elaborate show of kissing his wife and babies good-by, gave the children a few pfennigs to spend on sweets, and said not to worry about the baby—he would watch her. Please, he said, do not stay at Grandma's too late. It worked. The little family got on the train. The police did not question them. The truck driver watched, and, when the train left, he almost broke down. Later, he got on another train, and met his family at the Zoo station. That was his story.

The old commissioner asked him a few more questions about Brieseleng. The answers were correct. The old commissioner stood, and bowed formally. "Welcome," he said, "to Berlin, a free city. We are glad that you and your family have come."

The young man looked bewildered. He half stood, half sat. He waited for the other commissioners to ask questions. There were none. He began to smile. The gold teeth showed. Suddenly, he fled with the news.

Arigato Gozaimasu, Jonesy-San

Tokyo is schizophrenic. It is the dullest city by day, and the wildest by night. The eight million Japanese who live in Tokyo do not hate to see that evening sun go down. They just can't wait. No one begins to fly properly until the little band of dusty concord grape dies over the Sea of Japan. That's when the samisens swing. That's when five hundred night clubs, three thousand coffee shops, and ten thousand bars begin to glow.

My first view of this gigantic city was discouraging. It was 10 A.M. and I stood yawning and scratching myself at a high window in the Imperial Hotel. No foreigner should be permitted to see Tokyo in the morning. It looks like a runaway Hoboken. The sky is gray; the buildings are all gray; the air of the city is gray-blue with smoke; the people look like things in the bottom of a teacup; there is a low humming noise, the soft incessant roar of the city which, once heard, never leaves the consciousness.

It is flat dead-out dull, like the second reading of the treasurer's report of the Parent-Teachers Association. Bathing, shaving and leaving the hotel for a closer look is an act of courage. The taxis are driven by kamikaze pilots who flunked. All private automobiles are driven by dreamers. It is easier to get killed in Tokyo than any city in the world, and it is the only metropolis in the world which posts a lethal scorecard at intersections so that, if the dead total—let us say—499, a Japanese motorist has the option of changing it to a nice round number at once.

My wife is much younger, and more agreeable, than I. She is the kind who reads all the guidebooks and likes to address people in their native language. This has led to some surprised looks, and eyebrows arched to the hairline, if any.

Festooned with cameras, we left the hotel to meet my friend, Mr. David Jones of Pan-American World Airways. He had volunteered to steer us to a few clipjoints and I was so eager to be taken that I signed several Travelers Cheques in advance. We met him at his office, and, when I introduced Kelly to this dark, intense man, she bowed too low and too long and said, "Arigato Gozaimasu, Jonesy-San" which is a polite thank you. For what, I don't know.

Jones is accustomed to Americans, having been one in San Francisco in his youth. He looked at me and said, "What's with her?" and I explained that she was in her Japanese mood. This mollified him, because Jonesy-San is in a perpetual Japanese mood. He has been in Tokyo six years and speaks Japanese, and even sings Japanese songs and reads the Japanese national mind. His wife calls him Lafcadio.

He has a built-in patience when listening to tourists. The ridiculous questions they will ask fall into this pattern: "Where can I buy a Japanese Happi Coat?" "Are cameras cheaper here than anywhere else?" "Do the Japanese secretly hate us because we dropped the bomb?" "How do I translate yen into dollars if there are three hundred and sixty of them to one of ours?" "Are the Mikkimoto pearls real?" "The Japanese women aren't on a bearing of ninety degrees, are they?"

Jonesy-San took us on a drive to see the emperor's palace in downtown Tokyo. One can't see the palace. Peaceable persons are permitted to drive up to the palace moat. The far side is lined with huge gray stones forming a wall. The moat is stocked with

royal carp. Beyond the wall, a few pines and cypresses lift their
branches high enough to look over at the people.

We spent time watching the Japanese people. They are caught
in a monumental tailoring problem. They want to face West, but
think East. The men wear fedoras and clothing which could come
from Robert Hall stores. The women—especially young ones—
wear wool skirts, flat-heeled shoes, blouses and short coiffures.
Except for the almond eyes and saffron complexions, they could
be natives of Olathe, Kansas.

The older women wear elaborate flowered kimonos, obis looking like scout knapsacks in the back, and clog sandals. They look
like the Japan of the picture books. That is, until your eyes follow
one along a sidewalk and the kimono turns into a little restaurant
with signs saying "Spaghetti and Meat Balls; Hotta doggu."

Almost all of this is a result of the American occupation of
Japan. A century ago, Admiral Perry opened the ports of Japan to
the world. General MacArthur inflicted democracy on these
people, and Elvis Presley gave them the music and the lyrics.
H.I.H. Hirohito is still the most revered personage among the
3,004 islands of Japan, but he is a constitutional monarch with
proscribed, ceremonial power. The people love him with oriental
inscrutability, but they seldom see him. As the years of bitter tea
add up, he has more and more time for his poetry and his stamp
collection, and he is consulted less and less in matters of politics.

In downtown Tokyo, the sound of pneumatic hammers and the
cry of goggled welders is incessant. Tokyo gets bigger and bigger.
There are more and ever more office buildings. For sixteen years,
the Japanese have been building on the one third of Tokyo which
was blackened by the U.S. Air Force fire raids of March and April
1945.

A superhighway runs from Tokyo down through Kamakura and
the toll-booth collectors have the same scornful look for a ten-
thousand-yen note as their American brethren have for a twenty-
dollar bill. Wages are low, but so are prices. It is ironic that the
two most prosperous nations (based on percentage of economic
expansion) are the defeated ones: Germany and Japan. In the
past six months, I have visited both and they are not only climbing
the economic ladder faster than the others, but are in a benevolent
mood to send CARE packages to the United States, if the need
becomes pressing.

This is not only a tribute to the natural industry of these peo-
ples, it also depicts the penalty of winning a war. Germany and
Japan, as losers, are not allowed to have big armies and navies.
Thus the winners deprived them of the fun of spending forty

billions of dollars each year on armaments, which is what the United States and the Soviet Union are doing. This led to much lower taxes in Japan and Germany, which led to more risk capital, which led to more businesses, greater employment, more national prosperity, more subsidization of merchant ships and railroads and superhighways, bigger and better hospitals, more grants to universities and a general aura of national good health. The losers will still accept a few hundred million apiece from the United States, under the Point Four program or direct foreign aid, but only to keep Uncle Sam from feeling moody about it.

We toured the city with Jonesy-San, and stopped in at St. Ignatius Loyola Church. It was empty and dim, as all churches are in the late afternoon, and what I recall was a sad wooden sign in the center aisle. It was in two languages and it said: "Ladies, watch your handbags."

Davey dropped us off at the Imperial for an hour or two, and went home to dress for a night out. I did not shower, preferring to remain dirty and sullen. For a while, I dozed. Kelly, who was at a make-up table trying to decide who she was going to be that night, dropped a bobby pin and I came up off the bed in a sitting position.

It was dark out. Time to dress. In an hour, Jonesy-San met us in the lobby with his lovely wife. It is a big lobby and, all over it, Japanese families were bowing low to each other. National politeness is always difficult to decipher. In America, the proper response to an introduction is, in many cases, the word "Hi." This is not synonymous with "high," nor is it to be confused with the old-fashioned "How do you do?"

It is "Hi" and is sometimes accompanied by a friendly grin and a half salute from the area of the right temple. The Japanese feel that this lacks respect. So, no matter how many times a group may meet in a given day, they bow low—the lowest bow is accorded to the seniors by the juniors—and give a happy smile in addition to the murmuring of polite words. At one time, there was an additional sucking in of breath, which induced the sound of a hiss. The intent was "May my unworthy breath not soil you," but this was dropped as being a little much, after the introduction of American mouthwashes.

The two faces of Tokyo were sharply defined when we left the hotel. Darkness is benevolent to the people and the landscape. The city glitters with colored neon lights. One sign was a five-story neon hand, with index finger pointed up. On the tip, a real sports car spun slowly. Other signs flashed news in Japanese. Another was a diminishing spiral in white neon edged with lavender. The blending of colors, the size of the signs, the great number of them obliterate the gray tone of daylight industry and rub a flush of rouge on the night sky above the city.

The drenching deluge of soft color also improves the workaday faces of a million people. It brightens the expression; dapples dark eyes with flecks of orange and crimson, heightens the skin tone, causes the kimonos and obis to look like a mass scene in an old kabuki play, and stripes the automobiles and taxicabs with a thousand moving hues, which blend and glow and die.

In joy, the Japanese are childlike with expectancy. They talk happy talk and think happy thoughts and reflect good will to strangers, even when they are bumped in crowds. This is the mood of the Ginza, which is a combination of Broadway, the Strand and Kurfürstendamm as they might be rendered by Otto Preminger. The Ginza is a street in downtown Tokyo, but it is also a district.

Hundreds of years ago, there was a silver foundry on this street. Gin—with a hard G—means silver coins. Za is foundry. The Ginza makes an almost ideal adult Disneyland because here one can find any type of entertainment, from the cultured formal dances and plays of old Japan to the cheapest house of prostitution, where one is called softly by a girl silhouetted in a window.

The American-style night club, with its brassy band, its young vocalists crooning "Mississippi Mud" in Japanese and that old concomitant, Scotch on the rocks, is everywhere. The big motion picture palace, with its elaborate stage presentation in the form of a condensed musical comedy, the young Japanese crooner in long sideburns and fluffed hair and blue slacks and white yachting jacket, is here too.

The geisha house—the true geisha house—serves dinner on a low table while the guests sit tailor fashion on mats, and the girls, made up in floury talcum and black brittle wigs, execute the slow dances to the fluttering of a paper fan and the sorrowful plunk of the samisen—this too can be found in the Ginza. The geishas, practiced only in poise and conversation and tittering jokes and games, pour the *sake*, sit with the guests and play match games, take a piece of cigarette paper and roll it into a diminutive ballet dancer doing an arabesque, then put a drop of water on it and watch in fascination as the tiny ballet dancer moves her arms gracefully and pirouettes.

Jonsey-San took us to a downstairs place first. He said it was a Zen Buddhist den and to please stand in silence in the presence of the nuns. We promised. He led us through a heavy black curtain into a room. There was a blast of bedlam, which sounded like a score of jukeboxes at top volume playing "You Do Something to Me." There were forty tables in neat rows and a score of voluptuous Japanese girls executing, vertically, motions which are associated with the horizontal.

Some Japanese men sat drinking and ogling, and elbowing each other to attract a buddy's attention to one of the wilder "nuns." The girls wore black pony tails which hung to the waist. They also wore skin-tight white toreador pants and blouses with necklines which can only be described as anatomically compelling. The girls served drinks to the customers, cracked jokes, hummed the tunes pulsing on the jukebox, and approached the male customers gyrating with one hand on the pelvis and one behind the neck. These girls do not earn much serving drinks. However, they will entertain the thought of a private exhibition of talent for sums ranging from thirteen dollars American to twenty-eight.

Jonesy-San listened to the jokes in Japanese, laughed uproariously, and translated for us, omitting the old prelude about "this one loses something in translation." The girls are always busy. When they are not working up an after-hours assignment, they embrace each other, giggle, and explore each other in braille. A ruddy American customer, Jack Sullivan, owner of a restaurant in Spring Lake, New Jersey, sat at a front table snapping his fingers and studying the girls with radiant eyes. "Sex Kittones," he said approvingly. Perhaps. But the sex play here was so exaggerated that it was amusing rather than aphrodisiacal. Its target was sex in caricature. When two of the girls flanked the manager of the place, a Japanese about four feet tall, and pressed him to their bosoms, the result was hysterical laughter.

We drove to a restaurant opposite the U.S. Embassy for dinner. This, as Jonesy-San knew, was the opposite side of the Japanese scale of entertainment. It was a quiet place of black and white sliding partitions, a private room, mats on the floor, and a dining room table not much higher than the mats. The proprietress met us at the door to the dining room, crouched on her knees. She bowed low, Jonesy-San bowed. The murmured words of greeting and appreciation were gravely uttered and heard with dignity.

The thinnest, reddest strips of beef were served and the diners clasped them with ohashi (chopsticks) and dipped them in a pot of boiling water three times. This is enough to cook the strips to a warm gray color. There is a great deal of animated conversation and the strips are dipped into one or two of the multitudinous small cups of sauces.

Afterward, the waitress put fresh vegetables into the water which had cooked the strips, and made soup. The meal is as prescribed as a concerto for strings; the eating and the conversation move swiftly as though certain courses had to be punctuated with mass laughter, and others with an oral riposte. Raw fish and seaweed sounds unappetizing to occidental ears, but it is good.

Afterward, all the arigatos were whispered and Jonesy-San, who was now equipped with two eyeballs of *sake*, drove us to a Ginza coffeehouse for dessert. It was a place of three floors, on the first of which was a cashier's desk and, in a glass case, replicas of creamy desserts. The guests selected their sweets, the cashier wrote the order in Japanese, and handed the slip of paper to Jonesy-San.

We walked up two flights to a booth on the third floor. In the front, where a stage might be, was a huge square hole adorned with mirrors. The floor show, we learned, is on an elevator which travels slowly, almost imperceptibly, from floor to floor. There is a band which plays fair American jazz, and three almond-eyed Andrews sisters, who harmonize to Japanese lyrics. The effect is like spinning a Chordettes record backward, by hand. The elevator made three passes at our floor before we left. The young men and ladies in the booths around the floor sat staring at each other solemnly, sometimes pausing to sip coffee or to summon a waitress, but they showed no animation beyond ears attentive to music. We were beginning to tire, but Mr. and Mrs. Jones were beginning to bud.

They urged us on to a stage show, and here again the feeling of East meeting West head on is compelling. The girls link arms and kick in unison like the Rockettes, the pit orchestra comes up on a rising stage, the sets are more elaborate than on the average American stage, but the Japanese leading men give an illusion of an old Elvis Presley or a young Bing Crosby.

From there, we drove to a small neighborhood bar. This one was not for tourists. It was for Japanese who want to sit at a small bar with irregular curves, and listen to three girls with ukuleles sing Japanese folk songs. They had a guitar accompanist, but there was no room for him behind the bar, and he sat, plunking and smiling, against a wall.

The local people drink bir-u out of large bottles and, when they achieve a slight alcoholic edge (which is easy with local brew), they tend to become romantically saddened, and they hum the folk songs with tilting heads and many cracked notes. The girls sang a long ditty about a train to Osaka, a rambling funny train which stopped at every crossing to permit the passengers to disembark and have fun. In one stanza, the train stopped near a seashore, and all the gay passengers got off and went swimming.

In the local bars, there is a happy cameraderie between the performers and the customers. The barflies requested certain numbers, and the girls sang well, taking short rests between numbers. Jonesy-San assured me that the spirit of these places is sentimental, but not sexy. The male customers make no personal approach to the girls, and the performers, for their part, giggle shyly and cover their mouths with their hands when the applause is loud and long.

The lavatory in this particular little bar was coeducational. It was in a small room, behind a curtain. The men's room came first so that the few ladies at the bar who wanted to powder up had to pass through the male section first, with its huge vertical ash trays. This did not disturb the Japanese women.

In truth, the Japanese people dissociate normal bodily functions from sex. In most Asian countries, it is common to walk into a men's room and find a woman attendant holding towels. The Japanese also bathe in a family manner, rising as one in a public tub to bow gravely and nudely to friends who have just arrived.

The little neighborhood bar was voted best of the evening by the Bishops and the Joneses. At some early hour, we left. The Ginza was still festooned with lights and people. Old ladies in darkened corners sold tiny bouquets; cabdrivers opened doors for passengers, and both parties bowed low; families strolled in slow disarray, the men a pace or two in front examining the still photos of nudes in front of the clubs, the women in kimonos and wooden sandals, chatting in low tones and averting their eyes from the direct gaze of strangers.

Here and there, a drunk hesitated in his journey, lurched sideways and exchanged happy greetings with the passing families. The intoxicated ones were mostly young men in late teens or early twenties, and none of them had female companionship. Each one was alone, or with a group of drunken young men. The prostitutes, at this hour, travel in pairs. Some were in Western dress; some in Chinese skirts split almost to the hipline; a few appeared to be demure in brocaded kimonos.

However, even these responded when the drunks stopped to exchange greetings. Sometimes this led to whispered conversations and the men split up to go off with separate girls. It seemed awkward, to watch a tiny Japanese girl link arms with a tall Japanese who could not maintain more than a semblance of equilibrium, and watch her try to keep him in a vertical position as she walked down the dark narrow streets.

We returned to the Imperial Hotel. The lobby was empty except for a bellman in uniform and a cashier who punched an

I.B.M. machine while staring dreamily at an old abacus. We got
our room key and rode the elevator to the eighth floor. It had been
a long night and, in many ways, an edifying one.

"Daylight will be here soon," Mrs. B. said. She yawned into a
pair of empty gloves and lines of weariness showed through the
make-up. I loosened the knot of a tie. "Yes," I said. "In an hour or
two, Tokyo will put on its dull expression—the inscrutable one,
shall we say?"

"Say it," she said, "and be damned to you. I'm tired."

A Home Overlooking Washington

This is a beautiful city. It was always beautiful and I have never
stood within it without catching my breath. Like Pompeii, it is
prettier without people. The snowy buildings, the broad avenues,
the sun-spangled streams and the kelly-green hill are entrancing
by themselves. Add to this black streams of people, thousands of
taxicabs and trucks, the smoke of industry, and you have less.

In this city, I know the places, not people. Always my favorite
spot is the Custis-Lee mansion at the top of Arlington Cemetery.
The house is as it was when Robert E. Lee stood between the
fluted columns before the beginning of the Civil War. The view
was down across the cascading glen-dimpled hill to the smooth
Potomac River. Beyond it he saw the City of Washington and the
Capitol without a dome.

He was a colonel, a good tactician, a hard and fair discipli-
narian. They offered him command of a Union Army and he
thought about it and said no, that his first loyalty was to the Old
Dominion where he lived. It must have been hard for him to say
this because he knew that, in a war, the first territory the North
would take would be his wife's home.

It was a good solid home for a man looking toward retirement.
The beams under the ground floor were whitewashed tree trunks.
In the basement the big iron tubs for washing hung on pegs. The
cooking fireplace was surrounded with black pots. Upstairs there
was gracious living: a dining room with cut-glass chandelier, a
music room, a small west room where a tutor taught the Lee
children and the children of the slaves.

He said no and he took his family away and lost his home. He fought well and honorably and savagely with fewer men and less money than the North, and so their vengeance was spiteful. They not only occupied his mansion; they desecrated it as well. And when the war was done, the North buried its hero dead on the sunny slopes in front of the mansion. Today it is called Arlington Cemetery.

There are other places I visit. And other dreams I dream. I go to Ford's Theatre and I walk across the street to Peterson House where they carried Lincoln to die; the National Cathedral, within the purple shadows of which Woodrow Wilson prayed that he could make brothers of nations; the Smithsonian Institution, where Lindbergh's plane hangs.

There is the Capitol, where Andrew Johnson showed up ill and drunk for Lincoln's second inaugural; Lafayette Park, on the north side where Secretary of State Seward was assaulted by a murderous maniac named Lewis Paine; down the river a place called Mount Vernon, where the rich farmer, George Washington, lived in style with his hunters, his dogs, his wine cellar, until, when he felt the heaviness of time on him, he drew a map and said: "Bury me here and build a little place of brick. Red brick." It is still there and he is still there.

There is the Jefferson Memorial and the Lincoln Memorial, and the Executive Mansion where Tad Lincoln once played on the oak lawns with his goats. Today, it is full of people who are too busy to see it.

Miami

This city is, in a sense, a beautiful woman with an inferiority complex. She has a need to be told, every day, how gorgeous she is and how much she is loved. She shies from the strangers who come to her room, but without them she would die. She preens herself constantly as though, if a palm frond was out of place, she would look dowdy.

I have loved her since 1925. That's a long time for a one-sided affair. She is more breath-taking now than then. Like a willow, she grows more beautiful with age. She's big too, with hips spreading all the way from Snapper Creek to Opa Locka. If one takes in a few of the small towns which should be part of Miami, the population runs close to half a million.

The weather is incomparable. One afternoon I stood in front of the Jordan Marsh store. The temperature was sixty-six and I wore a sport shirt. A woman went by with two little children. They wore heavy sweaters and little snow hats with the side flaps down. Miamians feel that sixty-six is cold. To my way of thinking, it was good swimming weather.

The cost of living here is not high. The fishing is of the finest. The homes, even in the lower middle-income group, are arrayed in bright colors behind palm trees. At Tropical Park, you lose your money in a glass-enclosed, air-conditioned turf club. At the Dania Jai-Alai Fronton, the play is so swift and exciting that you go home forgetting whether you won or lost.

There are things I do not like about Miami, too. A man can love a woman and still spot a crooked seam. The radio stations are among the worst in the country. The disk jockeys are obsessed with making weird sounds and the announcers try to make an ordinary weather report sound as though a Russian missile were on its way. Everything is uttered at the top of the lungs at top speed.

The policemen alienate visitors by watching for out-of-state cars and stopping them. They ask to see your license, and how long you plan to stay in Miami. If you say, "Oh, a couple of months," they tell you that you have to buy Florida plates. They also believe that he who hands out the most summonses is the best policeman.

Take it from the one who comes from a family of policemen, Miami cops scare tourists. I have received no summonses, but my New Jersey plates have caused me to be flagged down three times so far.

There are, it seems, more motels than people here. They stand shoulder to shoulder on the highway and, in spite of the sunny weather all year round, they advertise "Heat." The beach, from Daytona to Key West, is as beautiful as any I've seen on the French and Italian Riviera, but, along Collins Avenue in Miami Beach, the big hotels screen it like shower curtains.

Topographically, the whole state is a bowling alley. It's as flat as a playboy on Sunday morning. When Miami was laid out, around the turn of the century, the founding fathers decided to do it in the form of a cross. There is a northeast section, a southeast, a northwest and a southwest. The streets are numbered.

The city grew eastward in giant strides, so that the northwest and southwest sections appear to have squeezed the other two into Biscayne Bay. Besides, there are arteries like this: Northwest 5th Street, Northwest 5th Avenue; Southwest 5th Street, Avenue, Terrace. Asking a Miamian how to get somewhere is about as reliable as telling time on an automobile clock.

Miami is big and getting bigger. In 1925, I lived on Northeast 38th Terrace. I tried to find it the other day. It's gone. An overpass cuts through it to the airport. In my time, it was near the northern limit of the city. Today it is listed as part of "Downtown Miami."

The newspapers are good enough to rank with any in the land but they too are obsessed with weather. They will publish a photo of a snowflake from any other part of the United States. The idea, of course, is to keep the visitors in Miami. Show them how cold it is back home.

The beautiful lady's feelings of inferiority show the most in this. A million people come to this county because it is beautiful and restful and warm. They will remain here as long as their money holds. Even if the weather back home is mild, they will stay here because Miami and romance are synonyms.

She looks attractive even when she steps out of a tropical shower. . . .

Fort Pierce, Florida

It is 10 P.M. The town is asleep. At the drive-in theater one big eye is open. A squad car moves up Orange Street past the dark stores. No one is on the sidewalk. At Ann's Restaurant a man wipes the crumbs from the counter. The gas station across the street has a light on.

In the drugstore, the woman behind the counter yawns and looks at the wall clock. The big trailer-trucks roll up Route One from Miami to New York. At this point, they have covered 119 miles. They move fast and, when a green light changes to orange, they snort with impatience as they pull down. Fort Pierce is a light.

The county prison has three floors. There are two broken wicker rockers on the porch. No one uses them. No inmate is allowed on the porch. The place is dark and whitewashed and somewhere inside a Negro sings "Come to Me, My Melancholy Baby" and the clear notes feel their way through the bars to the dark freedom outside.

On the third floor rear, Joseph Peel—a judge accused of engineering the killing of a judge—sits on the edge of his bunk, looking out across the street, and beyond to the beautiful Indian River and the winking stars. He is a bright man and he has been able to figure out everything in life except how to get on the other side of this window.

Diagonally across the street is the New Fort Pierce Hotel, which isn't new. It has broad marble flagstones running through a big lobby. A few elderly people sit before the television set. A stout woman fans herself with a newspaper. It is a hot night.

There were lights on, nice colored lights, a little while ago in the lot on the far side. The old men were playing shuffleboard and shouting taunts to each other. The lights are out now. The men are in bed.

A Pan-American billboard shows a beautiful Japanese girl kneeling before a tiny teak table. "Why Not Have Tea In Tokyo Tomorrow?" the sign asks. Well, why not? A big Florida East Coast diesel pours through the city southbound followed by eighty-three freight cars—a drunken swaying boa constrictor with a headlight.

The big man with the brief case—Phillip O'Connell, state attorney—walks around the swimming pool of Quality Court's Southern Aire to rooms occupied by his legal assistants. Mrs. O'Connell calls out, "They have lights on the putting green, Phil." She cannot tempt him from his work, which is the ceaseless fight against malefactors, putting them on the inside of barred windows and keeping them there.

Over at South 29th and Palm Boulevard a car backfires twice and dies in front of the First Freewill Baptist Church and the young man at the wheel dies a little too because he just bought it, and he just bragged about it, and now his girl sits in silence and stares at him. She says, "What now, big shot?" He owes twenty-three more payments, that's what.

There is a scent of jasmine around the courthouse but the Negro woman who mops the floor smells only ammonia. She knows every stone in this floor and has known them for years. On the other side of town, Sally Latham, a writer, sits with two pillows propped behind her in bed. She is composing a poem and sometimes a new line comes swiftly, and sometimes it hides and defies her.

It is ten thirty now, and the street lights stare down at empty macadam and concrete. In the dark, the oranges and grapefruit ripen on the trees and over at Indian Creek golf course, a wild duck sits on a nest of reeds and contemplates a little lake and the freight cars standing on a siding.

Fort Pierce is quiet. In the silence, I can hear an air conditioner
stop....

Madrid

A lovely ciudad, this Madrid. It is beautiful and yet remote, asking love but never giving it, pleading for understanding but never
listening. Madrid is 2,200,000 people. It is tall skyscrapers, an
empty palace, small cars, buzzing motorcycles, tile roofs, millions
of roses, Franco, a pale bedspread of a sky with scattered pillows,
big park trees lighted with green floodlights at night, fireworks,
bullfights and holy days.

It is the biggest city in Spain, and one of the newest. It sits on a
marbleized, sandy plain in the center of the country, like a Moor-
ish mirage. The boulevards are broad, and the plazas are huge
circles built around statues and fountains and formal gardens. A
house without pots of flowers and window boxes is either empty
or occupied by non-Madrilenos.

At one thirty, siesta begins and the shops close, the shutters are
drawn, and all Madrid goes to bed. At four thirty, the shops
reopen until seven thirty, and the city comes to life between 9 P.M.
and 1 A.M. In Spain, every city has an old cathedral, but Madrid is
now building its first one—La Almudena.

The Plaza de Toros is the Yankee Stadium of bullfighting. The
corrida begins at 6 P.M. Seats on the shady side are more expensive than on the sunny side. Three matadors fight a total of six
bulls in two hours and ten minutes. The object of the corrida is
not the kill, but to show man's domination over the animal
world.

More than half the population of Spain does not attend bullfights. When a matador does poorly, the crowd whistles. Someone
always yells derisively: "Mañana sera otro día" (Tomorrow is another day). Another favorite expression is heard from the laborers
who are expected to work too hard: "Lo barato es caro" (The
cheap is expensive). Some men earn eighty cents a day.

Recently, Generalissimo Franco learned that Madrid taxi drivers were paid sixty cents a day, and got a dollar in tips and
commissions. Overnight, he doubled the wage to three twenty.

Ironically, there are wealthy families who can afford to hire servants to take care of their dogs. The goal of the Spanish government is to create a middle class to leaven the sandwich of the very poor and the very rich.

In actuality prices almost match the poor man's wallet. The price of steak for a family of four is a dollar fifty. A chicken costs sixty cents. Rent for two rooms is fifteen dollars a month. The new government apartments in the La Casa de Campo section cost as little as five dollars a month for laborers.

For the American tourist, no capital in Europe matches the bargain of a trip to this city. A room at a good family hotel costs about three dollars a day; a steak dinner at Paco's in Madrid Antigua is a dollar and a quarter. A car, with driver-guide, averages ten dollars a day, and, within the city, or near it, are such sights as El Escorial, the Valley of the Fallen, the Prado, Segovia (where Queen Isabella was crowned in a castle still standing); Alcala de Henares, where Cervantes wrote *Don Quixote* and where St. Ignatius of Loyola decided to found the Jesuit Order; the royal palace; Toledo, Avila, and flamenco dancers.

A house can be bought on the edges of this city for five thousand dollars. A living-in maid gets twenty-five dollars a month. A combination chauffeur and gardener is paid fifty dollars a month. Food, as noted, is extraordinarily cheap and so are services, like gas and electricity, phone, etc.

It is a proud and good place, this city. I have visited it four times and I like it better each time. The people are overladen with courtesy and good manners, down to the humblest ditchdigger. They are aware that for a quarter of a century, they have lived in isolation, apart from Europe, and apart from Africa across the Straits of Gibraltar. Now they are ready to rejoin Western Civilization.

It is 1:30 P.M. Okay, Pedro. Turn down the bedspread. . . .

Las Vegas

The city is a stalk of asparagus in the bottom of a chipped bowl. It is surrounded by a lemon desert inside a rim of chocolate mountains. A century ago, the Paiutes ambushed the tourists in their covered wagons. Today, automation does the same work; nineteen thousand slot machines lie in wait for fourteen and a half million palefaces in air-conditioned Cadillacs.

No one bets on the rising sun in Las Vegas because the ninety thousand natives know it is 8-to-5 that it will come up over Sunrise Mountain every morning. If it doesn't, somebody is tilting the planet. Gambling here is as wide open as a rattan door after a hurricane, but it is also honest, because the operators know they can become rich on a house edge ranging between 7 and 10 per cent.

Betting is Nevada's biggest industry. About three hundred million dollars will be wagered this year. Prim old ladies stand before nickel slot machines in grocery stores, watching the spinning cherries and lemons stop in the wrong places. There are slot machines at the airport, in drugstores, arcades, lobbies, souvenir shops, barbershops, everywhere but in the Western Union office. It is assumed that penitents in that place are wiring home for more money.

There is a two-mile boulevard called The Strip. This is the lavish part of Las Vegas. On it are the big hotels: The Sands, Desert Inn, Tally-Ho, Tropicana, Hacienda, The Dunes, New Frontier, The Stardust, Riviera, Thunderbird and Sahara. Each spends between fifty and eighty thousand dollars a week for lavish shows seen free by the guests.

The Stardust and Sahara take in more gambling money than the others, but Wilbur Clark's Desert Inn has a reputation for being a lucky place for the sporting crowd. It was at the Desert Inn that a young man picked up the dice, put down a dollar, and said he didn't know how to play.

He rolled twenty-eight straight passes. Each time he won, he took back most of his winnings and bet only a little. When he left, he had $750. Gamblers who bet on the kid won $150,000. If he had let his winnings ride twenty-eight times, the young man would have won $268,435,456, and would now own the State of Nevada.

From Las Vegas to Reno, 448 miles, there are twenty-seven thousand slot machines, but most of them are here. The Federal Government collects two hundred fifty dollars per machine per year. The state, county and city take another two hundred. To earn this amount, plus a profit for the owner, the machine is kept working twenty-four hours daily. Altogether, the gambling industry pays $13,600,000 a year in taxes and license fees.

The late Senator Pat McCarran lifted Nevada out of the mining and smelting business and literally put it in the chips. He nodded a gaming bill through the legislature at Carson City in 1935.

Within a short time, most of the compulsive gamblers were heading West. The rich stars and producers of Hollywood are 290
miles away, and the cloak and suiters of Seventh Avenue are two
thousand miles east. Both make this Mecca regularly.

There is more here than gambling. There are seven radio stations, three TV stations, six hospitals, good schools and eighty-
three churches and thirty-one-hundred swimming pools. However,
gambling is a blessing to Las Vegas and Nevada. Because of it,
there are no franchise taxes, no inheritance, corporate or personal
taxes. Property tax is five dollars per hundred of assessed valua-
tion.

There are more silver dollars here than anywhere in the world.
One gambler, armed with twenty and a plane ticket home tried
his final hours of bad luck at the Desert Inn craps table one
morning. He ran the twenty dollars up to $75,000. A floor man
reminded him that he barely had time to make his afternoon
plane.

"You fellows are all alike," the gambler said. "Always trying to
save the house some money. I'm sticking." He stuck. By sundown,
he had lost everything and borrowed cab fare to get to McCarran
Field. He arrived just in time to miss the plane.

Greenfield Village

Successful men destroy the time of their youth. When they become rich, they try to buy it back. Henry Ford is a good example.
He killed the horse and put the country on wheels. He died bringing the horse and buggy back to Greenfield Village.

The snow was percale white as we drove slowly through the
past. The children and I sat behind two husky horses—Dick and
Dan—and Kelly pulled her collar tight around her neck. The
hooves thudded on the hard snow and the horses breathed long
plumes in the cold blue air.

There were blacksmith shops and old pharmacies with big colored jars in the windows, barns, brickyards, forges, log cabins, a
cotton gin, a windmill and a covered bridge. Henry Ford put
twenty-three million dollars into the village before he died in
1947. "When we are through," he said, "we shall have reproduced
American life as lived . . ."

What he has done is a good thing. He has recaptured the authentic America of his boyhood days. Every beam of every building is exactly right. When he bought the home in which he was born, Henry Ford had every stick brought with it. Thomas A. Edison came here one time to look at the shop in which he had invented the electric light.

"Well?" said his friend Henry. Edison, deaf and old, looked up at his skinny round-shouldered confrere. "It's ninety-nine per cent accurate," Edison said. Henry Ford was not amused. "How did we miss by one per cent?" he asked. Edison smiled. "It's cleaner than when I worked in it," he said.

Ford also bought Sarah Jordan's boardinghouse, and brought it from South Orange, New Jersey, to Greenfield Village. Mrs. Jordan used to feed Edison's assistants. When he invented the mazda bulb, he waited until New Year's Eve, 1879, and strung wire from his laboratory to Mrs. Jordan's dining room and, using wet cell batteries, watched the room light up. Now the boardinghouse is here.

There is nostalgia and sentimentality in all this. There is more than that. There is history and vanity in it. Ford started the village accidentally. He began to collect old things; items which evoked memories. He was seldom far from his huge River Rouge Plant and, when the collector's items became cumbersome, he had to find a place for them.

Dearborn is a suburb of Detroit, and Greenfield is now a public museum. Ford, I think, wanted to show from what humble beginnings he had sprung. He was working in an Edison power plant in Detroit for $45 a month when he got the idea for his horseless carriage. No one can take it from him—he came a long, long way.

His first car is still here. Ford was thirty-three years old when he bought a two-cylinder gasoline engine, four bicycle wheels, a chain drive, the front seat of a buggy, an electric bell, two springs, some pipe for an exhaust, a hand brake, and a rod for a tiller, "kicked her over," and started down Bagley Avenue with the wind whistling through his hair at twenty miles per hour.

Any invention is only half a story. The other half is what was done with it. Ford devised mass production as we know it. He blue-printed the conveyer-assembly line, putting an automobile together as it moved slowly down a long factory room. I worked for him in his Kearney Plant when I was a kid. I had to put the upholstery on the front seat, and tuck it under, as the car went by.

It required three weeks for me to discover that I had no time for scratching, so I quit. But he paid well—five dollars a day at a time when few men earned that much. I took my money and made a down payment on one of Gaston Chevrolet's whizzers. Ford was a hard man, but more than just to his employees at a time when unions were weak and management was strong.

He made mistakes. Who doesn't? He made Eagle Boats for Uncle Sam in World War I. The first one came off the line about four months before the war ended. Later, he chartered a steamer called *Oscar II* and sent a peace mission to Europe in a forlorn hope that greedy statesmen would listen to an industrialist. He was a reactionary and, at one time, was accused of anti-Semitism, although Jews worked without hindrance in his plants.

He's been dead nearly two decades, and orange smoke pours out of his River Rouge Plant and Dick and Dan pull tourists through Greenfield Village. There is a black walnut building which interested me. It is the Logan County Courthouse in which Abraham Lincoln practiced law from 1840 until 1847. It contains the judge's bench, the gavel, counsel table, clerk's desk and feather quill, and something more: The rocking chair in which Lincoln sat the night he was shot by John Wilkes Booth.

Here also one can find the Wright Brothers' bicycle shop from Dayton; nineteenth-century locomotives; early harvesters; a Conestoga wagon; an old-time barbershop; a harness shop; red barns; an old railroad station; the first harvesters and sewing machines—spinning wheels and looms.

On the second floor of the museum, I found the most revealing keepsake of all. It is a red, lacy heart, the valentine Henry sent to Mrs. Ford on their fiftieth wedding anniversary. . . .

Communism in Amana

The city sits like a sardonyx stone mounted in an emerald ring. On one side is a valley so rich that the soil is like devil's food cake and the shade of the old trees softens the sparkle of the Iowa River. Here, in a place called Amana, pure communism was tried before Karl Marx wrote *Das Kapital*.

A group of Germans, led by Mr. Cristian Metz of Büdingen, Germany, had broken from the Lutheran Church and had come to America to seek the utmost Christian life. They believed that some men are inspired by God, and they called themselves Inspirationists. Buffalo, New York, was their first stop, but it was too materialistic, so they found this valley in Iowa and moved a thousand people into it.

It was called Amana, a word from the Song of Solomon, which means to "remain true." Metz and his industrious Germans desired to remain true to the simplicity of Christ, to live apart from the rest of the world in stark piety. The elders formed a group called The Amana Society, and incorporated it in 1855.

In time, Amana prospered and had twenty-five thousand acres and seven villages along the riverbanks. No man was paid for his work; each one labored for all. The crops were good, the cattle were fat. The trustees of the corporation gave money to a man who had to have a doctor, or a dentist, and it doled out money for clothing. A woolen mill was built; a flowing stream was dug from the river to the mill and Amana harnessed the water at a little waterfall. They baked their own bread on hearths, built their own slaughterhouse, opened butcher shops and general stores. Each family was ordered to live in a given village, a given house. There were no kitchens and no living rooms in these houses—just sleeping quarters.

The communal kitchen fed everyone, and everyone was well fed. In good times and bad. Amanaites ate about five meals a day, and averaged forty-eight hundred calories per person. The people were plump and old-fashioned. When a boy became serious about a girl, the trustees moved them as far apart as possible—seven miles. The boy was then told that if he truly loved the girl, he would not mind sweating in the fields all day, and walking seven miles to see her at night. The elders believed that love could survive this ordeal for one year. If it did, the elders sanctioned marriage. The girl dressed in black; so did the boy, and they touched the palms of their right hands together before the elders' table in the temple. Words of marriage were pronounced over them.

Divorce is unheard of among the Amanaites. So is crime. In 109 years there has never been a murder, a rape, a felonious assault or a holdup. Juvenile delinquency is nipped in the bud in school. Discipline is important to adults as well as children. The people never had a crucifix in their church, never listened to music except the guttural sound of their own hymns. They worked hard, and obeyed their elders.

The food they ate consisted of seven main dishes, one for each day of the week. They cured hams Westphalian style, and bacon too. They even made their own furniture of native cherrywood. The elders laid down twenty-four rules for Amana living, and everyone had to live those rules or face excommunication in church.

The community protected everyone from the cradle to the grave. The Amana cemetery, on a hillside, is screened by huge pines. The headstones are all of one size. People are buried chronologically, by date of death. Families are not buried together. The entire plan was Christian communism, executed perfectly.

It died a violent death in 1932. There was a depression. The neighboring city of Cedar Rapids began to flaunt its cars and radios at Amana. The young members became restive. Forty-seven of the younger men appeared before the elders and demanded a new corporation, a hybrid of socialism and capitalism. They called it "co-operative." The elders were forced to surrender. The total worth of Amana was only $2,500,000 after seventy-seven years of work, and the population was only fourteen hundred. Many members had left because they felt that communism was too harsh.

I walked through an Amana Village. It was warm and the trees were in leaf again. The fields were tilled. Amana has socialized medicine, dentistry, funerals and hospitalization. The big industries are still owned by the corporation. But the people live as capitalists. The houses are now individual family homes. The men keep what they earn. Television antennae grow from chimneys. Radios enunciate Rock 'n Roll. The young people drive convertibles. Drinking and smoking are permitted. Under capitalism, the corporation is now worth $16,400,000.

Moscow papers please copy. . . .

The Sins of a City

The last of the sun throws a million sequins against the windows of New York. Then it dies, and night comes quickly, rolling upward from the streets like a dark shade.

High over Coney Island, a falling star scratches a wet match across the sky and the city below bursts into a flame of light. It blazes like a forest of stately sequoias. The city is ready to offer its nightly sacrifice to the great god Tailfin.

Under the lights are 7,850,000 people. Of all the people in the United States, 4.5 per cent live here. They exist in a vertical world of masonry and macadam, squeezed and stultified in elevators, kitchenettes, offices and subway trains. They walk fast, think fast, race to work, hurry home, and, in the middle of a church service, study their watches pettishly. Time is Tailfin's chief apostle.

New York is 320 square miles of land. Most of it consists of islands. There are 34,000 acres of parks, 18 miles of sandy beach, 725 playgrounds. There are rivers, spidery bridges, tunnels, and, somewhere in the molten lava of headlights, 8,000 stolen automobiles. It is a city of lofty charity, yet steeped in degradation. The pigment of the people ranges from the albino Swede to the dusty dark of the West Indian. Their impulses range from the woman who gave milk to needy children, down to the meek little Albert Fish, who cut them up and ate them.

Hundreds of thousands of New Yorkers speak no English. On the Lower East Side, it's Yiddish; on the Upper West Side it's Spanish; in Yorkville it's German; in Cherry Hill it's Italian. People of many tongues build the Tower of Babel.

New York is a place where one can look down on a cross or spire. It is a place of good families, expensive living, cheerful chiselers, cherubs, criminals, loose women and tight men, piety and passion, angles, generosity, study, fun, skyscrapers, robbers, policemen, television stations, psychiatrists, riches, poverty, ambition, despair, and, like any other city, sudden death.

The thing that is different about this city is that it is losing its sense of values. Since 1946, it has been dropping its morality as though goodness is a fake.

The churches are crowded. So are the prisons. One of these groups understands true contrition. Crime moves upward and the population declines. New York City averages almost a murder a day. Every time the morning sun washes the cold spires with gold an average of three more women have been raped; sixteen armed robberies have been committed; ninety-two homes have been burglarized; $16,000 in merchandise has been stolen; thirty persons have been beaten, stabbed, shot or maimed; sixty-seven grand larcenies have been detected; four persons have been arrested for peddling narcotics; six hundred men and women have been picked up for minor offenses; three men have abandoned their families; three hundred and forty abortions have taken place; forty-one cars have been stolen; two pickpockets have been booked; seven prostitutes are in cells; two hundred children are in trouble with the law.

None of this is to be taken as an index that New York is the most criminal of cities. Far from it. The combined populations of Chicago, Philadelphia, and Los Angeles approximate that of New

York. They had 558 murders last year. New York had 354. In fact, according to the Federal Bureau of Investigation's annual crime report, New York is below the national average in cases of forcible rape and burglary, as well as murder. New York is being used as a case history here because it is still the Big Apple—easy to peel, easy to cut, easy to dissect.

Crime has always been a part of man's life. It is as ineradicable as love. Twenty centuries ago, when there were no prisons, the punishment for all crime was death. The Jews stoned their lawless citizens; the Romans crucified as many as six thousand a day on the public highways. Three centuries ago, the picking of pockets was a capital offense in England. At the public hangings, more pockets were picked than at any other time.

Crime and a city are like a temperature and a patient. There is a reading, even in the healthiest of times. The higher the temperature, the sicker the city. The fever chart indicates illness; it never tells the cause. The chart in New York is high. There were over three hundred thousand crimes great and small last year. This is a wrong every 1.7 seconds around the clock. It amounts to a punishable offense committed by one out of every twenty-six persons in the city. Some of these, sadly, were policemen. One, the worst in modern law enforcement history, robbed an old lady, beat her, killed and raped her. He was tracked down and arrested by his fellow officers.

The temperature is high, and it moves higher. Figures are meaningless. Murders increased 12.7 per cent in a year. So did the cost of automobiles. If, for example, it is pointed out that seven hundred homosexuals are arrested each year, the figure is misleading because it hides the fact that there are 38,300 homosexuals who are not in jail.

Writers talk of the pulse of the city as though in the wrist of the metropolis one can detect the fibrillations and impending embolisms. For this, it would be better to look to the children of New York. These are the electrocardiograms of our culture.

Civilizations are not built on legislatures and laws. They are built on families. The stronger the spiritual, emotional and physical values of the family, the better the children. The better the children, the healthier the nation. There are 1,500,000 persons in New York under the age of twenty-one. They live 4,700 to the square mile. About 5 per cent of them (75,000) are arrested each year. This is not as good as their parents, who average 3 per cent arrests (222,000). However, arrests do not tell the story of youthful crime because scores of thousands of children commit crimes each year for which restitution is made and no record is kept. The crime figure for children is probably close to 9 per cent. Even that has no impact.

Try it this way: Last year twenty-one boys under the age of sixteen were tried for murder; fifty girls under sixteen were arrested for armed robbery; 1,892 boys were charged with felonious assault; fifty-two girls too young to drive were apprehended for stealing automobiles; ninety-three boys set homes and shops on fire; two girls, barely in their teens, were held for selling narcotics; 407 boys and twenty-three girls, all under the age of sixteen, were charged with sex crimes. No one was arrested on a charge of being a wayward minor.

What does the average bad boy look like? Take a look. He is seventeen. His frame is thin. He walks in a casual crawl. His shoes are heavy and well-shined. So is his hair, which is combed straight back along the sides and permitted to puff a little on top. He likes sweaters and skin-tight slacks. His sideburns are long, his temper is short. He has pimples, a spurious disdain for the girl at his side, a switchblade knife or zip gun in his pocket, a package of cigarettes, two to four dollars, and a perpetual tension which he feels but cannot explain. He cracks his knuckles, laughs immoderately at small jokes, goes berserk when his dignity is affronted.

He despises his mother or his father and, on the street, refers to that person with four-letter words. One parent is an alcoholic, or jobless, or the parents quarrel chronically. The boy is a victim of overdoses of discipline and love, or none of either. In adolescence he becomes a rebel. He is fond of anything which runs counter to his parents. This includes his choice of music, girls, entertainment, school, dress, church, hours, cleanliness and speech. On impulse, he will upset ash barrels, break windows, defy a policeman, beat up an old man, snatch a purse, force a window or a girl. He despises respect, cultivates contempt.

He likes homogeny. He hangs out in gangs. There are sixty criminal gangs of boys roaming the streets of New York at night. There are 150 other gangs with police records. There are five hundred more inching toward crime.

Over thirty thousand youngsters were arrested on serious charges last year. Does it shock you to learn that a few hundred of them were seven years of age? In the sixteen-to-twenty-year group, 18,760 arrests. It is here that the new cult has arisen. These are the ones to whom God is a pair of tail fins: these are the ones who want to tear down the Tower of Babel.

Statistics will not tell the story. There are, of course, many millions more of good, law-abiding people than bad people in the

Big City. Those are the ones who make New York a mecca of
education, entertainment and culture for the rest of the nation.
However, the good are becoming mute and frightened in the presence of the bad.

One cannot learn much about the humans by looking a percentage in the eye. It is necessary to look at an individual and in him
see all of the others. Can you weep for Mrs. Marks? She never did
anything wrong in her life. It is possible also that she never did
anything right. She calls herself a good mother. She sat in Lieutenant Nelson's office in the 20th Detective Squad waiting for the
word. Her son, Micky, she reported, had been missing for a week.
He was fifteen. (Do you detect anything wrong with Mrs. Marks
so far?) Would the police try to find him? The police would. They
found him. They didn't know how to tell her the news. The boy
was living in Greenwich Village with an old man. He didn't want
to come home.

Still, the story of New York City is not a story of juvenile
delinquency. The young set headlines, but the old manufacture
the young. The unfit sire the misfit. Even good parents are hurt in
the huge temple of the god Tailfin. No frieze can capture the
expression on the faces of a mother and father called in by the
police in a murder case, to be told: "Your boy had the gun."

It is night. It is quiet, but nobody fools the 24th. The precinct
has been around a long time. The worst crime rate in New
York City is here. So are the best policemen. There is no tick to
the wall clock. It sneaks from second to second. The only sound is
the police radio asking for an ambulance at 125th and Lenox. A
Negro police lieutenant stands behind the desk, showing pictures
of his grandchildren.

This is a soft evening. It is six thirty and nothing has happened
in "The Pressure Cooker." Down the hall to the right, Captain
Fred Blahnick initials reports. He is tough and friendly. He has
deep wavy hair, brown eyes, a wife and three daughters. He looks
like a pug who has been out of the ring one season too many.

Blahnick is the boss. He controls the area from 86th Street to
125th, from the Hudson River to Central Park West. It measures
1.38 square miles. In it are 208,000 people. They are squeezed
cheek to cheek. In the same area are Columbia University, Grant's
Tomb, Teacher's College, Juilliard School of Music, St. Luke's
Hospital, the Cathedral of St. John The Divine, Riverside Church,
Sydenham Hospital, twenty other churches and synagogues, nine
public schools, four parochial schools, eleven playgrounds, twenty-
five hotels, 758 rooming houses and 411 places which sell liquor.

"The pressure cooker" precinct is outside its own area, at 423 West 126th Street, a skinny boarded-up store in an old red brick building. Inside, 338 policemen and forty detectives are on the roster. Outside, in the concrete hunting preserve, the unwanted ones live. They are 75 per cent European Caucasian, 16 per cent Puerto Rican; 9 per cent Negro.

These are the mean ones. They live four, five and six to a room. The halls are dark and dirty: The rats inch along the floors like sleepy brown rabbits. Roaches stop and start across a sleeping baby's face. A gas range boils rice in a lavatory. One family saws a hole in the floor and uses it as a toilet; the room below is untenanted. A police car stops and four bricks drop from a roof and the windshield comes in on two policemen.

"The pressure cooker" waits. It is Friday night. This is pay night. Booze night. Fight night. The 24th Precinct averages thirteen arrests a night. It will do better this evening. It is warm out and warmth breeds violence.

An old lady with a face like a pale prune comes into the 24th. She has five children with her. "My daughter ran away with a man," she says angrily. "You take care of the children." The desk lieutenant, Alfred Gray, comes out quickly. He tells the woman that the police will not take care of the children. The old woman turns around slowly. When she jerks her head at the youngsters, they follow. She does not cry. The hands clasp and unclasp.

Gray is back behind the desk. A plain clothesman comes in with a girl. She isn't pretty. She looks tired. The charge is that she solicited the policeman for five dollars. The lieutenant takes the monotonous history. The girl gives an incorrect name. "All I want," she says softly, "is to phone a man who will post bail for me." She knows the legal ropes.

Blahnick comes out with some sheets. "I'm going home to get something to eat. I'll be back. Is Bednarsky still out?" Bednarsky is still out. He is Lieutenant Belek Bednarsky, in charge of the four-to-twelve platoon. He is a tough and fair cop. He is in a squad car, cruising the district. Out there he has thirty men on foot; nineteen others in eleven cars.

Lieutenant Gray is two bites into a sandwich when two Negroes are brought in. One is tall and holds his hand over his mouth. He looks sick. The little one giggles. They are under arrest for receiving stolen property. A policeman caught them dragging 111 pounds of meat across a sidewalk. The prisoners said they had bought it for fifteen dollars. They couldn't remember from whom. Gray books them. He asks the routine question: "Do you use drugs?" Both men nod. They are heroin addicts. The tall one says it costs him twenty dollars a day. He needs a fix now. He has cramps. The little one spends ten dollars a day on heroin. He doesn't need anything at the moment.

Bednarsky comes in with a blond man. The prisoner got into an argument with his best friend. The blond one held his friend by the hair and drew with a knife. The injured one is in Sydenham Hospital.

The lieutenant finishes the booking. He also finishes his sandwich. He is listening to the police broadcast when the door swings open and two Puerto Ricans come in with two policemen. The charge is rape. They saw a woman stagger to her room drunk. They waited until she fell asleep. Then they battered the door.

The stout Puerto Rican woman came in. Her purse was snatched yesterday. She went looking for the man today. He is a young Irishman. Out of the 208,000 people in the area, she found him. The police, she says calmly, are bringing him in. They found her social security card in his pocket.

It isn't eight o'clock yet and five winos are led in. They lean against each other. One wants to sing. One wants to cry. They were picked up at Columbus Avenue and 106th Street. A bright-looking policewoman comes in with a Negro woman. The charge is fortune-telling.

A sad-looking Negro is booked for stabbing his girl. She gave the wrong answers to the right questions.

Bednarsky leaves with a patrolman. The lieutenant sits up front. The single gold bar on his shoulder picks up a gleam from a street light. He understands his district. It's a vicious jungle and his dark eyes snap back and forth across the windshield like nervous wipers. He feels sorry for the people, but he cannot forgive filth.

At 94th and Amsterdam, the car stops. This is the worst crime area in the worst crime precinct. It looks peaceful in the dark. There are five-story tenements. A few doors away is Public School 93. In the faint light, a billboard can be seen proclaiming that Miss Rheingold "Saluda A Puerto Rico." There are garbage cans and children with pale faces and uncombed hair. Short women with big bosoms cross the street. Only the bottoms of their sweaters are buttoned.

On the far side of the street is Peggy and Bill's Beauty Shop. It is closed. Up the street toward Central Park West are the old brownstones, the rooming houses. This is where the chiseler humbles his brown brother. He charges the Puerto Rican fifteen dollars a week for a small room and no heat. Then he hires him at hard labor for $1.05 an hour and sells him old sticks of furniture for hundreds of dollars. The so-called white man's contempt is obvious.

The men are young. They stand in twos and threes on stoops. Their clothes are flashy. The shoes are gleaming yellow, the trouser cuffs pinch the ankle, the ties are florid, the hair is wet onyx. The squad car creeps up a trench of parked cars. A Negro woman comes out. "Make 'em stop!" she pleads. "They throw stones. They break windows all summer." The woman points in the dark across the street. "Now it's going on winter." The lieutenant gets out. He disappears in the dark to talk to the Puerto Rican boys. The boys promise not to throw stones.

The lieutenant and the driver investigate a couple of domestic complaints. They carry flashlights. The people remember Bednarsky. Tough and fair. Some of the old men remove their hats as he passes. There is one twenty-watt bulb in a five-story hallway. The smell is bad. The lieutenant stumbles over a couple halfway up a staircase. He calls the janitor to go with him. The janitor is tall and self-assured. He has deep pockmarks and he speaks a little English. He represents the landlord. He collects fifteen dollars a week from every room on every floor. This old house takes in $1,625 a month from thirty cells of broken plaster. This comes to $19,500 a year, much more than the house is worth.

On the third floor, Bednarsky goes into a back room. Two grown couples sleep across one bed. A woman sits in a chair near a heater watching. In the hall, a chipped statue of the Sacred Heart stands on top of the garbage pail. An old rosary is still around the neck.

There are shouts from below. The lieutenant and his driver hurry down. They shove their way through shouting Puerto Ricans. A man sits on the floor, half in, half out of his apartment. His trousers are open. He rubs his fat belly. Pain scars his face. His wife sits in the room with a nude baby in her arms, watching her man. She shows nothing. The man wants to die. He swallowed rat poison. Two little youngsters watch from a double-deck bed. The radio plays Spanish music. He speaks no English. He sits rubbing his belly and he looks at his wife and children and, in the midst of pain, tears come. His shoulders shake as though he is laughing and the sobs bring his face to the floor.

The lieutenant has no time for tears. He asks questions in English. The poison, he learns, is on the floor behind the refrigerator. Why? he asks. The wife replies in Spanish. Her man could not get a job. He did not want relief checks. He is a coward who wants to die and she spits on his memory.

Bednarsky gets the poison. It is smoky paste. The lieutenant finds milk. The suicide does not want it. Bednarsky pulls his head straight back and dumps the fluid. It goes into the dark mouth, down the throat, over the shirt front and down the chest. He points to a man who speaks English. "Get me some warm water and a box of salt. Pronto." The man hurries. The suicide begins to get ill. Bednarsky looks at his driver. "Call an ambulance. This one can be saved." He looks around the room. It is newly painted. The linoleum is spotless. The only odor is from the kerosene stove. When the hot water is ready, the lieutenant pours the salt in. The suicide is sick. He pleads no. Bednarsky bends his head back. The man drinks.

The woman watches. The shoebutton eyes show nothing. The ambulance takes twenty-two minutes to arrive. The woman holds the nude baby in one hand, and with the other, shuts off the radio. She watches the attendants take her man away. He was a good man until he lost his self-respect.

The lieutenant orders everybody out of the little room. The people move reluctantly. He shoves a little money in the woman's hand. "Your husband will be all right," he says, nodding. "El O.K." he gets back to the 24th as Captain Blahnick walks in. Lieutenant Gray nods to both of them. "A quiet night," he says. "A nice quiet Friday." Blahnick shrugs. "It's early, Al. Give it time."

Bednarsky permits himself a small smile and a small joke. "The night's so young," he murmurs, "and we're all so beautiful."

The 20th is noisy. On the ground floor, a gray-haired lieutenant tries to straighten out two cheap gamblers who want to kill each other. The police radio is up. Out front, two detectives talk to a stool pigeon who is a master at studying the cracks in sidewalks. Two others walk the creaky stairs to the second floor. This is the 20th Squad Detectives Room.

There are a half-dozen cheap desks with phones. Three detectives check out evidence on the telephones. There is a little office to the right; a big cage of wire to the left. Lieutenant Jake Nelson calls two detectives into his office. He's the boss. He is a dark, slender man who smokes a pipe. Nelson has been in touch with the 24th, which is adjacent to the north. It is a quiet Friday there and here.

He sends Walter Daino and Walter Bentley out on a burglary. They are young and willing. A woman at Riverside Drive and 72nd Street has phoned in that her apartment has been burglarized while she was away. "Get going," Nelson says. They get.

Down front they nod to Detectives George Joannides and Daniel Fogerty, still talking to the informant.

Daino and Bentley hurry to the apartment house. It is a smart place with a doorman and an elevator operator and soft lights and end tables in the lobby. Their eyes miss nothing. The elevator takes them to the ninth floor. Daino knocks. A fortyish woman with thick glasses opens it. The detectives introduce themselves. She tells them to come in.

They remove their hats. A few questions are asked. Bentley examines the bedroom while Daino studies the windows and doors. The apartment looks immaculate until the bedroom is reached. The woman cannot look at it. Bureau drawers are dumped on the twin beds. Papers and clothing are on the floor.

"In my closet," she says, pointing, "is a stone marten cape and two fur coats. Untouched." The detectives look. They feel the place with their eyes. "What was taken?" A four-carat diamond ring. "Insured?" No. "Where did you get it?" From my husband. "Where is he?" Dead twelve years. Daino comes into the bedroom. He smiles at Bentley. "Spring locks," he says.

They go back to the front door. Bentley stands inside. Daino is outside with a piece of celluloid. The door is locked. The piece of celluloid is inserted between the door and the jamb. It moves downward. It hits the lock and the door springs open. The woman cannot believe it. "You need more than a spring lock, lady." Last year there were 33,806 burglaries. That's almost four an hour.

Daino looks around. "It wasn't a sympathetic burglar," he says. A sympathetic burglar disturbs nothing. He replaces everything he moves. He picks a small, expensive item—like one ring in a box of jewelry—and takes it and hopes that he can sell it and move on before the burglary is discovered. There was nothing sympathetic about this one.

The two detectives get back to the precinct on West 68th Street and find a parking space. They move up the steps together, dividing the work which must be done. From the squad room comes the scream of a woman. It comes from good lungs.

They move through the little swinging gate. A young Negro woman is screaming and stripping her clothes. A gray pleated skirt goes off first. Then a slip. She tears it two ways. She stands before the detectives in a pair of tight briefs, mules with plastic heels, and a shoelace bra. Saliva is on her thick lips. She's plump and curvesome. "You dirty——!" she roars at the big policeman. "You kicked me in the stomach. I'm three months pregnant and if anything happens to that baby, I'm coming back to kill you, you——!"

Daino tries to use a phone. He can't hear the operator. The woman screams. The big cop stands looking down at her. Joannides tries to talk to her. She shoves him off. Fogerty tells the big cop to leave the room.

Lieutenent Nelson questions the policeman. He was cruising in a car. He saw two women fighting. They were rolling in the street. One has a record as a lesbian. Big Sam picked them up as a housewife would lift two chickens. He held them apart. This one, the screamer, came out of the crowd kicking and biting. Big Sam shows the teethmarks on his wrist. He ordered her into the car. She dropped to the sidewalk and taunted: "Make me."

The cop grabbed two ankles and pulled until she was in the squad car. He didn't kick her, he says. He looks apologetically at his feet. Size nineteen. "Can you imagine anybody being kicked by one of these?"

Lieutenant Nelson asks for a report and he asks for witnesses. He summons a policewoman and tells the Negro girl how to make a complaint against Big Sam. He calls Joannides and Fogerty and sends them off to 74th Street on a bar stickup.

George Joannides in a gray fedora with turned-up brim, two hands clasped behind the topcoat, and wise eyes which have tracked crooks and murderers for thirty-five years. Fogerty has a big smile and square teeth. He is always shopping for baby bottle nipples.

They go to a pizza place. It is dark and smells of stale beer. The jukebox is playing "Mack the Knife." Joannides gets the old Greek chef at a rear table for a chat. Fogerty talks to the owner up front. A girl sits at the bar, crying softly. It was she who came to the locked front door this morning and asked the chef to let her in. She wanted a drink of water. The chef says they talked in the kitchen for twenty minutes. Then a man came through the front door with a gun. "Stay where you are, old man," he said. "Stay right where you are. You too, sister." They stayed. The man stole liquor. It required eight trips to carry out fifty-seven bottles. Joannides asks the chef what he was doing in the back for twenty minutes. The old man says nothing.

They take the owner, the chef and the girl back to the West 68th Street station. The girl cries all the way and smokes all the way. They walk up to the squad room. The plump one is still screaming. The tone is hoarse. Tears give her skin a dark satin sheen.

Joannides and Fogerty take statements from the owner and the chef. They ignore the weeper. She is led to a big cage. Inside, she breaks down completely and sits on the floor to cry.

A detective gets to the other girl. He whispers. She listens a little and hollers a little. "Come on, kid. Put your clothes on. If he hurt you, file a complaint. How about those fingerprints?" Joannides and Fogerty shake their heads and leave for dinner. The time is nine fifteen. The colored girl will not put her clothes back on. She agrees to the fingerprinting.

The detectives take her to a desk beside the cage. He starts to roll her fingers in ink. "Don't help me," he says. She keeps rolling her fingers. "Don't help me, kid," he says. The girl bursts into laughter as uncontrollable as the tears. "When you been through this as often as me," she says, "you can do it yourself."

In the office, a young woman in restrained frenzy comes in. She asks Lieutenant Nelson to find her little boy. He is five years old. When did she last see him? At 8 A.M. He has been gone thirteen hours. An alarm goes out to the squad cars to find a little man of five. The woman clasps and unclasps her handbag. Nelson asks her to sit outside. He watches her leave and he removes his pipe to think about her.

In a half hour, Joannides and Fogerty are back. They come into the squad room slowly. The girl from the pizza place gets up and grabs the bars of the cage. "Hey, you," she shouts, "I want to talk to you." They pay no attention. They sit at a desk. The young woman becomes angry. "You could at least have the decency to answer me," she shouts.

Joannides winks at Fogerty. "Meditation," he says, "sometimes pays off." The girl's voice cracks. "Will you answer me? Will you please answer me? I want to make a statement. The fellow with the gun this morning is my boy friend."

Across town, a gray gorilla of a man walks up East 49th Street. He passes the neat trees with the street lights coming down through the branches, and he turns into a Tudor-style home. This is the 17th Precinct. The windows are leaded. The gray one walks through the precinct, nodding a little, and walks up two flights. A sign says "homicide."

He is Lieutenant Daniel Mahoney. He is in charge of the Homicide Squad Manhattan East. There are no murders this evening and Mahoney wants no murders. He gets behind his desk and calls for the ledger. Sergeant Thomas Buzanga brings it. Mahoney is short and gray. Buzanga is tall and brown-haired and talks with a little puff of the lips like Humphrey Bogart.

They go over the old cases in the ledger. Mahoney likes to see them all cleaned up. It will never be. They keep trying, as all the other homicide squads do. New York averages almost a murder a day and, in the past year, the Detective Division solved 322 out of

354. In Mahoney's district, which is the East Side of Manhattan from the Battery to Harlem, they have had ninety-three killings in a year and ninety are marked closed.

There is no magic. The Homicide Squad has no brilliant flashes, no astounding deductions. Their job is not to take over a case, but to assist the detectives in whatever squad area the killing occurred. They take little bits and pieces and they keep fitting and refitting them together. The cases always fall into a pattern. An old pattern. Once they see the outlines, Mahoney and Buzanga and the others in Manhattan East can almost recite the rest.

The one that worries them is called the psychotic murder. These are the senseless, pointless ones which follow no pattern. There is no robbery, no jealousy, no love, no revenge, no passion, no racket —nothing.

The girl on the East Side. She was on a bed. She wore nothing. Her body had been stabbed so many times that the doctors couldn't agree. They thought it might be thirty-seven. All they knew about her was that she thought she could sing, and couldn't, and she tried to be good, and couldn't.

Mahoney's men picked up all the sex suspects. Thirty days' work produced nothing. Then a girl screamed one night in a small East Side apartment. Three neighbors phoned Police Headquarters. The cars got there fast. Two were in front of the building, one was in back. The one in back saw a man climb a fence. They chased him into a cemetery and got him. They brought him back to the apartment. He was short and blond and friendly. The girl was terrified. She said he tried to tear her clothing. He had a knife. It wasn't homicide, but Mahoney and Buzanga wanted to take a look. They asked him if he had ever stabbed a girl. No, he hadn't. "You're sick, pal. You want to involve your family in a thing like this? You have two nice kids. We know you did it. It will take a little time to iron the wrinkles out of it, but you did it and you know it. Medical care is what you need. How about it?"

It went on like this a long time. Then the blond man broke. He met the girl who thought she could sing at a bus stop. He talked. She smiled. He was invited to her place. When he got there, he moved fast. His biggest thrill was inflicting pain. Her clothes came off and he bit and stabbed her. Afterward, he felt quiet and happy.

Buzanga went to the killer's apartment. He met his wife and the two children. He asked the wife if she had noticed anything peculiar about her husband. "Like this?" she asked and opened a closet door. Inside, the blond man had hung a photo of a nude. Buried in the middle was a knife.

The psychotic killings make Mahoney grayer. The colored cab-driver was a one-time wrestler. He strangled two girls: one with a telephone wire, one with his big hands. The only clue was that both had dates with a cabbie. Mahoney went through the hack files until his eyelids burned.

It required seven weeks of work. And every evening of that time they sat in Homicide East waiting to hear an alarm that he had found a third girl. When they got him, they were out of breath and so was he. "Don't tell the newspapers I'm a sex criminal," he whined. "Say I'm a burglar. You got to do this for me, fellows. I got a kid five years old."

It was a quiet Friday evening. All over the city, policemen sat watching.

The van moves by the big depressing pile of stone on Centre Street and around the block and down to the back of Police Head-quarters. It stops and a policeman gets off and unlocks the heavy wire door at the back. "O. K." he says, and holds the door open. Two women get out. The older one clutches the fur collar tight against her throat.

Another van pulls up. A young Negro gets out. He is crying. A short man with gray hair squints against the cold morning sun. A tall man of dignity steps down. The policeman motions for them to head down the back stairs. They go without looking at the city around them.

Inside, they are led through the catacombs of the law. In a big room, Sergeant Winfield Wray yells at the cop: "In there. Put them in there." He motions to a big cage. The policeman puts them in there. The lives of these people will be a succession of cages. They are parakeets without plumage. They can talk but they do not sing.

Sergeant Wray finishes making a mug shot on the big copy camera. He motions to the policeman. "One at a time," he says. The middle-aged woman is brought out first. She has been finger-printed. Now she poses for a front view and a side view. A number is hung around her neck. She has been here before, but she always feels the indignity.

Sergeant Wray calls for the next one. And the next. He and his assistants photograph 36,500 felons each year and there is not time for pity. There are 445,000 mug shots in the New York police file. It is dull work. Once in a great while, something unusual happens. The sergeant once turned a Negro's face side-wards and the color came off on his hand. The prisoner was white.

Another time, one of his assistants was out in a field, photographing a pretty schoolgirl. She was dead. On her way across an empty field, the child had been raped and strangled. Behind the body was a wooden garage.

Every time the police photographer looked into the camera, a ray of light kept coming from the garage wall. He examined the wall. In tiny letters, the girl had scratched the name "Nick" with her pointed fingernail before she died. It was Nick.

Upstairs in the big damp gymnasium, thirty detectives sit in the gloom. The prisoners are led across a lighted stage with horizontal lines showing their heights. The two women squint in the glare. Out in the darkness, Deputy Inspector John Ronayne stands at a lectern He conducts the morning lineup. Before him he has the record of each prisoner. He tells the two women that they are shoplifters. The older one shakes her head no. Inspector Ronayne tells her that she and her girl friend were caught with four men's suits wrapped around their waists. The older one speaks: "No," she says. "We were walking in the store. The man ahead of us dropped the suits. We were brushing them off when the policeman came."

The young colored boy is charged with snatching a purse. There was four dollars in it. He worked as a delivery boy. "Why did you do it, Roy?" The boy swallows. "My parents don't know I'm on drugs," he whispers. "I need twenty dollars every day."

The dignified man is on next. He stole a police shield, impersonated an officer, and tried to blackmail a homosexual. His downfall was that the homo had no shame.

The gray-haired one is a pension treasurer. He also likes horses. He is $2,400 short and he admits that he forged checks. The prisoners file through swiftly, a moment or two onstage, a lot of time off. The difference between them and the rest of the city is that they do their thinking late.

On the second floor, the Police Commissioner steps into his office. He is Stephen Patrick Kennedy, fifty-three, handsome and hard. He runs a tight force. In 1929, he started as a policeman. Now, after working his way through all the ranks—and law school —he is a civilian again. He must ask for a permit to carry a gun.

He is the twenty-fifth commissioner, and the seventh to come from the ranks. He is married, has a son, and lives in a two-family house in Bayside, Queens. He's a loner, and, if he has a weakness, it is that he never learned to delegate authority. Kennedy wants to be in on everything that happens in the department and to the department. To his way of thinking, a policeman is not a sociologist and not a lawyer. He's an enforcer. "He has a job to do, and if he does it honestly and intelligently, he gains respect. That's a lot more important than being liked."

He calls First Deputy Commissioner James Kennedy to his office. These men are not related. The deputy is all cop. He wears a splash of snow on the sides of his head and he finds it difficult to concentrate on anything not concerned with police business. He has spent three days trying to track a big floating dice game. The two men talk. The deputy knows where the gamblers' pickup car operates. It averages five new passengers every few hours. It cannot be tailed because the driver always makes it a point to turn down a dead-end street and then double back to see if a police car is following. Deputy Kennedy has been tailing him three blocks at a time. He is close to the crap game.

Down the hall, James Leggett leaves his desk in a hurry. An old gangster is dead in Brooklyn and Mr. Leggett wants to do some work. Mr. Leggett is a stout southpaw, and chief of the Detective Division. He has put in thirty-six years as a policeman and he is an advocate of the long sweat school of detection. Mr. Leggett draws a grim joy from his work. He never feels sorry for a criminal. He feels that the lawbreaker's job is to try to hide and his job is to find him. His division is one eighth of the New York force, but they make 60 per cent of all felony arrests and solve 33 per cent of all lesser crimes.

A woman was found on a roadside with her head crushed by a rock. There were no clues. Chief Leggett ordered his men to investigate the lady's girl friends. Then he summoned one. "You know where Louise was that night," he said. The woman said she didn't. She was indignant. Leggett nodded. "Okay," he said softly, "I think I'll call your husband in and tell him about that bartender you hang out with." The woman almost fainted. She wept. She pleaded. She told the chief that Louise had been at a certain tavern that night and a stranger had offered her a ride home. Leggett was satisfied. "Tell me," he said, "how do you get away with it? I mean, you and the bartender?" The woman looked away. "My husband thinks I'm bowling," she said.

The detectives went to the bar and, in time, found the suspect. He broke. He had taken Louise in his car. She was intoxicated. At a lonely part of the trip, he led her out of the car and kissed her. She bit his lip and wouldn't let go. He picked up a rock. Louise let go.

There are 24,000 men in the New York department and they are divided into many bureaus. There are eighty patrol precincts in the five boroughs, besides which there are the Pickpocket Squad, Homicide Squad, Special Frauds, Automobile Unit, Stolen Property Bureau, Forgery, Special Services, Vice, Missing Persons, District Attorney's Squad, Narcotics, Police Laboratory, Ballistics, Bomb Squad, Safe and Loft, Criminal Intelligence, Traffic Division, Patrol, Burglary.

In the past year these men worked on 31,902 felonies, 96,771 misdemeanors, 2,345 prostitution cases, 20,418 gambling offenses, and 47,494 disorderly conduct charges. Beside this, they gave out 1,900,000 summonses for traffic violations.

Last year, policemen appeared in court to assist in the prosecution of 26,909 serious crimes. There are five district attorneys in five counties within the City of New York and they fight hard for convictions. Almost nine thousand felons went free, 3,614 were discharged on their own recognizance, fifty-nine died awaiting trial.

On the fifth floor of headquarters there is a room with six big switchboards, a dozen small ones. This is crime's pinball machine. The lights blink saffron, a male voice growls, "Police Headquarters," and a citizen asks for help or information. The departmental switchboards around the city accept 3,600,000 such calls a year. Most of the calls ask for an ambulance or for police assistance in a dispute. Monday morning is burglary day. Businessmen, returning from a weekend, find their shops ransacked at this time. All emergency calls go through the small boards. The patrolman listens, repeats a location, writes it on a sheet, jams it in a pneumatic tube and it shoots to a room next door where two patrolmen handle radio stations KEA 394 and KEB 291. The two announcers, through relays, can contact all police cars, police planes, boats, precincts, ranking officers, ambulances and police boats in a few seconds. In the city, there are 725 police cars, four helicopters, fourteen boats.

Across the street, Lieutenant John Cronin runs through a list of names. He is a pleasant man with gray hair and he is in charge of the Missing Persons Bureau. Sometimes, the sins of New York become too great for the living to beat. They walk out. Leave. Disappear.

Every year, ten thousand New Yorkers—enough to populate a small city—walk out into the darkness. In time, most of them are found or come home again to try once more. In an average year, the Waterfront Squad and the Bowery group find 2,665 bodies. Fifty are never found. Who? Why? Most of them are sensitive persons who, like the twenty-four thousand narcotics addicts, cannot face the harshness of New York.

The sins of the big city are many, but the greatest, the most unforgivable of all, is what New York is doing to its young.

ABOUT THE AUTHOR

Born in Jersey City, New Jersey, in 1907, JIM BISHOP became a member of the fourth estate early in life. He went from St. Patrick's School and Drake's Secretarial School to the *New York News* as a $12-a-week copy boy. He was taught the fundamentals of writing by a noted columnist, Mark Hellinger, at the *New York Mirror*. In 1943 he was appointed war editor of *Collier's* magazine and later became executive editor of *Liberty* magazine. He was subsequently director of the literary department of the MCA agency, the founder of Gold Medal Books, and executive editor of the *Catholic Digest*.

The author of more than a dozen books, Jim Bishop originated "The Day" style of writing, and his *The Day Lincoln Was Shot, The Day Christ Died,* and *A Day in the Life of President Kennedy* were all bestsellers. The Bishop family now lives in Hallandale, Florida.